161 185461 4

D1429224

# Two week
# loan

Pleas  ret
date
C.

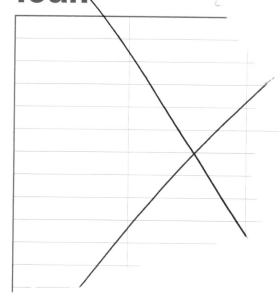

# NATIONAL SECURITY AND THE D-NOTICE SYSTEM

# National Security and the D-Notice System

PAULINE SADLER
*Curtin University of Technology, Western Australia*

**Ashgate**

**DARTMOUTH**

Aldershot • Burlington USA • Singapore • Sydney

© Pauline Sadler 2001

Published by
Dartmouth Publishing Company
Ashgate Publishing Limited
Gower House
Croft Road
Aldershot
Hampshire GU11 3HR
England

Ashgate Publishing Company
131 Main Street
Burlington, VT 05401-5600 USA

Ashgate website: http://www.ashgate.com

**British Library Cataloguing in Publication Data**
Sadler, Pauline
 National security and the D-Notice system
 1. National security - Great Britain 2. National security -
 Australia 3. government and press - Great Britain
 4. Government and the press - Australia 5. Freedom of
 information - Great Britain 6. Freedom of information -
 Australia
 I. Title
 323.4'45'0941

**Library of Congress Control Number:** 2001091648

ISBN 0 7546 2170 7

Printed and bound by Athenaeum Press, Ltd.,
Gateshead, Tyne & Wear.

# Contents

# Table of Cases

*Fraser* v *Evans* [1969] 1 QB 349.

*Gallagher* v *Durack* (1983) 152 CLR 238.

*GCHQ* case (see under *Council of Civil Service Unions* v *Minister for the Civil Service* [1985] 1 AC 374).

*Gouriet* v *Union of Post Office Workers* [1978] AC 435.

*Grant* v *Headland* (1977) 17 ACTR 29.

*Hinch* v *A-G (Vic)* (1987) 164 CLR 15.

*Izuora* v *R* [1953] AC 327.

*John Fairfax & Sons Ltd* v *Cojuangco* (1988) 165 CLR 346.

*John Fairfax & Sons Ltd* v *Police Tribunal of NSW* (1986) 5 NSWLR 465.

*John Fairfax Publications Pty Ltd* v *Doe* (1995) 130 ALR 488.

*Johnston* v *Director of Public Prosecutions* (1989) 97 FLR 424.

*Khorasandjian* v *Bush* [1993] QB 727 (CA).

*Kitcat* v *Sharp* (1882) 52 LJ Ch 134.

*Klass* v *Federal Republic of Germany* (1978) 2 EHRR 214.

*Kruger* v *Commonwealth* (1997) 190 CLR 1.

*Lange* v *Australian Broadcasting Corporation* (1997) 189 CLR 520.

*Langer* v *Commonwealth* (1996) 186 CLR 302.

*Leander* v *Sweden* (1987) 9 EHRR 433.

*Leask* v *Commonwealth* (*Leask*) (1996) 187 CLR 579.

*Levy* v *State of Victoria* (1997) 189 CLR 579.

*Lord Advocate* v *Scotsman Publications Ltd* [1990] 1 AC 812.

*Lord Advocate* v *Scotsman Publications Ltd* 1988 SLT 490

*Lovell* v *Lewandowski* [1987] WAR 81.

*Malone* v *Metropolitan Police Commissioner* [1979] 2 All ER 620.

*McGinty* v *State of Western Australia* (1996) 186 CLR 140.

*Microsoft Corporation* v *Marks* (1996) 139 ALR 99.

*Miller* v *TCN Channel Nine Pty Ltd* (1986) 161 CLR 556.

*Morison* v *Moat* (1851) 68 ER 492.

*Muldowney* v *State of South Australia* (1996) 186 CLR 352.

*National Mutual Life Association of Australasia Ltd* v *G.T.V. Corporation Pty Ltd* [1989] VR 747.

*Nationwide News Pty Ltd* v *Wills* (1992) 177 CLR 1.

*New York Times Co* v *US*, 403 US 713 (1971).

*Nicrotherm Electrical Co Ltd* v *Percy* [1956] RPC 272, (on appeal) [1957] RPC 207.

*Onus* v *Alcoa of Australia* (1981) 149 CLR 27.

*Parry* v *Crooks* (1981) 27 SASR 1 (Court of Appeal).

*Peek* v *NSW Egg Corporation* (1986) 6 NSWLR 1.

*Pidduck* v *Molloy* [1992] 2 FLR 202 (CA).

*Pollard* v *Photographic Co* (1889) 40 Ch D. 345.

# Table of Statutes

# 1 Introduction

## National security and the D-Notice system[1]

It seems to be generally accepted that there is some government information which should remain secret and information relating to national security matters is the type of information most often cited in this context (Barendt, 1996; Campbell and Whitmore, 1975).[2] At the same time secrecy should not be misused in order to obscure government mismanagement or iniquity (Bok, 1982; Lustgarten and Leigh, 1994; Lee, Hanks and Morabito, 1995). In other words the public interest in the non-publication of certain government information must be balanced with the public interest in openness in government.

The D-Notice system sits at the centre of this tension between secrecy and openness in government. The D-Notice system is an arrangement between the government and the media whereby the media agrees not to publish certain government information which is sensitive on the grounds of being a threat to national security. The system exists only in the U.K. and Australia, and has been described as 'uniquely British' (HC 773, 1980, para. 12).

In Israel the Military Censor has broad powers to censor publications. There is also an agreement, first signed in 1949, between an 'Editors' Committee' of the daily press and the Israel Defence Force Authorities, whereby certain newspapers accept 'advisory censorship' from the Military Censor. In return, criminal proceedings will not be brought against newspapers which are party to the agreement (Seegal, 1991). Although the Israeli system bears similarities to the D-Notice system, further comparison will not be undertaken. Israel is continually under the threat of war or terrorism so the situation there is more akin to wartime censorship in the U.K. or Australia. In the U.S.A. President Kennedy considered introducing a system similar to the D-Notice system after the Cuban crisis, but the members of the press with whom he raised the idea dismissed it without hesitation (Marshall, 1967).

The D-Notice system is administered by a committee consisting of representatives from the media on one side and from the government, or from government departments, on the other side. The system is voluntary and extra

1

legal, that is, there is no legal requirement for the media to participate and the system itself provides for no legal penalties in the event of a breach.

## The parties involved and the issues

The main parties, or 'sides', involved are the government, wishing to suppress sensitive information, and the media desiring to publish. Both claim to represent the public interest, but for different reasons. In the narrowest of senses the subject matter of this book is the interests of government pitted against the interests of the media. In a broader sense, the subject matter of this book is the right of the government to censor certain material, weighed against the right of the general public, represented by the media, to have full and frank disclosure of government activities.

Neither the government nor the media can properly be described as objective participants in disputes of this nature because their own interests are inextricably tied to the competing public interests they purport to represent. While the government claims the public interest in suppressing material for the safety and welfare of the general public, their real reasons may have more to do with suppression of potentially embarrassing revelations. Similarly the media claim of representing the public interest by revealing information may have little to do with promoting the interests of the general public. The question then arises as to whom, or what, *does* weigh the competing interests objectively - that is, who looks after the interests of the general public? The answer seems to be that there is a major deficiency in the operation of the D-Notice system and in the legal alternatives to the system: the public interest, that is the interests of the general public, is not sufficiently represented in the former and is often not sufficiently recognised by the judiciary in the latter.

The 'public interest' or, as it has just been stated, 'the interests of the general public', is a concept at the core of this book. In the context of the issues examined, this means the interests of the general public in having only that material suppressed which is genuinely prejudicial to national security.

## Structure of the book

This book begins with a review of the three main philosophical arguments used to justify a free speech principle. Chapters 3 to 5 are mainly narrative and begin with an examination of the history and operation of the D-Notice system in the U.K. This commences with the political background leading to the introduction of the system and continues by closely following its development and charting the major events that have taken place until the present day. Much of the early historical material was obtained by examination of original cabinet and war office documents held in the Public Record Office in Kew. The current operation of the system in the U.K. is outlined, followed by the history and operation of the system in Australia. Finally there is also a look at issues such as the financial cost of complying with the system and misuse of the system by the government.

As noted earlier, D-Notices are supposedly extra-legal, that is they are voluntary and have no legal backing. In both the U.K. and Australia, however, the government has utilised civil actions against media organisations in order to secure by injunction prior to publication the suppression of sensitive information. The criminal law has been used in the U.K. to punish media defendants subsequent to publication. Chapters 6 to 8 examine the legal protection of sensitive material, starting with the use of the criminal law in the U.K. This involves a detailed look at the Official Secrets Acts (U.K.) passed between 1911 and 1989. The provisions of these Acts have been the main instruments of punishment for the publication of government information, sensitive or otherwise. The very existence of these provisions may prevent the publication of sensitive material because the threat of potential prosecution may act as a deterrent. The equivalent legislation in Australia, the *Crimes Act 1914* (Cth), is then considered.

For the media the use of the criminal law generally follows publication, but the government would prefer that the information not be published in the first place. The next matter to be investigated is therefore the potential for the use of injunctions to restrain a breach of the criminal law, for example to prevent a breach of the Official Secrets Act 1989 (U.K.). The discussion includes the use of injunctions to restrain a contempt of court. It will be seen that the use of injunctions in these circumstances is not as dependable as in the civil law, and Chapter 8 looks at the way in which the government in both the U.K. and Australia have applied the civil law to suppress publication of information. There is a detailed analysis of the use of breach of confidence in this context, and a briefer look at copyright. In effect the issues discussed in these chapters comprise the main alternatives to the D-Notice system for the protection of sensitive information.

Chapters 9 to 11 cover a number of concepts that are interwoven into the matters that have been already been discussed, but have not been examined in their own right. Chapter 9 investigates the meaning of the key phrases 'national security' and 'the state', then inquires into whom or what balances the interests of national security against the competing public interest of openness in government, manifested by publication. Chapter 10 examines the tension between freedom of speech and the suppression of information, and considers the question of what circumstances justify censorship. Chapter 11 looks at manipulation of the news by government and by the media. This is followed by examination of the role of the judiciary in determining cases, either criminal or civil, that come before courts where the publication of sensitive information is in dispute. Chapter 11 helps to gain a better understanding of whom or what balances the competing public interests in suppression or disclosure. Finally the conclusion makes recommendations based on the examination of the above issues.

## Notes

[1]    For the sake of continuity the term 'D-Notice system' is used in any general references to the system in this book even though it has been called the 'DA-Notice system' in the U.K. since 1993. References to the system in books, reports and articles include many variations in citing the name. For the sake of simplicity and uniformity, the 'D-Notice system' will be the name used throughout this book when general reference is being made to the system in either country.

[2]    For an argument that there is little justification for keeping national security information secret see Toohey (1994). In 1997 the present author sent out a survey to print media editors and electronic media news editors in the U.K. and Australia. One of the questions was: 'Do you consider that there is certain information which, in the interests of national security, should not be published?' Six respondents, all from the Australian media, answered in the negative.

## References

Barendt, E. (1996), *Freedom of Speech*, Oxford.

Bok, S. (1982), *Secrets - On the Ethics of Concealment and Revelation*, New York.

Campbell, E. and Whitmore H. (1975), *Freedom in Australia*, Sydney.

HC 773 (1980), *Third Report from the Defence Committee (Session 1979-80), The D Notice System*, London.

Lee, H., Hanks, P. and Morabito, V. (1995), *In the Name of National Security: The Legal Dimensions*, Sydney.

Lustgarten, L. and Leigh, I. (1994), *From the Cold: National Security and Parliamentary Democracy*, Oxford.

Marshall, G. (1967), 'Comment', *Public Law*, vol. Winter, p. 261.

Seegal, Z. (1991), 'Security Censorship: Prior Restraint (After the Schnitzer Decision)', in S. Shetreet (ed), *Free Speech and National Security*, Dordrecht.

Toohey, B. (1994), 'A Case for Greater Openness', in A. Bergin and R. Hall (eds), *Intelligence and Australian National Security*, Canberra.

# 2 The Right to Freedom of Speech

This book examines the operation of the D-Notice system to determine if the system provides a satisfactory way of deciding whether or not certain confidential government material should be suppressed. The essence of the issues involved is the government's right to censor certain material versus the public's right to be informed - or censorship versus freedom of speech. This presupposes that freedom of speech is a right that can legitimately be weighed against the government's right to censor information. The focus of this chapter is to justify the presupposition.

In the Western democracies freedom of speech is accepted as being one of the fundamental basic rights, whether or not those rights are entrenched in the constitution of a country or formally adopted in some other way. Where there is no constitutional protection of human rights, for example Australia, and 'rights' are therefore residual, the word 'value' might be more appropriate. Barendt (1996), uses 'value' in this context. The acceptance of freedom of speech as being one of the fundamental rights is reflected in the International Covenant on Civil and Political Rights (ICCPR), Art. 19(2) of which recognises the importance of freedom of speech. Both the U.K., in 1976, and Australia, in 1980, have signed and ratified the ICCPR. Neither country has incorporated the ICCPR into domestic law. The U.K. is also a party to the European Convention on Human Rights (ECHR), Article 10(1) of which protects freedom of expression; the ECHR was incorporated into domestic law in November 1998 by the Human Rights Act 1998 (U.K.). The Act came into force in Scotland in July 1999 and in England in October 2000.

There are a number of different, and perhaps to some degree competing, philosophical bases for justifying a free speech principle. The three main theories are the argument from truth, the argument from democracy and free speech as an aspect of self fulfilment. In the context of this book it is necessary to examine these philosophical justifications in order to determine whether one or more of them alone or in combination is sufficient to justify the proposition that free speech is a factor to be taken into account when any restriction is contemplated. Before examining the three main arguments it is worth making a couple of general observations.

5

Schauer (1982, pp. 3-6), takes freedom of speech to be an 'independent principle', 'principles' being 'the currency of political philosophy'. By 'independent principle' he means a principle that can stand alone without being reliant on any larger principle for its existence or justification. He prefers to see free speech as being an independent principle rather than being an instance of the broader principle of liberty, an approach he would find 'troubling'. If it were an 'instance' of a larger principle, acceptance of the 'instance' would require acceptance of the larger principle, whatever that may be.

Schauer also takes freedom of speech to be an 'other-regarding' act because it has an effect on others. Speech can cause harm to the speaker, harm to others, harm to society and, when military secrets or lies about the government are disclosed, harm to the 'governing apparatus' of the state. He questions whether there is in fact a category of acts that are self-regarding, that is, harming only the individual involved in the act, but says that if there is such a category, speech does not fall within it.

Other-regarding acts, because of the potential of harm to others, are, generally speaking, acts that may legitimately be subjected to control by the state. Despite this, as will be seen below, free speech is seen as a right worthy of protection from any such governmental interference or control, mainly because the government cannot be trusted to make the necessary distinction between truth and falsity. These comments may be said to justify the case for the validity of either the argument from truth or the argument from democracy, or both.

## The three main free speech theories

*The argument from truth*

The argument from truth has a long pedigree extending back to Milton's *Areopagitica* written in November 1644. Milton made reference to the search for truth being hampered by government regulation via the licencing of publications. It is, however, John Stuart Mill with whom this theory is most usually associated. Barendt (1996, p. 8), for example, uses the heading 'Mill's argument from truth'. According to Mill (1859, p. 33):

> If all mankind minus one, [*sic*] were of one opinion, and only one person were of the contrary opinion, mankind would be no more justified in silencing that one person, than he, if he had the power, would be justified

in silencing mankind. Were an opinion a personal possession of no value except to the owner, if to be obstructed in the enjoyment of it were simply a private injury, it would make some difference whether the injury was inflicted only on a few persons or on many. But the peculiar evil of silencing the expression of an opinion is, [*sic*] that it is robbing the human race; posterity as well as the existing generation, those who dissent from the opinion, still more than those who hold it. If the opinion is right, they are deprived of the opportunity of exchanging error for truth: if wrong, they lose, what is almost as great a benefit, the clearer perception and livelier impression of truth, produced by its collision with error.[1]

Mill divided the chapter entitled *Of the liberty of thought and discussion* into two parts. The first part addressed the situation where the suppressed opinion may possibly be true (1859, p. 34):

To refuse a hearing to an opinion, because they are sure it is false, is to assume that *their* certainty is the same thing as *absolute* certainty. All silencing of discussion is an assumption of infallibility [*Mill's emphasis*].

The focus of the first part was to point out the dangers of 'the assumption of infallibility', as Mill termed it. Governments, and individuals, should properly inform themselves before forming opinions, and only then should they act upon the opinion. The second part of the chapter looked at when the suppressed opinion may possibly be false. For Mill the difficulty with this sort of suppression was that the truth, without challenge, was worth little.

One criticism of the argument from truth as described by Mill is that it assumes that the truth is worth pursuing, and that the truth, or whatever most closely approximates the truth, will ultimately be elicited from unrestricted freedom of discussion. That the truth is something intrinsically worth pursuing is not a matter of controversy, but, as both Schauer (1982) and Barendt (1996) point out, why should the truth necessarily emerge triumphant from unregulated discourse?[2] Another criticism is that Mill's theory advocates that there should be absolutely no restrictions by the state on speech, regardless of the truth or falsity of the statements being made. Schauer is of the view that this absolutism is the weakest point of Mill's arguments, but he does not think that an argument should be rejected because 'its proponent overstates the case' (1982 p. 23). Clearly, however, governments do restrict speech when there are other overriding interests, such as the interests in promoting harmony by restriction of racially offensive speech. Providing that the rationale for imposition of the restriction can be freely discussed, the curtailment of free speech may be regarded as legitimate.

Throughout his discourse on freedom of expression Mill refers to 'opinions', and he refers specifically to 'morals, religion, politics, social relations, and the business of life'. Of subjects such as mathematics he says: 'The peculiarity of mathematical truths is, that the argument is on one side. There are no objections and no answers to objections' (p. 66). Mill leaves unclear the status of the application of the argument from truth in relation to statements of fact and statements which may contain both fact and opinion.

## The argument from democracy

The argument from democracy applies only to a particular form of government, unlike the argument from truth which suffers from no such limitation.[3] Even so, in a general sense, both theories are connected (Schauer, 1982; Schauer, 1994). Indeed Schauer (1982) makes the remark about the argument from democracy that 'much of its strength derives not from its independent force, but from the extent to which it is a discrete and important subset of the argument from truth' (p. 45).

The argument from democracy holds that in order for citizens to effectively participate in the democratic process they must be properly informed, and so there should be no restrictions on speech. In addition, freedom to criticise government officials makes them accountable to the electorate. In 1977 the Royal Commission on the Press (U.K.) described freedom of the press on the basis of this theory, and Barendt describes it 'as probably the most attractive and certainly the most fashionable free speech theory in modern Western democracies' (1996, p. 20).

Both the argument from truth and the argument from democracy are goal based and utilitarian, in that they focus on the rights of the recipient. The argument from democracy, however, also focuses on the rights of the speaker. It would seem also that the argument from democracy applies to information as well as to opinions.

One of the main objections to the argument from democracy is that the principle is self limiting. If the people are sovereign, and no restrictions may be placed on that sovereignty, then how is any limitation on speech justifiable? Indeed, how is any free speech principle justifiable because that limits the right of democratically elected representatives to act on behalf of the sovereign electorate without impediment. For Barendt, the solution may lie in recognising that, while the argument from democracy is pre-eminent, there is more than one relevant justification for a free speech principle. Therefore the argument from democracy may be seen as relating primarily to freedom of political speech, and being of limited application.

Consistent with this approach is the view that restraint may be legitimate if a distinction is made between public law and private law rights. When the publication relates to a private individual, restraint may be more acceptable because there is no third party, or 'public', interest in the material being revealed. When the publication relates to the government, there is more likely to be a public interest in the material being revealed in order that the workings of government are open to scrutiny. Thus where the competing right of an individual is concerned, for example the right to an untarnished reputation, the right to freedom of speech does not carry the same weight as it does when the 'public interest' is involved.[4] Despite the problems, Barendt considers the argument from democracy to be pre-eminent among the free speech theories of the twentieth century.

*Free speech as an aspect of self-fulfilment*[5]

Free speech as an aspect of self-fulfilment is based on the liberal concept that individuals have certain basic human rights, regardless of whether or not these rights are given to them by law (Dworkin, 1977).[6] Free speech is one of these rights, and should not be restricted even if it is in the interests of the majority to do so. There are two branches of this argument. The first is that free speech is necessary to individual development and any restrictions on speech will hinder self development and self improvement. The difficulty with such an approach is that it is hard to justify the special position of speech in relationship to other factors which may equally promote self development, such as food, shelter and a good education. In this context free speech seems to be merely an indistinguishable component of a more general libertarian claim (Schauer, 1982; Barendt, 1996).

The second branch of this argument relates to individual choice and the right to dignity. Dworkin (1977), one of the main proponents of this aspect of the theory, sees the basic human rights as 'strong' rights against the government, but he points out that even these rights are not absolute and the State may be justified in overriding them when the rights of others are at stake, or if the benefit to the majority interest is sufficient. He also refers to them as 'paradigm rights' (p. 197), and for him the government could not override these rights on 'the minimal grounds that would be sufficient if no such right existed' (p. 192). In some instances, however, where a law invades an individual's rights against the government, these rights may trump a law made in the general interest. In such a case the individual has a right to disobey the law in question.

Dworkin considers that the basic human rights are based on a concept of equality:

> Citizens governed by the liberal concept of equality each have a right to equal concern and respect. But there are two different rights that might be comprehended by that abstract right. The first is the right to equal treatment, that is, to the same distribution of goods or opportunities as anyone else has or is given ... The second is the right to treatment as an equal. This is the right, not to equal distribution of some good or opportunity, but the right to equal concern in the political decision about how these goods and opportunities are to be distributed (p. 273).

He sees the second right as being fundamental, and the basic human rights arise from the requirement that each individual be treated as an equal. Thus the emphasis is placed on personal, or 'internal', preferences - the choice of one person is equal in value to the choice of another person. Dworkin explains the distinction between internal and external preferences in terms of choices that affect the individual on a personal level (internal preferences), as opposed to more general choices which do not have the same direct effect (external preferences).

Schauer says that, in the context of free speech, Dworkin's basic human rights approach proposes that each person's ideas carry equal weight. When an individual's ideas, or the expression of those ideas, are suppressed, the inference is that society takes those ideas to have less value than the ideas of others. 'Society is saying that his ideas, and by implication he himself, are not worthy. He is not deserving of treatment as an equal member of society' (1982, p. 62). This leads to the main criticism of Dworkin's theory which is that, as Schauer puts it, people are not equal in their abilities, including the credibility and intellectual soundness of their ideas, but this does not exclude them from being treated equally.

Unlike the argument from truth which is essentially goal based, that is favouring the interests of the audience, and the argument from democracy which may favour the interests both of the speaker and of the audience, both branches of the argument that free speech is a basic human right favour the speaker. Both branches are centred on the right of the speaker to express himself or herself without restriction, and while the audience may benefit from the speaker's views, this is incidental to the main focus.

Further criticisms applying to the theory in general are, firstly, that because it is focused on the speaker, it would seem to deal only with ideas and opinion rather than fact and information. A second criticism is that, being about self-fulfilment, it does nothing to explain how free speech theories apply to non-natural legal persons such as corporations.

## Conclusion

There are other free speech theories but these tend to be variations on the three main arguments.[7] In the context of this book it is not necessary to conclude which of the theories individually, or in a combination of two or more, are sufficient to justify a free speech principle.[8] The theory which is most relevant to the subject matter of the book is the argument from democracy. The information which is the subject matter of the D-Notice system is facts and information, rather than opinion and ideas, and the reason for arguing against restriction is that, as will be seen in later chapters, the government may use the system to conceal ineptitude, mismanagement or corruption. The criticism that may be applied to the argument from democracy, that it is limited in its application and may apply only to political speech, are of no consequence in this context. It also has the advantage of focusing on the rights of both the speaker and the recipient.

Having accepted that, in principle, freedom of speech is a right worthy of protection from interference, it is also recognised that it is not an absolute right and in some cases, such as in the interests of national security, interference may be legitimate.[9] The subject matter of the book is whether the D-Notice system sufficiently balances the competing interests of free speech and national security by restricting only that information which genuinely threatens national security.

## Notes

[1]   Mill wrote his treatise *On Liberty* in 1859; the version referred to was published in 1992 by The Legal Classics Library, New York. The rather curious punctuation is copied directly from the text. For a detailed discussion on Mill's approach to freedom of expression see Ten (1980). For discussion on the argument from truth generally, including criticisms, see Barendt (1996) and Schauer (1982).

[2]   For a detailed discussion on the 'value of truth' see Schauer (1982), Barendt (1996) and Campbell (1994).

[3]   Schauer (1982) defines his use of 'democracy' not 'as rule *for* the people, but as rule *by* the people' (p. 37) [*Schauer's emphasis*]. He says: 'The entire argument is generated by

the single principle of a sovereign electorate' (p. 40). This approach is echoed in some recent Australian High Court judgments (see Ch. 10).

[4]   Macmillan Patfield (1996) questioned the meaningfulness of the public/private distinction. The comments were made in the context of formulating a free speech theory in relation to copyright, but the breach of confidence cases examined in Chapter 8 illustrate that the public/private distinction is still a live issue for the courts, at least in that particular legal area.

With respect to the right of an individual to an untarnished reputation, the ICCPR and the ECHR permit derogation from the right to freedom of expression 'for respect of the ... reputations of others'. ICCPR Art. 19(3)(a), and 'for the protection of the reputation ... of others', ECHR Art. 10(2).

[5]   This is Barendt's heading (1996, p. 14); Schauer (1982) canvasses this argument in his chapter entitled 'Individuality and free speech'. See also Campbell (1994, p. 33) who says: 'Self-expression/self-development/self-determination/autonomy arguments for freedom of expression are perilous in their potential for tautology [*endnote omitted*]'.

[6]   Dworkin (1977) is one of the main proponents of this theory. He comments, 'Some philosophers, of course reject the idea that citizens have rights apart from what the law happens to give them. Bentham thought that the idea of moral rights was "nonsense on stilts" ' (p. 184). The notion that free speech is one of the basic human rights is supported by its incorporation into the ICCPR and ECHR and in the First Amendment to the Constitution of the United States of America.

[7]   See, for example, Scanlon (1986 and 1979). Scanlon's theory is based on individual autonomy and is a variation on the rights based theory.

[8]   Both Schauer (1982) and Barendt (1996) seem to intimate that while no one theory individually is satisfactory to justify a free speech principle a combination of two or more may be sufficient to fit the differing circumstances where free speech is an issue.

[9]   The recognition that freedom of expression is not an absolute right is reflected in the relevant provisions of the ICCPR and the ECHR which allow for exceptions, including, inter alia, the interests of national security.

## References

Barendt, E. (1996), *Freedom of Speech*, Oxford, pp. 8, 14, 20.

Campbell, T. (1994), 'Rationales for Freedom of Communication', in T. Campbell and W. Sadurski (eds), *Freedom of Communication*, Aldershot, p. 33.

Dworkin, R. (1977), *Taking Rights Seriously*, London, pp. 184, 192, 197, 273.

European Convention on Human Rights, Art. 10.

Human Rights Act 1998 (U.K.).

International Covenant on Civil and Political Rights, Art. 19.

Macmillan Patfield, F. (1996), 'Towards a Reconciliation of Free Speech and Copyright', in E. Barendt, S. Bate, J. Dickens (eds), *The Yearbook of Media and Entertainment Law*, Oxford.

Mill, J.S. (1859), *On Liberty*, reprinted by The Legal Classics Library (1992), New York, pp. 33, 34, 66.

Milton, J. (November 1644), *Areopagitica*, reprinted by Cambridge University Press (1918), Cambridge.

Royal Commission on the Press (U.K.) (1977), *Final Report*, London.

Scanlon, T. (1986), 'A Theory of Freedom of Expression', in R. Dworkin (ed), *The Philosophy of Law*, Oxford.

Scanlon, T. (1979), 'Freedom of Expression and Categories of Expression', *U. Pittsb. L.R.*, vol. 40, p. 519.

Schauer, F. (1994), 'Free Speech in a World of Private Power', in T. Campbell and W. Sadurski (eds), *Freedom of Communication*, Aldershot.

Schauer, F. (1982), *Free Speech: a Philosophical Enquiry*, Cambridge, pp. 3-6, 23, 37, 40, 45, 62.

Ten, C. L. (1980), *Mill on Liberty*, Oxford.

# 3 History of the D-Notice System in the U.K. to 1945

## Introduction

The D-Notice system commenced in 1912 with the formation of the Admiralty, War Office and Press Committee in the U.K. Chapters 3 to 5 concentrate on the events responsible for shaping the development of the D-Notice system and examine the way in which the D-Notice system works in the U.K. and Australia at the present time. These chapters show how the various competing interests, in particular the interests of the general public, were balanced during the development of the D-Notice system, and are now balanced, if at all. Much of the historical material comes from original documents, such as letters and minutes of meetings, which are stored at the Public Record Office in Kew, London.[1]

## Brief historical background: 1850-1912

On a number of occasions in the second half of the 19th century the U.K. press published information detrimental to government interests. The inadequacies of English military equipment in the Crimean War (1854-1856) were exposed by *The Times*, and similar reports about the navy appeared in the *Pall Mall Gazette* in 1884. In 1858 the *Daily News* disclosed the contents of two confidential despatches sent from the Lord High Commissioner of the Ionian Islands to the Colonial Office. The story compromised the purpose of a visit to the Ionian Islands that Gladstone was making at the time (Williams, 1965).

In 1878 leaks from the Foreign Office of details of a recently concluded secret agreement between England and Russia appeared in *The Globe*. These leaks were traced to Charles Marvin, a poorly paid clerk in the Foreign Office, who was subsequently tried for the theft of a document from the Foreign Office. Because he had repeated the information to *The Globe* from memory and the document had never left the Foreign Office, the case was stopped by the presiding magistrate who found that the charges had not been established (Williams, 1965; Aitken, 1971; Vincent, 1998).

In an effort to stem the damaging flow of leaks the Official Secrets Act was passed in 1889. The preamble stated the Act was 'to prevent the Disclosure of Official Documents and Information'. Few prosecutions took place under the Act, and all except one were concerned with military or naval secrets, so it did appear to stop the leaks to the press from sources within government departments.[2] According to Williams (1965) the one exception was the use of official information for economic purposes - a supply clerk working for the Navy at Woolwich Dockyard was prosecuted for offering a contractor official information on contracts and prices.

Problems with obtaining convictions under the Official Secrets Act 1889 led to unsuccessful attempts in 1896 and 1908 to amend it. The problems related to the public interest defence in each provision and having to prove the unauthorised communication was intended to be contrary to the well-being of the state. On 11 May 1908 the Lord Chancellor, Lord Loreburn, had the following to say in answer to a question about whether the government intended to proceed with the amendments to the Official Secrets Bill:

> The LORD CHANCELLOR (Lord Loreburn): My Lords, I propose to postpone the Second Reading of the Official Secrets Bill. I met a few days ago a deputation representing the Metropolitan Press on this subject, and they informed me of their anxiety lest this Bill should interfere with the legitimate enterprise and freedom of the Press. His Majesty's Government have no such design, I need hardly say, and if I entered upon detail I could show that a great deal of misunderstanding exists as to the clauses of the Bill and their effect. But it should be clear that anyone in the Press conducting his duties honourably would be quite safe. I told the deputation that I would be very pleased to receive from them any communications or criticisms directed to this object, or to safeguard legitimate enterprise; and no doubt I shall soon have an opportunity of considering them ... On the one side is the necessity of respecting the just freedom of writing and of publication; on the other side is the danger to the public interests of the publication of important secret documents or information, either of a military or civil character. What I should like is that, if possible, those interested should arrive at a common agreement with the Government. I do not know if it is possible. I hope it may be, and I have thought it better to postpone the Second Reading in that hope, although, of course, this does not signify that the Government have any intention of dropping the subject.

The 1908 amendments were subsequently allowed to lapse. In the meanwhile the activities of the press in publishing strategic information to the detriment of England, particularly during the Crimean War and the Boer War, had infuriated the military authorities. In 1898 the English newspapers published details of the 'composition of garrisons of all home defended ports ... the existence of submarine defences at Portsmouth, Falmouth and other ports ...'. On 1 March 1899 the Adjutant General at the War Office, Sir Evelyn Wood, wrote a memo which indicated that the institution of formal press censorship in wartime had been contemplated, but ultimately rejected. The memo also recognised the financial loss that might occur when a newspaper was conscientious and withheld publication (PRO WO 32/6381).[3]

On 27 September 1899 two newspapers, *St James Gazette* and *The Globe*, quoting directly from a Reuters telegram, gave full details of the strength that day (27 September 1899) of the camp at Dundee in North Natal. Some form of censorship was in place during the Boer War, as is evidenced by the following exchange in the House of Commons on 27 July 1900:

> Captain SINCLAIR: If you want the people of this country to form a sound and wise judgment as to the war, keep them informed. It is one of the liberties and rights of the country that they should be informed, responsible as they are in supporting the Government. It is the greatest regret to me that the Government have been so reticent in this matter of the publication of the despatches ... Our complaint is not confined to the non-publication of the despatches. It refers also to the censorship. Censorship which is purely military and for military purposes no one has any title or right to object to. It is absolutely necessary to an army in the field, and we must submit to the discretion of the Commander-in-Chief, whoever he may be. When the censorship is no longer military but is also political - because that is what the censorship in South Africa has been - I believe it becomes a great danger ...
>
> We find in South Africa, also, the prohibition of newspapers under martial law. At the present moment, two newspapers, and two newspapers alone which took a side opposed to the war - *Ons Land* and the *South African News* - have their circulation prohibited ... that seems to disclose a most serious state of things.
>
> Mr WYNDHAM: It *is* a serious state of things; that is what makes the course of action necessary.
>
> Captain SINCLAIR: The hon. Gentleman is too experienced and far-seeing a man not to know that the liberty of the press is one of the essential liberties of persons living under the British constitution. You may be doing a very dangerous thing in suppressing all expression of opinion, and you may be furthering your policy in but a very slight degree if you make such stringent and severe measures as these ...

These two extracts sum up well the great difficulties involved in attempting to balance the competing interests of keeping the public informed on the one hand, and on the other hand keeping certain information secret for reasons of national security. It is interesting to note that as early as 1900 there was concern in Parliament that censorship legitimately invoked in the interests of military security should not be extended to become political censorship. This is a concern that has not diminished with time, and which the D-Notice system has done nothing to allay.

The war in South Africa and the defeat of the Russians by the Japanese in 1904 kept alive the idea of press censorship. The Russian defeat was seen as the latest in a long list of examples of where the English press had given the advantage to the victors in a number of conflicts by revealing strategic military information about the vanquished (Towle, 1975; Palmer, 1984). In the words of Palmer (1984): 'It all added up to a single lesson: the essential weapon of modern warfare was secrecy, and that, as far as the administrators were concerned, meant shutting up the press' (p. 228).

In 1905 drafting began on the Publication of Naval and Military Information Bill which would have given legislative force to formal press censorship in wartime, the earlier consideration (and ultimate rejection) of which was outlined in Wood's letter of 1899. The Committee of Imperial Defence (CID), the group responsible for initiating the drafting of the Bill in 1905, recognised that a press backlash would spoil any chance it had of a trouble free passage through Parliament.

The Secretary of the CID, Sir George Clarke, sought the assistance of Sydney Brooks, a freelance journalist, to sound out the attitude of the editors and proprietors to the Bill, and, if required, to convince them that it was necessary (Lovelace, 1978). In January 1906 Brooks wrote a lengthy letter, in essence asking the following questions:

> (1) Are you prepared to support a Bill making the publication of all news of naval and military movements, not authorised by the responsible authorities, penal?
> (2) Are you prepared to accept and advocate the principle that such a Bill should be passed with powers to make it operative by order in Council when the Government of the day so decides?
> (3) Are you willing to attend a Conference of the leading editors of the United Kingdom at the offices of the Committee of Imperial Defence, should such a conference be thought advisable for the further discussion of the details of the Bill in question? (PRO Cab 17/91)[4]

A majority of the respondents were, for the most part, supportive of the proposed Bill. An examination of the correspondence in question (about one hundred and five responses, dated from late 1905 to the first few months of 1906) shows that just under half fully supported the idea, a further fourteen percent agreed but with reservations, nineteen percent wanted a conference to discuss the matter, sixteen percent disagreed, and a few reached no conclusions at all (PRO Cab 17/91). Lovelace (1978, p. 308) says Brooks 'gained the almost unanimous support of the leading proprietors and editors throughout the country',[5] whereas Palmer (1984, p. 229) says 'most did not - at least not in detail'.

In 1907 *The Times* reported on the annual conference of the Institute of Journalists. Discussion about the Publication of Naval and Military Information Bill took place. Delegates at the conference urged the Institute of Journalists to watch its passage through Parliament:

> [T]o secure (1) that, in accordance with the promise of the first Lord of the Admiralty (Lord Tweedmouth), in the House of Lords, on July 13, 1906, there be placed no restriction on comment or criticism based on facts which are common knowledge; (2) that no penalty shall be inflicted upon any owner, publisher, or seller of, or contributor to, a newspaper, unless it be proved that he wilfully and knowingly published, circulated, or contributed information which the court may hold to come within the provisions of the statute; and (3) that any person convicted under the Act by a petty sessions Court shall have a right of appeal to the High Court of Justice.
> The attempts to suppress the circulation of news had broken down in nearly every civilized country. In following the course they were taking the conference believed they were protecting the interests of the country at large, for the policy of secrecy in regard to war led as an inevitable consequence to the concealment of jobbery, corruption, and sometimes of crime.[6]

The end result was that the Bill did not proceed because the War Office perceived that opposition by the press would prevent the Bill from being passed by Parliament (Lovelace, 1978; Palmer, 1984).

In the years following the failure of the 1908 amendments to the Official Secrets Act the government started taking the threat of espionage more seriously. This was due to the obviously hostile intent of Germany accompanied by an increase in German spying activities in England. The 1889 Act was replaced by the Official Secrets Act 1911 in the August of 1911 - the new legislation went through Parliament quickly and without debate, passing all its stages in one day only (Seely, 1930; Vincent, 1998). England was in crisis at the time with a very real threat of war; in June 1911 a German gunboat was sent to Agadir in Morocco, starting a period of international crisis which lasted until November 1911. At the same time there was the imminent start of the much publicised trial of a German accused of spying (Williams, 1965).

In September 1911 the *Morning Post* printed an article entitled 'Guardianship of British Forts' detailing the defences of many of the fortifications on the East Coast of England.[7] The issue of press censorship, which had been simmering under the surface since the shelving of the Publication of Naval and Military Information Bill, came once again to the fore. The Permanent Secretary at the War Office, Sir Reginald Brade, was briefed by the CID to negotiate with the press. This time instead of approaching the editors as Brooks had done, Brade went to the Newspaper Proprietors Association and entered confidential negotiations with the leading proprietors (Lovelace, 1978; Palmer, 1984).

This was the background which gave rise to the introduction of the D-Notice system.

## The history of the D-Notice system in the U.K.: 1912-1945

*1912-1914*

Following two conferences in 1912, between representatives of the press and service representatives, the Joint Standing Committee (Admiralty, War Office and Press Committee) was organised. The Joint Standing Committee (Admiralty, War Office and Press Committee) will be referred to in the history up to 1918 as the Joint Standing Committee. This was the name commonly used in documentation until 1918 when the committee became known as the Admiralty, War Office, Air Ministry and Press Committee.

In a memorandum dated 5 November 1912, Sir Reginald Brade (PRO DEFE 53/1) outlined the situation leading up to the negotiations between government and press:

> The discussion at the meetings of the standing sub-committee of the Committee of Imperial Defence which deals with the co-ordination of departmental action on the outbreak of war, brought prominently to notice a certain weakness in the system of the precautionary measures to be adopted in the period of tension or strained relations which might be anticipated before an actual outbreak of war between this country and a foreign power ...
> The chief obstacle in the way of securing concealment lies, of course, in the newspaper Press and in its freedom from Government control.
> While these considerations were being debated at the sub-committee, and

before a conclusion had been reached, the crisis of the summer of 1911 occurred, and the War Office had occasion to go more closely into the question of the control of the Press. Certain newspapers published items of military news which it was obviously contrary to the public interest to make generally known, especially at that moment, and verbal remonstrances were addressed to the editors. Apologies were freely forthcoming but the War Office authorities were impressed with their helplessness in the matter, and it was clear to them that no strong reliance could be placed upon any scheme of precautionary measures unless some special measures for dealing with the Press could be included.

There appeared to be two alternatives open; one was some form of statutory control, and the other a friendly arrangement with the dominant Press interests. The former was being considered by a sub-committee of the Committee of Imperial Defence, and seemed, moreover, not to be a suitable method of securing the silence of the newspapers before the actual outbreak of the war. The authorities accordingly decided to attempt the latter.

Details of the 1912 conferences are contained in a document entitled *Notes of Proceedings of Conferences held at the Admiralty on 13th August and 16th October, 1912, to consider the establishment of a Joint Committee of Official and Press Representatives to deal with the publication of Naval and Military news in times of emergency* (PRO DEFE 53/1).

Some of the political and bureaucratic manoeuvrings going on in the background are set out in a letter sent just before the second conference (PRO CAB 17/91):

Dear Colonel Seely                          8th October 1912
                        Press Censorship
Mr Churchill informed me last night that he is too heavily pressed with work at the Admiralty to continue to act as Chairman of the sub-committee inquiring into the question of press censorship in war, though he would like to remain a member. He thought that perhaps you would be willing to relieve him of the Chairmanship.

2. This inquiry was commenced over 2½ years ago and has hitherto rather hung fire, first owing to the difficulty of inducing the Press to support a Press Censorship Bill, which it was then proposed to introduce, and afterwards owing to changes in Ministerial appointments rendering it difficult to push the matter along.

3. Now, however, the question appears ready for settlement. Mr Brade and Sir Grahame Greene have practically completed a 'friendly arrangement' with proprietors of newspapers, by which the latter will submit to a voluntary censorship, though they would oppose the passage of a bill passed in time of peace.

4. The principal task that remains for the sub-committee therefore is to arrange the departmental responsibility for bringing in the Bill on the outbreak of war, and the machinery for press censorship both voluntary in peace and compulsory in war.
Etc, etc. M. Hankey.
(M.P.A. Hankey, Committee of Imperial Defence)

Colonel Seely became Secretary of State for War in June 1912, having been Under Secretary of State for War for the previous year or so. He was also on the Committee of Imperial Defence (Seely, 1930). The sub-committee referred to in the above letter, a sub-committee of the Committee of Imperial Defence, was made-up entirely of politicians and government officials and was completely separate from the Joint Standing Committee. The latter was comprised of members of the press and representatives of the War Office and Admiralty (PRO CAB 16/27). At one of the first meetings of the Joint Standing Committee the press side successfully clarified some issues of concern. These issues were mainly to do with the arrangement being 'to prevent disclosure of information as to facts and not to stifle comments on policy', and a desire that all the press should be treated equally (PRO DEFE 53/1). These concerns of the press were outlined again a month later, this time by the government side, in the minutes of the *Standing Sub-Committee of the Committee of Imperial Defence Enquiry Regarding Press and Postal Censorship in Time of War. Press Censorship. January 31, 1913* (PRO CAB 16/27).

The system was to be voluntary, and as it was not connected directly with any statute there was no need for Parliamentary approval. Williams (1965, p. 81) suggests that in 1912 'the idea of voluntary censorship was in vogue' because it was in 1912 as well that a group of film producers approached the Home Office and said that 'for their own sakes and in the public interest, they were prepared to set up at their own expense a censorship body'. As a result the British Board of Film Censors was set up.

The formal constitution of the Joint Standing Committee was drawn up by Ernest Parke, secretary of the Newspaper Proprietors' Association (Lovelace, 1978; Palmer, 1984). The heading of the constitution is officially recorded as follows (PRO ADM 116/4082):

Note on the constitution and machinery of the Joint Committee of Admiralty, War Office and Press Representatives for the informal censorship of naval and military information in time of peace.
Dated 10.1.1913.

The Constitution is also included as part of another document headed *Standing Sub-Committee of the Committee of Imperial Defence Enquiry Regarding Press and Postal Censorship in Time of War* (CAB 16/27; DEFE 53/1). The rather intriguing shift from 'in Time of *War*' in one document to 'in time of *peace*' in the Constitution is not explained anywhere. A later visit to the PRO established that no mistake had been made in copying the wording, and confirmed that there was no obvious explanation in the material available.

Parke, referred to as 'Prefect Parke' by Palmer (1984, p. 234), and the secretary of the committee were on immediate call if the Admiralty or War Office had a matter of emergency to be dealt with. The procedure under paragraph 4 of the constitution, for the communication to the Press of items to be suppressed, is detailed in a memo by Brade, dated 10 December 1912, and headed 'Joint Standing Committee of Admiralty, War Office and Press Representatives'. The memo was not addressed to anyone but 'Sir Graham Greene' was hand written at the top (PRO DEFE 53/1):[8]

> When a case arises in which either the Admiralty or the War Office wish to arrange for suppression of any item of news, Mr Robbins will be at once communicated with and if time permits, the Committee will be assembled. If the matter is extremely urgent, Mr Robbins will communicate with Mr Parke and a decision will be arrived at on the spot. In all cases the decision can be communicated to the London Press by letter or by telephone. In the majority of cases the provincial Press can similarly be communicated with by letter, but in some cases it will be necessary to telegraph or telephone. Mr Robbins has explained that owing to the frequent changes in newspaper offices and for other reasons, there may be some difficulty in providing that a decision communicated by telegram shall reach the responsible official in a provincial editor's office in such a way that there will be no risk of violation of secrecy or serious loss of time ...
>
> Mr Farnall [*of the General Post Office*] was inclined to think that if the telegrams were sent from the Press Association to the Central Telegraph Office of the General Post Office, the latter could arrange before telegrams were sent that there should be at the other end to receive them a responsible officer upon whom reliance could be placed; and by whom they could be passed safely on to the various editors.

The 'Mr Robbins' referred to was the manager of the Press Association and a member of the Joint Standing Committee.

In this arrangement with the media the government had ostensibly traded off the benefit of mandatory legislation, imposing censorship during 'times of emergency', with voluntary censorship that would apply even in peace time. Clearly there was no question of the interests of the general public being taken into account independently during these early stages of development of the D-Notice system. Even though the arrangement with the press in itself fostered a different kind of public interest to that represented by the government, the government was simply being expedient.

In December 1912 'Service' journals and newspapers also agreed to participate in the system (PRO DEFE 53/1). In January 1913 a procedure was initiated whereby editors could refer confidential or apparently secret information to the Admiralty or War Office for advice. Editors were to address communications to the 'clerk in waiting' at the Admiralty or the War Office (this title was to be used by the two departments for that purpose and in that connection only), and such references were to be dealt with promptly In no case would an editor be asked to refrain from publishing any news unless it was genuinely secret (PRO DEFE 53/1). A memo from Brade dated 10 March 1913 confirmed the discussion that took place during a meeting of the Joint Standing Committee on 3 February 1913. In this discussion an indication was given of the type of news in regard to which editors were advised to consult with the Admiralty or War Office before publication. The class of information listed as always being likely to have a bearing on secret matters included any information relating to plans or proposals of the naval or military authorities dealing with new ships or armaments, new methods of utilising the armed forces in warfare, and new defences (PRO DEFE 53/1; Cmnd 1681).

By playing on the voluntary nature of the agreement between the service departments and the press, Brade had succeeded in achieving what the War Office wanted and the committee worked very successfully between October 1912 and the outbreak of war in August 1914. For example, a meeting of the Joint Standing Committee was held on 3rd February 1914 to ask the Press to refrain from publishing information on the firing experiments being conducted by HMS Hood (PRO DEFE 53/1). At the meeting held on 27 July 1914 it was agreed that a circular should be sent out requesting the press to refrain from publishing any information regarding the movements of ships, aircraft and troops without first communicating with the department concerned (PRO DEFE 53/1).

Some of the items that were not published included embarkation practice at Southampton by the British Expeditionary Force (BEF), increased works at Woolwich and other naval and non-government dockyards, and a suppression on the whereabouts of the BEF in mid 1914 until it had arrived at its destination in France (PRO CAB 16/27; Seely, 1930; Lovelace, 1978; Palmer, 1984). Seely was at the time the Secretary of State for War (Seely,

1930). By the end of July 1914 the newspapers were complaining about each other, some having rung the Admiralty for advice while others had published the same material without any attempt at clearance (PRO DEFE 53/1).

Meanwhile neither Parliament nor the public knew anything about the formation of the Joint Standing Committee. On 22 January 1913 Mr Winston Churchill, then First Lord of the Admiralty, made a veiled reference to it in answer to a Parliamentary question (H.C. Deb., vol. 47, col. 388-389, 22 January 1913). At a meeting of the Joint Standing Committee in July 1913, mention was made of the publication by the *Gaelic American* of a letter circulated to the newspaper press by the press members of the Committee. The letter in question brought to the notice of editors the arrangements made by the Committee for the suppression of news (PRO DEFE 53/1). Despite these hints in Parliament and the press, the existence of the Joint Standing Committee and of its successor, the Services, Press and Broadcasting Committee, remained unknown to the general public until 1961 (Williams, 1965). The mere fact that the system operated in secret to withhold information from the general public raises the prospect that the interests of the general public were not likely to be independently evaluated.

*Wartime censorship: 1914-1918*

In August 1914, at the beginning of the first world war, the Press Bureau was formed to censor information prior to publication by the Press (PRO DEFE 53/2). The purpose of the Press Bureau was discussed in the House of Commons on 25 August 1914:

> Mr. King asked the Under-Secretary of State for War whether a censorship of the Press has been, or will be, set up; and whether all items of war news must be passed before publication by the Press Bureau or other authority?
> The UNDER-SECRETARY of STATE for WAR (Mr. Tennant): a Press Bureau has been established which, during the continuance of hostilities, will arrange the distribution of news of naval and military matters to the Press, and to which the newspapers will refer in regard to news which in the national interests it is not advisable to make public. The arrangement applies to news and matter of that description.

The voluntary arrangement with the press for suppression of sensitive news items was thus suspended and, regardless of any obfuscation of the situation by the government, replaced by full censorship for the period of the war. The circular announcing the establishment of the Press Bureau was sent out to the press participants by the Joint Standing Committee on 8 August

1914. The press were advised that inquiries regarding the advisability of publishing information directly or indirectly connected with the war should be made to the Press Bureau (PRO DEFE 53/1).

Compliance with the edicts of the Press Bureau was notionally voluntary, but the Defence of the Realm regulations, passed on 12 August 1914, carried heavy penalties for the publication of sensitive material (Lovelace, 1978; Palmer, 1984). It was on 31 August 1914, in answer to a Parliamentary question relating to the Press Bureau, that Mr F.E. Smith, Director of the Bureau, told Parliament about the beginnings of the Joint Standing Committee. This was the first time that the Joint Standing Committee had been spoken of openly in Parliament, but, as mentioned earlier, its existence was not generally known until much later.

The Press Bureau passed on to the press information provided by the War Office and Admiralty, and, like the Joint Standing Committee before it, sent out private and confidential notices requesting that other items of information not be published. These notices were known as 'D-Notices' and several hundred were sent out during the war (Palmer, 1984). The goodwill built up prior to the war with the establishment of the Joint Standing Committee was quickly destroyed by the treatment of the press when the war broke out. Lord Kitchener banned war correspondents from accompanying the British troops, so the press 'were forced to rely on the terse, opaque accounts by "official spokesmen" or quotations taken from foreign newspapers' (Lovelace, 1978, p. 315).

The treatment of the press was the subject of criticism both in the press and in Parliament (H.C. Deb., 31 August 1914; H.C. Deb., 12 November 1914; Towle, 1975; Lovelace, 1978). In particular, according to Williams (1965) '[t]he establishment of the Press Bureau in 1914 led to protests about the eccentricity of censorship which cropped up regularly throughout the war years' (p. 77). Bainbridge (1984) describes the censorship of newspapers at this time as being 'both capricious and inconsistent' (pp. 76-77).

Despite the censorship of sensitive information, the press did at least remain free to criticise and freely express opinion. The right of the press not to be punished for robust criticism was supported by Sir Stanley Buckmaster, the Solicitor General, who replaced the unpopular and erratic Smith as Director of the Press Bureau in November 1914 (Lovelace, 1978).

The Joint Standing Committee remained in existence and continued to meet at fairly regular intervals throughout the war years, with about nineteen meetings taking place between August 1914 and the end of the war in 1918. While the main role of the Joint Standing Committee had been taken over by the Press Bureau, the representatives continued to discuss issues of concern to the press. At the meeting of 18 December 1914 the liability of the press to punishment in the event of contravention of directions issued to them was considered. The press representatives emphasised the difficult position in which the loyal press were placed if the government refrained from proceeding against the newspapers who disobeyed (PRO DEFE 53/1). The meeting of 14 January 1916 decided that punishment of minor press offences was not serious enough to warrant the interference of the DPP. Members of the Joint Standing Committee were of the opinion that it was undesirable to formulate any scheme for dealing with any minor press offences other than the procedure provided by the Defence of the Realm Act (PRO DEFE 53/1).[9]

*1919-1938*

The Press Bureau was closed in April 1919 (PRO DEFE 53/2). The Admiralty, War Office and Press Committee was revived when the war ended (Palmer, 1984), and included the Air Ministry for the first time.[10] Because the committee had as its original purpose the suppression of material prejudicial to military operations in time of war it did not have much of a role in times of peace. Palmer (1984) states that there was an attempt in the early 1920s to include in its purview matters of political sensitivity. It was proposed that a representative from the Foreign Office should sit on the committee to determine what foreign news 'in its political aspect' should be subject to a D-Notice (p. 238).[11]

While the suggestion of a widened scope for the subject matter of D-Notices was accepted by the press representatives, as the result of a trick by the War Office according to Palmer, the idea was ultimately vetoed by the Committee of Imperial Defence (CID). The Chairman of the CID, Lord Salisbury, well understood the political damage that would follow if details of the agreement were to be seized upon by those sections of the press not forming part of the committee. Palmer's sources for this information are not clear, but some of his assertions are substantiated by the minutes of the meeting of the Admiralty, War Office, Air Ministry and Press Committee, dated 7 July 1922 (PRO ADM 116/4082; PRO DEFE 53/1), and the minutes of the conference of the CID held on 16 October 1922 (PRO CAB 4/8).

Some four months after the CID conference a letter was sent by Captain M.P.A. Hankey, Secretary of the CID, to Sir Oswyn Murray, Assistant Secretary of the Admiralty and Chairman of the Admiralty, War Office, Air Ministry and Press Committee. The letter seems strangely out of tune with the minutes of the above mentioned meetings, and it would make more sense if the date was 1922 rather than 1923, but this date appears in two separate references. The letter does seem to indicate that the idea of suppressing political information was not quite extinct, regardless of the opinions expressed at the July 1922 meeting of the Admiralty, War Office, Air Ministry and Press Committee (PRO ADM116/4082; PRO DEFE 53/1):

> Offices of the Cabinet
> 18th February, 1923
>
> My Dear Murray
>
> The report of the meeting between you, Creedy, Nicholson and myself on the question of using the Admiralty, War Office, Air Ministry and Press Committee to circulate to the press requests from other Departments for the non-publication of information of various kinds has not been formally before the Committee of Imperial Defence.
>
> In the circumstances I am inclined to think it would be advisable not to raise it officially to be recorded on the Minutes of your half-yearly meeting. If, however, you could informally sound the press side of your Committee on the subject, I think it would be useful. If, for example, you were to ascertain for certain that the press representatives would resent the use of your Committee for stopping the publication of political information, even in the event of strained relations or war, it would be better to avoid using this machinery for the purpose, as it would be deplorable if anything were done to weaken your admirable organisation.
>
> Yours sincerely
> M.P.A. Hankey

A separate issue that was discussed at the meeting of 7 July 1922 was the question of sending notices to Irish newspapers. When the subject was raised, Sir David Duncan suggested leaving the matter to the next meeting when Ireland would be more settled (PRO ADM 116/4082; PRO DEFE 53/1):

> Mr Robbins said he had had a letter from Sir Robert Baird, who was strongly of the opinion that it would be impolitic to circulate the notices amongst the Editors of the Free State papers. During the War the Department concerned decided what should be done with each particular 'Parker'.[12] In some cases they were sent generally; in other cases not to Irish papers at all; and in other cases to the North of Ireland papers only. He thought it ought to be laid down that the responsibility for sending a particular 'Parker' must rest with the Department concerned.
>
> Lord Riddell thought Sir David Duncan's proposal was a practical way out of the difficulty. They should await the turn of events.

Eventually it was agreed to adjourn the question of Ireland until the next meeting. In the meantime ' "Parkers" were not to be sent to Ireland; but the issuing Department might consult with Mr Robbins as to his writing a special letter to some of the North of Ireland papers' (PRO ADM 116/4082; PRO DEFE 53/1). The Admiralty, War Office, Air Ministry and Press Committee held a meeting on 12 October 1923, and after that there is not much recorded about its activities for a number of years.[13]

A document dated January 1937 and entitled *Secret Report of the Service Press Officers' Committee to consider the principles which should govern the preparation and distribution of Admiralty, War Office, Air Ministry and Press Committee D. Notices and to make recommendations thereon* contains some interesting insights into the working of the system. The following extracts illustrate the relevant points (PRO DEFE 53/2):

> 2. ... The Committee came into being shortly after the Official Secrets Act, 1911, but it was constituted on a purely voluntary basis and derived no legal authority from that, or any other, Act of Parliament. That position continues.
>
> 3. ... The Air Ministry was added in 1919 and the title was then enlarged to its present form, the 'Admiralty, War Office, Air Ministry and Press Committee' ...
>
> 4 (i) ... It is efficient, speedy, and commands the confidence of the press. Indeed, it may fairly be remarked that the Notices have more authority by their issue through this channel than if they went direct from their official source or origin; editors realise that they have been seen by and have the endorsement of the Press side of the Committee. This is clearly of value ...
>
> 5 ... From the beginning each department has been responsible for the initiation of Notices affecting its immediate interests and has provided the Secretary with the framework of the Notice ...
>
> 6 ... (ii) From a small list in 1912, the number receiving Notices at the beginning of the war in 1914 had risen to nearly 500 and had increased further to approximately 1500 when the armistice came. It continued to rise until 1932 when it reached a peak figure of about 1800 ... it was reduced in 1934 ... to about 1600 ... the number of recipients is now 1120 ...
>
> (iii) The total number of Notices issued to date is approximately 890; of these about 20 were issued before the Press Bureau was opened in August 1914, about 747 up to the time of closing the Bureau in April 1919, and about 123 since ...
>
> 18 ... (iii) We observe that the D. Notice scheme has not been applied in any form to the publisher of books on defence subjects and we regard it as a weakness that there is no control on the publication of information through this channel. We accordingly suggest that the Publishers Association of

Great Britain and Ireland should be advised of the existence of the D. Notice procedure and the co-operation of their members sought ...

C.P. Robertson, Air Ministry (Chairman)

E. Buran [*the signature was not clear, so this may be an incorrect spelling*], Admiralty

A. Manson [*the signature was not clear, so this may be an incorrect spelling*], War Office

23rd January 1937


Appendix 2 ...

6. The work undertaken by the Committee is entirely non-political and does not deal with foreign affairs or with civil or political questions. There is no question of the machinery being employed for any purpose beyond the preservation of secrets on defence matters, the publication of which would be harmful to the interests of the country ...

8. If on any occasion a question is raised involving a new principle the subject is discussed by the Committee before action is taken. The rights and freedom of the press are therefore fully safeguarded, both by the constitution of the Committee and in the day to day machinery.

Several points, in particular, in the above document are noteworthy. One of these is the huge number of recipients of the Notices. It is really quite surprising, and a reflection on the relationship between the press and the government, that the system remained unknown to the general public for so long when so many people were involved. It is also interesting that the document reiterates that 'the work undertaken by the Committee is entirely non-political and does not deal with foreign affairs or with civil or political questions'. A further point of note is that it took so long for books to be included in the system.[14]

According to Palmer (1984), after the First World War the idea of another major conflict occurring was unthinkable and there was no real need to reconvene the committee at the end of that war. The continuation of the D-Notice system after the First World War demonstrated the reluctance of the War Office to simply let go of such an opportunity of encouraging press restraint. For Palmer, the relative inactivity of the system, illustrated by the fact that the committee did not meet regularly after 1923, shows the lack of a role to justify its existence between the wars. Palmer says that the committee did not meet again for 23 years after 1923, as it 'reverted to a state of suspended animation' (p. 239), but since he undertook his research at the Public Record Office more material has become available. In fact, as noted, the committee did meet in that period, and there are other indicators, such as memos, confidential acquaints, circulars to newspapers and the continued existence of the D-Notices themselves, which illustrate that the system had not entirely fallen into disuse.

*The nomenclature of D-Notices*

One explanation for the name 'D-Notices' is that the 'D' stands for 'Defence'.[15] A letter dated 18th October 1932 written by C. Robertson of the Air Ministry Press Section gives another explanation (PRO ADM 116/ 4082):

> [T]he Press Bureau issued during the War several kinds of notices, each class having a different letter. There were 'A' notices and so on. The letter 'D' happened to be allotted to 'Parker' messages. It has no other significance and does not stand (as I once thought myself) for the word 'Defence' although it is, on that account, rather appropriate.

'Parker' was a code word which would communicate to Postmasters during the First World War what was required of them and which would convey nothing to any other person. It came from 'Parke' a War Office official concerned with the arrangements (PRO ADM 116/4082). The word 'Parker' appears on the telegram sent out to postmasters in 1912 when the system was instituted, and in that context was used to indicate where the confidential message would be inserted. A letter dated 25 July 1919 comments on the history of the code word 'Parker' (PRO DEFE 53/1):

> General Post Office,
> London,
> 25th July, 1919
>
> Dear Sir Edmund Robbins
> With reference to your inquiry about the origin of the word 'Parker' used in connection with the distribution of the Press Bureau notices during the war, I have looked up the official file.
> You will remember that the system of advising the Editors through the Post Office was first set up at the end of 1912, and it was considered undesirable to include in the telegrams sent to Postmasters *en clair* an instruction to communicate with the Editors. It was, therefore, necessary to adopt a code word which would communicate to the Postmasters what was required of them, and which would convey nothing to any other person. According to my recollection, the word 'Parker' was selected because Mr Parke is named in the printed War Office Memorandum dated 3rd December 1912.
> After the system was adopted for the regular distribution of urgent notices of the Press Bureau, the word 'Parker' continued to be used both here and

at the Press Association as a convenient means of referring to the system.
Yours very truly,
A.R. Kidner

Unfortunately the memo referred to, dated 3 December 1912, is not on file, but it is a possibility that the 'Mr Parke' was' Mr Ernest Parke who represented the Newspaper Proprietors' Association and who was actively involved in the institution of the system. Parke was one of the people on immediate call if a matter of urgency arose, so it may have been his name that appeared in the War Office memo.

The term 'Parkers' is used in the minutes of the Admiralty, War Office, Air Ministry and Press Committee, 7 July 1922 and the meeting held on 12 October 1923 mentions 'a "D" notice ("Parker")' being issued requesting the newspapers not to publish details of the 'new capital ships' (PRO DEFE 53/1). Although 'Parker' is used in correspondence between Sir Oswyn Murray and Sir Herbert Creedy in mid 1932, the name 'D notice' seems to be in common usage by late 1932 (PRO ADM 116/4082; DEFE 53/1). It appears, for example, in correspondence between Air Vice Marshall Burnett and Rear Admiral Usborne in February and April 1932 (PRO ADM 116/4082). In a letter sent by Mr H. Robbins[16] to Murray on 21 September 1932 a reference is made 'to the correspondence Sir Herbert Creedy has had with you concerning "Parker" telegrams (D. Notices by wire) ...' (PRO ADM 116/4082; DEFE 53/1).

The 1937 *Secret Report of the Service Press Officers' Committee to consider the principles which should govern the preparation and distribution of Admiralty, War Office, Air Ministry and Press Committee D. Notices and to make recommendations thereon*, already mentioned earlier, included the following observation (PRO DEFE 53/2):

> (vii) During the Great War 1914-1918 Notices continued to be issued under the auspices of the Committee but were allotted by the Press Bureau the letter 'D' by which name they have since become known. We think the question of associating the word 'Defence' with their designation should be considered and, if there is no legal or other objection, we advise the adoption of the title 'Defence Notices'. We consider that it might have a useful psychological effect amongst newspaper staffs, and tend to make them more careful in dealing with them in working hours and to prevent reference to them outside their offices.

These references illustrate that the information to be suppressed was intended to relate to defence information. They also illustrate that the government wished the press to be conscious of the secrecy and seriousness of the operation of the system.

*1938-1945*

During the Second World War full censorship again replaced the D-Notice system, and the committee apparently took no part in the organisation of the Ministry of Information press bureau (Palmer, 1984). Between October 1939 and May 1940 the News and Censorship Divisions were removed from the Ministry of Information, and formed into a separate organisation, the Press and Censorship Bureau which became the responsibility of the Home Secretary. During this time the Minister of Information was not involved in the issuing or censoring of news. The division went back to the Ministry of Information in May 1940 when Lord Reith took over from Lord Macmillan as Minister of Information (Thomson, undated).[17]

At the commencement of the war the Director of Censorship was Vice-Admiral Usborne, who had previously been Director of Naval Intelligence. Usborne's successor in May 1940 was Sir Walter Monckton, who was Director-General of the Press and Censorship Bureau. Monckton's 'Chief of Staff' was Sir Cyril Radcliffe who followed on as the next Director-General. Both Monckton and Radcliffe were barristers and more at ease with the cut and thrust of arguing with newspaper editors than Usborne who expected simply to be obeyed. Both these men ultimately became in turn the Director General of the Ministry of Information as a whole (Thomson, undated).

Francis Williams (1946), Controller of News and Censorship during the latter part of the war, said the censorship was voluntary, and so did Rear Admiral G.P. Thomson (Thomson, undated), who commenced the war as Deputy Press Censor, and spent the last five years of the war as Chief Press Censor. Both authors do point out that Defence Regulations applied, but add that there were very few prosecutions. If an item was mistakenly passed by the censor and published when it should have been suppressed, the member of press who had sought clearance was protected from prosecution (Williams, 1946). The Defence Regulations applied generally and not just to the press, so perhaps these two censors made the assertion that the censorship was voluntary on the basis that there was no special regime for the prosecution of offending members of the press.

Thomson claimed the prospect of prosecution under the Defence Regulations had no influence on the press, and he said editors and news editors submitted material for assessment because they did not want to assist the enemy in any way. Williams (1946, p. 20) said he knew of *no* case where a 'newspaper published deliberately or by accident information of material value to the enemy. Such prosecutions as there were concerned only minor and relatively unimportant infringements of the Defence Regulations'. Somewhat contradictorily, however, he later mentioned the prosecution, and subsequent suspension from publication for some time, of the Communist Party newspaper the *Daily Worker*. The *Daily Worker*, which was openly opposed to the war, was prosecuted under s2d of the Defence Regulations. Where Williams outlined how the wartime system worked, the description is interesting, and extraordinary, because he made no reference to the already established D-Notice System to which the passage could equally well apply.

Later on in the war there was an attempt by Cabinet to impose political censorship on the British press. This was brought on by British High Commissioners overseas, particularly in Australia and South Africa, who complained about the critical tone and nature of some of the messages being sent out of Britain by newspaper correspondents. Some of the reports complained of were taken from articles in British newspapers. These High Commissioners wanted to know why there was no effort to censor outgoing cables of this type. Outgoing cables were already censored with regard to sensitive defence matters, but political censorship was altogether different.

At this time the *Daily Mirror* was advised that unless it resiled from its critical policy the Defence Regulations would be used to suppress it. Williams (1946) described this as 'possibly the lowest ebb of the war in the Government's readiness to trust the good sense of the great mass of newspapers and people in Britain and the Dominions' (p. 67). Ultimately the 'tyranny' was avoided insofar as the British press were concerned, as Cabinet was persuaded not to force political censorship on British newspapers. One of the reasons for the idea being dropped was the certain knowledge that the British press would not accept political censorship voluntarily, and the backlash that would follow any kind of official or legal enforcement would be enormous. Political censorship was, however, imposed on outgoing cables sent by 'American, Dominion and neutral correspondents' from March 1942, even on material which had already been published in Britain. The censors, who were unhappy with the decision which was taken against their advice, interpreted the powers generously in favour of publication (Williams, 1946).

After a troubled beginning, the censorship procedure during the Second World War seemed to achieve a balance that was, for the most part, satisfactory to both the press and the government. Williams attributed this success to a number of factors, among these being the voluntary nature of the system, the fact that the censorship was not extended to include opinion, the co-operation of the newspapers, the (sometimes reluctant) appreciation by the government and individual Ministers that freedom of speech was a principle to be sustained even in times of war. His greatest praise was reserved for quite a number of the individuals involved, but in particular Rear Admiral Thomson.

## Notes

1.  The documents were sighted first hand by the author in a number of visits to the Public Record Office (PRO) during March and November 1997 and July 2000.
2.  For the background to the passing of the Act see Vincent (1998).
3.  This issue is discussed further in Chapter 5.
4.  It seems that Brooks sent the letter out in several batches as some posted in late 1905 speak of a letter of October 30th and some of the 1906 replies respond to 'your letter of January 30th'. The responses to this letter were, for the most part, very short and to the point. Among the responses was a letter from Christopher O'Sullivan of the *Limerick Echo*, Limerick, dated 3rd February 1906, which said the following: 'Dear Sir, In reply to your enquiry re publication of war news, I may say that I feel no interest in the matter, holding to the belief that the vast millions of money spent in brutalising humanity could be far more advantageously expended in Christianising portion of the King's realm not a stone's throw from Westminster. War is a practice of barbarism and a blot upon the fair name of any Christian nation'.
5.  Lovelace's conclusion is to some extent supported by CAB 16/27: 'In 1905 an individual appeal was made by Mr Sydney Brooks to nearly 200 editors of the leading London and provincial newspapers, most of whom replied that they were in favour of the legislation'.
6.  *The Times*, 19 September 1907: cited in PRO ADM 116/1058.
7.  Lovelace (1978, p. 395fn12) refers to *Forts*. Palmer (1984, p. 233) refers to *Ports* rather than *Forts*. Perusal of the newspaper ·in the British Museum's Newspaper Library showed the article (on p. 7 of the *Morning Post* dated 2 September 1911) to refer to 'Guardianship of British Forts' in the headline, but the text included reference to ports.
8.  The actual wording of paragraph 4 of the Constitution is as follows (POR CAB16/27): When a case arises in which either the Admiralty or War Office desire to take the initiative in arranging for the suppression of any item of news, the manager of the Press Association (Mr Robbins) is communicated with, and the Committee assembled. Except in the very rare instances, in which circumstances do not admit of even an hour's delay, the action contemplated by the Department concerned is suspended until the full Committee has been summoned. In the exceptional instances referred to, the official members may consult with such of the Press representatives as may happen to be in London, who will generally be Mr Robbins, and Mr Parke of the Newspaper Proprietors Association.

    The decision of the Joint Committee is communicated to the Press by Mr Robbins. In the case of the London Press it is conveyed either by letter or by telephone; but in the case of the Provincial Press special arrangements are considered necessary....
9.  For an account of the wartime situation in the United States of America where the provisions of the federal Espionage Act 1917 appeared to be contrary to the principles of the First Amendment see Chafee (1919).

10    As noted earlier the Admiralty, War Office and Press Committee was more commonly known as the Joint Standing Committee until 1918. 'The Air Ministry was added in 1919 and the title was then enlarged to its present form, the Admiralty, War Office, Air Ministry and Press Committee' (PRO DEFE 53/2). The minutes of the meeting dated 14 May 1920 are headed Admiralty, War Office, Air Ministry and Press Committee - this is the first time contemporaneous official documentation mentions the Air Ministry (PRO DEFE 53/1). PRO ADM 116/4082 contains several references to the Admiralty, War Office, Air Ministry and Press Committee. One is a letter dated 17 July 1922 referring to a meeting of the Admiralty, War Office, Air Ministry and Press Committee on 7 July 1922, and there are also letterheads from the committee secretary (one dated December 19th, 1932) carrying the extended title. Gowing (1974, p. 135) refers to 'the Admiralty, War Office, Air Ministry and Press Committee'. References elsewhere, however, including references in official documentation, do not include the Air Ministry in the title (Cmnd 1681, para. 126; Williams, 1965, p. 82). The committee will be referred to as the Admiralty, War Office, Air Ministry and Press Committee until after 1945 when it became known as the Services, Press and Broadcasting Committee.

11    According to Pincher (1968, p. 40) this issue came up again in the 1960s, 'The new secretary is also on record that state secrets, other than defence secrets, and especially those of the Foreign Office, fall within his blue-pencil baileywick [*sic*]. This is an extension of the D-(for Defence) Notice system that we must resist ...'

12    'Parker' is another name for a D-Notice; there is further explanation later in this chapter.

13    The activity that did take place is of no relevance to this book. For the period 1923-1937 see PRO ADM 116/4082 and PRO DEFE 53/1.

14    In the late 1990s the monitoring of the contents of books forms a large part of the work load of the secretary of the Defence, Press and Broadcasting Advisory Committee.

15    That the 'D' stands for Defence seems to be commonly accepted. For example, Whitmore (1968, p. 449), ' "D" notices, which strictly are Defence Notices ...'; Marshall (1961, p. 225), 'The "D" (for "Defence") Notice ...'; Aitken (1971, p. 39) 'to issue D- or Defence notices ...'

16    Mr H. Robbins was the son of Sir Edmund Robbins and followed his father as secretary of the Admiralty, War Office, Air Ministry and Press Committee.

17    PRO DEFE 53/3 contains the script of a talk about censorship given by Mr C.J. Radcliffe, K.C., (Acting) Controller of the Press and Censorship Division, Ministry of Information. The talk, entitled 'How Censorship Works', was broadcast by radio on 31 December 1940.

## References

Aitken, J. (1971), *Officially Secret*, Birkenhead, p. 39.

Bainbridge, C. (1984), 'One Hundred Years of Journalism', in C. Bainbridge (ed.), *One Hundred Years of Journalism*, London, pp. 76-77.

Chafee, Z. (1919), 'Freedom of Speech in War Time', *Harvard Law Review*, vol. 32, p. 932.

Cmnd 1681 (1962), *Security Procedures in the Public Service*, para. 126.

Gowing, M. (1974), *Independence and Deterrence - Britain and Atomic Energy, 1945-1952 Vol. 2*, London, p. 135.

H.C. Deb., 4th series, vol. LXXXI, col. 1593-1597, 27 July 1900.

H.C. Deb., 4th Series, vol. 188, col. 673-674, 11 May 1908.

H.C. Deb., vol. 47, col. 388-389, 22 January 1913.

H.C. Deb., vol. LXVI, col. 8, 25 August 1914.

H.C. Deb., vol. LXVI, col. 372-374 and col. 453-511, 31 August 1914.

H.C. Deb., vol. 68, col. 123-139, 12 November 1914.

Lovelace, C. (1978), 'British press censorship during the First World War', in G. Boyce, J. Curran, and P. Wingate (eds), *Newspaper History from the 17th Century to the Present Day*, London, pp. 308, 315, 395fn12.

Marshall, G. (1961), 'Comment', *Public Law*, p. 225.

*Morning Post*, 2 September 1911, p. 7.

Palmer, A. (1984), 'The History of the D-Notice Committee', in C. Andrew and D. Dilks (eds), *The Missing Dimension: Government and Intelligence Communities in the Twentieth Century*, London, pp. 228, 229, 233, 234, 238, 239.

Pincher, C. (1968), 'Press Freedom and National Security', *Journalism Today*, vol. Spring, p. 40.

PRO ADM 116/1058.

PRO ADM 116/4082.

PRO CAB 16/27.

PRO CAB 17/91.

PRO CAB 4/8, 368-B CID.

PRO DEFE 53/1.

PRO DEFE 53/2.

PRO DEFE 53/3.

PRO WO 32/6381.

Seely, J. (1930), *Adventure*, London.

*The Times*, 19 September 1907: cited in PRO ADM 116/1058.

Thomson, G. (undated), *Blue Pencil Admiral*, London.

Towle, P. (1975), 'The Debate on Wartime Censorship in Britain 1902-14', in B. Bond and I. Roy (eds), *War and Society Vol I*, London.

Vincent, D. (1998), *The Culture of Secrecy - Britain, 1832-1998*, Oxford.

Whitmore, H. (1968), 'Censorship of the Mass Media: The "D" Notice System', *The Australian Law Journal*, vol. 41, p. 449.

Williams, D. (1965), *Not in the Public Interest: the Problem of Security in Democracy*, London, pp. 77, 81, 82.

Williams, F. (1946), *Press, Parliament and People*, London, pp. 20, 67.

# 4  History Post 1945 and Current Operation of the D-Notice System in the U.K.

*1945-1960*

In early September 1945 Thomson, as Chief Press Censor, sent out a letter to newspaper editors regarding the cessation of hostilities. The letter was headed 'Private and Confidential Letter to Editors' and said:

> [E]ven in peace time there are obviously some subjects about which information should be kept secret on security grounds. This matter is now under consideration by representatives of the Press and the Fighting Service Departments, and the necessary advice will be communicated to you at an early date ... (PRO DEFE 53/4; PRO DEFE 53/5).

On 3 October 1945 a meeting was held under the Chairmanship of Sir Arthur Street, Permanent Under-Secretary of State for Air. Sir Arthur told the meeting, which was attended by representatives from the press, that the Admiralty, War Office and Press Committee had been suspended at the outbreak of war but the Government would now like to see it revived. The meeting agreed that the committee would be revived, and a sub-committee was set up to select a secretary. At the next meeting, in November 1945, it was announced that Rear Admiral Thomson was to be secretary (**PRO DEFE 53/6**). Sometime fairly soon after the war the name of the Committee changed from the Admiralty, War Office, Air Ministry and Press Committee to the Services, Press and Broadcasting Committee (PRO DEFE 53/8).[1]

Thus at the end of the Second World War the committee was re-established but it was quite different to the pre-war body. The cold war with the Russian bloc filled the vacuum left by the cessation of open warfare with Germany, so the political climate was not the same as it had been after the First World War (Cmnd 1681). There were two major differences between the pre-war and post-war committees. The first difference was that the secretary was now a member of the services, albeit a very high ranking one, rather than a member from the press side. By 1962 the Permanent Under-Secretary of Defence chaired the committee on a permanent basis. The second difference was that the members representing the press tended to be working journalists rather than proprietors.

According to Palmer (1984, p. 241) '[t]he changes in the nature of the committee stemmed from its continuation with wartime censorship'. A booklet dated 1953 and entitled 'NEWS AND PRESS CENSORSHIP BUREAU - Press Censorship Division. DEFENCE NOTICES. March 1953' bears out the connection with wartime censorship. The loose leaf hardcover quarto booklet, carrying a warning notice that the contents are secret, has 169 paragraphs, and includes a detailed listing of 'Defence notices'. It is not clear what role it plays with respect to the individual D-Notices which were issued separately and listed in a different document. The booklet clearly contains information relating mainly to war-time, but, as the date of March 1953 places it well after the end of the war, it is rather a curiosity (PRO DEFE 53/7). If the document was meant to be current in 1953, rather than being simply a reprint of the D-Notices in effect during the war, it indicated a mindset still fixed on the type of censorship more appropriate to a time of outright hostility.

The question was raised at several meetings of the Admiralty, War Office, Air Ministry and Press Committee between 1945 and 1952 as to whether D-Notices should be circulated to the *Daily Worker*, the Communist Party newspaper. On the 8th November 1945 Mr William Will, a member from the press side, informed the Committee that he had discussed the matter of D-Notices with the editor of the *Daily Worker* and he had found the editor very willing to co-operate. The *Daily Worker* was to be sent a copy of each D-Notice. At the Committee meeting of 18th March 1948 it was suggested that there should be a review of the practice of sending D-Notices to the *Daily Worker*. On the 7th February 1951 the Committee discussed the *Daily Worker* and wondered whether all D-Notices sent to the newspaper would then be revealed to Russia; it was decided to refer the matter to the Press organisations to see what they thought. The minutes of the meeting held on 7th April 1952 show the *Daily Worker* issue had become one for a higher authority; a decision had been sought from the government which had recommended that certain D-Notices be withheld and the relevant Ministers had accepted this (PRO DEFE 53/6).

This somewhat arbitrary treatment of the *Daily Worker* is a good illustration of the rather peculiar nature of the D-Notice system. In the *Daily Worker* case there was genuine concern on the one hand that the information in the D-Notices (which in those days contained a great deal of extremely sensitive material in quite specific detail) would find its way straight to the 'enemy', thus defeating the purpose of the system. If, on the other hand, a newspaper is placed outside the system and is therefore apparently not a part of it, even though it is supposedly voluntary, it again defeats the purpose of the system. While the disquiet about the *Daily Worker* may have been warranted, the case raises the issue of whether the public interest is well served when the executive government makes such determinations about whether a media organisation is fit to be included on the circulation list.

In the period between 1945 and the early 1960s the system remained unknown to the public and neither the media nor the government were sufficiently dissatisfied with it to bring about any change in the way it operated. This was largely due to the efforts of the secretary, Rear-Admiral Thomson, who made a genuine effort to weigh the balance between the interests of the press in obtaining information and the suppression of material prejudicial to security (Palmer, 1984; Aitken, 1971).

There were a few breaches of the D-Notices, but these were usually accidental and the responsible editor contrite. Gowing (1974) relates an incident in 1951 when *The Daily Telegraph* wrote about an atomic bomb in the context of the tests in Australia, which infringed a D-Notice. The chairman of the committee complained, and the deputy editor, Malcolm Muggeridge, who was 'most distressed' to learn about the apparent infringement, responded, '[i]f this is indeed the case you may be sure the lapse was unintentional and that all requisite steps will be taken to avoid any further repetition of the offence' (p. 137).

According to Palmer the calm surface hid a growing undercurrent of unrest on the part of the press. He attributes this to the growing debate as to what is actually meant by the concept of the national interest, with the government taking a different view to that of the press. The press were becoming increasingly suspicious of the system, seeing it as a means of stifling political opinion. In 1956 a D-Notice was issued restricting stories on troop movements to the Middle East prior to the Suez Crisis. The Downing Street Press Officer, William Clark (1986), wrote in his diary on 13 August 1956: 'Certain facts are now becoming clear: ministers want the press to be quiet about our military preparations because they are politically embarrassing; but fool themselves into thinking they are only asking for military censorship in the national interest' (p. 173). The manipulation of the D-Notice system to suppress information that relates more to embarrassing political issues rather than to national security is a recurring criticism of the system. It illustrates the way in which the system fails to balance the competing interests, especially the right of the general public to be informed about the activities of government.

Also in 1956 the *Manchester Guardian* reported on plans for the development of a new supersonic bomber in what seemed to be deliberate contravention of a D-Notice. The purpose of the article was to comment on government policy with respect to the number of defence projects being undertaken. The commitment to the system was wavering, but apart from the 1956 incident, it was not until 1961 that the problems, and for the first time the whole D-Notice system, became public (Marshall, 1961; Palmer 1984).[2]

## 1961-1970

Much of the history of the D-Notice system during the 1960s is well recorded. What follows is a summary of the events that have most relevance to this book.

In January 1961 Gordon Lonsdale, Harry Houghton, Ethel Gee and Morris and Lona Cohen (alias Peter and Helen Kroger), known collectively as the Naval Spy Ring, were arrested and charged with espionage under Section 1 of the Official Secrets Act. A D-Notice was sent out by Admiral Thomson, secretary of the Defence, Press and Broadcasting Committee, regarding the committal proceedings which took place in early February 1961 (PRO DEFE 53/9). The authorities wanted maximum publicity of the hearing, with due attention paid to keeping certain matters secret in the interests of national security, as a way of scoring points against the Soviet Union in the Cold War. Lonsdale, the leader of the spy-ring, was a Russian born, Russian trained, agent who posed in London as a Canadian. The Krogers, who ran the communications centre from their house in Ruislip, were Americans who had been trained in Russia and who also posed as Canadians. Harry Houghton and Ethel Gee were both English and were both minor civil servants employed at the secret Admiralty base in Portland, Dorset. They passed on secrets acquired during their work in return for money (Bulloch and Miller, 1961). All five were found guilty; Lonsdale was sentenced to twenty five years' imprisonment, the Krogers were sentenced to twenty years each, and Houghton and Gee were sentenced to fifteen years each.

Bulloch and Miller (1961) recount the full story. Of interest is the mention of the D-Notice system; the book was published in 1961, so the D-Notice system had only just become known to the general public. Although the reference was to the system operating 'in peacetime' and being voluntary, it also says 'Admiral Thompson [sic], the Chief Censor' (p. 155). An extract from the D-Notice is also reproduced.

The publicity sought by the authorities for the Naval Spy Ring case contrasts with the desire of the authorities to keep the George Blake case as quiet as possible. Blake was an officer of MI6 and had spied for the Soviet Union for a number of years. On 3 May 1961 George Blake was tried for espionage offences under s1(1)(c) of the Official Secrets Act 1911. He pleaded guilty. Before the proceedings commenced a D-Notice was sent out requesting discretion in reports of the trial. The government had two reasons for wanting the case to be downplayed by the media. The first was to hide from the British public the ineptitude within MI6 that enabled Blake to operate undetected for so long. The second was to hide yet another spy scandal from the U.S. Congress when the Fuchs and Maclean cases had already seriously harmed Britain's reputation as a reliable secret-sharing ally (Pincher, 1981).

The British press complied, but foreign newspapers, freely available in the U.K., printed full details of the trial. This included the information subject to suppression, namely that Blake had betrayed several British agents and was a member of the 'well known but officially non-existent sixth branch of British Military Intelligence' (Marshall, 1961, p. 227). A second D-Notice was issued asking that there be no repetition in the British press of the material in the foreign papers (Marshall, 1961; Williams, 1965). Blake was convicted on five counts of unlawfully communicating information and sentenced to forty two years' imprisonment, but six years later he escaped from Wormwood Scrubs and went to Moscow (Pincher, 1981; Kalugin, 1994).

On 4 May 1961 the Prime Minister, Mr Harold Macmillan, was questioned in the House of Commons about any confidential statements he may have made to the press regarding subjects on which they must not report. The Prime Ministerial response was cryptic. A further exchange involving the Prime Minister took place on 11 May 1961 in answer to a question on notice. This time open reference was made to the D-Notice system:

> 41. Mr. Lipton asked the Prime Minister which Minister is responsible for preparing the D-list; how many copies are circulated; and to whom, in addition to newspaper editors, this document is sent.
> The Prime Minister: Ministerial responsibility for D-notices rests on the Minister responsible for the subject covered by the notice. The circulation varies according to the subject matter.
> Mr Lipton: We appreciate that the Prime Minister has little time for effective general supervision of our Secret Service. Is it not rather ridiculous to continue this relic of war-time censorship for the purpose of concealing information which a potential enemy already knows? Will he put copies of this document in the Library so that hon. Members can judge for themselves the futility of what was issued in connection with the George Blake case?
> The Prime Minister: No, Sir. It can hardly be described as a relic of war-time procedure, as it began in 1912. Secondly, I think that there were advantages in this procedure, and they have been of importance.

> Mr. Gaitskell: Is the Prime Minister aware that the question of the D-list
> and the handling of the Press in this matter is quite distinct from the
> broader issues of the Blake case ... Is he aware that there is a good deal of
> anxiety about how the D-list operated on this occasion ...
>
> Is it not the case that first the British Press was asked not to publish certain
> information, then not to publish what was in foreign newspapers, and was
> then allowed to publish it? Does this not suggest that the whole way in
> which this question of the D-list was handled was really very unsatisfactory
> on this occasion?
>
> The Prime Minister: No, Sir. I still think - and I have discussed this, but I
> cannot publicly discuss it - that there were reasons why some advantage in
> time was important.

The answers given explained very little and, if nothing else, the
answers are a good example of political adeptness at avoiding the issue. It
seems, however, that while occasional public references had been made to the
system in the past, and the system had still managed to remain secret, this time
it could not be kept secret any longer. Now at least the general public were
aware of the fact that the government and the media were making decisions,
supposedly in the public interest, as to what government information should,
or should not, be made public.

*The 'Spies for Peace' - 1963*

In 1963 a group supporting nuclear disarmament called 'Spies for Peace'
distributed a pamphlet containing details of the location of the underground
headquarters of regional seats of government. These regional government
headquarters were to be used in the event of a war emergency, nuclear or
otherwise. Some of them were already public knowledge, and the one at
Warren Row, Berkshire, had been visited during the Aldermaston March. At
the time there was already a D-Notice in existence which covered the location,
communications and physical characteristics of the individual regional
headquarters, so the press were prevented from republishing the material
contained in the pamphlet. Even so the information did appear in some
newspapers, including *The Daily Telegraph* (H.C. Deb, 23 April 1963).

On 23 April 1963 the Prime Minister, Mr Harold Macmillan, was
asked in Parliament why the D-Notice, or at least the part of it relating to the
location of the regional headquarters, should not be removed now that it was
generally known. He responded:

> The Press has accepted the restriction most loyally, and I should like to take this opportunity to pay tribute to their recognition that this was a sensible use of the D notice procedure ...
> Is he really saying that one out of every two people in the country could tell us the location? ... Of course not ... The D notice covers much more than the location ... I repeat that I am grateful to the Press for so loyally keeping to the requests made to them.

The documents available in the Public Record Office include quarterly lists of 'Live D-Notices', that is the D-Notices in force during the period. Unfortunately there is no detail, only headings, for these particular D-Notices, but there are two, either of which or both of which, might have referred to the information in question. The first D-Notice is '11.7.52 (104) *Regional Commissioner's Operational Headquarters*' and the second is '14.1.60 *Underground Operational Centres*' (PRO DEFE 53/9). The date indicates when the D-Notice was first issued. The last time these two D-Notices appeared was in the list dated 27 November 1961 which would indicate that neither were in operation in 1963. On the list dated 28 February 1962 there is a new D-Notice ('26.2.62 *National Defence*') which seems to be an umbrella D-Notice that included material from those D-Notices that disappeared between the two lists.

This was replaced in 1969 by 'D Notice No 8', entitled 'National Defence – War Precautions and Civil Defence'. The D-Notice covered certain types of buildings, structures and installations, including, inter alia, 'sites intended for headquarters or communication centres of government above local authority level in time of war'. It precluded disclosure of 'their defence purposes' and publication of 'their precise location, structural details, approaches or identifiable surface work' (PRO DEFE 53/19). Clearly the government was determined to retain control over this information, even though there was no remaining public interest in doing so.

*The 'Cable Vetting Sensation' (or the 'D-Notice Affair') - 1967*

The 'Cable Vetting Sensation' was to cause one of the biggest controversies about the operation of the D-Notice system in the 1960s. In February 1967 Chapman Pincher, defence correspondent for the *Daily Express*, was given the information that copies of all cables leaving England for overseas were taken to the Ministry of Defence offices in London. Pincher checked the story with a press officer in the Ministry of Defence, with the public relations officer for the General Post Office, and the then secretary of the Services, Press and

Broadcasting Committee, Colonel Leslie Lohan. None were able to fully satisfy Pincher that he should not run the story, but before going ahead he had a meeting with Lohan. Following the meeting Pincher was 'convinced that the original ruling that D-Notices did not apply had been fully justified' and Colonel Lohan 'was confident that he had carried out his brief' - his brief being to suppress the story on the instruction of the Foreign Office. There was no question about Pincher's full support of D-Notices; in his own words he said he regarded them as 'of the greatest value, and I would defend the system to the death' (Hedley and Ainsley, 1967, pp. 22, 25).

Pincher gave the story to his editor, explained the events that had occurred and a conference of senior editors and the legal manager of the paper was called. On the assurance by Pincher that no D-Notice applied the story went ahead. It appeared on the front page of the *Daily Express* of 21 February 1967 under the headline 'Cable Vetting Sensation'.

The Prime Minister, Mr Harold Wilson, certain that there had been a deliberate breach of two D-Notices and that the system was in disarray, said as much in Parliament. Pincher made a counter-attack in the *Daily Express* the following morning denying the allegations, to which the Prime Minister replied in Parliament the next day. After a number of further incidents, and pressure by the Opposition, the Prime Minister announced in Parliament on the 28 February 1967 that a Committee of Privy Councillors chaired by Lord Radcliffe had been appointed, the second Radcliffe Committee.[3]

The second Radcliffe Committee reported on 19 May 1967 (Cmnd 3309).[4] Colonel Lohan had resigned in the interim. The report found no breach of the D-Notices, nor any deliberate attempt to evade or defy the procedure. The report found there was 'not much in the way of alteration that can usefully be recommended', and while no-one associated with the system thought it to be perfect, it had nonetheless worked effectively (Cmnd 3309, para. 65).

What suggestions there were in the report for improvement mainly related to the role of the secretary and the composition of the government side of the Services, Press and Broadcasting Committee. With respect to the secretary, it was said that 'what is needed is a closer delimitation of the functions of the Secretary' (Cmnd 3309, para. 69). The report recommended that there should be a deputy secretary and the secretary should be 'properly informed as to the facts that lie behind any "D" notice request' (Cmnd 3309, para. 71). The report further recommended that two of the four Ministry of Defence representatives on the Services, Press and Broadcasting Committee should drop out and be replaced by the Permanent Under Secretary of the Home Office, and possibly the Deputy Under Secretary of State of the Foreign Office.

The finding in the second Radcliffe Committee's report that there had been no breach of the D-Notices did not please the government and its release was accompanied by a government White Paper (Cmnd 3312). The White Paper rejected the finding that there had been no breach of the D-Notices and made more far reaching suggestions for improvements to the system. The White Paper agreed that the secretary of the Services, Press and Broadcasting Committee should have unfettered access to secret information to assist in making decisions as to 'the applicability of any particular "D" notices'. It was noted, however, that, '[i]t is the practice that officials who have regular and constant access to information of a highly secret nature are required to go through certain security procedures' (Cmnd 3312, para. 34). These procedures are known as 'positive vetting'. In addition the White Paper concurred with the other changes recommended by the Report, the most important being that the Home Office and Foreign Office should be represented on the Services, Press and Broadcasting Committee.[5]

On 22 June 1967 the House of Commons acrimoniously debated the D-Notice affair. The Prime Minister was on the receiving end of some trenchant criticism but he persisted with his support of the White Paper in preference to the findings of the Radcliffe Committee Report.[6] In so doing he also made an extraordinary personal attack on Colonel Lohan, citing the long standing friendship between Colonel Lohan and Pincher as being the reason why Pincher was not sufficiently convinced of the material being subject to a D-Notice. In the end the motion put by the government approving the White Paper, noting the report and accepting the report's recommendations bearing on the D-Notice system, was passed on party lines. The final chapter in the D-Notice affair came with a debate in the House of Lords on 6 July 1967 when Lord Radcliffe took the most unusual step of entering the fray to criticise the actions of the government. This speech was reported on the front page of *The Times* on 7 July 1967 by Hugh Noyes, Parliamentary Correspondent, under the headline: 'D notices White Paper savaged - Scathing attack by Lord Radcliffe'.

What appears to be an overreaction by the government to the cable vetting story may be partly explained by the fact that the vetting was undertaken by Government Communications Headquarters (GCHQ). The existence of GCHQ was a secret at the time and remained so for a number of years more. The government's fervent desire to keep it a secret may account for the full-on attack (Lustgarten and Leigh, 1994).[7] Pincher himself (1978) offers a different explanation, but as this was published in 1978 (so may have been written at the time when the existence of GCHQ was still unknown to the general public) it is possible that the GCHQ theory is the correct one:

Inside the office we suspected that Wilson's attack was not unconnected with various articles about Marcia which had appeared in the *Evening Standard*, the *Express* sister evening paper. Events were to show, however, that the real reason was much more interesting and had originated from the extraordinary Tory MP for Arundel, Captain Henry Kerby.

Wilson himself told me recently that what really underlay the whole D-notice affair was a tip in writing from Kerby that Lohan, who was strongly anti-Labour, was giving Tory MPs, including himself, ammunition for embarrassing parliamentary questions and still more embarrassing supplementary questions mainly on issues affecting defence matters. From that moment, Wilson told me, he was determined to sack Lohan but some legitimate excuse had first to be found ...

Suddenly the publication of the cable-vetting story with Lohan's failure to induce my editor to suppress it presented a ready-made excuse for the hatchet-job. At the same time it could be used to settle some old scores with the *Daily Express* and with me (pp. 235-237).

'Marcia' was Marcia Williams, later to become Lady Falkender, who at the time was Harold Wilson's political secretary. A report in *The Guardian* on 13 April 1999, making reference to recently released documents in the Public Record Office, supports Pincher's version. *The Guardian* says also that Lohan was paid £500 a year by MI5 to spy on journalists.

Whatever the real reasons for the reaction of the government to the cable vetting story, it appears that the system was being manipulated by the government to cover up a politically embarrassing situation rather than one that had genuine national security implications. In this case the government quite certainly did not represent the interests of the general public.

*The secrecy surrounding MI5 and MI6 and the revelations of October 1967*

During the 1960s the U.K. government used the D-Notice system in its attempts to keep MI5 and MI6 as secret as possible. A series of letters sent out by the secretary of the Services, Press and Broadcasting Committee to press members during 1963 and 1964 illustrate the need for constant reminders of the government concern for continued secrecy (PRO DEFE 53/10). In October 1967 the *Sunday Express* and the *Daily Express* ran some articles on the British Intelligence Services. In direct contravention of a D-Notice still in force at the time ('27.4.56 *Secret Agents and Counter Agents*'), the *Daily Express* revealed, in a front page story on 19 October 1967, the names of the heads of MI5 and MI6 as being Martin Furnival Jones and Sir Dick Goldsmith respectively. The story was written by David English, Express Foreign Editor, and headlined 'Britain's Spy Chiefs named in America'.

The *Daily Express* asked why the information should be suppressed in the U.K. when it was being published in the United States, and commented further:

> The suspicion must therefore arise; Is the D-Notice system being used and extended, not to maintain the security of the state but to suit the convenience of the Government?
> The Daily Express is deeply concerned lest the D-Notice system should become a form of censorship.
> If there is to be censorship in this country then it can only be enforced by an Act of Parliament. It cannot be allowed to come about by stealth.
> The Prime Minister must demand in Parliament the right of censorship, and take the consequences of such a challenge to the freedom of the press (p. 10).

Pincher (1968) suggests suppression of the names had more to do with the privacy of the heads of MI5 and MI6 than with national security.

*1970-1979*

The last available quarterly list in the PRO, dated November 1963, gives 18 D-Notices and 13 Private and Confidential letters (PRO DEFE 53/10). In the late 1960s there was a review of the individual D-Notices (PRO DEFE 53/19):

> In 1965 it was agreed that the Working Party on Security Restrictions on the Collection and Publication of Information should review all the 'D' Notices – other than those dealing with the Security Services, Cyphers and Communications which would be dealt with separately – with a view to dispensing with those no longer essential and to simplifying the remainder as far as possible.

Following the 'Cable Vetting Sensation' in 1967 this process was accelerated, and by the summer of 1967 the Working Party had prepared revised drafts of the D-Notices. Between mid 1967 and February 1969 these revised drafts went backwards and forwards between the Services Press and Broadcasting Committee and the Working Party, undergoing 'further simplification and rationalisation' (PRO DEFE 53/19). Eventually the first set of the revised notices, twelve in all, was published on 16 August 1971. Meanwhile in

October 1970 the Services, Press and Broadcasting Committee had changed its title to the Defence, Press and Broadcasting Committee.[8]

## The Jonathan Aitken case - 1970

In January 1970 the *Sunday Telegraph* printed a story revealing details from a report by Colonel R.E. Scott on the Biafran war in Nigeria. In the report, entitled *An Appreciation of the Nigerian Conflict*, Colonel Scott, the Defence Adviser to the High Commission in Lagos, had made a detailed assessment of whether either side in the war would be able to overcome the other in the next couple of months. The report was critical of the war effort on the part of the Nigerian army, which was being supported by the supply of arms from the British government. While the report had been prepared by an official of the British government, it was not an official document in the true sense. The report had been passed to the newspaper by Mr Jonathan Aitken, a working journalist and aspiring politician, who was unaware that it was confidential. It had been given to him at a dinner party without any comment as to its secrecy and the story had been offered to the newspaper by Aitken via the medium of a literary agent, with any proceeds to go to charity (Aitken, 1971).

Prior to running the story the *Sunday Telegraph* had cleared it by telephone with Vice-Admiral Sir Norman Denning, successor to Colonel Lohan as secretary of the Defence, Press and Broadcasting Committee. Sir Norman Denning's advice was that no D-Notice would be breached because the story concerned the forces of a foreign power. Aitken understood this to mean that the clearance gave the story complete legal immunity.

The Nigerians immediately expelled Scott and a full scale inquiry into the source of the leak was undertaken by Scotland Yard. When the trail led to Aitken he was charged under s2(2) of the Official Secrets Act 1911 - this section covers any wrongful communication of information or the receipt of information which has been wrongfully communicated.[9] Others charged at the same time were Mr Brian Roberts (editor of the *Sunday Telegraph*), the Sunday Telegraph Ltd and Colonel Douglas Cairns (Senior British member of the International Team of Military Observers in Lagos) who was alleged to have passed the report to Aitken's source. The source from whom Aitken received the document claimed that the confidentiality of the document had been made clear to Aitken from the outset. The source was not charged, neither was Mr Hugh Fraser, a Member of Parliament to whom Aitken had also given a copy of the report (Aitken 1971).

The story caused a furore in the press, both over the wide drafting of the relevant section of the Official Secrets Act and the selective way in which charges were laid. The trial lasted three and a half weeks, and the accused were acquitted on all counts, the jury finding that the activities of the defendants did not fall within the prohibitions of s2 of the Act.[10]

Prior to the Aitken case the media participants in the D-Notice system were of the view that clearance from the secretary of the Defence, Press and Broadcasting Committee gave immunity from prosecution under the Official Secrets Act. For it to be otherwise defeated the purpose of the committee and made its existence unnecessary. An alternative view is that while information may not be covered by a D-Notice it may, nonetheless, be covered by the Official Secrets Act (Fairley, 1990). The types of material covered respectively by D-Notices and the Official Secrets Act was not, and still is not, identical (the Act was amended in 1989). While the secretary of the Defence, Press and Broadcasting Committee may give an opinion on whether a D-Notice applies to the information, that is the limit of his mandate.

While the 1960s were punctuated by highly publicised events involving the D-Notice system, the situation changed in the 1970s. In view of the perceived failure of the system to be effective in censoring what the government regarded as sensitive information, a different approach was taken, the government turning to legal avenues to protect sensitive information. In turn the press lost interest in a process in which, as they saw it, the other side clearly played by a different set of rules. Because the system relies on co-operation between the government and the press, it did indeed appear to break down after the Jonathan Aitken case.

*1980-1989*

As far as major newsworthy events relating to the D-Notice system are concerned, the 1970s and 1980s were quiet years in comparison to the 1960s. In August 1980 the House of Commons Select Committee on Defence (the Defence Committee) published its report on the D-Notice system (HC773, 1980). The (rather voluminous) minutes of evidence appended to the report contain some fascinating insights from witnesses.

This was the first time a committee of the House of Commons had reviewed the system, and the report outlined how the system was working, or (perhaps) not working, during the 1970s in contrast to its more effective operation during earlier times. The report listed the four main criticisms of the D-Notice System that arose from the evidence given. The first criticism was that it was a form of censorship couched in very wide terms, so there was a perception that the government was trying to prevent open discussion of an expansive range of national security issues. The second criticism was that freedom of the press was compromised by participation in the system:

> This was strongly believed by those in press and broadcasting who opposed the D Notice system. They are in a minority among those who submitted evidence to us but they come from among those publications which take a serious interest in defence matters. The written evidence received by the Committee revealed the *New Statesman, Defence* magazine and London Weekend Television (under certain conditions) against the system. The editors of the Press Association and of the *Guardian* and the *Sunday Times* (but not the staff of these two newspapers) were also against. Other critical views came from several journalists submitting evidence in their personal capacities. The fact remains, however, that the majority of the evidence from the media serves to reflect acceptance of the system (para. 20) [*footnotes omitted*].[11]

The third criticism related to the confusion between the D-Notice system and the law, specifically the operation of the Official Secrets Acts. Compliance with a D-Notice did not preclude prosecution under the law, and defiance of a D-Notice did not necessarily lead to prosecution. The fourth criticism was that the system had fallen into disuse and was unnecessary.

From the evidence heard by the Defence Committee, the conclusion was reached that the D-Notice system was at that time not fulfilling the role for which it had been originally constituted. Despite all this, the Defence Committee found that there was still a role for the D-Notice system, provided some changes were made. The first of these changes related to the publication of the subject matter of the D-Notices, except for classified material, to avoid the misconceptions about the system that arose from unnecessary secrecy. The D-Notices should be published in 'a document (whether or not it is called a D Notice is immaterial) which would traverse much of the ground of the present D Notices and provide in generally accessible form as much guidance as possible about what is sensitive and what is not without doing damage to national security' (para. 29). The finer detail would be contained in appendices which would not be published.

The Defence Committee recommended that responsibility for drafting D-Notices should rest with the Ministry of Defence, the Home Office and the Foreign and Commonwealth Office, but would be issued after consultation, which could be done *ad hoc*, with the media. It was also recommended that the secretary of the Defence, Press and Broadcasting Committee should be 'seen to be the servant of the whole Committee and not just of the Ministry of Defence' (para. 36). To this end, the office of the secretary should not be located in the main Ministry of Defence building. An alternative would be to disband the system and rely on an *ad hoc* system where the media could consult the relevant Ministry when necessary, but the Defence Committee expressed a preference for the retention of the system.

The Defence Committee returned to the issue of the D-Notice system and the operation of the Official Secrets Act (para. 40):

> There is the question ... of whether or not compliance with a D Notice should guarantee immunity from prosecution or constitute a valid defence in court. We think that these are logical proposals. Before the law can be changed, there may be difficulties in providing an absolute guarantee but meanwhile we think that the Government should make it clear that prosecution would not normally be initiated where there had been a genuine attempt to comply with a D Notice.[12]

While the Defence Committee was compiling its report, the Defence, Press and Broadcasting Committee expressed an intention to 'review all aspects of the existing system' (HC773, 1980, Appendix 24, p. 146). As a result of criticism in the report, the D-Notices were rewritten and were no longer classified as 'confidential'. The secretary of the Defence, Press and Broadcasting Committee did become more a servant of the whole of the committee, but his office remains in the main building of the Ministry of Defence. Despite the reassessment of the operation of the system, and the reforms aimed at loosening the grip of the Ministry of Defence, there was no suggestion that the public interest may not have been sufficiently represented by the participating parties.

In the 1980s the government tried a different way to suppress information supposedly prejudicial to national security. Rather than use the Official Secrets Act to prosecute the publisher after the information had already been published, as had been done during the 1970s, the government started to use instead the civil action of breach of confidence. The advantage of a breach of confidence action is that an injunction may be granted to prevent the publication taking place at all, in other words a prior restraint on speech. In contrast it is rare for an injunction to be granted to prevent a breach of the criminal law.

While on the subject of prejudice to national security, and concerning information at least some of which would also have been the subject of one or more D-Notices, the *Spycatcher* case made the most headlines in this context. *Spycatcher* was a book of memoirs written by former MI5 officer Mr Peter Wright. Wright resigned from MI5 in 1976 and retired to live in Australia where he began to write his book in the mid 1980s. The book included information gained during his time with MI5 to the disclosure of which the U.K. government objected on the basis that it prejudiced the interests of national security in Britain. The litigation was commenced in the U.K. by the granting of interim injunctions in July 1986 to prevent the memoirs from being published in *The Guardian* and *The Observer* newspapers. It continued until the House of Lords decision in the summer of 1988 when the government finally lost its action for a permanent injunction.[13]

In 1987 the BBC proposed to examine the issues raised by the *Spycatcher* case in a radio series called *My Country Right or Wrong*. The producer of the first programme, Anne Sloman, spoke to the secretary of the Defence, Press and Broadcasting Committee, Admiral Higgins, before recording commenced. She gave him a summary of all the items involving former and present members of the security services. Where there may have been a conflict with the D-Notice system, she read him the entire item. The secretary's response to all this was a 'no advice' comment.[14] Indeed Admiral Higgins himself was due to take part in the programme - but first he wanted a full transcript, which the BBC refused to hand over (Fairley, 1990).

Shortly before the programme commenced the government obtained an injunction based on a breach of confidence action. The Attorney-General, Sir Patrick Mayhew, was asked in Parliament by John Morris on 4 December 1987 why this was not censorship 'of the kind emulated by every tinpot dictatorship; and were not these programmes discussed with the security services and the D-notice committee, who were satisfied with the generality of the programmes?'. Sir Patrick tartly responded:

> There is no question of censorship in the action I took yesterday on behalf of the Government. However, there is every question connected with the duty of the Government to protect the confidentiality that is owed to them by members and former members [*of MI5*]. Had the BBC been prepared to meet the reasonable request of the Treasury Solicitor to see the passages of the transcript limited to the contributions from members and former members of the service, great difficulty would have been overcome.

Under a court ordered discovery of documents the BBC was forced to hand over the tapes to the government for examination. It was not until some six months later, after the tapes had been found not to contain anything sensitive, that the BBC was able to broadcast the programme (Robertson, 1989).

There was other similar activity in 1987. An article headed 'News – Spy in the Sky' (Author not identified, 1987) reports that in January 1987 injunctions were granted against the *New Statesman* and the BBC programme *Secret Society*. The injunctions were ordered to prevent revelations, by investigative journalist Duncan Campbell, relating to the secret British Zircon project which was planning to launch a British spy satellite. Another article headed 'UK News' (Author not identified, 1987) reports that in May 1987 the Attorney-General obtained a temporary injunction to restrain the publication of a book, *GCHQ - The Secret State*. The article does not say who wrote the book. At the same time the Attorney-General also successfully requested that all existing manuscripts be surrendered. The articles provided no further information as to the legal basis for the granting of the respective injunctions.

At about the same time Mr Anthony Cavendish, a former MI6 officer, wrote his memoirs in a book called *Inside Intelligence*. Cavendish sought authorisation from the government to publish the book, but authorisation was refused.[15] In late 1987, following the government's refusal to clear the book for publication, he gave out nearly three hundred as 'Christmas cards'. While he was criticised for his actions by the government, no action was taken against him following his assurance that he would not distribute any further copies (Walker, 1990). On 27 December 1987 *The Sunday Times*, which had obtained a copy of the book, published an article about it, and it was the intention of *The Observer* also to publish similar material. On 1 and 2 January 1988 the Attorney-General was granted injunctions, based on actions for breach of confidence, restraining *The Observer* and *The Sunday Times* respectively from publishing any further details from the book relating to the British security and intelligence services. The injunctions were subsequently modified, on 15 January, to allow publication as long as sensitive material relating to national security or the author's work as an intelligence officer was not included.

On 5 January 1988 *The Scotsman* featured a front page story outlining the Cavendish story, having received a 'no advice' comment from Admiral Higgins, secretary of the Defence, Press and Broadcasting Committee, beforehand. The Lord Advocate immediately obtained an interdict (injunction), again based on breach of confidence, against *The Scotsman* to prevent any further revelations. The interdict was later recalled and an application for reinstatement of the interdict was refused by the Lord Ordinary on 23 February 1988. The refusal was upheld by the Second Division and the House of Lords.[16]

Counsel for the Lord Advocate argued that the issue was the fact of disclosure, rather than what was disclosed. This argument failed in both the Second Division of the Court of Session and in the House of Lords, but had the argument been based on the contents of the Cavendish story the result may well have been different. Whatever the result, the D-Notice system was the real casualty as the government resorted once more to the Courts, contradicting the advice (or rather the 'no advice' ) given to the editors by the secretary of the Defence, Press and Broadcasting Committee.

An updated version of *Inside Intelligence* was eventually published in hardback in 1990 and in paperback in 1997.

*1990-*

In 1993 the system was revised following a review announced by the Minister of State for the Armed Forces in October 1992 (Ministry of Defence, 93/06). The Defence, Press and Broadcasting Committee undertook the review and the aim 'was to make the system more transparent and relevant in the light of international changes and the increased emphasis on openness in Government' (MoD, 93/06, p. 1). The wording of the individual notices was tidied up, and some changes were made to allow discussion of civil defence issues and of non-classified matters pertaining to conventional weapons (Lustgarten and Leigh, 1994).

The name of the notices is now Defence Advisory Notices (DA Notices) and the committee is now named the Defence, Press and Broadcasting Advisory Committee. The number of notices was reduced from eight to six, and these came into effect on 1 August 1993. The eight D-Notices that were circulated in November 1989 were entitled: Defence Plans, Operational Capability, State of Readiness and Training; Defence Equipment; Nuclear Weapons and Equipment; Radio and Radar Transmissions; Cyphers and Communication; British Security and Intelligence Services; War Precautions and Civil Defence; Photography etc. of Defence Establishments and Installations. The two D-Notices dropped in 1993 were 'War Precautions and Civil Defence' and 'Photography, etc. of Defence Establishments and Installations'. The six DA Notices effective from 1993 were: Operations, Plans and Capabilities; Non Nuclear Weapons and Operational Equipment; Nuclear Weapons and Equipment; Ciphers and Secure Communications; Identification of Specific Installations; United Kingdom Security and Intelligence Services (MoD, 93/06).

The DA Notices were updated and reduced in number to five in May 2000. These five are: DA-Notice No. 1 'Military Operations, Plans and Capabilities'; DA-Notice No. 2 'Nuclear and Non-Nuclear Weapons and Equipment'; DA-Notice No. 3 'Ciphers and Secure Communications'; DA-Notice No. 4 'Sensitive Installations and Home Addresses'; DA-Notice No. 5

'United Kingdom Security and Intelligence Services and Special Forces' (www.dnotice.org.uk/index.htm).

## Censorship during the Falklands War and the Gulf War

Before concluding the review of the history of the DA-Notice system in the U.K., it is of interest to examine briefly the censorship of news during the most recent military conflicts.[17] During the Falklands War, due to the isolation of the war zone and the way in which the war was conducted, control of information by the U.K. authorities was absolute. News was censored at the source, and also by the Ministry of Defence. In the Falkland Islands the material was vetted by military PR officers who 'became censors as well as advisers' (Mercer et al, 1987, p. 172). With the field censorship and the insistence that material then be cleared by the Ministry of Defence, what evolved was a system of double vetting.

During the Gulf War advances in satellite technology, and the ability of journalists in the field to transmit live coverage as it happened, led to a different approach which involved field censorship rather than a centrally co-ordinated system. Detailed Ground Rules were issued to reporters, some of whom were allowed to accompany active service units provided they complied with field censorship - this field censorship seems not to have been unduly restrictive. In addition a document entitled *Guidance to Editors* encouraged editors to discuss certain matters with the Ministry of Defence before publication. This regime replaced the D-Notice system during the war (Lustgarten and Leigh, 1994)

Over one thousand journalists covered the Gulf War, but were subjected to a 'controlled information environment' in which the coalition managed the media in a way that produced what to the military was 'a desired view', although it was not necessarily accurate (Taylor, 1992, pp. 11-12). The strictness of military control over information meant that all the journalists were working from the same limited material. Taylor (1992, pp. 268) describes it as 'monopoly in the guise of pluralism' and 'secrecy disguised as publicity', and says it could be compared to the handling of information by the Ministry of Information in the U.K. during the Second World War. Perhaps unsurprisingly Taylor makes no reference to the D-Notice system.

## The current operation of the Defence, Press and Broadcasting Advisory Committee (DPBAC)

Much information about the operation of the system was provided, or confirmed, by Rear Admiral David Pulvertaft, secretary of the DPBAC from November 1992 to November 1999. The Ministry of Defence 'Open Government Document' on DA-Notices, issued in 1993, set out how the system operates:

> The Press and Broadcasting members respond to proposals from the government departments concerned and advise the Committee on those areas of information in which it may be reasonable to invite guidance reflecting the interests of national security. Official proposals may not be issued in DA Notice form without the consent of the Press and Broadcasting members ...
>
> The DA Notices are intended to provide to national and provincial newspaper editors, to radio and television organisations and to relevant book publishers general guidance on those areas of national security which the Government considers it has a duty to protect. The Notices, together with a General Introduction, details of the Committee and how to contact the Secretary, are widely distributed to editors, producers and publishers and also to officials in Government departments, military commanders, chief constables and some institutions. The Notices have no legal standing and advice offered within their framework may be accepted or rejected partly or wholly ...
>
> Although the system is normally applied through the standing DA Notices, should it be found necessary to issue a DA Notice on a specific matter, the Government department concerned will agree a draft of the proposed Notice with the Secretary who, from his experience, can advise upon the form and content which are likely to make it acceptable to the press and broadcasting members. The Secretary will then seek the agreement of both sides of the DPBAC to the draft and, if it is obtained, issue the text as a DA Notice (MoD, 93/06, pp. 9-10) [*the spelling of 'government' and 'Government' is copied from the text*].

This is much the same as the way the system operated in the 1960s (Cmnd 1681).

The DPBAC usually meets twice a year, in spring and autumn. Its normal business is to receive reports from the secretary on the 'guidance sought and advice offered' since the last meeting, and to review the DA-Notices currently in force. As well as responding to queries, the secretary is pro-active in that he keeps a watch for publications which have the potential to infringe one or more D-Notices.

The DPBAC now has its own home page on the Internet (www.dnotice.org.uk/index.htm).[18] The information provided includes a general introduction, the DA-Notices in full, the names and work title of the current members of the committee, and the name and contact details of the secretary and deputy secretary. There is the text of a talk given by the current secretary, Rear Admiral Wilkinson, to the Society of Editors in May 2000, and a Frequently Asked Questions (FAQs) section. In addition, as an acknowledgement of the increasing requirements for openness, a synopsis of the minutes of the six monthly meeting of the DPBAC, starting with the one held on 17 May 2000.

The committee is chaired by the Permanent Under-Secretary of State, Ministry of Defence, and there are three other government members representing the Home Office, the Ministry of Defence and the Foreign and Commonwealth Office. The press and broadcasting side select one of the thirteen members nominated by the media as chairman of their side and vice chairman of the committee. The committee has a full time secretary, usually a retired two star officer of the Armed Forces, and a part-time deputy secretary (MoD, 93/06; www.dnotice.org.uk/index.htm). In November 1999 Rear Admiral David Pulvertaft's term as secretary expired, and he was succeeded by Rear Admiral Nick Wilkinson.

The media side of the committee is represented by three nominees from the Newspaper Publishers Association (representing the national newspapers), two nominees each from the Newspaper Society (representing the regional newspapers) and the Periodicals Publishers Association (representing magazines such as *Janes* publications), and one nominee each from the Scottish Daily Newspapers Society, the BBC, ITV, ITN, SKY and the Press Association (a total of thirteen).[19] In September 2000 there are twelve Press and Broadcasting members listed on the website, the Scottish Daily Newspaper Society seemingly not being represented at the time (www.dnotice.org.uk/committee.htm). There is mention of eventual membership by 'Internet authorities' (www.dnotice.org.uk/faqs.htm).

The media side are all working journalists or managers and are nominated by their respective organisations. The DA-Notice system is funded by the Ministry of Defence, and the current cost per annum, which includes salaries, is about £105K. The DA-Notice system applies to the Internet, but only to publications on U.K. websites. The issue of whether U.K. Internet Service Providers are 'publishers' is unresolved.

The general introduction on the website contains the following comments of note:

> 1. Public discussion of the United Kingdom's defence and counter terrorist policy and overall strategy does not impose a threat to national security and is welcomed by Government. It is important, however, that such discussion should not disclose details which could damage UK national security ...
> 3. When these notices were first published under their new title of Defence Advisory Notices in 1993, they reflected the changed circumstances following the break-up of the Soviet Union and Warsaw Pact. The 2000 revision has allowed an overall reduction of the scope of the notices while retaining those parts that are appropriate for the current level of threat that involves grave danger to the State and/or individuals. Compliance with the DA-Notice system does not relieve the editor of responsibilities under the Official Secrets Act.

In December 1998 the Freedom of Information Bill was introduced into the House of Lords. Rear Admiral Pulvertaft's term as secretary of the DPBAC was due to expire in late 1998 but his term was extended for a year so that the necessary changes could be made to the system while he was still in office. In September 2000 the Bill was still progressing through Parliament. As 'national security' is a category of exemption in the Bill, the issues relating to the application of Freedom of Information to the DA Notice system may revolve around the definition of national security. In recognition of this, the DPBAC considered, with some difficulty it would seem, the definition of national security, as recorded in the minutes of the May 2000 meeting (www.dnotice.org.uk/records.htm):

> Definition drafted for General Introduction to DA-Notices not satisfactory. Agreed that any definition would either be too short and general to be consistent with precision of revised Notices, or very long to try and cover all eventualities. Agreed therefore to insert instead a phrase showing context of scale, involving 'grave danger' and 'the State' (in terms of national interest) and 'people' (whether collectively or individually).

## The role of the secretary of the Defence, Press and Broadcasting Advisory Committee

The effectiveness of the system depends very much on the secretary of the committee (Cmnd 1681; Joint Working Party of JUSTICE and the British

Committee of the International Press Institute, 1965; Cmnd 3312; HC773, 1980). The first two secretaries after the Second World War, Rear Admiral Sir George Pirie Thomson, Press Censor during the War, and Colonel Sammy Lohan,[20] maintained a close relationship with working journalists. Both made a conscious effort not to suppress any material unless it was necessary in the interests of national security. Palmer (1984) says of Admiral Thomson in this context:

> He gained the press's trust and respect by passing much matter that government departments wanted censored. 'Is there a genuine security objection? I would ask ... hundreds of deleted passages I have marked "stet" because I could not see that there were proper grounds for secrecy'. Added to an unprecedented degree of national cohesion, Thomson's approach produced remarkably good-humoured acceptance of censorship (p. 241) [*footnote omitted*].

The relationship between the secretary and the media has on occasion also been one of friendship following years of shared experiences. This was so in the case of Colonel Sammy Lohan and journalist Mr Chapman Pincher. As mentioned earlier, their friendship led to the downfall and resignation of Colonel Lohan in the wake of the 'D-Notice Affair'.

The secretary is appointed for a three year, renewable, term. The government pays his salary, but he is supposedly a servant of the committee and not a government official. When interviewed by Lustgarten and Leigh (1994), Admiral Higgins 'identified three requirements for the post as including: (1) knowledge of how Whitehall works; (2) sufficient seniority to ring up and speak on terms of equality with senior editors and civil servants; and (3) being a retired person and therefore not susceptible to pressure' (p. 271).

This was reiterated by Rear Admiral Pulvertaft in an interview in 1997. Rear Admiral Pulvertaft said that, although he was paid by the Government and had an office in Whitehall, he was a servant of the Committee and played the role of the independent broker, a phrase he used repeatedly, between the media and the bureaucrats. Lustgarten and Leigh say Admiral Higgins, the previous secretary, 'saw his role as that of "honest broker" between the media and the government' (p. 271). The internet site for the system says: 'The Secretary DPBAC (the DA-Notice Secretary) is the servant of the Government and the Press and Broadcasting sides of the Committee' (www.dnotice.org.uk/notices.htm) and '[h]e works for the Committee, and is similarly independent' (www.dnotice.org.uk/faqs.htm).

Rear Admiral Pulvertaft said the reason for having a retired ex-serviceman as secretary is because he is security cleared, he knows his way around Whitehall, and he is not a career civil servant. The office is in Whitehall for security purposes as the secretary has access to secret files, in order to be well informed when he has to give advice, and it would not be practicable for these files to leave Whitehall, say for example if the secretary were to have his office in Fleet Street. While most secretaries of the Committee have been from the Navy, this is coincidental; Rear Admiral Pulvertaft had competition from the members of the other services for his job.

Rear Admiral Pulvertaft talked of the role of the secretary as being like walking a tightrope and he made the comment that 'Lohan fell off'. The secretary actively promotes the system among editors, and Rear Admiral Pulvertaft recognised that the DA-Notice system represents just a tiny sliver of the business of both editors on the one side and departmental officials on the other. When the DA-Notice Committee meets twice a year the secretary reports as to what he has been doing. Having regular meetings is, in the view of Rear Admiral Pulvertaft, another of the reasons why the U.K. system has survived. During these meetings if either side complains to him that he has not looked after their interests sufficiently, and they are quick to make such complaints if they feel it necessary, he takes note. This has a balancing effect and helps to keep his approach even handed. [21]

Rear Admiral Pulvertaft had irregular but frequent contact with the print media; he would expect to have about one contact a week from newspaper editors, less from the broadcast media - probably about one a month for radio/TV. When asked for advice, the secretary will either say the material is subject to a DA-Notice, and therefore should not be published, or give a 'no advice' comment rather than actually giving clearance to anything. Much of his time is taken up with books and he goes through publishers' forecasts looking for titles that might carry sensitive material. About six books a year require close attention, and these are very time consuming. He goes through the books with the authors suggesting how the book might be changed (such as using a false name or leaving some bits out).

Rear Admiral Pulvertaft said he did not try to stop stories as a whole, only the highly classified detail, and he would suggest leaving a bit out of the report, or altering the wording. No editor had refused to cooperate. [22] Sometimes something had been printed or aired that should not have been, but he did not rebuke those responsible, rather he discussed the matter with them and reminded them of the existence of the system in the hope that the publication of sensitive items would not happen again. He was also careful to keep requests for advice confidential, in order that other media organisations are not alerted to the potential scoops of their rivals.

Rear Admiral Pulvertaft said it was preferable for matters not to get to the court stage - this often resulted in more publicity about the disputed material which might otherwise have remained known only to a few. Having lawyers representing government departments 'rattling the bars in the background' was not helpful to the cooperative approach. Officials from government departments would on occasion ask him to try and restrict something; if he said the information was not subject to a DA-Notice, 'they would get all sad with him'. Even though the system in the U.K. is running smoothly at present, he appreciates that he cannot afford to be complacent. He is very aware of what happened to Colonel Lohan, and if those circumstances happened again he believed it would be extremely damaging to the system.

Having a secretary who is nominally independent of the government advances the public interest. The government may want the suppression of material which does not genuinely threaten national security, for example where the material reveals ineptitude. If the secretary is a member of the administrative, as was the case when the Australian system was functioning, the system appears weighted in favour of government interests.

## Summary of the history and operation of the DA-Notice system in the U.K.

The D-Notice system was instituted 'to deal with the publication of Naval and Military news in times of emergency' (PRO DEFE 53/1). The early history shows that the government sought to control the publication of information through a formalised 'old-boys' network rather than risk the odium of overt censorship through legislation. When the D-Notice system was first established there may have been some legitimacy in excluding the general public from knowledge of the existence of the system, but the system remained locked into its wartime origins long after the emergency had passed. Even after the system became known to the general public, there remained the view that the committee members were the best placed to decide what should or should not be made known to the public.

If lack of public controversy is a sign of success in more recent years, it is clear that the successful operation of the DA-Notice system in the U.K. for the past few years is largely due to the public relations skills of the secretary. Having a secretary who is an 'independent broker', and both easily accessible and approachable, helps to ward off suspicion of the system. Even so, it is still by any measure a comfortable arrangement between the media and the government. Although both sides claim to be serving the public interest, a closer examination in later chapters of these claims will show that neither side is sufficiently objective. Both sides primarily serve their own interests in the guise of serving the public interest. As there are no independent members on the committee to objectively ascertain whether or not suppression is in the interests of the general public, the interests of the general public are not adequately represented.

## Notes

1    The headings in DEFE 53/6 change in mid 1954 and remain consistent thereafter, whereas the letterheads in 53/8 alter in mid 1952. The first letterhead bearing the new title is dated 11 July 1952. The use of the old letterheads may have been to finish old stocks of stationery. There is an earlier reference to the 'Services and Press Committee' in ADM 1/20905 dated December 1946-March 1948. The committee will be referred to as the Services, Press and Broadcasting Committee until 1970 when it became the Defence, Press and Broadcasting Committee.

2    Palmer (1984, p. 246) refers to *The Guardian*, Marshall (1961, p. 226) to the *Manchester Guardian*. The *Manchester Guardian* became *The Guardian* in 1959-1960.
On the issue of when the system first became generally known, there is no reference to this in the material presently available in the PRO. Most commentators seem to accept 1961 as the relevant date: see Marshall (1961, p. 225); Williams (1965, p. 85); Williams (1968, p. 23); Supperstone (1981, p. 259); O'Higgins (1972, p. 56) refers to 'a practice which remained hidden from the public view for thirty years before even a whisper reached the public, and for even longer before its general outline was made known in 1962'. For a different date altogether see Robertson and Nicol (1990, p. 333); they say: 'The Committee was established in 1912, shrouded in secrecy: for forty years its existence was not publicly known'. There is an associated footnote which refers to Williams (1965); Williams clearly states 1961, so perhaps Robertson and Nicol mean fifty years rather than forty years. See also Hooper (1987, p. 223) who says: 'The existence of the D-notice committee was not publicly revealed until 1952'; Hooper provides no specific references by which this date can be substantiated.

3    The first Radcliffe Committee was appointed in 1961 'to review procedures and practices in the public service' following the George Blake trial (Cmnd 1681, p. iii). This first committee also made a thorough examination of the D-Notice system.

4    It proved to be very difficult to see a copy of Cmnd 3309. There is no copy held in Western Australia and a search of other libraries in Australia failed to locate a copy for loan. The White Paper response, *The 'D' Notice System* (1967) Cmnd 3312, is held in the National Library in Canberra and was available for a short term loan through the interlibrary loans service. Eventually a copy of the Report, that is Cmnd 3309, was found in the Senate Library of London University (but not available on loan) during a research trip to the U.K. in 1997.

5    In 2000 representatives from the Home Office, Ministry of Defence and the Foreign and Commonwealth Office are members of the Committee. Whether the changes to the

government side came about as a result of the recommendations put forward in 1967 or were made after 1980 when the House of Commons Select Committee on Defence reviewed the system is not clear from the literature.

[6] For comment on the relationship between Harold Wilson and the press, with particular reference to the D-Notice affair, see Margach (1978).

[7] The revelation of the existence of GCHQ was subject to a D-Notice until November 1977 when GCHQ became public knowledge as a result of the Aubrey, Berry and Campbell committal proceedings, see Chapter 6. Lustgarten and Leigh (1994) say the existence of GCHQ was not publicly acknowledged until fifteen years after the 'D-Notice Affair' which would be 1982. This date, 1982, does not accord with other writers, for example, Aubrey (1981) Robertson (1998). Aubrey, a defendant, and Robertson, counsel for Campbell, were involved in the 1977 proceedings.

[8] The information in the last two sentences comes from a letter written to the author in April 1997 by Rear-Admiral Pulvertaft, secretary (in 1997) of the Defence, Press and Broadcasting Advisory Committee. The information available in the Public Record Office in July 2000 ended with DEFE 53/19 'Revision of D Notices (Nos 1-9, 12 and 13)', which was released on 1 January 2000. The last date in DEFE 53/19 is 10 March 1969. DEFE 53/20 'Revision of D Notices (Nos 1-9, 12 and 13)' remains closed until 1 January 2002.

[9] The legal aspects of this prosecution, and the relationship between the D-Notice system and the Official Secrets Act 1911, are discussed in Chapter 6.

[10] *R v Cairns, Aitken, Roberts and the Sunday Telegraph.* The case was unreported but a write-up appeared in *The Times* newspaper on 4 February 1971.

[11] The question of whether the D-Notice system does compromise the independence of the media was included in a survey of the U.K. and Australian media in 1997 by the present author. 55% of the U.K. respondents answered 'No', 9% answered 'Yes' and the remainder left the question unanswered; 44% of the Australian respondents answered 'No', 47% answered 'Yes' and the remainder left the question unanswered.

[12] For further analysis of the report see Jaconelli (1982). For the response of the Secretary of State for Defence, which was positive, see Cmnd 8129.

[13] *A-G v Guardian Newspapers Ltd (No 2)* [1990] AC 109. The government's case was based on breach of confidence.

[14] The 'no advice' response was adopted following the Jonathan Aitken case (Lustgarten and Leigh, 1994). Whereas the secretary will indicate when material may be prejudicial to national security, he does not now give clearance to any material, instead saying something such as: 'I shall offer no advice' (Fairley, 1990, p. 431).

[15] *Lord Advocate v Scotsman Publications Ltd* [1990] 1 AC 812. There is no reason given in the case for the refusal of the Government to allow Cavendish to publish his book.

[16] *Lord Advocate v Scotsman Publications Ltd* 1988 SLT 490, and [1990] 1 AC 812.

[17] For a detailed discussion on the relay of information during the Falklands War see Mercer et al (1987) and for the Gulf War Taylor (1992).

[18] The original DPBAC home page was: www.btinternet.com/~d.a.notices

[19] The Newspaper Publishers' Association was originally known as the Newspaper Proprietors' Association; it is not known exactly when the change of name occurred but it was at least 20 years prior to 1997.

[20] Thomson was secretary from 1945-1964. Lohan was secretary from 1 Jan 1964 to early 1967.

[21] The question of who looks after the public interest is a different matter; for a discussion on the way both the government and the media manipulate the news see Chapter 11.

[22] Fairley (1990, p. 438), includes a survey of the print media editors in the U.K. He says: 'A questionnaire sent ... to eighty-three editors of national and local newspapers and periodicals revealed fairly widespread participation in the system, but that actual use of it is infrequent, the majority of editors seeking advice, at most, only once or twice a year. However, eighty four per cent (thirty-seven editors) of those who replied felt that, in the light of recent Government behaviour, they would be more influenced by the advice of their lawyers than by that of the Secretary of the D Notice Committee'. The following footnote appears in Fairley's text: 'Sixty-four per cent of the forty-four editors who replied, claimed to participate in the system'.

A similar question was included in a survey of the U.K. and Australian media in 1997 by the present author. The response from both countries was overwhelmingly that the advice of lawyers would be more influential.

# References

*A-G* v *Guardian Newspapers Ltd (No 2)* [1990] AC 109.

Aitken, J. (1971), *Officially Secret*, London.

Aubrey, C. (1981), *Who's Watching You?*, London.

Author not identified (1987), 'News – Spy in the sky', *Media Law and Practice*, vol. 8, p. 34.

Author not identified (1987), 'UK News', *Media Law and Practice*, vol. 8, p. 118.

Bulloch, J., and Miller, H. (1961), *Spy Ring, The Full Story of the Naval Secrets Case*, London, p. 155.

Clark, W. (1986), *From Three Worlds*, London, p. 173.

Cmnd 1681 (1962), *Security Procedures in the Public Service*, p. iii.

Cmnd 3309 (1967), *Report of Committee of Privy Councillors appointed to inquire into 'D' Notice matters*, para. 65, 69, 71.

Cmnd 3312 (1967), *The 'D' Notice System*, para. 34.

Cmnd 8129 (1981), *The D Notice System, Observations presented by the Secretary of State for Defence*.

*Daily Express*, 19 October 1967, pp. 1, 10.

*Daily Express*, 21 February 1967.

DPBAC home page: www.dnotice.org.uk/index.htm

Fairley, D. (1990), 'D Notices, Official Secrets and the Law', *Oxford Journal of Legal Studies*, vol. 10, pp. 431, 438.

Gowing, M. (1974), *Independence and Deterrence - Britain and Atomic Energy, 1945-1952 Vol. 2*, London, p. 137.

H.C. Deb., vol. 639, col. 1616, 4 May 1961.

H.C. Deb., vol. 640, col. 636-638, 11 May 1961.

H.C. Deb., vol. 676, col. 27, 31, 23 April 1963.

H.C. Deb., vol. 742, col. 274, 28 February 1967.

H.C. Deb., vol. 748, col. 1989, 2080, 2084, 2085, 2088-2089, 22 June 1967.

H.C. Deb., vol. 123, col. 1227, 4 December 1987.

H.L. Deb., vol. 284, col. 775-783, 6 July 1967.

HC773 (1980), *Third Report from the Defence Committee (Session 1979-80), The D Notice System*, August, para. 20, 29, 36, 40; Appendix 24, p. 146.

Hedley, P. and Aynsley, C. (1967), *The D-Notice Affair*, London, pp. 22, 25.

Hooper, D. (1987), *Official Secrets*, London, p. 223.

Jaconelli, J (1982), 'The "D" Notice System', *Public Law*, p. 37.

Joint Working Party of JUSTICE and the British Committee of the International Press Institute (1965), *The Law and the Press*, London.

Kalugin, O. (with Fen Montaigne) (1994), *Spymaster*, London.

*Lord Advocate* v *Scotsman Publications Ltd* [1990] 1 AC 812.

*Lord Advocate* v *Scotsman Publications Ltd* 1988 SLT 490.

Lustgarten, L. and Leigh, I. (1994), *In From The Cold: National Security and Parliamentary Democracy*, Oxford, p. 271.

Margach, J. (1978), *The Abuse of Power: The War between Downing Street and the Media from Lloyd George to Callaghan*, London.

Marshall, G. (1961), 'Comment' *Public Law*, pp. 225-227.

Mercer, D., Mungham, G. and Williams, K. (1987), *The Fog of War*, London, p. 172.

Ministry of Defence Open Government Document No. 93/06, *The Defence Advisory Notices: A Review of the D Notice System*, pp. 1, 9-10.

Official Secrets Act 1911 (U.K.), s1, 2.

O'Higgins, P. (1972), *Censorship in Britain*, London, p. 56.

Palmer, A. (1984), 'The History of the D-Notice Committee', in C. Andrew and D. Dilks (eds), *The Missing Dimension: Government and Intelligence Communities in the Twentieth Century*, London, pp. 241, 246.

Pincher, C. (1968), 'Press Freedom and National Security', *Journalism Today*, vol. Spring, p. 37.

Pincher, C. (1978), *Inside Story: A Documentary of the Pursuit of Power*, London, pp. 235-237.

Pincher, C. (1981), *Their Trade is Treachery*, London, pp. 151-152.

PRO ADM 1/20905.

PRO DEFE 53/1.

PRO DEFE 53/4.

PRO DEFE 53/5.

PRO DEFE 53/6.

PRO DEFE 53/7.

PRO DEFE 53/8.

PRO DEFE 53/9.

PRO DEFE 53/10.

PRO DEFE 53/19.

*R* v *Cairns, Aitken, Roberts and the Sunday Telegraph* (1971) unreported, but see *The Times*, 4 February 1971.

Robertson, G. (1989), *Freedom, the Individual and the Law*, London.

Robertson, G. (1998), *The Justice Game*, London.

Robertson, G. and Nicol, A. (1990), *Media Law*, London, p. 333.

Supperstone, M. (1981), *Brownlie's Law of Public Order and National Security*, London, p. 259.

Taylor, P. (1992), *War and the Media - Propaganda and Persuasion in the Gulf War*, Manchester, pp. 11-12, 268.

*The Guardian*, 13 April 1999.

*The Times*, 7 July 1967, p. 1.

*The Times*, 4 February 1971.

Walker, N. (1990), 'Spycatcher's Scottish Sequel', *Public Law*, p. 354.

Williams, D. (1965), *Not in the Public Interest: the Problem of Security in Democracy*, London, p. 85.

Williams, D. (1968), 'Official Secrecy in England', *Federal Law Review*, p. 23.

www.dnotice.org.uk/index.htm

# 5 History and Operation of the D-Notice System in Australia

## Introduction of the D-Notice system in Australia

The D-Notice system in Australia has not commanded as much attention over the years as its counterpart in the U.K. Whitmore (1968) attributes this to several things; some thirty years later his words are, for the most part, still valid. He says in the first place that, with one possible exception, the Australian D-Notices deal with genuine matters of defence. His second point is that the print and electronic media in Australia have never had specialist military correspondents of the calibre of those in the U.K., such as Chapman Pincher for example. In addition the system does not seem as well known among editors in Australia as it is in the U.K.,[1] and those that do know of it may simply ignore it rather than forgo a good story.

The D-Notice system in Australia had its origins in the Cold War period immediately after the Second World War. The Chifley Government (1945-1949) was advised by Sir Frederick Shedden, Secretary of the Australian Defence Department, to introduce a D-Notice system in Australia. Press coverage of a series of leaks of classified information on defence matters in the late 1940s led to consideration of amendments to the *Crimes Act 1914* (Cth). These amendments did not come about until 1960, but in late 1950 Prime Minister Menzies took steps to introduce a D-Notice system relating only to issues of national security. On 14 July 1952 the first meeting of the Defence, Press and Broadcasting Committee took place at Victoria Barracks in Melbourne, with the Prime Minister acting as Chairman (Maher, 1995). The Australian system was identical to the one operating in the U.K. and was introduced after discussions between the two governments (Whitmore, 1968; Maher, 1995).

## Number and contents of Australian D-Notices

According to Maher (1995) 'the secretaries of six Commonwealth Departments and about a dozen proprietors' representatives' were present at the inaugural meeting, and agreement was reached on eight D-Notices. These covered: 'UK atomic tests in Australia, aspects of naval shipbuilding, official ciphering, the number and deployment of Centurion tanks, troop movements in the Korean War, weapons and equipment information not officially released, aspects of air defence, and certain aerial photographs' (Maher, 1995, p. 140). The Commission of Inquiry into the Australian Secret Intelligence Service (1995) (Samuels Report) gives the original number of D-Notices as being seven, but they are not listed. Defence, Press and Broadcasting Committee, (1983, p. 1) says 'the number of Notices was reduced from seven to four in 1974' intimating also that the original number was seven, but again these are not listed.

The original D-Notices were reduced to four in 1974 and these were: No. 1: Technical information regarding navy, army and air force weapons, weapons systems, equipment and communications systems; No. 2: Air operational capability and air defences; No. 3: The whereabouts of Mr and Mrs Vladimir Petrov; and No. 4: Ciphering and monitoring activities. In 1977 a fifth notice relating to the Australian Secret Intelligence Service (ASIS) was added, the government thereby formally acknowledging the existence of the Service for the first time (Samuels Report, 1995).

In 1982 the D-Notices were revised and have remained unchanged since. They are; No. 1: Capabilities of the Australian Defence Force, Including Aircraft, Ships, Weapons and Other Equipment; No. 2: Whereabouts of Mr and Mrs Vladimir Petrov; No. 3: Signal Intelligence and Communications Security; No. 4: Australian Secret Intelligence Service (ASIS) (Defence Press and Broadcasting Committee, 1983). Petrov was an agent of the KGB. Petrov, and his wife Evdokia, who was also a career officer with the KGB, defected to Australia in 1954. The Petrovs' whereabouts in Australia was the subject also of a U.K. D-Notice (PRO DEFE 53/8, D-Notice - 3.9.54). D-Notice No. 3 relates to the highly secretive Defence Signals Directorate (DSD) and to those elements of the Defence Force which operate in conjunction with DSD to form the Australian Signal Intelligence (Sigint) Organisation.

**The history of the D-Notice system in Australia: 1960-present day**

*1960-1969*

The D-Notice system in Australia remained a secret for many years after its introduction in 1952. Its existence was not exposed to the Australian public until 15 July 1967 when Richard Farmer wrote a piece in *Nation* under the headline 'D-noticed out of print'. The revelation in the article about the existence in Australia of a D-Notice system led to questions being asked in Parliament on 4 October 1967:

> Mr DEVINE - My question is directed to the Prime Minister. I ask: Are D security notices used extensively by his Government to give directions to the Australian Press, radio and television? ...
> Mr HAROLD HOLT - Mr Speaker, there is a D notice system operating in this country along very much the same lines as that which operates in Great Britain under the Government of the United Kingdom. I do not have the detail of how this is applied in particular circumstances ...

The issue was raised again on 8 and 9 November 1967 by Mr Devine in a question upon notice to the Prime Minister. The reply sets out how the system operated at the time.

> Mr Devine asked the Prime Minister:
> 1. Who are the members of the Defence Press and Broadcasting Committee?
> 2. Is it part of this Committee's responsibility to recommend the issue of D notices to press, radio and television?
> 3. How many D notices are currently operating and to what subjects do they relate?
> Mr Harold Holt - The answer to the honourable member's questions is as follows:
> The Defence Press and Broadcasting Committee is a committee established by agreement between the Commonwealth Government and press, radio and television interests in Australia.
> The Committee consists of fourteen members, with Government members in a minority. I do not feel that it is appropriate that I indicate current membership by name. However, nine members represent a cross-section of the morning, evening and provincial press, and broadcasting and television stations. Five members represent the Defence group of Departments.
> The Committee's function is not to recommend, but in fact to issue D notices to press, radio and television. A D notice is a confidential request in the interests of national security not to make public specific matters referred to in the notice. The system is a voluntary one and non-compliance carries no penalties.
> A request for a D notice originates with a Government department and is referred to the committee, which can either approve, refuse or suggest amendment. When it approves the committee's secretary issues the notice on a confidential basis to editors and managers. If it does not approve, the notice does not issue.

The number of D notices currently in force is small and it is not in the national interest to disclose the precise number or the subjects to which they relate.

The Defence Press and Broadcasting Committee renders a valuable public service and it is appropriate to record the Government's appreciation of its work.

Whitmore (1968) criticised the secrecy in which the detail of the system was shrouded, commenting that there seemed no reason why the number and content of D-Notices should not be made public. Nonetheless Whitmore discreetly refrained from filling in the detail, saying it would be 'improper' (p. 452). Campbell and Whitmore (1975) comment:

Perhaps the most unsatisfactory aspect of this particular exercise in security censorship is that it existed for so long without the general public being informed of its existence. Both the Government and the press were at fault. It is the ultimate in censorship to conceal the very existence of a system of censorship however informal it might be (p. 333).

Campbell and Whitmore conclude their comments on the D-Notice system by observing that it did not seem to have been used during the Vietnam war. There was, however, much criticism by journalists of the heavy handed censorship that did take place, and which was conducted by service censors guided by rules drafted in Canberra.

*1970-1979*

The Australian public was first alerted to the existence of the Defence Signals Directorate, the highly secret electronics intelligence unit, by *The National Times* of 12-17 February 1973. The article was headed 'Why our troops are staying in Singapore':

Although its operations are top secret in Australia (and its existence never referred to by government) the existence of the DSD and its mode of operation have been described by the American radical leftist magazine 'Ramparts'. In an issue last year 'Ramparts' claimed that the Australian DSD is associated in an international electronics intelligence 'swap' with the National Security Agency of the United States (p. 1).

The following week, in the edition dated 19-24 February 1973, *The National Times* reported that the DSD revelations had brought about a storm of controversy, including an accusation by the Prime Minister, Mr Gough Whitlam, that the newspaper had breached a D-Notice. Even the Leader of the Opposition, Mr Billy Snedden, called for action to be taken against the offending journalist, Mr Fred Brenchley. The newspaper's response was to point out that the technical material had already been published in *Ramparts*, copies of which were available in both the Parliamentary and National libraries in Canberra.

During August 1973 *The National Times* continued its campaign for more openness in the operation of secret government intelligence agencies by carrying stories on the Joint Intelligence Organisation (JIO), the Australian Security Intelligence Organisation (ASIO), the Australian Secret Intelligence Service (ASIS) and the Defence Signals Directorate (DSD) (*The National Times*, 20-25 August 1973). The connection between the Australian organisations and the British intelligence gathering system was also outlined, the report in the 6-11 August edition saying: 'Prime Minister Whitlam ... refuses to acknowledge publicly the existence of ASIS' (p. 19). As a result of the publicity during 1973 the D-Notice system became widely known and the Prime Minister eventually acknowledged that it needed to be updated.

In December 1973 the Defence, Press and Broadcasting Committee met in Canberra. It was at this meeting that the number of D-Notices was reduced to four, and the decision was taken to issue a booklet containing details of the D-Notices and their operation (*The National Times*, February 25-March 2 1974; *Nation Review*, 9-15 February 1978). From then on the number of D-Notices and their substance was no longer confidential information.

In the 25 February-2 March 1974 edition *The National Times* again broke a story relating to issues covered by the D-Notice system. Under the headline 'Why Australians know less than the Chinese' the newspaper told of how a Taiwanese Chinese translator working for an Australian Electronic Intelligence Unit in Asia had defected to China. *The National Times* pointed out in the report that it was unable to disclose details of where the unit was operating and what the unit did because this would be in breach of the D-Notice system. A meeting of the emergency sub-committee of the Defence, Press and Broadcasting Committee, held the day before publication, had informed the newspaper of the potential breach, despite the fact that the proscribed information was known to the Chinese and had also been reported in other Australian newspapers the previous year. The article does not name the other Australian newspapers that had reported the information the previous year. The editorial in the same issue again criticised the lack of openness in government.

Once again *The National Times* was the first media outlet to report a new development in the D-Notice system when a fifth D-Notice came into force in late October 1977. The new D-notice prohibited disclosure of information relating to ASIS, the government having decided to acknowledge publicly for the first time the existence of ASIS but at the same time wanting to prevent publication of any specific details about the organisation.[2] Initially the intention was that the fifth D-Notice should be in place only temporarily, but a meeting of the Defence, Press and Broadcasting Committee in Sydney on 24 November 1977 agreed to retain it indefinitely. The front page of the same issue of *The National Times*, dated 31 October-5 November 1977, carried a story on new powers to be given to ASIO under the heading 'More Power than the FBI'.

*Nation Review* on 9-15 February 1978 reported that the Australian Journalists Association (AJA) 'is considering full opposition to the "D" notices cabal between press and government'. The story carried the headline 'The "D" Notice System - What the Press isn't Saying'. Following a review of the system, including some stringent criticism of its operation both in Australia and the U.K., the newspaper gave an edited version of the AJA recommendations to its members:

> 1. The Australian Journalists Association opposes the voluntary censorship embodied in the 'D' notices system. It points out the system was introduced in peacetime without any informed discussion as to why the public's right to freedom of information should be summarily abridged. Information about the system was kept secret from the public for many years, violating the onus on censors to justify their actions.
> 2. The Association calls on all media companies to relinquish their membership on the Defence, Press and Broadcasting Committee as being inimical to the traditions of journalism and to the public's right to freedom of information (p. 15).

The next week *Nation Review* followed up by publishing in full the five existing D-Notices and the names of the government and media representatives then on the Defence, Press and Broadcasting Committee. The headline was 'D Notices Part two: Blank Spaces'. Part of the article included an addendum to the AJA report of the previous issue. The addendum was supplied by Mr Laurie Oakes, then the political correspondent of the Melbourne *Sun News-Pictorial*. Oakes said that although the fifth D-Notice on ASIS was to be retained, the retained version had been revised and was an improvement on the original.

Several other items were listed in the addendum, the following being the most noteworthy. Information about the provisional D-Notice on ASIS, and its contents, had been revealed first by *The National Times*. The D-Notice included a request that the names of current and former employees of ASIS remain confidential, but that edition of *The National Times* named former ASIS employee Mr H. Barnett as the new deputy head of ASIO.

> The editor of the *National Times* received a rocket from the Defence Department for breaching the very 'D' notice the paper had quoted. This shows how 'D' notices can prevent the reporting of news. The background of a new deputy head of the domestic security and intelligence service is obviously both newsworthy and important (p. 6).

There was also some comment made on the deaths of the Australian journalists at Balibo in Timor in 1975. According to the addendum, the DSD picked up Indonesian army messages within hours of the attack on Balibo 'reporting that the newsman had been killed by Indonesian troops and their bodies burned'. Because of D-Notice number 3 (relating to ciphering and monitoring activities) nothing concerning DSD can be published, the result being that certain vital information was not available to the public. 'Apart from anything else, in the case of the Balibo deaths it prevents the hypocrisy of the Australian Government then in power (and of the present Government which also has access to the file containing the signals) from being exposed' (*Nation Review*, 16-22 February 1978, p. 6).

The final comment in the addendum was that the operation of the D-Notice system should be more open to public scrutiny. The suggestion was that there should be more publicity about the system in the news media, including information about the approval or withdrawing of D-Notices.

*1980-1989*

Thirty years after the defection of Mr and Mrs Vladimir Petrov the release by the government of secret papers relating to the incident raised a flurry of interest in 1984. When on 24 September 1984 *The Age* purported to reveal their whereabouts, this information being subject to a D-Notice, the newspaper was immediately advised by a government official that this 'was in the view of the relevant Government authorities a clear and deliberate breach of a D notice'. According to Mr G. Mawer, then Secretary of the Defence, Press and Broadcasting Committee, 'all the media representatives on the committee had been specifically reminded on 20 September' of the existence of the relevant

D-Notice. *The Age* went on to report that it had also been offered rights to a photo said to be a current one of Vladimir Petrov, but had chosen not to publish it 'as it considered it to be an invasion of privacy' (*The Age*, 25 September 1984, p. 16).

*1990-*

Almost ten years elapsed before the next major D-Notice story broke. This particular issue centred on publicity about ASIS. During 1993 and 1994 certain leading daily newspapers published ASIS-related stories, alleging operational and administrative inefficiencies within the Service. The Minister for Defence, who was Chairman of the Defence, Press and Broadcasting Committee, alerted the respective editors to the existence of the D-Notice relating to ASIS. The editors responded by saying either that they did not know the system still existed, or that they were unaware of the D-Notice specifically relating to ASIS (Samuels Report, 1995).

On 21 February 1994 the Australian Broadcasting Corporation (ABC) broadcast a *Four Corners* programme about ASIS. While the D-Notice had not been drawn to the attention of the ABC by the committee beforehand, despite the content of the programme being known in advance, the ABC did apparently consider the terms of the D-Notice prior to the broadcast. The programme aired allegations about ASIS made by two former officers of the service and the wife of one of them. Like the earlier media stories on the subject, the programme was critical of the service.

On 23 February 1994 Senator Gareth Evans, then Minister for Foreign Affairs and thus responsible for ASIS, announced a judicial inquiry 'into the operations and management of ASIS' (Samuels Report, 1995, p. xx). The Commission of Inquiry into the Australian Secret Intelligence Service was made up of the Honourable G.J. Samuels AC, Q.C. and Mr M.H. Codd AC, and they reported to the government on 31 March 1995. Part of the *Report on the Australian Secret Intelligence Service* (Samuels Report) remains secret but a public edition was tabled in Parliament on 24 April 1995.[3]

As a part of its investigation the Commission of Inquiry examined the effectiveness of the D-Notice system as the means of preventing publication of sensitive information relating to national security, and thereby also details about ASIS. The conclusion reached in the Samuels Report was that the system appeared to have fallen into disuse. The Defence, Press and Broadcasting Committee had not met since 1982, and there was ignorance of the system or of the content of the individual D-Notices. Two opposing views as to the future of the system were put forward in the Samuels Report. On the one hand 'the clear view of the media is that the D-Notice system should be revived, not buried' (para. 11.8), whereas ASIS proposed that major problems beset the system and it should be replaced by a voluntary code of conduct.

In the middle of all this activity, a review of the D-Notice system had been undertaken by the Defence Department in December 1993. The review came about because of the proposed ABC *Four Corners* programme on ASIS and a DSD related story in a Melbourne newspaper, and also because of the recently completed British review of the system. The Australian review concluded that the system should be restored and the individual notices revised. As a result the ASIS D-Notice was redrafted and submitted to the Minister, but the establishment of the Commission of Inquiry into ASIS halted the review and consideration of the redraft.

The Samuels Report recommended the reconstitution of the D-Notice committee which should then review the content of the D-Notices. The report suggested the members of the committee should be editorial staff rather than newspaper owners, and that Ministers should be involved in discussions relating to the redrafting of D-Notices that affected their particular portfolios. In view of the fact that the committee had not met since 1982, the report saw no further purpose for the continuation of the committee once the D-Notices had been satisfactorily redrafted. If another major redraft of the D-Notices were to take place it could be recalled. In place of the committee the report recommended the establishment of a permanent secretariat to the committee which would take over the administration and communication of matters relating to the D-Notice system. Specific advice on individual D-Notices would be given by the relevant government department.

Before there was any time for proper consideration to be given to the Samuels Report, another major news story about ASIS with D-Notice implications hit the headlines. On Saturday 27 May 1995 *The Sydney Morning Herald* carried a front page story written by David Lague in Canberra and Michael Millett in Tokyo, under the headline 'How we spied on China'. The story alleged that a joint operation between the Australian and United States governments resulted in a 'massive spying operation against the Chinese Embassy building in Canberra'. Australian technicians, with the assistance of 30 or so US National Security Agency (NSA) officers, installed a network of fibre optic listening devices costing about $5 million while the Embassy was being built. An injunction obtained by the Australian government in the New South Wales Supreme Court on 21 April 1995 restrained *The Sydney Morning Herald* from publishing the story, which the paper had known about since March.

However, yesterday the ABC revealed details of the operation in a special 5 pm news bulletin. At 6.15, Fairfax lawyers went back to the Supreme Court where Justice Bryson varied some of the orders made in April.

The *Herald* remains subject to other orders which prevent it from publishing certain details of the operation. The Federal Government last night obtained similar orders against the ABC ...

The US is understood to have unrestricted and direct access to all the intelligence gathered from the Chinese Embassy but has restricted Australia's access to some of this information.

This has led to fears that the US Government may have access to sensitive commercial information about Australia-China trade that may disadvantage local exporters.[4]

Also on the front page under the heading 'The Battle to publish spy report', *The Sydney Morning Herald* said further that on the instructions of the *ABC* Managing Director, Mr Brian Johns, a story relating to D-Notices had been withdrawn from the *ABC* television news on the evening of Thursday 25 May. Contrary to the requests of the Australian Government Solicitor, the *ABC* ran the story in a special extended news bulletin on Friday 26 May. On page 4, headlined 'ABC defies bid to quash spy report', *The Sydney Morning Herald* also described how it was *ABC* staff who forced the issue over the eventual broadcasting of the item by holding a protest meeting and passing a resolution calling on Johns to allow the story to be aired. Similar stories and headlines appeared in other newspapers, for example *The West Australian* on 27 May 1995: 'Defiant ABC runs China bug report' (p. 6). On the morning of Friday 26 May Mr Alan Jones had also reported on Radio 2UE in Sydney that he had information about certain spying allegations which he would reveal the next day. Mr Jones and Radio 2UE were promptly injuncted, on the basis of a breach of confidence action, to refrain from further comment.

Once the news had reached the public domain, more information about the role of *The Sydney Morning Herald*, which had hitherto been subject to a suppression order, became publicly available. David Lague, Foreign Affairs Correspondent based in Canberra for *The Sydney Morning Herald*, was the first journalist to prepare the story for publication. As mentioned in the above extracts from *The Sydney Morning Herald*, on 21 April 1995 the government was successful in obtaining a temporary injunction against the John Fairfax Group to restrain publication of the story following an application to the New South Wales Supreme Court. Both the case, which is unreported, and the terms of the injunction were subject to a suppression order. Immediately following the *ABC* broadcast on Friday 26 May 1995, John Fairfax Ltd returned to the court and the terms of the injunction were revised allowing publication of an amended version of the story in *The Sydney Morning Herald*.

The government agreed to discontinue its action for breach of confidence against John Fairfax Ltd on 29 May 1995, but once again the terms of the agreement were subject to a suppression order. John Fairfax Ltd, David Lague, Radio 2UE, Alan Jones and the ABC applied to the court on 31 May 1995 to retain documents and affidavits handed over by the government in support of its application for the injunction against publication. Bryson J, in a reserved judgment handed down on 26 June 1995, rejected the application (*West Australian*, 27 May 1995; Maher, 1995; Author not identified, 1995, 'Gareth's Suppression Capers').

In a Ministerial Statement in Parliament on 1 June 1995 the Minister for Foreign Affairs at the time, Senator Gareth Evans Q.C., officially responded to the Samuels Report. Senator Evans announced a review by the government which would include draft amendments to the *Crimes Act 1914* (Cth) making secondary disclosure an offence. The amendments were intended to catch those, in most instances the media, who disclose sensitive government information leaked to them by third parties already covered by provisions in the *Crimes Act*. In addition the government intended to 'update and reinvigorate the D-Notice system', but Senator Evans was critical of the role of the media:

> ASIS makes a good story, precisely because it is shrouded in secrecy. In these circumstances, the media is prone to exaggerate facts, and even experienced and responsible journalists are prone to suspend their powers of judgment and good taste in the pursuit of a good spy story. The Commissioners found that, in some instances, journalists had published allegations about ASIS which they had good reason to suspect were untrue. In some other cases, they made no attempt to verify the accuracy of the claims made to them. I hope the media will take note of these observations ... (Senate Deb., No. 8, col.723, 1 June 1995).

The Australian Press Council discussed the issue of the D-Notice system following consultation with editors. The Council drafted a submission to the government, but the then Chairman, Professor David Flint, made it clear he was opposed to putting the system on a statutory footing (Author not identified, 1995, 'News'):

> Indeed, legislation which would allow the censoring of information in peacetime on the grounds of national security seems incompatible with our democratic values. Such legislation could be unconstitutional and violate

our international human rights commitments. Above all, the fundamental right of the Australian people to be informed must remain paramount as it is in comparable democracies (p. 4).

In late 1995, following the controversy surrounding the publication of information about the alleged bugging of the Chinese Embassy in Canberra, the government, represented by the then Minister for Defence, Senator Robert Ray, and senior executives from some of the media organisations met to discuss the reinvigoration of the D-Notice system. *The Sydney Morning Herald* declined to attend. The meeting broke down in stalemate - the media proprietors wanting a deal whereby they would make the D-Notice system work if the government dropped the secondary disclosures amendments to the *Crimes Act* (*Sydney Morning Herald*, 14 December 1995).

The media voiced serious concern at the nature of the tough measures being proposed by the government, which included fines of $1 million for a prohibited broadcast or publication. Among these commentators were David Lague in *The Sydney Morning Herald* on 14 December 1995, under the heading 'Media chiefs baulk at crackdown on secrets' (p. 3) and the Australian Press Council in its 1996 *Annual Report*. On 15 September 1997 the defence writer for *The Australian*, Don Greenlees, under the heading 'Howard moves to censor secrets', also criticised the moves (p. 1). In the same issue Greenlees said under the heading 'Media censorship boils down to a matter of trust': 'The idea of jail terms ... was later dropped. But the $1 million fines stayed' (p. 13).

Following the elections in 1996, and the consequent change of government from Labor to Liberal, the issue of revival of the D-Notice system was 'the subject of ongoing consideration by the National Security Committee (NSC) of Cabinet'.[5] The most recent developments are discussed immediately below.

## How the system works (or, rather, used to work) in Australia

In Australia the system, when operative, has worked rather differently to that in the U.K. The government side in the Australian system is embedded in the executive and in the bureaucracy, without the interface of any 'independent broker' between them and the media side. The Chairman is the Minister for Defence, the executive secretary is a bureaucrat from the Ministry of Defence in Canberra, and the system operates under the administrative responsibility of the Minister for Defence.

A D-Notice is a communication issued to the media on the authority of the Defence, Press and Broadcasting Committee. It outlines subjects which bear upon defence or national security, and requests editors to refrain from publishing certain information about those subjects.

The basic principles underlying the system are as follows:

- it operates through the Defence, Press and Broadcasting Committee under the Chairmanship of the Minister for Defence. Membership of the Committee comprises representatives of the media and Government;
- a D-Notice originates from a request by an Australian Government Department which considers there is substantial reason, in the interests of national security, for restraint by the media in publishing particular information;
- D-Notices are issued to the media only on the authority of the Defence, Press and Broadcasting Committee. The Committee can approve, reject or amend Notices brought before it. The system is an entirely voluntary one, offering advice and guidance only. Non-observance of a request contained in a Notice carried [*sic*] no penalties. In the end, it is for an editor to decide whether to publish an item of information, having regard to national security requirements ... (Defence, Press and Broadcasting Committee, 1983, p. 1).

The media representatives on the Committee in 1982 were: Australian Newspapers Council (the President), News Limited, John Fairfax and Sons Ltd, Herald and Weekly Times Ltd, *The Age*, Regional Dailies of Australia Ltd, Australian Consolidated Press Ltd, West Australian Newspapers, Federation of Australian Commercial Television Stations, Australian Newspapers Council (the Secretary), Australian Provincial Press Assoc., Australian Broadcasting Commission, Federation of Australian Radio Broadcasters, Peter Isaacson Publications Pty Ltd, Special Broadcasting Service, Australian Magazine Publishers Association. The government side was represented by four members: the Secretary, Department of Defence, the Chief of Defence Force Staff, the First Assistant Secretary, Policy Co-ordination Division, and the Director, Joint Intelligence Organisation. The list includes names, business addresses and telephone numbers.

Maher (1995) describes how the Committee operated:

In its early days, the D Notice Committee met only when a new D Notice was proposed. The Committee secretary would make telephone contact with the proprietor's representatives. It seems that in many (probably most) cases, the issue of a D Notice was agreed to in that informal setting. Otherwise, it was intended that the committee meet formally once a year (p. 140).

As already indicated, the simple answer to the question of how the system works in Australia in 2000 is that it does not work at all. The committee has not met since 1982, and this was the last time the individual D-Notices were revised (Samuels Report, 1995). The D-Notice relating to the Petrovs in particular is out of date; although Evdokia Petrov was reported to be still alive in 1995, Vladimir Petrov died in Melbourne in 1991 (*The Sydney Morning Herald*, 27 May 1995).

It is difficult to obtain any information about the system. In October 1996 it took a number of phone calls over a period of days to the media office of the Department of Defence in Canberra to procure a copy of the official booklet on the D-Notice system. The booklet states:

> The function of the Executive Secretary of the Defence, Press and Broadcasting Committee is to administer the D-Notice system and to provide advice to the media, in consultation with the appropriate authorites [*sic*], on enquiries about matters which fall within the range of subjects covered by D-Notices. The advice and services of the Executive Secretary are always available to editors and others who have enquiries on D-Notice matters. The addresses and telephone numbers of the Executive Secretary and the alternative officer are shown below ... (Defence, Press and Broadcasting Committee, 1983, p. 7).

Several further phone calls to the Department of Defence, starting with the number given in the booklet for the executive secretary, finally led to the information that at present there is effectively no D-Notice committee (and thereby no secretary) because the committee is 'in abeyance' while Parliament decides how and if it should be reconstituted. The official said that Parliament would arrange talks with the media proprietors and the question of how to reconstitute the committee would be discussed in Parliament. The choice of the word 'Parliament' seemed curious, given that 'Parliament' in the general sense has never previously been involved with the establishment or the running of the committee either in Australia or the U.K.

Letters sent to various government Ministers and to the Department of Defence between 1997 and 1999 asking for more details eventually resulted in some helpful and informative responses. One letter said that Mr G. Mawer was the secretary of the committee when the last formal meeting was held in 1982, and that Mr Brian Oxley was the last active secretary, relinquishing the position in January 1990. At the time this letter was written in 1997 the National Security Committee of Cabinet (NSC) was considering the issue of reviving a D-Notice system. Because the consideration was ongoing, further details about the form of the proposed new system were unavailable. The

Intelligence Policy Section of the Department of Defence would ultimately form the secretariat for any new D-Notice system. In addition the comment was made in this letter that '[t]he committee was never formally placed in abeyance. Rather, it just fell into disuse'.

A background briefing on the D-Notice system sent with one of the replies provided, inter alia, the following information:

> Consultation with the media was carried out during September and October 1995 by a small group headed by the Chairman of the Secretaries' Committee on Intelligence and Security (SCIS) and the then Minister chaired a meeting with media representatives on 13 December 1995.
>
> The outcome of the meeting was inconclusive. In response to continuing reservations among the media, the Minister approved further consultations with the media pending the introduction in 1996 of legislation dealing with secondary disclosure. These further consultations were placed in abeyance pending the outcome of the election.
>
> The new Government is yet to decide on the issues of amendments to the *Crimes Act* and reinvigorating the D Notices. In the meantime, Defence is continuing to develop its proposal for renewed consultations, and is offering an advisory service to the media along the lines originally proposed.

One reply advised that the NSC was dealing with the issue of amendments to the *Crimes Act* (in relation to secondary disclosures) together with the reinvigoration of the D-Notice system. No further comment on the matter of amendments to the *Crimes Act* would be available until a decision had been reached by the NSC. Another letter said that in September 1997 the NSC directed 'that the Minister for Defence and the Attorney-General should meet with the media to discuss the feasibility of a voluntary D-notice system for the protection of national security information'. Such a meeting was held in May 1998 with the following outcomes:

> • There was strong support for the Government's approach of seeking a workable voluntary system before pursuing legislation; and
> • It was more or less readily agreed that the media and Government should be able to cooperate to reduce the damage that could be done by publication of some types of material, and acceptance of the legitimacy of the Government seeking to establish such cooperation, in that it was not contrary to Australia's principles of press freedom ...

What has not been agreed anywhere yet is how the new D-Notice system would operate. And what continues to frighten the media off is the possibility (however remote) of penalties for secondary disclosure after they have ignored the D-Notice principles.

By late 2000 there have been no further developments. It is always possible that no decision will be made unless a trigger occurs, if, indeed, a decision is ever made.

Rear Admiral Pulvertaft mentioned that he had received visits from Australian officials looking to revamp the Australian D-Notice system, and to this end seeing how the English system operates. He could see two differences between the DA-Notice system in the U.K. and the D-Notice system in Australia, and in his view these differences were seminal:

1. The system in the U.K. has continued uninterrupted and has been regularly reviewed and updated to keep it current. The Australian system had not been properly updated for years - the D-Notice concerning the Petrovs was probably entirely unnecessary by now and in his view it was these sorts of things that made the media wonder about the relevance of the system.

2. The Secretary in the U.K. plays a pivotal role in the successful operation of the system. The Secretary is accessible and available and plays the role of the 'independent broker'. The Australian system simply has the two sides facing up to each other, that is, government versus the media, so on the one hand there is the government being overly secretive and on the other hand the media seeking maximum openness.

In the absence of an operative procedure such as the D-Notice system it falls to the journalists and editors themselves to decide, in the interests of national security, what sensitive government information should or should not be published. This may be based on tests such as 'imperilled lives'. Pincher (1968) albeit speaking of the U.K. experience in the 1960s, says: 'No editor I have known ever wants a scoop at the expense of national security' (p. 38). Schauer (1982) speaks of the United States doctrine of 'clear and present danger' (p. 198). Whether the interests of the general public are sufficiently taken into account if it is left to the media to make the decisions as to publication or otherwise of sensitive material is open to question.

**Summary of the history and operation of the D-Notice system in Australia**

It would seem to be a very difficult task to successfully raise from the dead something which is regarded with such suspicion both by the media and by the government. The phoenix the Labor government appeared to have in mind in late 1995 was not a creature with which the media would willingly co-operate, and co-operation is fundamental to the viability of a system of voluntary self-censorship such as the D-Notice system. Certainly the interests of the general public would not be served by a system so heavily weighted in favour of government interests. The more conciliatory approach of the present Liberal government may achieve more success, but it will be difficult to convince the media that they need such a system when they have done quite well without one since 1982.

**The financial cost of the D-Notice system to the media - the U.K. and Australia**

It was recognised as early as 1899 that newspapers would suffer economically if censorship, either self censorship or government censorship, on matters relating to national security was imposed. In 1899 Sir Evelyn Wood well understood the financial loss that might occur when a paper is conscientious about not printing material that is potentially sensitive (**PRO WO 32/6381**):

> The editorial staff do not possess sufficient expert knowledge to discriminate between what may be published with impunity and what should be suppressed; they must either publish the whole or suppress the whole, the latter course involving perhaps serious financial loss on any paper which is patriotic enough to pursue it systematically, while other papers are nullifying the utility of such suppression by themselves publishing the same news.[6]

Any delay in the publication of a potential scoop increases the risk of other media outlets airing it first. In 1981 *World in Action* had to delay by two weeks, at the request of the IBA, a story on security leaks at the GCHQ in Hong Kong. This story was done in conjunction with *The New Statesman* and *The Daily Mirror* who ran the story without the two week delay, thus negating much of the newsworthiness of the *World in Action* programme. In 1987 the BBC was forced to delay by six months the broadcasting of an edition of *My Country Right or Wrong* dealing with the *Spycatcher* case. The *Sydney*

*Morning Herald* had been held up by five weeks in the running of the story regarding the alleged bugging of the Chinese Embassy, which at the beginning was exclusive to that newspaper. It was mainly due to *ABC*'s defiance of the government's wishes that the story eventually entered the public domain, but at the expense of a scoop for the *Sydney Morning Herald*.

The commercial downside to the media of attempted compliance is one of the matters which should be taken into account whenever there is any review of the system. Obviously the purpose of the D-Notice system is defeated if the media as a whole are not involved, in that they are all made aware of the system and the individual D-Notices and agree to comply. If some break ranks, either to ensure the 'scoop' remains theirs, or for some non commercial reason, the conscientious participators in the system will eventually follow suit. As far as the public interest is concerned, it is not healthy for there to be a delay in the publication of stories about government activities when these activities are not genuinely related to national security issues. This is a situation where the interests of the media and the interests of the general public coincide.

## Misuse of the D-Notice system

It is clear from the examination of the history of the D-Notice system that the subject matter of D-Notices is intended to be of the sort that relates to issues of national security. An attempt was made in the 1920s to widen the scope to include D-Notices covering foreign news 'in its political aspect', but this did not eventuate. It is worth recalling that from the outset the press were concerned about the possible misuse of the system. As noted earlier, however, one of the major criticisms of the system is that it has been used for the wrong purposes. D-Notices might be used to cloak government ineptitude, or to hide other matters that have nothing to do with 'military' affairs, or to prevent government embarrassment, or even to prevent criticism of government policy.

There are many examples. The D-Notice issued in the period before the Suez crisis has already been discussed in this context. The attempted suppression of evidence given during the George Blake trial was due to government embarrassment at having the scandal of a Soviet KGB agent such as Blake working for MI6 revealed to the British public. Attempts in 1961 to extend the D-Notice system in the U.K. to include all information relating to weapons systems was opposed on the basis that the real purpose was to prevent criticism of government policy (Palmer, 1984). A story by R. Farmer in *Nation* on 15 July 1967, headed 'D-noticed out of print', said:

In Britain a former editor of the magazine 'Aeronautics', Major Oliver Stewart, claimed in March 1962 that there was a grim and efficient censorship of the British press which effectively prevented informed criticism of defence measures because so little of the picture was open to public scrutiny (p. 5).

On 23 April 1963 Mr George Brown asked in the House of Commons:

> May I ask the Prime Minister whether he is aware that the country is very puzzled by what is a secret here and what is embarrassing? Does he not see the difference? There are references to regional seats of Government, publication about which I could well understand would be embarrassing, but not necessarily secret ...

On 29 May 1963 Lord Balfour of Inchrye said in the House of Lords:

> I do not believe that there is a Minister in the Government who could put his hand on his heart and say that he does not know of cases where 'D' notices and the public relations system have been used to cloak individual or departmental failures ...

A further example is the 'Cable Vetting Sensation' in 1967. The U.K. government was embarrassed by the Chapman Pincher story revealing that all cables leaving the country were being scrutinised by government officials, and was afraid that such a revelation would cause a diplomatic furore. Yet another example is the Jonathan Aitken case in 1970 where the leaked information concerned the forces of a foreign power. The U.K. government was embarrassed by the criticism of a foreign power to whom arms and support were being given, but there was no question of British national security being compromised as a result of the story appearing in the media.

The D-Notice system has been used on at least one occasion to provide incorrect information to the media. In July 1963 the editor of *The Daily Telegraph*, Mr Colin Coote (later Sir) pressed the Foreign Secretary, Lord Home, for the name of a KGB defector who was in Britain for interrogation by MI5. MI5 feared for the safety of the defector, and was angered by the persistent requests from the newspaper which refused to accept that publication would endanger the defector's life. MI5 contrived via the medium of the secretary of the Defence, Press and Broadcasting Committee, Colonel Lohan, to spoil *The Daily Telegraph's* scoop. It was done by having the name released in a D-Notice statement over the Press Association wire service. To confuse the issue further, in what Pincher has described as 'another extraordinary incident in MI5's strange machinations', the name was given as Anatoli Dolnytsin when in fact it was Anatoli Golitsin (Pincher, 1978, p. 69).[7] Kalugin (1994) says Anatoly Golitsyn, Kalugin's spelling, which is most likely the correct version, a high ranking KGB officer, defected in 1961, in which case the only people who did not know the name of the defector in July 1963 were probably the British public. Kalugin says the KGB knew about the defection in 1961. Pincher (1968) also claimed that the government, inadvertently, admitted to a misuse of the D-Notice system in seeking to suppress through the system the names of the heads of MI5 and MI6.

The misuse of the D-Notice system was recognised by a joint working party of representatives of JUSTICE (British Section of the International Commission of Jurists) and of the British Committee of the International Press Institute, chaired by the Right Hon. Lord Shawcross Q.C. In their 1965 report the joint working party concluded:

> 66. We did however get the impression that 'D' notices have occasionally been issued to prevent discussion or disclosure of matters which are not vital to national security or which have been already published in foreign newspapers, where the purpose was to protect a department rather than national security. We regard such a practice as undesirable and would not criticise any newspaper which published such material if it was certain that it could not harm the public interest (Joint Working Party of JUSTICE and the British Committee of the International Press Institute, 1965).

In Australia the latest occasion when D-Notices reached the headlines was with respect to the Chinese Embassy Bugging Affair in 1995. The overwhelming suspicion of the media is that the issue at stake was embarrassment to the government at being found out, rather than any genuine threat to national security (*The Sydney Morning Herald*, 14 December 1995).

**Summary - Chapters 1-5**

The restriction on the publication of information relating to defence or national security matters put in place by the D-Notice system is unusual. It is an agreement, or a collusion, between the government and the great majority of the media over what the media will, or will not, print. The public interest is not sufficiently represented by the U.K. system, but the U.K. system as it presently functions provides a better balance of the competing interests than did the Australian system when it operated. The D-Notice system may also better balance the public interest than journalists and editors themselves making unilateral decisions as is now the situation in Australia.

The D-Notice system works on voluntary agreement, so notionally at least the press has some choice as to what it publishes. While the interests of the general public may not be properly represented on the committee, the system may be seen as preferable to legal restrictions. The different legal ways in which the governments in both the U.K. and Australia have attempted to prevent publication of this class of information is examined in Chapters 6-8.

## Notes

[1]   This particular comment is interesting in the light of the surprisingly good response to a survey of the Australian media sent out in 1997 by the present author. Over 90% of the respondents said they were aware of the existence of the system.

[2]   In their book on the ASIS Brian Toohey and William Pinwill (1989) describe the introduction of the D-Notice on ASIS on the same day as the government publicly acknowledged the existence of the spy service. Their book was censored by the government and the entire contents had to be cleared by ASIS and the Department of Foreign Affairs and Trade before publication.

[3]   The Samuels Report is also mentioned in Chapter 6.

[4]   The injunctions against the *Sydney Morning Herald* and the other media organisations involved in the breaking of the story were based on breach of confidence actions. The issue of the use of breach of confidence to gag the media is discussed in Chapter 8.

[5]   This information came in a letter in May 1997 from the office of the then Minister for Defence, the Hon. Ian McLachlan AO MP in response to enquiries about the revival of the D-Notice system and amendments to the *Crimes Act*. The letter noted 'the Government's commitment both to protecting principles of freedom of speech and to protecting national security information'.

[6]   Other parts of this memo are referred to in Chapter 3.

[7]   See also Pincher (1981) and Palmer (1984).

## References

Australian Press Council (1996), *Annual Report No. 20*, Sydney.

Author not identified (1995), 'Gareth's Suppression Capers', *Gazette of Law and Journalism*, vol.32, p. 2.

Author not identified (1995), 'News', *Australian Press Council News*, vol. August, p. 4.

Campbell, E. and Whitmore, W. (1975), *Freedom in Australia*, Sydney, p. 333.

Defence, Press and Broadcasting Committee (1983), *Australian D-Notices*, Canberra, pp. 1, 7.

H. of R. Deb., col. 1643, 4 October 1967.

H. of R. Deb., col. 2865, 8 & 9 November 1967 (Answers to Questions).

H.C. Deb., vol. 676, col. 26, 23 April 1963.

H.L. Deb., vol. 250, col. 904, 29 May 1963.

Joint Working Party of JUSTICE and the British Committee of the International Press Institute (1965), *The Law and the Press*, London, para. 66.

Kalugin, O. (with Fen Montaigne) (1994), *Spymaster*, London.

Maher, L. (1995), 'ASIS "D" Notice Controversy', *Media Law Reporter*, vol.2, p. 140.

*Nation*, 15 July 1967, p. 5.

*Nation Review*, 9-15 February 1978, p. 15.

*Nation Review*, 16-22 February 1978, p. 6.

Palmer, A. (1984), 'The History of the D-Notice Committee', in C. Andrew and D. Dilks (eds), *The Missing Dimension: Government and Intelligence Communities in the Twentieth Century*, London.

Pincher, C. (1968), 'Press Freedom and National Security', *Journalism Today*, vol. Spring, p. 38.

Pincher, C. (1978), *Inside Story: A Documentary of the Pursuit of Power*, London, p. 69.

Pincher, C. (1981), *Their Trade is Treachery*, London.

PRO DEFE 53/8.

PRO WO 32/6381.

Schauer, F. (1982), *Free speech: a Philosophical Enquiry*, Cambridge, p. 198.

Senate Deb., No. 8, col. 716-726, 1 June 1995.

*The Age*, 25 September 1984, p. 16.

*The Australian*, 15 September 1997, pp. 1, 13.

The Commission of Inquiry into the Australian Secret Intelligence Service (1995), *Report on the Australian Secret Intelligence Service*, Canberra, para. 11.8; p. xx.

*The National Times*, 12-17 February 1973, p. 1.

*The National Times*, 19-24 February 1973.

*The National Times*, 20-25 August 1973.

*The National Times*, 6-11 August 1973, p. 19.

*The National Times*, February 25-March 2 1974.

*The National Times*, October 31-November 5 1977.

*The Sydney Morning Herald*, 27 May 1995, p. 1.

*The Sydney Morning Herald*, 14 December 1995, p. 3.

*The West Australian*, 27 May 1995, p. 6.

Toohey, B. and Pinwill, W. (1989), *Oyster: The Story of the Australian Secret Intelligence Service*, Melbourne.

Whitmore, H. (1968), 'Censorship of the Mass Media: The "D" Notice System', *The Australian Law Journal*, vol.41, p. 452.

# 6 The Use of the Criminal Law in Relation to the Disclosure of Sensitive Information

## Introduction

The history of the D-Notice system contained in Chapter 3 to Chapter 5 shows that the original purpose of the system was to prevent the publication of sensitive information relating to matters of defence or national security. It was, and still is, intended as a means of control over a specific type of information. For the government the D-Notice system, providing it works, is perhaps the least controversial way of preventing this sensitive information from being published. Where the term 'sensitive information' is used from now on in this context, it means information that is sensitive in relation to national security matters. One of the cornerstones of the D-Notice system is that it is a non-legal, voluntary agreement between the government and the media. The system initially applied to the press because at the time of formation there was no radio or television, but reference to the 'press' would seem to exclude the electronic media which now also participates in the system. Therefore the word 'media' is used to include both.

Because the government does not want the material published, the element of choice by the media is, in government eyes, the system's weakness and disadvantage. For the media this is its strength and advantage. There have been occasions in both the U.K. and Australia when the government has resorted to the law to achieve the desired result, that is to prevent the non publication of material deemed, by the government, to be sensitive on national security grounds. When the government sidesteps the D-Notice system and turns to the law, the burden falls on the judiciary to weigh the competing interests, within the parameters allowable by the law.

The purpose of Chapter 6 to Chapter 8 is to consider the legal means available to the government to restrain the publication of material it considers to be sensitive on national security grounds, or to punish those who have already published such material. The reason for this analysis is to assess whether the D-Notice system is a preferable alternative to legal restraint for the suppression of this type of material. This will be done by examining whether the judiciary properly take into account the public interest (in other words the interests of the general public) in cases concerning the suppression of sensitive government information. The interests of the general public lie in having only that material suppressed which is genuinely prejudicial to national security. Where the nature of the legal action allows judges no discretion to balance the competing interests, this will be shown to give the advantage to the government at the expense of the interests of the general public.

## The use of criminal law in the U.K.

### Introduction

The government has used the provisions of s2 of the Official Secrets Act of 1911 (the Act), as amended in 1920, and its replacement contained in the Official Secrets Act of 1989, to prosecute those who publish sensitive information. The Official Secrets Act and the D-Notice system have a very close connection, and the history of the D-Notice system in England shows that the D-Notice system was designed to complement the workings of the Act. D-Notices could be used to clarify the meaning of the Act and to prevent revelations that were not strictly speaking within the ambit of the Act. Conversely the Act was always there in the background as a threat; when the D-Notice system did not work as the government would have wished, the Act was a useful implement with which to bludgeon the transgressing media.

Hooper (1987) describes the Act as hovering 'like a vulture over those connected with government service and the media' (p. 10). In Appendix 1 of his book Hooper lists a selection of cases brought under s2 between 1915 and 1986. Some half dozen of these cases (seventy three in all) involve journalists or the press; they do not include the cases discussed in this chapter. Pincher (1968) says: 'The Official Secrets Acts are rarely used against newspapermen, but the ever-present *threat* of their use makes them effective instruments of censorship' (p. 39) [*Pincher's emphasis*]. A full analysis of the workings of s2 of the Official Secrets Act 1911, and the Act of 1989, is not within the scope of this book.[1] It is, however, relevant to look at the interaction between the Official Secrets Act and the D-Notice system and to that extent the Act is examined.

It has become clear from official documentation, secret at the time, that when the D-Notice system was being organised the government side, from the outset, were not completely open in their dealings with the press. On 5 November 1912 Mr R.H. Brade, Assistant Secretary of the War Office, wrote a letter to the Secretary of State headed, 'Memorandum on the Formation of a

Standing Committee of Official and Press Representatives to deal with the Publication of Naval and Military News in Times of Emergency' (PRO DEFE 53/1). The following extract illustrates the difference between the approach to the arrangements which the government side adopted with the press, and the reality which was the secret underlay to the proceedings:

> I have referred ... to the 'helplessness' of the War Office in dealing with certain newspapers last summer. I ought perhaps to explain further that while this expression correctly conveys the situation at the moment when the cases had to be dealt with, and when we had not had time to receive legal advice as to the scope of the new Official Secrets Act, yet the power of the department is really not so meagre as would appear. After the editors' attention had been drawn to their action, I referred the papers to the Treasury Solicitor with the following minute:
> 'Our contention is that the publication of these articles is "prejudicial to the safety and interests of the State." Assuming that, could proceedings be taken against the publisher under Section 1. (c) of the Official Secrets Act, he having by publication "communicated to another person information which might be useful to an enemy?" '
> This was referred to Director of Public Prosecutions, who advised that on certain assumptions as to the correctness of the information communicated by the newspapers then in question, that information was or might be directly or indirectly useful to an enemy within the section of the Act quoted. And from this we have inferred that, in certain circumstances, this Act could be used against a newspaper. And I gather from conversation with Sir Graham Greene that, in a subsequent case in which the Admiralty were concerned, Sir Charles Matthews himself saw an editor and warned him that the Official Secrets Act might be used against him. We have a note on our official papers to the effect that the speedy passage of the Act through the House of Commons was due to a general understanding that the new measure was not directed against any new class, but against that at which the former Act was aimed, viz., the spy class* and that to use it against a newspaper merely for publishing news useful to an enemy would amount to a breach of faith with Parliament. But there is no record of this in the official versions of the debates ...
> *The marginal note to the first section is 'penalties for spying,' but I believe that such notes do not limit in any way the provisions of a Statute.

There are two items of note in particular that arise from the memorandum:

1.  Brade, who was a very active member of the Admiralty, War Office and Press Committee, representing the government side from its formation in 1912 through to December 1919, clearly took the view that the Official

Secrets Act remained to be used to punish offending newspapers, regardless of any agreement between the government and the press for the *voluntary* withholding of news items which were perceived to threaten the interests of national security. The media, meanwhile, were under the impression that, because of the abandonment of the Press Bill and the emphasis on the voluntary nature of the system, they were now trusted by the government (Lovelace, 1978; Palmer, 1984). Palmer describes it as 'a delusion' on the part of the press (p. 235).

2.  The memorandum talks about the operation of the system during 'Times of Emergency' or 'the period of tension or strained relations which might be anticipated before an actual outbreak of war' - there appears to be no mention of the peace-time use of the system. If it was originally only intended for use in 'Times of Emergency' it was apparently too useful to be allowed to wither away in times of peace. The system has mainly been used in times of peace and only during periods of declared war has it been held in abeyance, to be replaced by full censorship.

The voluntary agreement between the press and the government worked without any major differences of opinion from 1912 until the 1960s. Although a few events occurred which threatened the stability of the system before the 1960s, these were relatively minor and not sufficient to do serious damage or even to warrant publicity about the existence of the system which until then remained hidden from public knowledge. Displeased with the outcome of some of the events which took place in the 1960s and 1970s, from the 1970s onwards the government saw fit to use the legal system as a back up for (or an alternative to) the D-Notice system.

The reasons for the difference in approach by the government to the suppression of sensitive information are rooted in the development of the D-Notice system after the second world war. Palmer describes the revival of the system following the war as 'in effect, simply a continuation of wartime censorship with the sop of a channel for the press to air grievances thrown in as a concession to the formal cessation of hostilities' (p. 240). Furthermore, according to Palmer:

> The continuity with wartime censorship meant the system was now widely identified with the Official Secrets Act, and the Whitehall members of the committee did nothing to discourage that belief, once itself a closely guarded secret. The alternative to compliance was believed by everyone to be imprisonment (p. 242).

Pincher (1968) says: 'Only the British could call the D-Notice system voluntary. It is in fact an extension of the Official Secrets Acts which are already far too wide' (p. 30). The corollary to this perception of the system was the perception that clearance by the secretary of the committee of material for publication meant immunity from prosecution. The media thus continued to participate in the system under the misapprehension that they would be granted immunity in return for co-operation, and would be prosecuted if they did not co-operate.

As discussed in Chapter 4, in 1967 Mr Chapman Pincher found himself at odds with the system when he published in the *Daily Express* a story which the government thought was in contravention of one or more D-Notices then in force. A subsequent inquiry by a Committee of Privy Counsellors found no breach of any D-Notice had occurred, but the government persisted in its disagreement over this particular matter and issued a White Paper to this effect. The Attorney-General, however, found no evidence of the commission of any offence under the Official Secrets Act, so no prosecution took place relating to Pincher's disclosures (O'Higgins, 1972).

This clash between the government of the day and the press over the D-Notice system served notice on the media that the government would not take kindly to differences of interpretation of how the system should work, or of individual D-Notices. It also marked a point from which the media were less willing to smother information 'in the interests of national security' when the information did not readily fit this description.

Before examining in detail the use from the late 1960s of the Official Secrets Act 1911 in relation to sensitive information of the general kind protected by the D-Notice system, it is useful to outline the relevant sections of the Act and to determine the effect of these sections. Sometimes these provisions were used to protect sensitive information which may also have been subject to a D-Notice, but sometimes there was no overlap of this nature. The cases discussed below have been selected either because they have a direct connection with the enforcement of the D-Notice system, or because they involve the media in some way, or because they illustrate a milestone in the judicial interpretation of the Act relevant to the issues at hand.

*The Official Secrets Act 1911 (U.K.) - relevant sections and their effect*

The Official Secrets Act 1911 repealed, and replaced with extensions, the earlier Act of 1889 which the authorities had found to be too limited in its application. Section 1 of the 1911 Act related to espionage. The most relevant section, because of its effect on the press, was s2. Leave had to be obtained from the Attorney-General before a prosecution under the Official Secrets Act could be instituted.[2] Section 2 of the Act was particularly wide in its scope, it was in effect a catch all provision, and the judiciary seemed unwilling to interpret it narrowly.

An early example of this judicial reticence is *R* v *Crisp and Homewood* (1919) 83 JP 121 where the defendants were a War Office clerk and the director/secretary of a firm of tailors respectively. Crisp passed copies of documents containing particulars of contracts for officers' clothing to Homewood. The information would give an advantage to the firm in the tendering for government contracts, although it was accepted that there was no corruption involved. At first instance the magistrate in the Westminster Police Court found the Official Secrets Act did not apply to the offence. The Attorney-General appealed and the case came before Avory J in the Old Bailey. Comparing the 1911 Act with the Act of 1889, which he saw as being limited to spying, Avory J remarked that the 1911 Act went much further: 'It seems to me that s. 2 applies to any document or information of an official character which has been obtained by a person holding office under his Majesty' (p. 122-123). Even though Avory J said he regarded the case as a technical breach of the statute, the defendants were convicted. He ordered each to pay a fine of 40*s.*, and each to pay half the taxed costs of the prosecution.

In 1920 the Act was amended[3] and the new provisions contained within the amendments widened the scope of s2 considerably. In particular the elastic wording 'or in any other manner prejudicial to the safety or interests of the State' added to the potential scope of s2. The combined effect of the two Acts made s2 a formidable weapon in preventing leaks of any kind of information from government departments. 'In legal theory, it was a crime to reveal the number of cups of tea consumed each day in the MI5 canteen' (Robertson, 1989, p. 132).

In 1926 Major F. Blake, a former governor of Pentonville Prison, was tried and convicted for unlawfully communicating confidential information to a newspaper. The *Evening News* ran a story by Major Blake which included the alleged last minute confession of a condemned murderer. Blake's defence argued unsuccessfully that a disclosure must be contrary to the public interest to be covered by the official secrets legislation. The editor of the newspaper was not prosecuted (Aitken, 1971; Hooper, 1987).[4]

The application of the section to matters other than those relating to national security was supported by the government. Lord Normanbrook, who was the British civil service head at the time, said in 1957 that the Act would be contravened by any civil servant who disclosed any information which had not been released officially. This approach was maintained by his successor,

Sir Laurence Helsby (Campbell, 1967).

In 1958 two Oxford University undergraduates, Mr Paul Thompson and Mr William Miller, published in *Isis*, the Oxford University undergraduate magazine, details of monitoring stations along the Russian frontier. They acquired this information while they were in the Royal Navy Special Reserve on national service. They were charged under s2 of the Official Secrets Act and tried at the Old Bailey. The Solicitor-General prosecuted and at his request most of the trial was heard in camera. Thompson and Miller were both convicted and sentenced to three months' imprisonment. The conviction was the beginning of a serious effort by the government to keep secret the existence and activities of Government Communications Headquarters (GCHQ).[5] As noted previously GCHQ remained unknown to the general public until 1977. Following the appearance of the article in *Isis*, several newspapers ran the story; a D-Notice was immediately issued, and so the later editions did not carry it (Hooper, 1987).

In 1965 the Official Secrets Act was criticised in the report of the Joint Working Party of JUSTICE (the British Section of the International Commission of Jurists) and the British Committee of the International Press Institute:

> It is in matters not affecting national security that the Official Secrets Act lends itself to abuse or suspicion of abuse. There appears to be a climate of secrecy surrounding the workings of Government departments and public authorities which is particularly marked in this country ... This British tradition of secrecy is of long standing but has increased during this century. It is not generally realised, for instance, that until the passing of the Official Secrets Act of 1911, spying in peace-time was not even a criminal offence, whereas now the disclosure or improper use of the most harmless document can lead to prosecution. We feel that this does not make for good government since it can lead to protection of inefficiency and malpractice, stifle the needful exposure of public scandals, and prevent the remedying of individual injustices (para. 67).[6]

The report concluded that fear of the Act did not serve the public interest, and the criminal law should not apply to publications by the media that were not genuinely prejudicial to national security.

*R* v *Cairns, Aitken, Roberts and the Sunday Telegraph Limited*

The facts of *R* v *Cairns, Aitken, Roberts and the Sunday Telegraph Limited* (1971 - unreported) (the Jonathan Aitken case) have been covered in Chapter 4 when the case was discussed with respect to its implications on the D-Notice system. The prosecution in the committal proceedings had conceded that the case did not concern national security and the prosecution's insistence that the publication of the report had compromised the relationship between Britain and Nigeria was not supported by the evidence (Aitken, 1971). The defence also proved that all the detail in the Scott Report was already public knowledge. It was decided at the committal proceedings, however, that a prima facie case had been made out on the charges under the Official Secrets Act, so the case was sent to trial.

The trial of Aitken and his co-defendants for offences under s2 of the Official Secrets Act took place at the Old Bailey before Caulfield J in early 1971.[7] The prosecution advised the jury that 'the meaning of confidential information was information whose unauthorised disclosure would be contrary to the interests of the State' in this case the Scott Report. Even if the content of the report were public knowledge it was the protection of 'uninhibited reports and assessments' that was at stake (Aitken, 1971, p. 156). The prosecution case against Aitken was that he knew he was being entrusted with just such a classified document in the strictest confidence. The case against Roberts and the *Sunday Telegraph* was that they had deliberately ignored the warnings of both Mr Johann Welser of the Foreign Office, and of Vice-Admiral Sir Norman Denning, secretary of the D-Notice Committee, that they might be contravening the Official Secrets Act by publishing the Scott Report (Aitken, 1971).

According to Aitken the evidence given by Welser during the trial was confusing and inconclusive. Denning gave evidence that Mr Gordon Brook-Shepherd, assistant editor of the *Sunday Telegraph*, summarised the report for him paragraph by paragraph. Denning told Brook-Shepherd that as the contents of the report did not refer to U.K. national forces, the report did not affect U.K. national security and so was not covered by the D-Notice system. Denning said he had added that if it was an official document it would be covered by the Official Secrets Act. He commented that he was no expert on what would, or would not, be covered by the Act, and while D-Notices are distinct from the Act they may cover the same information.

When it came to deciding whether there was a case to answer, the defence argued, in the absence of the jury, that s2 of the Act was intended to discipline public servants who leaked information, but should only apply to private citizens when the information related to matters of national security. This was refuted by the prosecution who claimed that the Crown regarded all official information - whether classified or not - as covered by s2. 'The whole structure of government would fall down if people had complete freedom to communicate any document that was not a document useful to an enemy', using as an example budget leaks (Aitken, 1971, p. 171). After two and a half days of legal argument Caulfield J found there was a case against each of the accused and the issues should be put before the jury.

Following the case for the defence, Caulfield J summed up for the jury, having the following to say about the independence of the judiciary and the freedom of the press:

> It may well be that prosecutions under this Act can serve as a convenient and reasonable substitute for a political trial, with the added advantage of achieving the same end without incurring the implied odium. Nevertheless I urge you most strongly to dismiss from your minds, now that this Court is seized of the matter, any political prejudice one way or the other ...
> It may well be that this trial is important to the Press of this country. We all recognise, do we not, that the opinion-forming and informing media like the Press must not be muzzled. The warning bark, you may think, is necessary to help in maintaining a free society. If the Press is the watch-dog of freedom, and the fangs of the watch-dog are drawn, all that will ensue is a whimper, possibly a whine, but no bite. And the Press so muzzled, you may think, becomes no more than the tenement of the political poor ...
> The 1911 Act achieves its sixtieth birthday on 22 August this year. This case, if it does nothing more, may well alert those who govern us at least to consider, if they have the time, whether or not Section 2 of this Act has reached retirement age and should be pensioned off, being replaced by a section that will enable men like Colonel Cairns, Mr Aitken and Mr Roberts and other editors of journals to determine without any great difficulty whether a communication by any one of them or a certain piece of information originating from an official source, and not concerned in the slightest with national security, is going to put them in peril of being enclosed in a dock and facing a criminal charge ... (Aitken, 1971, pp. 197-198).

The jury found the defendants not guilty on all counts, and Caulfield J took the unusual step of ordering that the defendants' costs be paid out of public funds.

*The Times* reported the case on 4 February 1971 under the heading 'No Duty in Law for Editor to Run to Whitehall, Secrets Case Judge Says' (p.2). The report set out the points summarised by Caulfield J for the jury and included some of the comments in his speech. The editorial on the same day, headed 'The Secrets Act Must be Reformed', commented on the acquittal and made special mention of the need to reform the Official Secrets Act (p. 15).

The case was an unpleasant defeat for the government. It showed up the flaws in s2 of the Official Secrets Act, in particular the lack of distinction in the type of information intended to be caught by the section and the selective way in which prosecutions were brought. The D-Notice system was also a victim. It became obvious as a result of the prosecutions in this case that the media had been basing their participation in the D-Notice system on an incorrect assumption, the assumption being that clearance from the secretary of the Defence, Press and Broadcasting Committee would give them immunity from prosecution under the Official Secrets Act.

Perhaps the media had been naive in not fully appreciating that D-Notices and offences under the Official Secrets Act were, and still are, two separate issues. If the media did understand the differences between the D-Notice system and the ambit of the Official Secrets Act, and it is hard to believe they did not, they were naive to think the government would not pursue by any means its objective of keeping information such as this out of the public view in the future. The information contained in the Scott Report was not sensitive to national security, but it was politically sensitive.

Vice-Admiral Denning had cleared the contents of the Scott Report from being subject to any D-Notices then in force, but, according to his evidence as mentioned above, had warned that if the Scott Report was an official document then it would be subject to the Official Secrets Act. This suggests that media defendants in this situation must then also take the further, and separate, step of determining whether or not their information is subject to the Official Secrets Act. Why should the media not simply cut out one of the steps by ignoring the D-Notice system, supposedly voluntary anyway, and concentrate solely on the Official Secrets Act? The vexed question of just exactly what is to be gained by seeking advice from the secretary of the Committee remains the subject of conjecture.[8]

The case illustrates the importance of the role of the judiciary in cases involving information that is alleged by the government to be sensitive on national security grounds. Writing a short time after the trial, Aitken makes reference to Caulfield J's summing up and the effect of the decision, enthusiastically forecasting reform of the Official Secrets Act and a future for journalists without having to face criminal charges simply for publishing information that is embarrassing or inconvenient to the government. Aitken also speaks of the judgment assuming 'an historic as well as a contemporary importance' (Aitken, 1971, p. 197).

Events since 1971 have shown that Aitken's optimism was misplaced - the war was far from being won and the case was a mere skirmish. Mr Richard Crossman wrote somewhat prophetically:

I am amazed by the naive enthusiasm with which it is now being argued that the Act should be scrapped and replaced by a new statute. A delight in secrecy and a passion for keeping the public in the dark still dominates Whitehall ... What makes anyone imagine that if Whitehall gets the chance it won't produce a young mastiff to replace the toothless old watch-dog? (Aitken, 1971, p. 218)[9]

Nonetheless, one of the causes for optimism at the time was the announcement by the government two weeks after the verdict that a Committee of Inquiry, under the Chairmanship of Lord Franks, was to examine s2 of the Official Secrets Act.

*Summary of the Franks Committee Report*

The Franks Committee Report (1972), the *Departmental Committee on s.2 of the Official Secrets Act 1911* (Cmnd 5104), came out in September 1972.[10] It covered the background to the Official Secrets Act, pointing out that the Official Secrets Bill was put forward in 1911 during the Agadir and Parliamentary Bill crisis to replace the 1889 Act which the government saw as inadequate. The 1911 Bill was a stronger measure which was aimed at spying and which was essential on the grounds of national security. Section 2 was not mentioned once in the Parliamentary debates and while the government did not conceal the fact that the new s2 was designed to impose a much tighter grip on all unauthorised documents, they did not draw attention to it. The 1911 Act was passed in one afternoon with little debate, but it had been long desired by the government and carefully prepared for years.

The Franks Report noted at the outset that 'there is an inevitable tension between the democratic requirement of openness, and the continuing need to keep some matters secret ... The tension has been increasing in recent years' (para. 1-2). The Franks Report said the Scott Report Affair and the resultant prosecution under the Official Secrets Act was not the only reason for the appointment of the Franks Committee to examine s2 of the Act. While Caulfield J in his summing up had suggested that s2 be 'pensioned off' he meant it should be replaced by new, clearer, provisions. Caulfield J remarked to the Franks Committee: 'I could add many other worries I have about this section, but perhaps it is sufficient to say that I think the section in its present form could be viciously or capriciously used by an embarrassed executive' (Hooper, 1987, p. 8).

The Franks Report found s2 to be a catch all provision - short, covering a great deal of ground and 'according to one calculation over two thousand differently worded charges can be brought under it' (Cmnd 5104, para. 16). Between 1945 and 1971 there had been twenty three prosecutions involving thirty four defendants of whom twenty seven were convicted and six were acquitted. Nearly two thirds of these defendants were Crown Servants or former Crown Servants. Only two cases since 1945 had involved professional journalists. Over one third of the cases (involving information) concerned information on defence, national security or intelligence. One third involved police or prison information, and three cases involved information relating to international affairs. Section 2(1)(a) 'which creates the offence of unauthorised disclosure, contains nothing to imply directly that mens rea is an ingredient of the offence' (para. 20). Supperstone (1981) and Thomas (1986) both suggest that no mens rea is required for s2(1).[11]

The Franks Report acknowledged that s2 had a widespread deterrent effect, and views on it ranged from unqualified approval, from the government, to total rejection, by the media. The Report recommended that the Official Secrets Act should be confined to espionage and not leakage of information; it found journalists to be resentful of being lumped in with spies and traitors. A brief summary of the D-Notice system concluded that '[t]here is no direct relationship between the system and the Official Secrets Act, and nothing in the "D" Notice System relieves an editor of his responsibilities under the Acts' (para. 65).

The Franks Report proposed that s2 should be repealed and replaced by an 'Official Information Act' which should apply only to official information which would be categorised according to the nature of its confidentiality. The top category would be classified information relating to defence, or internal security, or to foreign relations, or to the currency or reserves, the unauthorised disclosure of which would cause serious injury to the interests of the nation. The consent of the Attorney-General would be required for a prosecution to take place, and secondary offences would apply - that is, *any* person who communicates information which he knows or has reasonable grounds to believe falls within that classification would be subject to prosecution.[12] Nothing was done by the government to implement the recommendations of the Franks Committee.

## *R v Aubrey, Berry and Campbell*

*R v Aubrey, Berry and Campbell* (1978 - unreported) (the *ABC* case) involved Mr Crispin Aubrey, a staff reporter on *Time Out* magazine, Mr John Berry, an ex-soldier who had been involved with the interception and analysis of radio communications during his time with Signals Intelligence, and Mr Duncan

Campbell, a freelance journalist specialising in defence and government communications. In 1977 they were charged with nine offences under various sections of the Official Secrets Act. The charges followed the publication of an article written by Campbell and Mr Mark Hosenball in the May 1976 issue of *Time Out*.

The article, entitled 'The Eavesdroppers', revealed that the purpose of GCHQ was to carry out electronic eavesdropping. GCHQ was still secret at the time and a D-Notice was in force which proscribed the revelation of its existence to the public in the U.K., even though its existence was already well known to the Warsaw pact countries. Robertson (1998) says: 'The subject was blanketed by "D" notices, the curious and very English system whereby the country's newspaper editors - all of them - cravenly complied with directives from a committee dominated by the security services and the armed forces' (p. 106). *Time Out*, however, was not a party to the D-Notice system (*R v Secretary of State for the Home Department, ex parte Hosenball* [1977] 3 All ER 452).

Berry read 'The Eavesdroppers' and made arrangements to meet Aubrey and Campbell to talk about his experiences with Sigint in Cyprus. It was following a three hour meeting between the three at Berry's flat, recorded on tape by Aubrey, that the three were arrested and charged. Much of the information which led to the charges was already in the public domain - albeit in a variety of different publications, but the 'mosaic' or 'jigsaw' of pieces put together as a whole was the subject of the government's complaint.[13]

When the *ABC* case eventually came to trial before Mars-Jones J at the Central Criminal Court in October 1978, the number of charges had been reduced to three. Berry was convicted under s2(1)(a) of communicating information and sentenced to six months imprisonment suspended for two years. Campbell was convicted under s2(2) with receiving information and Aubrey was convicted under s7 of the 1920 Act of abetting the receipt of information; these two were given conditional discharges. Campbell and Aubrey were each ordered to pay costs of £2,500 towards the prosecution costs, Campbell £2,500 towards his own costs, and Aubrey one third of his own costs, which amounted to £10,000 (Nicol, 1979; Aubrey, 1981; Suppertsone, 1981; Eisenschitz, 1985; Thomas 1986; Hooper, 1987; Robertson 1989; Robertson, 1998). Aubrey (1981) was one of the defendants, and his book tells the story of his involvement. Robertson (1998) was on Campbell's defence team, and he describes the case in a chapter entitled 'Ferrets or Skunks? The ABC Trial'.

During the trial a bizarre exchange took place which typifies the obscurity surrounding the provisions of the Official Secrets Act. Lord

Hutchinson Q.C., Campbell's counsel, while cross examining prosecution witness 'Colonel B' (Colonel H. Johnstone), asked him how secrets were classified (Hooper, 1987):

> 'What remains secret is what is designated secret by whoever makes the designation,' he replied, without shedding too much light on the subject.
> 'You mean the rules that are laid down for what is and is not secret are themselves secret?'
> 'Yes,' was his unflinching reply (p. 117).

*Events during the 1980s*

A memorandum dated 6 June 1980 submitted to the Defence Committee of the House of Commons by the BBC in 1980 elaborates the concern of the media regarding the operation of the Official Secrets Act and its effect on the D-Notice system. 'Thus, editors continue to be concerned about the lack of certainty surrounding the workings of the Official Secrets Act, suspended over many journalistic activities as one eminent lawyer has put it "like a sword of Damocles held by an extremely rusty chain" ' (HC 773, Minutes of Evidence, 8 July 1980, p. 43 para. 4 [*there are many separate days on which evidence was given, some of which start afresh with paragraph 1, some do not, without any apparent consistency*]). During the 1980s the government continued to make use of s2, and indeed while Sir Michael Havers was Attorney-General there were more s2 prosecutions than had been brought under any other Attorney-General. In most of these cases national security was not an issue (Lustgarten and Leigh, 1994).

*R v Ponting*

While the convictions in the *ABC* case may have been reasonably satisfactory in the eyes of the government, the result in the 1985 case of *R* v *Ponting* [1985] Crim.L.R. 318 was not at all welcome. Ponting's case had nothing to do with D-Notices, and neither for that matter did it have anything to do with the jeopardy of national security, but is worthy of mention because it was one of the reasons for the reform of s2 of the Official Secrets Act.

Mr Clive Ponting OBE was a senior civil servant in the Ministry of Defence who gave information to an MP, Mr Tam Dalyell, regarding the sinking of the Argentinian ship the *General Belgrano* during the Falklands War. This information enabled Dalyell to show that there had been ministerial deception in the official version of events put before the House of Commons and the public. The government kept the information from the public during the trial by using s8 of the Official Secrets Act 1920, which allows that 'all or any portion of the public shall be excluded during any part of the hearing ...' and s4 of the Contempt of Court Act 1981, which allows that 'the publication of any report of the proceedings, or any part of the proceedings, be postponed ...' (Hocking, 1993).

The defence conceded that the information had been obtained by Ponting through his position in the civil service, and that he had passed it to Dalyell without authorisation. Ponting claimed in his defence that Dalyell was, as provided for in s2, 'a person to whom it is in the *interest of the State* his duty to communicate' the information, because Parliament should be informed of the ministerial deception. In rejecting this interpretation, the trial judge, McCowan J, equated 'interests of the State' to 'the policies of the Government of the day', not necessarily the Conservative government which was in power at the time, but the government in power at the relevant time. McCowan J held that 'on a proper construction of s2, there was no requirement of *mens rea* for this section further than an intention to commit the *actus reus*', and he was quite prepared to stop the case and direct the jury to find the defendant guilty (*R v Ponting*, 1985, p. 319). Following submissions from the defence and a request from the prosecution that the question should go to the jury, the jury was allowed to make up its own mind and it 'followed its own collective conscience' resulting in a decision of not guilty (Thomas, 1986, p. 497). This was a surprising outcome in view of McCowan J's clearly expressed opinion as to what the verdict should be (Eisenschitz, 1985; Thomas, 1986; Lustgarten and Leigh, 1994).

Thus, in the *Aitken* case and in the *Ponting* case there are two completely different judicial interpretations of the intent required for a breach of s2. In the former case Caulfield J indicated that the defendant, to be guilty, must know that the information was being disclosed in breach of the Act. In the latter case McCowan J viewed the section as effectively one of strict liability. Lee, Hanks and Morabito (1995) consider that McCowan J's interpretation of 'interests of the state' may be defensible:

> It is not only that the courts' processes and expertise are poorly suited to addressing and resolving the types of issues implicit in the concept of the 'interests of the state' ... it might also be said that judicial deference to the executive's policies is the appropriate response in a political system constructed on the value of representative democracy and in which the executive can claim a legitimate mandate for its policies...
> This is not to dismiss the criticism of the deference to the executive's judgment shown by McCowan J in *Ponting* ... It must be conceded that the

reading given to s 2(1) in *Ponting* (and, by analogy, the ruling which would be given to s 79(3) of the Australian *Crimes Act*) allows those provisions to be used for the protection of the sectional interests of a political party or faction: publication of information which could establish dishonest or corrupt dealing, or which could lay the foundation for calling the current government to account in the appropriate political forums can effectively be discouraged through the threat of prosecution (p. 153) [*footnote omitted*].

The first paragraph of the quote appears to compromise the separation of powers doctrine. The role of the judiciary in determining issues related to national security interests, and the approach of the judiciary to these issues, is examined in detail later in this book.

*The Official Secrets Act 1989 (U.K.) (OSA 1989)*

In 1989 the Official Secrets Act was reformed, but it was not reformed in the way that the media wanted, or had expected, following the recommendations of the Franks Committee. Section 2 of the 1911 and 1920 Acts was repealed and replaced by the 1989 Act, which covers disclosure of official information. Section 1 of the 1911 Act still remains in force to cover espionage. While the 1989 Act was still in the Bill stage, Robertson (1989) likened the changes to s2 as replacing 'a blunderbuss with an Armalite rifle' (p. 141).[14]

One of the differences between the new and the old provisions is evident immediately. In the 1911/1920 provisions the reference was to 'any person holding office under H. Majesty'. Section 1(1) of the 1989 Act[15] refers more specifically to '[a] person who is or has been a member of the security and intelligence services; or, a person notified that he is subject to the provisions of this subsection' thus allowing the provisions of s1, the old s2, to be extended to others who may have contact with the security services, for example senior police officers. Lustgarten and Leigh (1994) report that all Metropolitan Police Special Branch officers of the rank or Inspector or above - more than 100 people - have received notification.

A second noteworthy difference is less obvious; the 'interest of the State' defence that helped the jury acquit Clive Ponting does not appear in the 1989 Act. During the bill stage of the Act, former Prime Minister Edward Heath was critical of this omission. He says: 'Unfortunately, the lack of public interest defence is integral to the bill's failure to weigh the right of the individual against the possible abuses of state powers' (Heath, 1989, p. 10). In addition, the inability to prove the chain of culpability which led to Jonathan Aitken's acquittal in *R* v *Aitken* has been overcome in the 1989 Act by the inclusion in the relevant sections of the words 'disclosed (whether to him *or another*) ... without ... authority ...' [*emphasis added*] (OSA 1989, s5(1)a(ii) and (iii), s6(1)(a)).

The material divulged by Aitken, the Scott Report, was not subject to a D-Notice because it did not concern the national security of the U.K. The 1989 Act includes a section, s3, specifically relating to 'International relations', and the disclosure is 'damaging' if 'it endangers the interests of the United Kingdom abroad, seriously obstructs the promotion or protection by the United Kingdom of those interests or endangers the safety of British citizens abroad ...'. Thus another loophole is closed which might otherwise allow acquittal by a jury in similar circumstances, that is, where the information does not directly relate to U.K. national security.

Different sections of the 1989 Act cover the different types of information which it is an offence for a Crown servant or government contractor to disclose. Section 1(1) deals with 'Security and intelligence', s2 with 'Defence', s3 with 'International relations' and s4 with 'Crime and special investigation powers'. A Crown servant or government contractor in the categories of security and intelligence, defence, and international relations 'is guilty of an offence if without lawful authority he makes a damaging disclosure'. In each of these sections there is a definition of the circumstances in which a disclosure is deemed to be damaging, but these are widely framed and would be relatively easy for the prosecution, with the support of government evidence, to establish (Palmer, 1990). For example:

> 1(4) For the purposes of subsection (3) above a disclosure is damaging if-
> (a) it causes damage to the work of, or any part of, the security and intelligence services; or
> (b) it is of information or a document or other article which is such that its unauthorised disclosure would be likely to cause damage or which falls within a class or description of information, documents or articles the unauthorised disclosure of which would be likely to have that effect.

In each of these sections there is also a defence. Once the prosecution has established that the disclosure is 'damaging' according to the provisions of the Act the onus shifts onto the defendant 'to prove that at the time of the alleged offence he did not know, and had no reasonable cause to believe, that the information, document, or article in question was such as is mentioned in subsection ... above or that its disclosure would be damaging within the meaning of that subsection' (OSA 1989, s1(5), s2(3), s3(4)). It may be very difficult for a defendant to show he had 'no *reasonable* cause to believe' in the face of the prosecution's evidence.

For a member of the security and intelligence services, and a person notified that he is subject to the provisions of the subsection, it is an offence to make a disclosure of 'any information, document or other article relating to security or intelligence' without lawful authority (s1(1)). There is no reference to 'damaging' and the defence relates to not knowing, or having no reasonable cause to believe, that the 'information, document or article in question related to security or intelligence' (s1(5)). The provisions relating to 'crime and special investigation powers' (s4) are similar. Therefore in these two categories, that is, the categories of 'security and intelligence' provided for in s1 of the Official Secrets Act 1989, and 'crime and special investigation powers' in s4, the simple fact of disclosure would in most circumstances be sufficient for a conviction.

The sections which apply to third parties such as the media are s5 and s6. Section 5 covers 'Information resulting from unauthorised disclosures or entrusted in confidence', and s6 covers 'Information entrusted in confidence to other States or international organisations'. Both sections refer to a 'damaging' disclosure and the damage is assessed in the same way as it would be in relation to s1, s2 and s3 (s5(3), s6(2) and s6(4)). Prosecutions under the Act must be instituted with the consent of the Attorney-General, and the penalty is a maximum two year prison term or a fine or both.

The lack of a public interest defence in any category shifts the focus to the fact of disclosure and away from the reasons for disclosure. Palmer (1990) points out that the test of harm provided for in the Act as a defence is inadequate. If the trial judge decides that matters of conscience have no bearing on the legal issues relating to unauthorised disclosure, the jury may not find out why the disclosure was made.

Lustgarten and Leigh (1994) comment further that s1 with its strict liability provisions which prevent disclosure by a member of the security and intelligence services will 'in many instances not preserve secrecy, but merely freeze public knowledge in the state it happened to reach when the Act and concurrent policy change took effect' (p. 236). There is also an anomaly in cases where a member of the security or intelligence services discloses information to a third party who also discloses it; for the first defendant the disclosure is in itself an offence, and for the second defendant the disclosure (of the same information) must be 'damaging' to be an offence (Lustgarten and Leigh).

In addition, s5(1)(a) subsections (i) and (ii) refer to 'a Crown servant or government contractor' whereas s1, s2, s3 and s4 say 'a person who is or has been a Crown servant or government contractor'; the obvious implication from this is that it is not an offence under s5 for a third party, such as a journalist, to make a 'damaging' disclosure of information, obtained from a *former* government servant (although the government servant will have committed an offence). Ewing and Gearty (1990) refer to the omission of 'former' from s5 as a 'drafting "cock-up" ...' (pp. 196, 201). As the omission was brought to the government's attention during the passage of the Bill through Parliament the charitable interpretation is that it was not the 'drafting cock-up' it would appear to be.

These provisions of the Act were referred to in *Lord Advocate* v *Scotsman Publications Ltd* [1990] 1 AC 812, although the Act was not yet in force. Lord Jauncey said: 'Upon the assumption that section 5 was intended to apply to confidential information deriving from past as well as present members of the security services, an assumption which may well be unjustified having regard to the obscurity of the language ...' (p. 830).

The interaction between the 1989 Act and the present DA-Notice system is much the same as with the 1911 Act. The 1989 Act contains more detail than the 1911 Act as to the offending type of disclosure of information, and clearly some of the DA-Notices currently in force cover the same ground. An example of this is s2(4) of the Official Secrets Act 1989 which defines the meaning of 'defence':

> (a) the size, shape, organisations, logistics, order of battle, deployment, operations, state of readiness and training of the armed forces of the Crown;
> (b) the weapons, stores or other equipment of those forces and the invention, development, production and operation of such equipment and research relating to it ...

DA Notice No 1 'Military Operations, Plans and Capabilities, covers, inter alia (www.dnotice.org.uk/dan1.htm):

> (a) details of present or future operations, methods, tactics and contingency planning, to meet particular hostile situations and to counter threats of terrorist attacks;
> (b) details of the state of readiness and operational capability of individual units or formations whose involvement in such operations is current or may be imminent ...

DA Notice No 2 'Nuclear and Non-Nuclear Weapons and Equipment' requests 'that disclosure or publication of highly classified information about nuclear and non-nuclear defence equipment, or equipment used to counter threats of terrorist attacks of the kind listed below should not be made without first seeking advice' (www.dnotice.org.uk/dan2.htm):

> (a) nuclear weapons, highly classified information on:
>> (1)  the detailed designs of nuclear weapons and the technologies for producing them;
>> (2)  operational details;
>> (3)  detailed security arrangements for the storage, transport and development of nuclear weapons and associated fissile materials;
>
> (b) non-nuclear defence and counter-terrorist equipment, highly classified information on:
>> (1) design details, technical specifications, materials;
>> (2) performance figures and operational capabilities;
>> (3) areas of vulnerability to counter-measures.

The DA-Notices are of assistance in filling in the gaps left by the legislation (Fairley, 1990). Clearly any journalist who publishes material subject to a DA-Notice that is the same but more specific than the provisions of the Act leaves him or herself open to prosecution.

It should be noted, however, that the 1989 Act does not entirely blanket the same ground as the DA-Notice system. There are two situations where the DA-Notice system applies when the Act does not. First, as mentioned earlier, s5 of the 1989 Act relates to damaging disclosures made by third parties of information given to them by presently employed Crown servants. The offences under the Act relating to damaging disclosures made by the Crown servants cover them even after they have left their government employment, but the Act does not cover disclosures to third parties by former Crown servants. The DA-Notice system fills the void to some extent by applying to journalists who receive information which is subject to a DA-Notice from a former Crown servant.

Second, s5 of the Act applies to information originally disclosed by Crown servants or government contractors. In the event that the journalist's original source is not a Crown servant or government contractor the DA notice system will apply, for example where the information is obtained through the journalist's own endeavour (Fairley, 1990). Another example of how this might arise would be from a situation similar to one which occurred in 1967. Classified documents from the Department of Defence became scattered while awaiting destruction by pulping. Pages marked 'restricted' were found by members of the public who handed them to the police. The pages might have instead have been handed to the media (H.C. Deb., 17 March 1967).

Until late 1997 there were no prosecutions under the 1989 Act. While no-one had been prosecuted under the 1989 Act, Scott V-C in *A-G v Blake (Jonathan Cape Ltd, third party)* [1996] 3 All ER 903, said George Blake, *in absentia*, had 'committed a breach of statutory duty' under s1(1), relating to disclosure of information by a member of the intelligence services (p. 910). The facts amounting to a breach of statutory duty was the submission to Jonathan Cape for publication in 1989 the manuscript detailing his work with MI6. The action was a civil action, argued on the basis of a breach of fiduciary duty. The Attorney-General did not plead any breach of statutory duty of the Act, because a conviction would not provide the remedy being sought by the Crown, which was 'to extract from the defendant any financial benefit he may obtain from publication of the book' (p. 906). The Crown lost. Blake had been convicted in 1961 for espionage offences under s1(1)(c) of the Official Secrets Act 1911. As earlier noted, he had escaped from Wormwood Scrubs prison, gone to Russia and was still living in Moscow at the time of this case in 1996.

In October 1997 Mr Richard Tomlinson, a former MI6 officer, was arrested and charged under s1 of the Act. 'The man ... is the first to be charged with such an offence since the Act was reformed in 1989 and the first MI6 officer since George Blake to be arrested on a secrets charge' (*The Times*, 3 November 1997, p. 1). Tomlinson had offered a publisher in Sydney a synopsis for a book about his work with the Secret Intelligence Service (*The Times*, 4 November 1997).

In the Bow Street Magistrates' Court in London on 24 November 1997 Tomlinson pleaded guilty to the charge of unlawful disclosure of information under s1 of the 1989 Act.

> After the hearing, John Wadham, Tomlinson's solicitor, issued a statement on his behalf which said: 'I wanted to plead not guilty to expose this hypocrisy, but the draconian nature of the Official Secrets Act makes this impossible. There is no public interest defence. I would have been guilty even if I had disclosed the colour of the carpets in the office' (*The Times*, 25 November 1997, internet version).

Tomlinson was sentenced to one year of imprisonment, and was released on probation after six months. Afraid of being re-arrested by the authorities in the U.K. he went to Paris, and was arrested, allegedly at gunpoint, by the French police who later released him without charge. He then went to New Zealand where he was served with an injunction 'sought by Britain - and sanctioned by the New Zealand government - preventing him from revealing details about MI6' (*Time*, 17 August 1998, internet version). It was reported in *The Times* on 12 December 1998 that Tomlinson, by then living in Switzerland, was the subject of new enquiries relating to a possible further breach of the Official Secrets Act. In May 1999 Tomlinson published on the Internet over one hundred names of alleged MI6 operatives, and while the government prevailed upon various Internet service providers to remove the information, mirror sites immediately appeared elsewhere (*The Times*, 14 May 1999).[16]

In August 1998 Mr David Shayler, a former MI5 officer, was arrested in Paris at the request of Scotland Yard. The British government wanted his extradition to face charges under s1 of the Official Secrets Act for divulging information about the operations of MI5 (*The Sunday Times*, 2 August 1998). In November 1998 a French court rejected the extradition attempt. The decision, which 'stunned' Whitehall, was made on the grounds the Shayler's arrest had political overtones (*The Guardian*, 19 November 1998, p. 1). The report in *The Guardian* mentions government gagging orders preventing the U.K. media from publishing details of Shayler's allegations, as does *The Sunday Times* report of 2 August 1998 and the *Time* report of 17 August 1998.

In August 2000 Shayler returned to Britain and was arrested as he left the ferry at Dover. He was taken to Charing Cross police station in London, charged with two offences under the OSA 1989 and released on bail.

> He has denied breaking the law and will rely on the new Human Rights Act in his defence. The legislation to be introduced later this year, allows for the disclosure of confidential information if it is deemed to be in the public interest (*The Daily Telegraph*, 22 August 2000, p. 6).

The author of this book asked Rear Admiral Pulvertaft, secretary of the DPBAC in 1997, if he had approached, or been approached by, Tomlinson regarding clearance for Tomlinson's book. The same question was asked regarding Shayler's publication. Rear Admiral Pulvertaft responded that while the DA-Notice system is open in principle, his work in actually applying the notices was conducted in strict confidence so he could not comment on 'involvement or non-involvement with the Shayler or Tomlinson cases'. In the book containing Shayler's revelations, published in 1999, the authors say they 'reluctantly' submitted the manuscript to the committee, which requested some minor changes (Hollingsworth and Fielding, 1999, p. ix).

In May 1999 Mr Tony Geraghty, a journalist and author of *The Irish War*, was charged with offences under s5 of the OSA 1989. Section 5 relates to 'Information resulting from unauthorised disclosures or entrusted in confidence' (margin note), in other words, secondary disclosures. The charges resulted from information in the book, which was published in 1998 and was never banned, about security and· intelligence operations and computerised surveillance systems used in Northern Ireland by British security forces (*The Times*, 14 May 1999).

A final salient point on the Official Secrets legislation, and one that is not often featured in discussion on these Acts, is that of the secrecy that surrounds the legal proceedings (Williams, 1965). Section 11(4) of the 1989 Act, repeating the provisions of s8 of the 1920 Act, permits the exclusion of the public from a hearing, except during the passing of sentence, on the grounds of national safety. Section 4(2) of the Contempt of Court Act 1981 gives further powers to the court to prevent publicity:

> In any such proceedings the court may, where it appears to be necessary for avoiding a substantial risk of prejudice to the administration of justice in those proceedings, or in any other proceedings pending or imminent, order that the publication of any report of the proceedings, or any part of the proceedings, be postponed for such period as the court thinks necessary for that purpose.

This is how the information which was the subject matter of the Ponting trial was suppressed.

Once the government becomes alert to the possibility that there is to be a disclosure of sensitive information which would fall within the ambit of the Official Secrets Act, the ideal situation would be to find some way to prevent the disclosure from occurring at all, or at least until it was no longer so damaging. The best way to achieve this would be by obtaining an injunction to prevent it from being published. The courts are, however, reluctant to grant an injunction to restrain a breach of the criminal law, an issue which is discussed more fully later.

From the mid 1980s the government resorted less to the Official Secrets Act and turned instead to the civil action for breach of confidence in order to obtain an injunction to prevent in advance the publication of the information. By the mid 1990s the media saw the Official Secrets Act as 'peripheral; of much greater concern was the possibility of civil injunctions, contempt of court, and "Special Branch rampaging through the office looking for [unrelated] national security material" ' (Lustgarten and Leigh, 1994, p. 263).

In 1997 the election of 'new' Labour in the U.K. brought with it the hope that the government would now be more open. Vincent (1998) says in his 'afterword' written in May 1997: 'It is possible that as in the time of the previous Labour Government, the Official Secrets Act will be abolished by neglect ...' (p. 325). Knightley reviewed Vincent's book in *The Sunday Times* on 1 November 1998 under the heading 'Why we are kept in the dark'. He (Knightley) remarks that following the arrest and imprisonment of Shayler and Tomlinson at the behest of the new Labour government ' ... it is too early to celebrate - Britain's traditional culture of secrecy has not yet been laid to rest' (p. 3).

It is indeed ironic that the first arrests under the Official Secrets Act 1989 should occur under a Labour government which at the same time was issuing white papers such as *Rights Brought Home: The Human Rights Bill* (October 1997) Cm 3782 and *Your Right to Know: Freedom of Information* (December 1997) Cm 3818. These white papers resulted in the Human Rights Act 1998, which incorporated the European Convention of Human Rights into domestic law in Scotland in July 1999 and England in October 2000, and the Freedom of Information Bill which was still working its way through Parliament during 2000.

In 1998 the Public Interest Disclosure Act was passed, which came into effect on 1 January 1999. This Act added a new Part (Part IVA) to the Employment Rights Act 1996 and protects certain disclosures made by workers, for example disclosure relating to criminal offences. Section 193 of the amended Employment Rights Act exempts from these new provisions notified Crown servants, the Security Service (MI5), the Secret Intelligence Service (MI6) and Government Communications Headquarters (GCHQ) (s11(3)). Section 43B(3) of the amended Employment Rights Act says: 'A disclosure of information is not a qualifying disclosure if the person making the disclosure commits an offence by making it'. Presumably this would include an offence against the Official Secrets Act 1989.

## The use of criminal law in Australia - the *Crimes Act 1914* (Cth)

The relevant provisions in Australian legislation are those contained within the *Crimes Act 1914* (Cth), specifically s70 in Part VI - *Offences by and against Public Officers* and s79 in Part VII - *Espionage and Official Secrets*. Section 70 relates to 'Disclosure of information by Commonwealth officers' and s79 relates to 'Official Secrets' with subsections (1), (3) and (6) being the most relevant to communications by the media.

The Official Secrets Act 1911 (U.K.) provided the model for the official secrecy provisions in the *Crimes Act 1914* (Cth), that is those in Part VII (H. of R. Deb., 21 October 1914); Lee, Hanks and Morabito, 1995). Section 78 of the *Crimes Act* relates to 'Espionage and similar activities', s79(1) and s79(3) relate to disclosures by Commonwealth officers, and the combination is the equivalent of s2(1) of the Official Secrets Act 1911. The provisions in s2 of the Official Secrets Act 1911 caught a wider range of disclosure, however, than the equivalent provisions in the *Crimes Act* because the latter are limited to the disclosure of information which it is the officer's 'duty to treat ... as secret' (s79(1)).

As already noted, s2 of the Official Secrets Act 1911 was replaced by the provisions of the Official Secrets Act 1989. The new provisions do not contain the defence of disclosure in the public interest, but this remains in the Australian legislation (Lee, Hanks and Morabito, 1995; Finn, undated). Section 70 has no historic link with the Official Secrets Act, coming instead from s86 of the Queensland *Criminal Code* (1889) (H. of R. Deb., 21 October 1914; McGinness, 1990).

Section 79(3) effectively duplicates s70, although in 1983 the then Attorney-General Senator Gareth Evans was of the opinion that the scope of s79(3) was wider than that of s70:

> Professor Sawer has argued in a recent newspaper article (*Canberra Times*, 10 August 1983) that the duty referred to in s.70 must mean a legal duty, i.e. one clearly imposed by some other statutory provision or rule of common law. He suggests that criminal courts would be very reluctant to construe an offence punishable by two years in gaol as extending to situations where the duty is merely a 'moral obligation arising from convention, reasonable expectation and honourable relations between colleagues'. This argument seems to me compelling in relation to s.70, where the direction to the courts to determine whether or not a duty exists is stark and unadorned. But it is rather less so in relation to s.79, to which Professor Sawer does not refer in the article cited.
> The difficulty is that in the latter section the courts are specifically directed to take account of, inter alia, 'the nature of the information' or 'the circumstances under which it was obtained'. It may be possible to read down s.79 and confine it to situations where there is some explicit pre-existing legal duty on the person in question, whether derived from particular statutory prohibitions, public service regulations, employment relationships, express or implied contractual obligations, fiduciary duties or something of that kind (as Professor Sawer has elsewhere suggested). But while the section so read down would still have some scope for operation, such a reading would give little or no effect to the statutory language requiring the court to look at the

circumstances of the particular case (Senate Deb., vol. 101, col. 3615, 9 December 1983).

The *Review of Commonwealth Criminal Law: Final Report* (1991) (also known as the Gibbs Committee report) supports this approach to the interpretation of the two sections. McGinness (1990), however, says it is doubtful whether the sections were intended to have any different effect. Finn (undated) would appear to be of the same view, pointing out that, 'so long as s.70 remains on the statute-books in its current form it renders criminal, [*sic*] conduct that may be exempted by s.79(3) - assuming the second exemption in s.79(3) allows some form of whistleblowing' (p. 243). Section 79(3)(b) exempts communication to 'a person to whom it is, in the interest of the Commonwealth ... his duty to communicate it' and so provides for a public interest defence. Section 79(6) of the *Crimes Act* is the equivalent of s2(2) of the Official Secrets Act 1911. It relates to information 'received' and thus applies to the media, the only defence being that 'he proves that the communication was contrary to his desire'.

Prosecutions under Part VII may only be instituted 'by or with the consent of the Attorney-General or of a person acting under his direction' (s85). The provision relates only to 'a prosecution under this Part ...', that is Part VII. There is no equivalent provision in Part VI. Putting the onus on the Attorney-General to initiate prosecutions provides some protection, and may explain why it has happened so infrequently (Lee, Hanks and Morabito, 1995).

No prosecution has been instituted against a Minister or ex-Minister under the official secrets provisions of the *Crimes Act* (Senate Deb., 9 December 1983). With respect to public servants, Campbell and Whitmore (1975) say that, '[f]or the most part offenders are dealt with quietly by the disciplinary process. It is impossible to guess at the frequency of disclosures to the press and other organizations; undoubtedly cases do occur but it appears that the legislation operates *in terrorem* fairly effectively' (p. 348).

Aitken (1971) tells of one case, which is unreported:

Official Secrets cases in Australia are extremely rare, the only recent example being a 1969 prosecution which resulted in a humiliating rebuff for the Crown. In this case a government official, Pratt, was accused of communicating information about the Government's trade and tariff policies to a well-known Canberra journalist, Mr Max Newton. The Canberra magistrate ruled at first instance that there was no case to answer, thereby implicitly upholding the view that Australia's laws of Official Secrecy apply exclusively to breaches of security even where civil servants are concerned (p. 216).

It would appear from the above that the journalist, Newton, was not charged with receiving the information. Campbell and Whitmore also comment on this case; *R* v *Pratt* (unreported 16 July 1969). They say Pratt was charged under s70. In *Johnston* v *Director of Public Prosecutions* (1989) 97 FLR 424, Miles CJ in the Supreme Court of the A.C.T. dismissed an appeal by a member of the Australian Federal Police against his conviction by a magistrate of charges under 70(1) of the *Crimes Act*.

One s79(3) case was *Grant* v *Headland* (1977) 17 ACTR 29, which illustrates the way in which the section covers careless disclosures as well as deliberate disclosures (s70 is the same in this respect). The appellant, James Grant, was a 19 year old probationary trainee with ASIO. In order to 'improve his competence as an employee and trainee' he made 'an overture to a foreign agency purporting to offer intelligence secrets' (p. 30). Smithers J, in the Supreme Court of the A.C.T., dismissing an appeal against conviction, found that the existence of the duty to treat information as secret is not dependent upon the person realising that the duty has arisen. The duty may arise by inference from the surrounding circumstances. In an illustration of the difficulty of balancing open justice with the interests of national security the appeal was heard in camera, but the decision was delivered in open court with the relevant information omitted.

In *Commonwealth* v *John Fairfax & Sons Ltd* (1980) 147 CLR 39, the Commonwealth Attorney-General in interlocutory proceedings attempted to obtain an injunction to restrain the publication of confidential government information. One of the grounds was to prevent a breach of s79 of the *Crimes Act*, and the application, although ultimately successful, did not succeed on this point.

*Australian Broadcasting Corporation* v *Cloran* (1984) 57 ALR 742 involved an application by the ABC and journalist Mr Chris Masters for the quashing of search warrants, issued under s10 of the *Crimes Act*, authorising the search of ABC premises and the home of Chris Masters. Lockhart J in the General Division of the Federal Court ordered that the search warrants be quashed because they did not specify the particular alleged offences complained of under s70 of the *Crimes Act*. According to His Honour s70 is a section providing 'a somewhat indeterminate number of offences' and the 'possible combinations of people who communicate information and of those to whom information is imparted are manifold' (p. 745).

Two other sections of the *Crimes Act* that may be used against the media are s5 and s7A. In 1997 an adviser on defence matters to the 1995 Labor government told the author of this book that section 5 would enable the government to construct a case against journalists who would technically offend simply by publishing the material. Section 5 (*Aiders and abettors*) provides that:

> [A]ny person who aids, abets, counsels, or procures, or by act or omission is in any way directly or indirectly knowingly concerned, or party to, the commission of any offence against any law of the Commonwealth ... shall be deemed to have committed that offence and shall be punishable accordingly.

The person aiding and abetting is charged under the substantive section (*Sherlock* v *Jacobsen* (1983) 13 ATR 935).

Section 7A (*Inciting to or urging the commission of offences*) makes it an offence to (a) incite to, urge, aid or encourage, or (b) print, or publish any writing which incites to, urges, aids or encourages the commission of offences against the law of the Commonwealth. *Walsh* v *Sainsbury* (1925) 36 CLR 464 and *Sullivan* v *Hamel-Green* [1970] VR 156 were two cases relating to offences under s7A, but both concerned incitement to the commission of offences contained in Acts other than the *Crimes Act*. The latter case did, however, involve 'publishing' in that the defendant distributed (which was found to be 'publishing') a pamphlet entitled 'Why Register for National Service?' which incited the commission of offences against the *National Service Act 1951-1968* (Cth). The penalty is imprisonment for twelve months.

If the public servant communicating the material is charged under s70, which provides no defence, rather than s79(3) which allows a public interest defence, the journalist who receives the material can be charged under s5 or s7A. If s5 were used the journalist would receive the same penalty as the public servant convicted under s70, imprisonment for two years, whereas s7A provides imprisonment for 12 months. By using s70 and either s5 or s7A there would probably be more likelihood of conviction of both parties.

Section 3A of the *Crimes Act* may also be relevant. Section 3A makes the Act applicable both in the Commonwealth and the Territories, 'and also applies beyond the Commonwealth and the Territories'. It would therefore bring within the ambit of the offences contained in s70 and s79 a person publishing outside Australia information which would render him or her liable to prosecution if he or she had published it in Australia (Gibbs Committee Report, 1991).

McGinness (1990) commented on the insidious nature of the secrecy provisions in the *Crimes Act*:

More generally secrecy provisions may conflict with the pursuit of open government by unnecessarily attaching criminal penalties to all unauthorised disclosures ... The fact that unauthorised disclosure of non-sensitive information is subject to criminal penalties is a powerful force in shaping official attitudes to the secrecy of government information generally. As Williams[17] observes, official secrets legislation serves to 'encourage timidity in the handling of official information which in the end deprives an administration of the scrutiny and criticism necessary for efficiency and responsibility' (p. 74).

## *The Review of the Commonwealth Criminal Law (Gibbs Committee Report)*

The final report of the Committee (commonly known as the Gibbs Committee), set up to review various aspects of the Commonwealth criminal law under the chairmanship of Sir Harry Gibbs, was published in December 1991. The Gibbs Committee Report criticised the sections of the *Crimes Act* relating to official secrets, on the basis that the provisions therein were catch-all provisions, wrong in principle and seriously defective in terms of law enforcement. In addition there was no distinction made between information which would cause real harm to the public interest if disclosed, and information which would cause no such harm if disclosed.

Three principles were taken into account when the Gibbs Committee reached its conclusions:

- it is unacceptable in our democratic society that there should be a restraint on the publication of information relating to Government when the only vice of that information is that it enables the public to discuss, review and criticise Government action;
- it is undesirable that the sanctions and machinery of the criminal law should be applied in relation to the unauthorised disclosure of all forms of official information and this should be avoided if possible; and
- there are some descriptions of official information that should be protected by the criminal law from unauthorised disclosure (para. 31.1).

The Gibbs Committee Report recommended that s70 and s79(3) be repealed and replaced 'with provisions under which the application of penal sanctions to unauthorised disclosure of official information is limited ... to specific categories of information no more widely stated than is required for the effective functioning of Government' (para. 35.1(a)). The 'specific categories' were listed as 'information relating to intelligence and security services, defence or foreign relations ... information obtained in confidence from other governments or international organisations' (para. 31.6, 35.1(b)).

The Gibbs Committee Report recommended that proof of harm should be a requirement in offences covering the disclosure of information relating to defence, foreign affairs and information from foreign States or international organisations. No proof of harm would be required in relation to disclosures concerning security or intelligence by members or former members of the intelligence and security services. By implication, because they are not mentioned as being exceptions in this regard, proof of harm would be required in relation to disclosure of information in the other categories by members or former members of the intelligence and security services.

In the draft *Crimes Amendment (No. 2) Bill* drawn up by the Gibbs Committee, Section 85DB(1) *Disclosure of security or intelligence information*, which refers to disclosures by members and former members of the security and intelligence organisations, makes mention only of 'any information relating to security or intelligence'. Present and former government officers or government contractors are covered by s85DB(2) which relates to 'damaging disclosure of any information relating to security or intelligence'. This gives rise to the assumption that relevant disclosures made by any party other than a member or former member of the intelligence and security services would require proof of damage to fall within the section.

Secondary disclosures, such as those published by the media, would be covered by provisions similar to s5 of the Official Secrets Act 1989 (U.K.), but the offence would apply only to a person 'who knows, or has reasonable ground to believe' that the information had been disclosed in certain proscribed circumstances (para. 31.42). The Gibbs Committee Report recommended prior publication as a defence to most of the offences - the defence would not be available to a member of the intelligence or security services. The Report declined to include a defence of public interest or iniquity, instead suggesting provision of a 'Special Counsel' to whom whistleblowers could make complaints (para. 32.2, 32.4).

The Gibbs Committee Report based its recommendations on the Official Secrets Act 1989 (U.K.), with the modification of the defence of prior publication and protection, in certain circumstances, for whistleblowers. The reliance on the U.K. Act is a source of criticism as the flaws in the U.K. model were already well documented before the Committee finished its report (Lee, Hanks and Morabito, 1995).

According to Carne (1993) there are two main reasons why the Gibbs Committee recommended a modified approach to official secrets law in Australia. One was the lack of successful prosecutions in the past, and the other was the reluctance of the High Court, that is Mason J in *Commonwealth* v *John Fairfax* (1980) 147 CLR 39, to grant an injunction to restrain a breach of s79 of the *Crimes Act*. He criticises the 'requirement of harm' provisions, saying they would concentrate the jury's attention on the *effect* of the conduct rather than the motive, and that the prosecution need only show that the damage is *likely* to result. Carne reserves his most trenchant criticism for the omission of a public interest defence saying:

> [T]he report implicitly assumes that the interests of the State are best served by public servants and others subordinating their opinions to that of the elected government in every circumstance ... Certain exculpatory statements ... suggest that the Committee believes that it is not in the public interest for the public to learn of anything in the nominated categories other than what the government thinks fit. This would be the case however outrageous or illegal those activities might be (p. 23) [*footnote omitted*].

While approving of the idea of categorising the different types of information to be protected, Zifcak (1989) makes criticisms that are similar to those of Carne. He thinks that the test of harm should be more stringent, and in each category it should be 'substantial' harm. Furthermore it should be the courts who determine the question of harm, rather than Ministers, or any special and independent tribunal set up for the purpose. Like Carne, Zifcak is of the view that there should be a public interest defence, although this would not be unqualified. For example the defence would not be available to a public servant unless redress had first been sought within the service. In addition the disclosure should relate to serious administrative misconduct which should outweigh statutory obligations of confidence, and the discloser must not be acting on unsubstantiated suspicion.

By late 2000 the recommendations of the Gibbs Committee had not been implemented, and there appeared to be no immediate likelihood of this occurring. In 1995 the Commission of Inquiry into the Australian Secret Intelligence Service, chaired by Samuels J, published its report (the Samuels Report). The Samuels Report recommended the re-establishment of the D-Notice system and suggested a 'defence of public interest' should be available for offences under s70 or s79 of the *Crimes Act*. The report made comment on the secondary disclosure recommendations of the Gibbs Committee:

> Although the existing s.5(1) potentially applies to journalists, the proposed new secondary disclosure offence is both an extension and a refinement of the present law. In particular, it would apply to a journalist who had no involvement in the primary disclosure. If enacted it would be seen by the media - with some justification in our view - as effectively replacing the

voluntary D Notice system with a system based on criminal sanctions. Media witnesses made clear their opposition to such a course. If this offence were created it would, in all likelihood, destroy the voluntary system. Accordingly, we recommend that the Government not proceed with the proposed offence of secondary disclosures at least until it has been established beyond reasonable doubt that the D Notice system is incapable of being made effective (para. 13.51) [*footnote omitted*].

The official government response to the Samuels Report was a Ministerial Statement made by Senator Gareth Evans Q.C., then Minister for Foreign Affairs (Senate Deb., 1 June 1995). Some of the recommendations were rejected, in particular the recommendations as to the inclusion in the *Crimes Act* of a defence of 'public interest' and the deferment of the introduction of the offence of secondary disclosure. The government also intended to revitalise the D-Notice system. This was described to the author by a journalist in 1997 as the 'carrot and stick' approach; if the 'carrot' (the D-Notice system) doesn't work, the government will resort to the 'stick' (the proposed amendment to the *Crimes Act* to include $1 million fines for secondary disclosures).

Although few journalists have been prosecuted for s70 and s79 *Crimes Act* offences, new offences relating to secondary disclosure would add to the existing threat and reinforce the deterrent effect. The introduction of secondary disclosure offences would not be in the public interest as the provisions may have a significant chilling effect on the media. In June 1995 Senator MacGibbon raised the issue of the amendments to the *Crimes Act* with Senator Evans, asking: 'How can you travel the world, Minister, and trumpet the values of a free press, when at home you are proposing to gaol journalists who might publicly report unethical or illegal conduct of the government? Is this the case of a double standard?' (Senate Deb., 7 June 1995). The resulting debate descended into an unedifying display of petulance from both sides of the Senate, but Senator Evans had the last word: 'I hope it will be possible to inculcate some kind of sense of responsibility among those who flap their gums on these issues but do not act in a way that is helpful and responsible when we are looking at larger issues of national interest ...'.

The change of government from Labor to Liberal in early 1996 saw the end to any immediate prospect of change to either the D-Notice system or the *Crimes Act*.

## Attempts

One final point with respect to the disclosure of sensitive government information which may be a breach of official secrets legislation. It is tempting to wonder whether the activity on the part of a media defendant in preparing to publish the material would amount to an 'attempt'. In *R* v *Olsson* (1915) 31 TLR 559 the Court of Criminal Appeal in the U.K. dismissed the defendant's appeal against his conviction for attempting 'for a purpose prejudicial to the safety or interests of the State, to obtain information calculated to be useful to an enemy' contrary to s1(1) and s4 of the Official Secrets Act 1911. Section 7 of the Official Secrets Act 1920 makes it an offence to attempt to commit any offence in the Act and the section applies to the 1989 Act. Section 7 of the *Crimes Act 1914* (Cth) makes it an offence to attempt 'to commit any offence against any law of the Commonwealth', which would therefore include s70 and s79. There appears to have been no prosecutions for attempt under either the Official Secrets Act 1989 or with respect to sections 70 and 79 of the *Crimes Act 1914* (Cth).

## Use of the criminal law - summary

Although the criminal law has seldom been used against the media in the context of the publication of sensitive government information, it nonetheless remains a potent alternative to the D-Notice system. The disadvantage for the government is that, for the most part, the use of the criminal law follows publication, meaning the information is no longer secret, but the threat of prosecution may be sufficient to prevent some disclosures. The cases examined in this chapter illustrate the crucially important role of the judiciary in balancing the various competing interests, but in particular the interests of the general public in having all information available except for the information that genuinely threatens national security. Where the law allows for no discretion on the part of judges, for example where provisions in official secrets legislation are so tightly worded as to result in strict liability offences, the government interest in suppression is greatly favoured.

## Notes

[1]    For a full and thorough analysis of the Official Secrets Act 1911, and in particular the workings of s2, see Hooper (1987).

[2]    The consent of the Attorney-General is required for prosecutions under the current

Official Secrets Act 1989: s9.

3   Amended by 10 & 11 Geo. 5, Ch. 75.

4   The case appears to be unreported as a search of primary sources failed to locate it.

5   Hooper (1987) and Aitken (1971) both say the case took place in 1958, Robertson (1998) says 1956.

6   For further references to this obsessive secrecy see, for example, Heath (1989) who says: 'We are the most secretive western democracy in the world' (p. 11). Edward Heath was the Conservative Prime Minister from 1970-74. See also Palmer (1984); Chapman (1963); Robertson (1998); and for an entire book on the subject, Vincent (1998, but especially pp. 9-18).

7   The trial is covered in detail in Aitken (1971).

8   See, for example, Fairley (1990). The question will be examined more fully in Chapter 8.

9   Aitken cites the *New Statesman*, 11 February 1971. The comments by Richard Crossman are somewhat ironic as it was his book, *Diaries of a Cabinet Minister*, that was the subject of the breach of confidence action in *A-G v Jonathan Cape Ltd* [1976] 1 QB 752.

10  Like Cmnd 3309, mentioned previously in Chapter 4, Cmnd 5104 is another Report that is not held in Western Australia and is unavailable for loan from any library in Australia. A copy of Cmnd 5104 was found in the Senate Library of London University (but not available on loan) during a research trip to the U.K. in 1997.

11  Thomas's 1986 article is substantially reproduced in Chapman and Hunt (1987) as Ch. 7; references are to the 1986 article.

12  For a full analysis of the Franks Report see Ewing and Gearty (1990).

13  On the issue of 'mosaic' or 'jigsaw' constructions of information, and in the context of national security in the United States of America, Dulles (1963) recounts how in 1951 the then Director of the CIA, Bedell Smith, gave a group of academics a list of unclassified and easily available documents. He asked the academics to put together from these documents 'an estimate of U.S. military capabilities'. After a few weeks work they produced an analysis that was so accurate 'that extra copies were ordered destroyed and the few copies that were retained were given a high classification' (p. 240).

14  Aubrey (1981) attributes the 'armalite rifle to replace a blunderbuss' comment to the then Home Secretary, Labour politician Merlyn Rees.
One of the mildest assessments of the 1989 Act comes from Justice E. Thomas, then a Judge of the High Court of New Zealand, now a member of the New Zealand Court of Appeal, who makes his comments from an antipodean distance; Thomas (1995).

15  The Official Secrets Act 1989 is 'an Act to replace section 2 of the Official Secrets Act 1911' (preamble). The 1989 Act starts with s1 which is confusing because this is in reality the old s2 of the complete Official Secrets Act 1911 to 1989. Section 1 (Penalties for spying) of the 1911 Act remains in place, so is not to be mistaken for s1 of the 1989 Act.

16  Some of the information can be found on the following rather dubious web site: http://www.1underground.com/Features/features253tomlinson.shtml
The website also includes an affidavit, allegedly deposed by Tomlinson, claiming that Henri Paul, driver of the car in which Princess Diana was killed, was an MI6 informant: http://www.1underground.com/Features/mi6-diana.shtml

17  The following footnote appears in McGinness' text: '*Supra* n 1, 208'.

Note: footnote 1 of McGinness' article refers to Williams (1968) whereas in fact the quote comes from Williams (1965) p. 208.

# References

10 & 11 Geo. 5, Ch. 75.

*ABC* v *Cloran* (1984) 57 ALR 742, p. 745.

*A-G* v *Blake (Jonathan Cape Ltd, third party)* [1996] 3 All ER 903, pp. 906, 910.

*A-G* v *Jonathan Cape Ltd* [1976] 1 QB 752.

Aitken, J. (1971), *Officially Secret*, London, pp. 156, 171, 197-198, 216, 218.

Aubrey, C. (1981), *Who's Watching You?*, London.

Campbell, E. (1967), 'Public Access to Government Documents', *The Australian Law Journal*, vol. 41, p. 73.

Campbell, E., and Whitmore, H. (1975), *Freedom in Australia*, Sydney, p. 348.

Carne, G. (1993), 'Official Secrets and the Gibbs Report: A Charter for Reform or a Tug of the Legal Forelock?', *University of Tasmania Law Review*, vol. 12(1), p. 23.

Chapman, B. (1963), *British Government Observed*, London.

Chapman, R., and Hunt, M. (eds) (1987), *Open Government*, Beckenham.

Cm 3782 (1997), *Rights Brought Home: The Human Rights Bill*.

Cm 3818 (1997), *Your Right to Know: Freedom of Information*.

Cmnd 5104(.1972), *Departmental Committee on s.2 of the Official Secrets Act 1911*, para. 1-2, 16, 20, 65.

*Commonwealth* v *John Fairfax & Sons Ltd* (1980) 147 CLR 39.

Contempt of Court Act 1981 (U.K.), s4.

*Crimes Act 1914* (Cth), s5, s7A, s70, s79, s85.

Dulles, A. (1963), *The Craft of Intelligence*, New York, p. 240.

Eisenschitz, T. (1985), 'Secrecy and Free Flow of Information in the UK', *European Intellectual Property Review*, vol. 9, p. 254.

Employment Rights Act 1996 (U.K.), s11, s43B.

Ewing, K. and Gearty, C. (1990), *Freedom under Thatcher*, Oxford, pp. 196, 201.

Fairley, D. (1990), 'D Notices, Official Secrets and the Law', *Oxford Journal of Legal Studies*, vol.10, p. 430.

Finn, P. (undated), *Integrity in Government - Interim Report 1*, Canberra, p. 243.

Freedom of Information Bill (U.K.).

Gibbs Committee (1991), *Review of Commonwealth Criminal Law: Final Report*, Canberra, para. 31.1, 31.6, 31.42, 32.2, 32.4, 35.1(a), 35.1(b).

*Grant* v *Headland* (1977) 17 ACTR 29, pp. 30.

H. of R. Deb. col. 265 and 269, 21 October 1914 (Second Reading).

H.C. Deb., vol. 743, col. 160-161 (Written Answers to Questions), 17 March 1967.

HC773 ((1980), *Third Report from the Defence Committee (Session 1979-80) The D Notice System*, August, Minutes of Evidence taken before the Committee, Mr Chapman Pincher, para. 446; Minutes of Evidence, 8 July 1980, p. 43 para. 4.

Heath, E. (1989), 'A State of Secrecy', *New Statesman & Society*, vol. 10 March, pp. 10, 11.

Hocking, B. (1993), 'What Lies in the Public Interest? A Legal History of Official Secrets in Britain', *Queensland University of Technology Law Journal*, vol. 9, p. 31.

Hollingsworth, M. and Fielding, N. (1999), *Defending the Realm – MI5 and the Shayler Affair*, London, p. ix.

Hooper, D. (1987), *Official Secrets*, London, pp. 8, 10, 117.

http://www.1underground.com/Features/features253tomlinson.shtml

http://www.1underground.com/Features/mi6-diana.shtml

Human Rights Act 1998 (U.K.).

*Johnston* v *Director of Public Prosecutions* (1989) 97 FLR 424.

Joint Working Party of JUSTICE and the British Committee of the International Press Institute, *The Law and the Press* (1965) London, para. 67.

Lee, H., Hanks, P., Morabito, V. (1995), *In the Name of National Security: The Legal Dimensions*, Sydney, pp. 153, 155, 162.

*Lord Advocate* v *Scotsman Publications Ltd* [1990] 1 AC 812, p. 830.

Lovelace, C. (1978), 'British press censorship during the First World War', in G. Boyce, J. Curran and P. Wingate (eds), *Newspaper History from the 17th Century to the Present Day*, London.

Lustgarten, L. and Leigh, I. (1994), *In From the Cold: National Security and Parliamentary Democracy*, London, pp. 236, 263.

Maher, L. (1995), 'ASIS "D" Notice Controversy', *Media Law Reporter*, vol. 2, p. 141.

McGinness, J. (1990), 'Secrecy Provisions in Commonwealth Legislation', *Federal Law Review*, vol. 19, p. 74.

*New Statesman*, 11 February 1971.

Nicol, A. (1979), 'Official Secrets and Jury Vetting', *Crim.L.R.*, p. 284.

O'Higgins, P. (1972), *Censorship in Britain*, London.

Official Secrets Act 1911 (U.K.), s1, s2.

Official Secrets Act 1989 (U.K.), preamble, s1, s2, s3, s4, s5, s6, s11.

Palmer, A. (1984), 'The History of the D-Notice Committee', in C. Andrew and D. Dilks (eds), *The Missing Dimension: Government and Intelligence Communities in the Twentieth Century*, London, pp. 235, 240, 242.

Palmer, S. (1990), 'Tightening Secrecy Law: The Official Secrets Act 1989', *Public Law*, p. 243.

Pincher, C. (1968), 'Press Freedom and National Security', *Journalism Today*, vol. Spring, pp. 30, 39.

PRO DEFE 53/1.

Public Interest Disclosure Act 1998 (U.K.).

*R* v *Aubrey, Berry and Campbell* (1978) unreported.

*R* v *Cairns, Aitken and Roberts* (1971) unreported.

*R* v *Crisp and Homewood* (1919) 83 JP 121, pp. 122-123.

*R* v *Olsson* (1915) 31 TLR 559.

*R* v *Ponting* [1985] Crim.L.R. 318, p. 319.

*R* v *Pratt* (unreported 16 July 1969).

*R* v *Secretary of State for the Home Department, ex parte Hosenball* [1977] 3 All ER 452.

Robertson, G. (1989), *Freedom, the Individual and the Law*, London, pp. 132, 141.

Robertson, G. (1998), *The Justice Game*, London, p. 106.

Senate Deb., No. 8. col. 716-726, 1 June 1995.

Senate Deb., No. 9, col. 987-988, 7 June 1995.

Senate Deb., vol. 101, col. 3615-3616, 9 December 1983.

*Sherlock* v *Jacobsen* (1983) 13 ATR 935, p. 936.

*Sullivan* v *Hamel-Green* [1970] VR 156.

Supperstone, M. (1981), *Brownlie's Law of Public Order and National Security*, London.

The Commission of Inquiry into the Australian Secret Intelligence Service (1995), *Report on the Australian Secret Intelligence Service*, Canberra, para. 13.51.

*The Daily Telegraph*, 22 August 2000, p. 6.

*The Guardian*, 19 November 1998, p. 1.

*The Sunday Times*, 2 August 1998.

*The Sunday Times*, 1 November 1998, p. 3.

*The Times*, 4 February 1971, pp. 2, 15.

*The Times*, 3 November 1997, p.1.

*The Times*, 4 November 1997.

*The Times*, 25 November 1997.

*The Times*, 12 December 1998.

*The Times*, 14 May 1999.

Thomas, Justice E. (1995), 'Secrecy and Open Government', in P. Finn (ed), *Essays on Law and Government, Volume 1, Principles and Values*, Sydney.

Thomas, R. (1986), 'The British Official Secrets Acts 1911-1939 and the Ponting Case', *Crim.L.R.*, p. 497.

*Time*, 17 August 1998.

Vincent, D. (1998), *The Culture of Secrecy - Britain, 1832-1998*, Oxford, pp. 9-18, 325.

*Walsh* v *Sainsbury* (1925) 36 CLR 464.

Williams, D. (1965), *Not in the Public Interest: the Problem of Security in Democracy*, London, p. 38, 87, 208.

Williams, D. (1968), 'Official Secrecy in England', *Federal Law Review*, p. 20.

www.dnotice.org.uk/index.htm

Zifcak, S. (1989), 'What Sir Harry Gibbs should decide: the disclosure of official information in Australia (Part 1)', *Freedom of Information Review*, vol. August, p. 38.

Zifcak, S. (1989), 'Secrecy, disclosure and the public interest: the disclosure of official information in Australia (Part 2)', *Freedom of Information Review*, vol. October, p. 50.

# 7 Injunctions to Restrain a Breach of the Criminal Law - U.K. and Australia

From the government point of view the most desirable outcome would be to prevent sensitive information from being published at all, and injunctive relief, as a legally enforceable remedy, would be the best way in which to achieve this end. It goes without saying that the extra-legal D-Notice system would also serve to suppress the information but, because the system is voluntary and the government cannot enforce any decisions not to publish, it is not as reliable as an injunction. The question arises as to why the two governments have not sought to restrain by injunction breaches of the respective official secrets legislation in their countries. The answer is that injunctions, a *civil* remedy, are not readily granted by the courts to restrain criminal acts (Aronson and Dyer, 1996; Author not identified, undated; Attorney-General's Department, 1994; The Law Reform Commission (Australia), 1985).

There is, nonetheless, a long line of cases where injunctions have been granted to restrain a breach of the criminal law. The procedure usually relates to a statutory offence, although it was first used in cases of public nuisance. For example in the case of *The Mayor and Commonalty and Citizens of the City of London* v *Bolt* (1799) 5 Ves. Jun. 129, an injunction (based on public nuisance) was granted by Lord Chancellor Loughborough to prevent the use of ramshackle old houses in London as temporary warehouses for the storage of sugar, which made the buildings dangerous to the public. In *A-G* v *Cleaver* (1811) 18 Ves. Jun. 212 Lord Chancellor Eldon, while admitting jurisdiction, stood over for trial by jury on the issue of fact an application by the A-G at the relation of individuals for an injunction (based on public nuisance) to prevent the defendants from continuing their manufacture of soap and soap by-products in Battersea. In *Crowder* v *Tinkler* (1816) 19 Ves. Jun. 618, Lord Chancellor Eldon granted an injunction limiting the amount of gunpowder the defendant could store in a newly built corning-mill until trial at the next Assizes of the issue of whether the corning-mill amounted to a public nuisance. It is clear from the terminology in these three cases on nuisance that the action was being dealt with as a criminal rather than a civil matter. Lord Diplock in *Gouriet* v *Union of Post Office Workers* [1978] AC 435, without citing any authorities, makes reference to this historical usage. In *Cooper* v *Whittingham*

(1880) 15 Ch 501, the plaintiffs were granted an ex parte injunction, based on s17 (breach of which was an offence) of the *Copyright Act* 1842 (U.K.), to restrain the defendants from importing for sale and from selling or retaining in their possession an issue of an American magazine carrying material pirated from the plaintiff's magazine. 'Importing for sale' was a statutory offence with a statutory penalty under s17. At a hearing before Jessell MR the injunction was continued with respect to 'selling and retaining in possession' and costs were awarded against the defendant.

These cases demonstrate, however, that until relatively recently, 'criminal law' has been used in the sense of breach of a public right rather than in the narrower sense of a breach of public order. 'In most of such cases its use would be futile; one does not obtain an injunction against a would-be burglar ...' (Sykes, 1953, p. 115). More lately English cases such as *Egan* v *Egan* [1975] Ch 218, *Pidduck* v *Molloy* [1992] 2 FLR 202 (CA), *Khorasandjian* v *Bush* [1993] QB 727 (CA) and Australian cases such as *Zimitat* v *Douglas* [1979] Qd R 454 evidence a willingness on the part of the courts to grant an interlocutory injunction to restrain criminal conduct such as assault on, or molestation of, the plaintiff. Dicta in *Parry* v *Crooks* (1981) 27 SASR 1 (Court of Appeal) support the granting of injunctions to prevent threatened or apprehended assaults, but 'in exceptional circumstances only' which did not arise in the present case, per King CJ (p. 9), with whom Mohr J agreed. Zelling J, in dissent, found the circumstances of the case did warrant the granting of an injunction to enjoin the defendant from assaulting the plaintiff. In *Corvisy* v *Corvisy* [1982] 2 NSWLR 557 McLelland J found the court did have 'power by injunction to restrain apprehended assaults, molestations etc' (p. 558), but, approving King CJ's approach, only in exceptional circumstances not present in the case before him.

The procedure generally relates to a statutory offence and it is injunctions to prevent a statutory offence which are relevant in the context of restraining an imminent breach of the official secrets legislation. In the statutory offence cases the application for an injunction is usually brought by the Attorney-General on behalf of individuals or on behalf of a public authority, or by a public authority acting on its own behalf if the statute so allows, to enforce a public right.[1]

In certain limited circumstances an individual may have standing to prevent the breach of the provisions of a statute. In the Australian context see, for example, *Onus* v *Alcoa of Australia* (1981) 149 CLR 27, where the appellants were found to have an interest in the subject matter greater than that of other members of the public and were thus held to have standing to commence an action to restrain a breach of the *Archaeological and*

*Aboriginal Relics Preservation Act 1972* (Vic). In *John Fairfax Publications Pty Ltd* v *Doe* (1995) 130 ALR 488, the Court of Appeal of the Supreme Court of NSW found the respondent had the requisite special interest, that being the possible interference with his forthcoming trial. This gave him standing to obtain an injunction to restrain the breach of the penal provisions of s63 *Telecommunications (Interception) Act 1979* (Cth) and thus prevent the appellant from publishing transcripts of his (the respondent's) telephone conversations obtained in the course of police surveillance. Compare, however, *Webster* v *Dobson* [1967] VR 253 where the plaintiffs were found to lack the requisite legal interest and standing in their application for an injunction to enforce the penal provisions of the *Electoral Act 1916-1966* (Cth).

The situation in the U.K. was stated as follows in *Gouriet* v *Union of Post Office Workers* [1978] AC 435: '[O]nly the Attorney-General can sue on behalf of the public ... and ... a private individual cannot do so on behalf of the public though he may be able to do so if he will sustain injury as a result of a public wrong', per Viscount Dilhorne (p. 494). Lord Diplock spoke of the court having jurisdiction to grant an injunction on behalf of an individual 'where the court is satisfied that grave and irreparable harm would otherwise be done to the plaintiff's private rights' (p. 500). The House of Lords in *Gouriet* overturned the broader approach to standing espoused by the Court of Appeal. For a discussion on 'this rather barren dispute about standing' see *John Fairfax Publications Pty Ltd* v *Doe*, per Kirby P (p. 506). In the context of official secrets legislation in both countries, however, it is difficult to envisage any party other than the Attorney-General desiring to make an application for injunctive relief.

When deciding whether or not to exercise its equitable discretion the court takes into account a number of factors.[2]

## Alternative remedies

One of the matters to be considered is whether alternative remedies remain available to deter the defendant. In *A-G* v *Bastow* [1957] 1 QB 514 the issue of alternative remedies arose because when the action was commenced not all the remedies under the relevant Act had been exhausted. In the period after the issue of the writ and before the hearing by Devlin J, the defendant continued to flout the law, was convicted for a second time under the relevant legislation, fined £100, which he failed to pay, and sentenced to three months imprisonment in default. By the time the case came before Devlin J, however, the maximum sentence had been passed on the defendant who had continued to defy the law. Therefore Devlin J was not called upon to decide the issue of other remedies being available. He did, nonetheless, appear to be of the opinion that once the Attorney-General had used his discretion to bring the action, it would be unusual for the court to refuse the application even when other remedies remained available. This point was approved in *A-G v Harris* [1961] 1 QB 74 and in *A-G v Melville Construction Co. Ltd* (1969) 67 LGR 309.

Feldman (1979) comments that this 'puts a political appointee in the seat which should be occupied by Her Majesty's judges, and threatens the traditional separation of powers between the judiciary and the executive' (p. 376). Evans (1980), referring in the accompanying footnote to 'curial deference to ministerial views', says: '[I]t seems that English courts will not refuse the Attorney-General an injunction to secure due compliance with the law except on very strong grounds' (p. 457). The issue of 'curial deference' will be examined more fully in later chapters.

On the issue when the procedure will lie, see *Cooper v Whittingham* (1880) 15 Ch 501, albeit for the protection of a private right, copyright, where Jessell MR stated:

> [I]t was argued that where a new offence and a penalty for it had been created by statute, a person proceeding under the statute was confined to the recovery of the penalty, and that nothing else could be asked for. This is true as a general rule of law, but there are two exceptions. The first of the exceptions is the ancillary remedy in equity by injunction to protect a right. That is a mode of preventing that being done which, if done, would be an offence. Wherever an act is illegal and is threatened, the Court will interfere and prevent the act being done - and as regards the mode of granting an injunction the Court will grant it either when the illegal act is threatened but has not been actually done, or when it has been done and seemingly is intended to be repeated. The second exception is that created by the *Judicature Act*, s. 25 sub-s. 8, which enables the Court to grant an injunction in all cases in which it shall appear to the Court to be just or convenient ... I think that in this particular case an injunction can issue on both those general grounds (p. 506-507).

## Whether the breach amounts to infringement of a public right

It is not enough merely for the provisions of the statute to be breached. The remedy by injunction only exists if a public right has been infringed (*A-G v Bastow*).

## Adequacy of the penalty imposed by the statute

In many cases the penalty provided, a fine, is insufficient to deter the defendant from continuing the breach. An example was *A-G* v *Harris* where the defendants had already been convicted on two hundred and thirty seven summonses and they signalled their intention to continue offending.

## Characterisation of 'injury to the public'

In *A-G* v *Harris* the question was raised as to whether 'injury to the public' in a specific sense was a requirement, or whether 'a larger and wider interest in seeing that the laws are obeyed and order maintained' was sufficient to amount to 'injury', per Pearce LJ (p. 95). Sellers LJ, Pearce LJ and Devlin LJ took the wider view as applying. Per Sellers J:

> It cannot ... be anything other than a public detriment for the law to be defied, week by week, and the offender to find it profitable to pay the fine and continue to flout the law (p. 86).

Pearce LJ did point out, however, that it would be better if Parliament put in place adequate legislative penalties rather than relying on the courts to deter law breakers with non statutory penalties.

As a result of the decision by the Full Court of the Victorian Supreme Court in *A-G (ex relatione Lumley) and Lumley* v *T.S. Gill* [1927] VLR 22 it seemed that a narrower approach would be taken by Australian Courts. An injunction was refused on the basis that an injunction would only be granted where the legislation was framed to protect a 'positive interest susceptible of enjoyment by His Majesty's subjects as of common right', per Dixon A-J (p. 33). Citing a line of English and N.S.W. cases, the limitation in *Gill* was disapproved by Menzies J, with whom Kitto, Taylor, and Windeyer JJ agreed, in *Cooney* v *The Council of the Municipality of Ku-ring-ai* (1963) 114 CLR 582.[3]

## Cases of emergency

Another reason for the granting of an injunction may be a case of emergency, such as in *A-G* v *Chaudry* [1971] 3 All ER 938. The relevant Act provided a sufficient penalty, but the two month time delay before the hearing of the case meant the defendants, who refused to give an undertaking to the court that they would cease their conduct, would continue to flout the law. The 'emergency' in this case was the continuing occupancy by guests of a hotel where there was a serious fire risk.

### Where the injury is irremediable or irreparable

In *A-G* v *Melville Construction Co Ltd* (1969) 67 LGR 309 an injunction was granted to restrain the defendant company from destroying the subject matter of the action, a stand of trees subject to a preservation order. The relevant Act provided penalties for cutting down trees subject to tree preservation orders, but the court acted immediately, without waiting to see if the penalties were adequate to prevent a breach of the law, because the damage, once done, was irremediable or irreparable. Megarry J speaks of 'irreparable harm' and 'irremediable injury' (p. 312). 'Irreparable injury' in the context of the right of the plaintiff to the granting of an interlocutory injunction means that other remedies would not be adequate compensation if the threatened harm eventuates. This case has particular relevance to information which is secret and subject to the Official Secrets Act 1989 or the *Crimes Act 1914* (Cth); the threatened harm, publication of the confidential information, is irreparable.

### Factors considered in *Gouriet* v *Union of Post Office Workers* [1978] AC 435 (*Gouriet*)

The case that is most cited in reference to the grant of an injunction to restrain the commission of a criminal act is *Gouriet* (Fairley, 1990; *Commonwealth* v *John Fairfax & Sons Ltd* (1980) 147 CLR 39). In fact the judicial comments on the issue are obiter, the decision turning on whether the plaintiff, Gouriet, had standing to bring the action. The House of Lords held that only the Attorney-General could bring the action, and the court did not have the authority to investigate his decision not to bring the action on behalf of the plaintiff, so the action failed on the threshold question of standing. Even so, all the judgments in *Gouriet* considered the issue of the granting of an injunction to restrain the threatened commission of a criminal offence.

Williams (1977) compares the use of injunctive relief to prevent a crime with the use of binding-over orders 'by which the aid of a court of justice may be "anticipatively invoked" before any crime has been committed'.

He found it 'perhaps surprising' that the only mention of this in *Gouriet* was by Lord Diplock (Williams, 1977, p. 707).

The following factors were considered in *Gouriet*:

## The Attorney-General's discretion

Lord Wilberforce made the point that this *civil* remedy (his emphasis) was exceptional and in all cases it was up to the discretion of the Attorney-General, in other words an individual could not bring an action.

> [T]his jurisdiction - though proved useful on occasions - is one of great delicacy and is one to be used with caution. Further, to apply to the court for an injunction at all against the threat of a criminal offence, may involve a decision of policy with which conflicting considerations may enter. Will the law best be served by preventive action? Will the grant of an injunction exacerbate the situation? ... Is the injunction likely to be effective or may it be futile? Will it be better to make it clear that the law will be enforced by prosecution and to appeal to the law-abiding instinct, negotiations, and moderate leadership, rather than provoke people along the road to martyrdom (p. 481)?

## Differences in the standard of proof

One of the problems adverted to by Lord Wilberforce is the possibility of a difference in the standard of proof between a contempt action for breach of the injunction, and the criminal offence which the injunction was intended to restrain. In the U.K. it seems to be accepted that the criminal standard of proof, 'beyond reasonable doubt', applies to both criminal and civil contempts. This emerges from cases such *Re Bramblevale* [1970] Ch 128 and *Dean* v *Dean* [1987] 1 FLR 517 and is discussed by Lowe and Sufrin (1996).

Until recently the situation in Australia was more complex, but was resolved by *Witham* v *Holloway* (1995) 183 CLR 525, in which the High Court held that the criminal standard of proof should apply to all forms of contempt. Even after *Witham* v *Holloway* some issues pertaining to the difference between civil and criminal contempts, mainly of a procedural nature, remain to be clarified (*Microsoft Corporation* v *Marks* (1996) 139 ALR 99).

*Complications arising*

Viscount Dilhorne in *Gouriet* referred to instances of applications for an injunction to restrain a breach of the criminal law as 'few in number and exceptional in character' (p. 489). He made reference to the complications that may arise:

> An enactment by Parliament defining and creating a criminal offence amounts to an injunction by Parliament restraining the commission of the acts made criminal. If the injunction in the Act is not obeyed - and in these days it frequently is not - the statute normally states the maximum punishment that can be awarded on conviction. If in addition to the enactment, an injunction is granted in the civil courts to restrain persons from doing the act already made criminal by Parliament, an injunction which does no more than embody the language of the statute, has that any greater potency than the injunction by Parliament contained in the Act? ... Repetition is not enforcement. The granting of such an injunction merely imposes a liability to fine or imprisonment for contempt additional to the maximum Parliament has thought fit to prescribe on conviction for the same conduct.
>
> Great difficulties may arise if 'enforcement' of the criminal law by injunction became a regular practice. A person charged, for instance, with an offence under section 58 or 68 of the Post Office Act 1953 has the right of trial by jury. If, before he commits the offence, an injunction is granted restraining him from committing an offence under those sections and he is brought before the civil courts for contempt, his guilt will be decided not by a jury but by a judge or judges. If he is subsequently tried for the criminal offence, might not the finding of guilt by a judge or judges prejudice his trial? This question is not to my mind satisfactorily answered by saying that juries can be told to ignore certain matters. It was suggested that this difficulty might be overcome by adjourning the proceedings for contempt until after the conclusion of the criminal trial. If that was done, the question might arise then as to the propriety of imposing a punishment in the contempt proceedings additional to that imposed on conviction for the same conduct in the criminal court (pp. 490-491).

## Review of the issues by Kirby P

Kirby P, in *Peek* v *NSW Egg Corporation* (1986) 6 NSWLR 1, reviewed the reasons why injunctions are so rarely granted in such circumstances. These are, in brief: the criminal process should not be interfered with by other courts;

if the legislature intended injunctive relief to be among the sanctions provided for by the relevant statute it should be included within the statute itself; where a fine is the only penalty in the statute an injunction would introduce the possibility of imprisonment 'which Parliament has expressly failed or declined to provide'; the procedure is different in civil and criminal courts; multiplicity of litigation is undesirable and, finally, it is sometimes plain the statute provides a complete code of the remedies available. Kirby P lists the exceptional circumstances as being where the criminal penalty is inadequate, where the party 'has evidenced a clear and unequivocal intention to continue to flout the criminal law, and there is a significant risk that if the party in breach is not stopped others will be encouraged to breach the law also' (pp. 3-5).

## Where the legislation provides an express or implied discretion

The provisions of the relevant legislation may allow for injunctive relief specifically or by implication. *ACR Trading Pty Ltd* v *FAT-SEL Pty Ltd* (1987) 11 NSWLR 67 and *Warringah Shire Council* v *Sedevcic* (1987) 10 NSWLR 335 concerned s124 of the *Environmental Planning and Assessment Act 1979* (NSW). This section provided that the Land and Environment Court 'may make such order as it thinks fit to remedy or restrain' a breach of the Act, which was found to include the discretion to grant or decline to grant an injunction. Both cases, in the NSW Court of Appeal, turned on the exercise of the discretion by the respective judges in the Land and Environment Court. *Becker* v *Muldowney* (1995) 120 FLR 322 concerned s132 of the *Electoral Act 1985* (SA) which specifically allows the granting of an injunction. In this particular case these provisions were not affected by a contemporaneous High Court challenge to the provisions of the Act the defendant was being restrained from infringing (but such a challenge to the validity of the respective act was, however, a factor to be taken into account).

## Restraint by injunction of threatened breaches of official secrets legislation

Breach of official secrets legislation by disclosure of confidential government information would give rise to irreparable injury in the sense that no penalty would remedy the fact that the information is no longer secret. Why then has injunctive relief not been sought to prevent threatened breaches of the legislation? An Australian case where this very question was subjected to judicial scrutiny was *Commonwealth* v *John Fairfax & Sons Ltd* (1980) 147

CLR 39. The Commonwealth Attorney-General sought an injunction to restrain a breach of s79 of the *Crimes Act 1914* (Cth). Having made reference to *Gouriet*, Mason J decided that the statute imposed substantial penalties and there was nothing in s79 to indicate that the rights of the Commonwealth should be supplemented by injunctive relief.

However Mason J did grant an injunction until trial on the basis of copyright in the articles, which were reproductions of government documents, being infringed. This was based on a civil infringement of the government's rights. It is open to speculation as to whether repeated infringements in defiance of the plaintiff's rights, especially if the plaintiff were the government, would give rise to an injunction to restrain the breaching of the criminal provisions in the *Copyright Act 1968* (Cth). *Cooper* v *Whittingham* (1880) 15 Ch 501 is an example of the granting of an injunction to prevent a breach of the criminal offences set out in s17 of the Copyright Act 1842 (U.K.).

Interestingly, and perhaps alarmingly, the Gibbs Committee Report (1991) recommended that the provisions drawn up by the Review Committee to replace sections 70 and 79(3) of the *Crimes Act 1914* (Cth) should be capable of enforcement by injunction at the suit of the Attorney-General. Particular reference was made to Mason J's judgment in *Commonwealth* v *John Fairfax & Sons Ltd*, and s80 of the *Trade Practices Act 1974* (Cth) was cited as a precedent for enforcement of the criminal law by civil injunction. These recommendations have not yet been implemented. The Commission of Inquiry into the Australian Secret Intelligence Service (1995) (The Samuels report) supported the recommendation of the Gibbs Committee with respect to injunctions, but with a proviso relating to narrowing the categories where an injunction would be granted with no proof of damage being required. These recommendations have not yet been implemented either.

In conclusion it may be said that in Australia at present, certainly as far as official secrets and s79 of the *Crimes Act* is concerned, Mason J's judgment in the *Fairfax* case makes it plain that an injunction will not be available to restrain the publication of secret government information. The situation in the U.K. may not be quite so clear cut, and will be examined again under the heading of injunctions to restrain a contempt of court.

## The use of injunctions to restrain a contempt of court

This particular discussion is prefaced by the acknowledgement that the law of contempt is extremely complex. What follows is a brief investigation, narrowly focused on the issue of injunctions to restrain the commission of a criminal offence; contempt of court being, in many instances, a criminal offence. The relevance of this discussion to the suppression of official secrets relating to national security becomes obvious in the analysis of the U.K. government's treatment of the *Spycatcher* disclosures in the late 1980s.

Contempts may be classified as being either civil or criminal:

> Under this scheme it can broadly be said that interference contempt is seen as criminal contempt and disobedience contempt as civil, although the position has been confused by cases in which the courts have talked of civil contempt which 'savours of criminality' ...
> In so far as contempt constitutes a crime it is best to regard it as a crime that is *sui generis* since there are a number of peculiarities associated with the offence ... (Lowe and Sufrin, 1996, p. 3) [*footnotes omitted*].[4]

Interference contempts covers such contempts as interference with the course of justice as a continuing process, for example 'scandalising' a court, interference with particular proceedings, for example subjudice contempts, and improper behaviour in court, for example refusing to answer questions. Disobedience contempts include breaching an undertaking to a court or disobeying a court order (Lowe and Sufrin, 1996).

Both forms of contempt are relevant to the suppression of official secrets relating to national security, but, as will be seen in the following examination, even what appears to be a disobedience contempt has been characterised as a criminal contempt in the present context. The law of contempt in the United Kingdom is partly statutory and partly common law. Strict liability contempts are subject to the Contempt of Court Act 1981 (UK), but even here the common law is still relevant. In Australia almost all of the law of contempt is non-statutory.

## The situation in the United Kingdom

### Confirmation of the procedure by the House of Lords

The first House of Lords decision to consider the issue of an injunction to restrain a contempt of court was *A-G* v *Times Newspapers Ltd* [1974] AC 273. Indeed Lord Reid indicates that it was the first time the House of Lords had considered the subject matter of contempt. The facts related to the proposed publication by *The Sunday Times* in 1972 of a story about the marketing by the drug company Distillers of the drug thalidomide - a drug which caused birth deformities when taken by pregnant women. *The Sunday Times* had already published one article which roundly criticised, on moral rather than legal grounds, Distillers for the amount offered by way of settlement to the deformed children (Knightley, 1998).[5] Distillers had drawn the attention of the Attorney-General to the first article, but no action had been taken.

Prior to publication of the second article, which contained detailed evidence pointing to the probable negligence of Distillers in selling the drug, the editor of *The Sunday Times* sent a copy to the Attorney-General. The Attorney-General obtained an injunction in the Divisional Court[6] to restrain publication of the article, on the basis that it would be a contempt of court because it related to proceedings that were 'pending'. The Court of Appeal[7] discharged the injunction on the grounds, inter alia, that the litigation was dormant. The Attorney-General successfully appealed to the House of Lords, and the injunction, in modified form, was restored. The reasons for allowing the appeal were that the material was considered to constitute a clear case of contempt, and it could not be said the proceedings were dormant.

In coming to their conclusions their Lordships made passing reference to the interests of freedom of speech. Lord Diplock said: 'Restraint of contempt of court, particularly where it takes the form of holding up litigants to public obloquy or "trial by newspaper", is a restriction on freedom of speech' (*A-G* v *Times Newspapers Ltd* [1974] AC 273, p. 312), but concluded that the restraint is justified if the contempt is sufficiently serious as in the instant case (p. 314). There is no reference to the propriety of obtaining an injunction to restrain the commission of a contempt of court, in the sense of it being an injunction to restrain an criminal act. In fact the procedure appears to have been so taken for granted as to be not worthy of comment.[8]

The decision of the House of Lords in *A-G* v *Times Newspapers* [1974] resulted in an application to the European Commission of Human Rights by *The Sunday Times*. The application was on the basis that the injunction violated Article 10(1) of the European Convention on Human Rights which provides for freedom of expression. The European Commission of Human Rights, by an 8 to 5 majority, and then the European Court of Human Rights, by 11 votes to 9, found the United Kingdom had violated Article 10(1) of the European Convention on Human Rights (*Sunday Times* v *U.K.* (1979) 2 EHRR 245).

Following the European Court of Human Rights decision, the Contempt of Court Act 1981 was passed which legislated with respect to contempts likely to interfere with the course of justice in particular proceedings, imposing strict liability. By s6 of the Act (*Savings*) the common law still applies to other forms of contempt.

*The Spycatcher cases - introduction of injunctions 'contra mundum'*

The *Spycatcher* cases marked a further development of the law in this area in the U.K. The case, or series of cases, centred on a book of memoirs entitled *Spycatcher* written by Mr Peter Wright, a former officer of MI5. The litigation over *Spycatcher* in the U.K. was extensive and complex. Two parallel series of hearings took place. The first series was the breach of confidence action against *The Observer* and *The Guardian*. The second series was the contempt of court action against *The Independent*, and other newspapers, for publishing material in contravention of the injunctions against *The Observer* and *The Guardian*. To further complicate matters, there was also an application for an injunction to restrain *The Sunday Times* from being in contempt of court by publishing excerpts from the book. This application formed part of the breach of confidence hearings against *The Observer* and *The Guardian*, but the judgments concentrated solely on breach of confidence without referring in any detail to the separate issues relating to *The Sunday Times*.

A very brief history of the proceedings relevant in this context, that is injunctions to restrain a criminal offence (the offence being contempt of court), is as follows. In September 1985 the U.K. government, through the Attorney-General (U.K.), began proceedings in N.S.W. to prevent publication of the book *Spycatcher*. The U.K. government's case was that the revelations by Wright amounted to a breach of confidence. On 22 and 23 June 1986 *The Observer* and *The Guardian* newspapers in England published an outline of the allegations that were going to be made in the Australian proceedings. On 27 June 1986 the Attorney-General (U.K.) obtained ex parte interlocutory injunctions before Macpherson J to prevent further publication of these matters by the two newspapers. On 11 July 1986 Millett J heard an application to vary or discharge those injunctions; he ordered that the injunctions be continued to the trial, and this order was affirmed by the Court of Appeal on 25 July 1986.[9]

On 27 April 1987 *The Independent* published a major summary of the allegations and statements in the book; on the same day the *London Evening Standard* and *London Daily News* gave a much shortened version of the story in *The Independent*. This appeared to be in direct contradiction of the injunctions restraining *The Observer* and *The Guardian*. As a result the Attorney-General committed the editors and the publishers of *The Independent* and the other two newspapers for contempt, notwithstanding that the outstanding injunctions restraining publication of the material had been issued against other parties. On 2 June 1987 Sir Nicolas Browne-Wilkinson decided on a preliminary issue of law that the law of contempt would not apply where the alleged contemnor was not a party to the injunction.

On 12 July 1987 *The Sunday Times* contained the first instalment of a serialisation of the book to coincide with publication of the book in the United States which occurred on 14 July 1987. On 13 July 1987 the Attorney-General started committal proceedings against *The Sunday Times* for contempt of court. On 15 July 1987 the Court of Appeal allowed an appeal by the Attorney-General against the 2 June finding of Sir Nicolas Browne-Wilkinson in relation to the action against *The Independent*, but without giving reasons at that stage. On 16 July 1987 the Attorney-General applied for an injunction against *The Sunday Times* to prevent further publication of the serialisation; the hearing was before Sir Nicolas Browne-Wilkinson and because of the Court of Appeal finding the previous day, an injunction was granted prohibiting publication the following Sunday. The injunction against *The Sunday Times* was to restrain the paper from committing a contempt of court by continuing the serialisation of the book.

On 17 July 1987 the Court of Appeal gave its reasons for the 15 July 1987 decision, namely that the defendants' actions were capable of amounting to criminal contempt, providing they had the necessary intent, where they knew of a court order to preserve the subject matter of an action pending trial, and had nonetheless interfered with the administration of justice by publishing the proscribed material.[10] This decision, in effect, made the original injunctions granted against *The Observer* and *The Guardian*, injunctions 'contra mundum', or, in the words of Lowe and Sufrin (1996, p. 219), 'a universal prior restraint order'. By their very nature injunctions 'contra mundum' suppress debate on the issue in question unless they are deliberately flouted, so, for all the public knows, there may be one or more of these injunctions in place at any given time.

It remains to be seen whether or not the incorporation in October 2000 of the European Convention on Human Rights into U.K. domestic law (as the Human Rights Act (1998)) would alter the outcome given similar circumstances. Section 12 of the Human Rights Act is entitled 'Freedom of Expression' and 'applies if a court is considering whether to grant any relief which, if granted, might affect the exercise of the Convention right to freedom of expression' (s12(1)).

As an aside, it is interesting to note the following from the 1988 litigation relating to the publication in *The Scotsman* newspaper of material from former MI6 officer Anthony Cavendish's book *Inside Intelligence*. The

Second Division in Scotland,[11] upholding the decision of the Court of Sessions, refused to grant an interdict against the *Scotsman* newspaper 'or any person having notice of said interlocutor', and thus declined to make the interdict 'contra mundum' (p. 491). The issue was not raised in the appeal to the House of Lords.[12]

## *The Spycatcher cases - injunctions to restrain a contempt of court*

Initially the Attorney-General had obtained an injunction covering a period of days to restrain *The Sunday Times* from further publication of the serialisation of *Spycatcher*. The Attorney-General's application for the extension of this injunction was part of the interlocutory proceedings pending trial on the issue of whether the disclosures would amount to a breach of confidence and should therefore be restrained indefinitely. These interlocutory proceedings included two other applications, one each by *The Guardian* and *The Observer* newspapers to discharge the interlocutory injunctions against them. These injunctions were based on a breach of confidence action by the government. The issue being examined here is the legal basis on which the injunction was granted against *The Sunday Times*.

Sir Nicolas Browne-Wilkinson V-C, who heard the three applications on 20-22 July 1987, explains it thus:

> The third application is technically one by the Attorney General against the Sunday Times claiming an injunction restraining the further publication of extracts from Mr Wright's memoirs called Spycatcher, the ground of the application in that case being that such publication would constitute a contempt of court in that it would thwart or frustrate the orders of the Court of Appeal made against the Guardian and the Observer.
> It is common ground that if I discharge the orders of 25 July 1986 made against the Guardian and the Observer, the Attorney General's claim for relief against the Sunday Times on the ground of contempt of court must also fail (*A-G* v *Guardian Newspapers* [1987], p. 319).

The earlier case against *The Independent*, the *London Evening Standard* and *London Daily News*,[13] which determined that their action in publishing material relating to the *Spycatcher* proceedings was capable of amounting to a criminal contempt, was based on s6(c) of the Contempt of Court Act 1981.

> 6. Nothing in the foregoing provisions of this Act-

(c)    restricts liability for contempt of court in respect of conduct intended to impede or prejudice the administration of justice.

This section expressly preserves the common law contempt of impeding or prejudicing the administration of justice. The original hearing against *The Sunday Times* is unreported, but it is assumed that the same section would apply as this was the section that was the subject of *A-G v Times Newspapers* [1992][14] in which the contempt case against *The Sunday Times* eventually reached the House of Lords. The penalties for contempt are set out in s14 of the Contempt of Court Act. Penalties include imprisonment, a maximum two years in the case of committal by a superior court (one month for an inferior court), and a maximum £2,500 fine for inferior courts, unlimited for superior courts. The section makes no mention of injunctions.

Because Sir Nicolas Browne-Wilkinson discharged the orders against *The Guardian* and *The Observer* the application for the continuing injunction against *The Sunday Times* was dismissed without discussion. Even though the Court of Appeal allowed an appeal by the Attorney-General, and thus *The Sunday Times* was also restrained from further publication, the case against *The Sunday Times* was not treated as a separate issue in the judgments. None of the judgments emanating from the House of Lords made any distinction between the application of the injunctions to *The Sunday Times* on the one hand, and *The Guardian* and *The Observer* on the other.

It is possible that the wording is clumsy and that in reality the injunction being sought was on the same basis as the one granted against *The Guardian* and *The Observer*, that is an injunction based on a breach of confidence action, not an injunction to restrain the commission of a criminal offence, namely a contempt of court. Without access to the decision of Sir Nicolas Browne-Wilkinson when he granted the original injunction against *The Sunday Times*, it is not possible to check this.[15] In the interlocutory proceedings, however, he quite clearly referred to the injunction as being to restrain a contempt of court; one assumes he would correctly remember the earlier hearing. Therefore the conclusion must be that by continuing the interlocutory injunctions until trial, the injunction against *The Sunday Times* was an injunction to restrain the commission of a criminal offence.

*The Spycatcher cases - characterisation of the particular form of contempt*

An issue in need of clarification at this point is the particular form of contempt that arises in the *Spycatcher* type of situation. The breach of an injunction falls into the category of 'non-compliance with court orders and undertakings' and is thus a civil contempt. In *A-G* v *Newspaper Publishing* [1987] the Court of Appeal characterised the breach of the relevant injunction as an interference with the due administration of justice, which is a criminal contempt. The House of Lords took the same approach also:

> I can see no reason in principle for distinguishing the position of a third party who aids and abets a breach of the order and one who intends to and does achieve a similar interference with or frustration of the order by means which do not involve assisting the person named therein to breach it. If a third party by such independent act renders nugatory a court order of whose existence he is aware, why should he not be liable for contempt as he would be if he had actively assisted the named person to defeat the operation of the order? In both cases the third party has, with knowledge, interfered with the course of justice, and in both cases he should in my view by [*sic*] subject to the same liability (*A-G* v *Times Newspapers* [1992] 1 AC 191, per Lord Jauncey, p. 230).

*The Spycatcher cases - relevance to official secrets*

In the context of official, secrets relating to national security, the procedure, and the resulting consequences, are as follows.[16] The government obtains an interlocutory injunction against one newspaper to restrain confidential information, until trial, and that injunction is 'contra mundum', as the Court of Appeal effectively decided by virtue of the decision in *A-G* v *Newspaper Publishing* [1987].[17] Breach of that injunction by a second newspaper, not a party to the injunction, would be a contempt, as decided in *A-G* v *Times Newspapers* [1992]. The government then hears that the second newspaper is about to print all or part of that information, and obtains an injunction against the second newspaper, not on the basis of joining the second newspaper in the existing breach of confidence action but on the basis of restraining the potential contempt involved in breaching the injunction.

That is what occurred during the *Spycatcher* litigation when Sir Nicolas Browne-Wilkinson granted an injunction against *The Sunday Times* on 16 July 1987 to restrain *The Sunday Times* from committing a contempt of court by publishing information subject to the separate injunctions imposed on *The Guardian* and *The Observer*. The injunction imposed on *The Sunday Times* to restrain the contempt of court remained in place through all the *Spycatcher* interlocutory proceedings in which *The Sunday Times* was a party.

*Criticisms of the procedure*

The procedure is questionable on three grounds.

1.    *It should be an 'exceptional procedure'*

The procedure involves an injunction to restrain a breach of the criminal law, which is an 'exceptional procedure'. It may, however, be justifiable because these particular cases fall within one of the few established exceptions, that is the damage done (by the disclosure) would be irremediable. It may also be a justifiable restraint on the basis that the media should not in any event be at liberty to flout court orders of which they have knowledge. This is regardless of whether or not the information in question has genuine implications for the interests of national security or whether the suppression is a cover-up for government ineptitude or embarrassment. In the words of Lord Reid:

> [C]ontempt of court has nothing to do with the private interests of the litigants ... a balance must be struck between the public interest in freedom of speech and the public interest in protecting the administration of justice from interference. I do not see why there should be any difference in principle between a case which is thought to have news value and one which is not. Protection of the administration of justice is equally important whether or not the case involved important general issues (*A-G* v *Times Newspapers Ltd* [1974] AC 273, p. 301).

Clearly where there is an irreconcilable conflict between the interests of the due administration of justice and the interests of freedom of speech the courts will give priority to the former (Lowe and Sufrin, 1996). Lord Reid's comment about the law of contempt having nothing to do with the private interests of the litigants cuts both ways; the implications of the involvement of the Attorney-General representing the government are discussed next in the second point.

2.    *The role of the Attorney-General*

In cases relating to injunctions to restrain a breach of the criminal law only the Attorney-General, or some other party authorised by statute or with a special interest, has standing to bring an action. In all the other cases, including other contempt cases not related to the issue of national security, the Attorney-General is acting on behalf of the public.[18] In the contempt of court cases associated with the breach of confidence actions relating to disclosure of information prejudicial to national security, the Attorney-General is acting on behalf of the Crown. In fact it is not the Crown in a general sense, but the Crown in the narrow sense of the executive, of which the Attorney-General is himself or herself a member. Sir John Donaldson MR, in one of the relevant breach of confidence cases, declared: 'The Attorney General is not personally the beneficiary of the right to confidentiality which he asserts, nor is the Executive. His claim is made on behalf of the state, that is to say, the general community' (*A-G* v *Observer Newspapers Ltd, The Guardian and Others* (1986), p. 799). This appears to be ignoring the reality of the situation. While it may be argued that the Attorney-General is acting on behalf of the public because national security is involved, there is obvious potential for criticism about lack of objectivity in the decision making process (Lowe and Sufrin, 1996; Zellick, 1985)

### 3.     *Differing liabilities*

The second newspaper's liability is at all times potentially a criminal liability,[19] whereas the first newspaper's liability is primarily a civil liability, for breach of confidence, and only becomes criminal liability if the injunction is breached. Even then, it may be the civil contempt of breaching a court order. If the second newspaper went ahead and published, it would seem to be rather odd for it to be tried for contempt of an injunction imposed to restrain a contempt. For the Attorney-General to frame the second newspaper's liability in the criminal law from the outset in this manner is a clever way of avoiding the outcry that would ensue from any attempts to obtain an injunction to restrain a breach of the Official Secrets Act in the U.K.

Effectively the second newspaper stands to be punished more than the first, and the message not to disable the legal process by destroying the subject matter of the action against the first newspaper, the confidential information, is clear. *The Observer, The Guardian* and *The Sunday Times* filed applications with the European Commission of Human Rights complaining the injunctions were an unjustified interference with their freedom of speech as guaranteed by Article 10 of the European Convention on Human Rights.[20] A majority of the European Court of Human Rights found that, certainly after the publication of *Spycatcher* in the USA in July 1987, the restraints violated Article 10.

## The situation in Australia

The issue of injunctions effectively 'contra mundum' has not arisen in Australia. The High Court has not yet had to decide cases such as *A-G* v *Newspaper Publishing* [1987] and *A-G* v *Times Newspapers* [1992]. In *John Fairfax & Sons Ltd* v *Police Tribunal of NSW* (1986) 5 NSWLR 465, McHugh JA, with whom Glass JA agreed, said on the issue:

> An order made in court is no doubt binding on the parties, the witnesses and other persons in the courtroom. But an order purporting to operate as a common rule and to bind people generally is an exercise of legislative - not judicial - power. Nevertheless, conduct outside the courtroom which deliberately frustrates the effect of an order made to enable a court to act effectively within its jurisdiction may constitute a contempt of court. But the conduct will be a contempt because the person involved has intentionally interfered with the proper administration of justice and not because he was bound by the order itself (p. 477).

In the most recent Australian case, *Commonwealth* v *Fairfax, David Lague, 2UE, Alan Jones and the Australian Broadcasting Corporation* (1995), all those who attempted to publish the information after the original injunction was granted were joined as co-defendants in the original action. The later injunctions were framed in breach of confidence, not in contempt of court. For all the blustering by the then Commonwealth government about the standards of the Australian media,[21] the point was apparently taken, whether consciously or unconsciously, that it was more appropriate for the legislature to take the necessary steps to frame criminal sanctions to prevent this happening than for the Attorney-General to be inventive with a contempt of court action.

## Notes

[1]   For comment on this point see, for example, *A-G* v *Sharp* [1931] 1 Ch 121, per Lord Hanworth MR.

[2]   The various considerations are weighed up to determine whether or not the balance of convenience favours the granting of an injunction. The great majority of cases under discussion involve interlocutory or interim injunctions rather than final injunctions. For a full discussion on the granting of injunctions see Tilbury (1990). Referring to the distinction between final and interlocutory injunctions, Tilbury says: 'The importance of the distinction lies in the function of the interlocutory injunction as a species of urgent relief. This is naturally reflected in the different application of discretionary considerations as between interlocutory and final relief. More surprisingly, it has

resulted in the existence of a relatively discrete body of law applying to interlocutory injunctions, sometimes at the expense of principle' (para. 6049) [*footnotes omitted*].

On the issue of the matters taken into account by the court when deciding on the exercise of its discretion in a particular case see Spry (1997).

3    For a discussion on this and other related issues see Meagher, Gummow and Lehane (1992).

4    See also *Australian Building Construction Employees' and Builders Labourers' Federation* v *David Syme* (1982) 40 ALR 518: 'It is true that proceedings for criminal contempt are, in some respects, *sui generis*. They are, none the less, plainly "criminal in character" (see, per Evatt J. *R* v *Wilson; Ex parte Kisch* (1934) 52 CLR 234 at 258). A finding of guilt of criminal contempt is a "conviction" (see *Izuora* v *R* [1953] AC 327 at 334-335) of an "offence" (see *Shamadasani* v *King-Emperor* [1945] AC 264 at 270: "so grave an offence as contempt of court")', per Full Court (Bowen CJ, Evatt and Deane JJ) (p. 522).

An examination of the three cases cited in *ABCE & BLF* v *David Syme* reveals that the quote attributed to *R* v *Wilson; Ex parte Kisch* (1934) 52 CLR 234, 258, is in fact from *R* v *Fletcher* (1935) 52 CLR 248, 'Summary proceedings for contempt are criminal in character and the respondents are therefore entitled to invoke the principle that guilt should be proved beyond reasonable doubt' (p. 258), and that *Shamadasani* should be *Shamdasani*. *Izuora* was a Privy Council appeal from the West African Court of Appeal, *Shamdasani* a Privy Council appeal from the High Court at Bombay.

5    Knightley (1998) gives a fascinating insight into the case from the point of the view of one of the journalists who was most involved in the story.

6    *A-G* v *Times Newspapers Ltd* [1972] 3 All ER 1136.

7    *A-G* v *Times Newspapers Ltd* [1973] 1 All ER 815.

8    Lowe and Sufrin (1996): 'It is well established that an injunction can properly be granted to restrain an obstruction to justice and in particular to certain publications or planned publications that are calculated to prejudice proceedings actually in progress or those about to be heard' (p. 499) [*footnote omitted*].

See, for example, *Coleman* v *West Hartlepool Harbour and Railway Company* (1860) 2 LT 766 and *Kitcat* v *Sharp* (1882) 52 LJ Ch 134; in both these cases a party to a trial was restrained by injunction from publishing material that was calculated to interfere with the fair trial of the action. The focus in the respective judgments was on preventing interference with a trial and there was no reference to any difficulty with granting an injunction in these situations. Cf *Brook* v *Evans* (1860) xxix LJ Ch 616 where an injunction was refused in similar circumstances.

9    These dates, that is 11 July 1986 for the Millett injunctions and 25 July 1986 for the affirmation of these order by the Court of Appeal, are given in *A-G* v *Guardian Newspapers* [1987] 3 All ER 316 (p. 318) and per Browne-Wilkinson V-C (p. 319). The dates seem at odds with the report of the Court of Appeal hearing in *A-G* v *Observer* (1986) 136 NLJ 799, this date being stated as 'Court of Appeal July 7, 1986' (p. 799).

10   *A-G* v *Newspaper Publishing* [1987] 3 All ER 276; Court of Appeal report starts at p. 289.

11   *Lord Advocate* v *Scotsman Publications Ltd* 1988 SLT 490.

12   *Lord Advocate* v *Scotsman Publications Ltd* [1990] 1 AC 812.

13   *A-G* v *Newspaper Publishing* [1987] 3 All ER 276.

[14]  *A-G* v *Times Newspapers* [1992] 1 AC 191; the House of Lords dismissed the appeal, upholding the decision of the lower courts that *The Sunday Times* had committed a contempt of court. The contempt case against *The Sunday Times* was joined in the Court of Appeal with the contempt proceedings against *The Independent*, the newspapers lost, but only *The Sunday Times* went on to the House of Lords. This contempt case against *The Sunday Times* is not to be confused with the separate case against *The Sunday Times* being discussed under the present heading and which relates to an injunction to restrain a contempt. The contempt action is mentioned here only to show that the original proceedings against *The Sunday Times* related to a criminal contempt and the present proceedings relate to an injunction to restrain that criminal contempt.

[15]  Efforts to obtain a copy of the judgment have proved fruitless; it is not available on Lexis, and a phone call to Lexis (Butterworths) in London in May 1997 confirmed its unavailability. Unreported judgments such as this one (that is, the ones not on Lexis) are kept by the Royal Courts of Justice for six years only, and the shorthand notes for two years only.

In response to an inquiry for information about this hearing, David Pannick Q.C. (who during the *Spycatcher* litigation was Anthony Lester Q.C.'s junior representing *The Sunday Times*) advised that, according to his recollection of events, there was no reasoned judgment. The injunction was granted without the matter being fully argued pending the hearing the following week, that is on 20-22 July.

[16]  In England at least. Post *Lord Advocate* v *Scotsman Publications Ltd* 1988 SLT 490 the courts in Scotland are unlikely to grant any interdict cast in wide terms, and unlikely to find that an interdict granted against one party is also effective against a third party not named in the original interdict.

[17]  For detailed comment see Lowe and Sufrin (1996). For comment on 'Orders which are of general application' and 'The position where the person enjoined is not in breach', see Miller (1989).

[18]  *A-G* v *Premier Line* [1932]; *A-G* v *Bastow* [1957]; *A-G* v *Times Newspapers* [1974]; Evans (1980). An exception to the generality of the comment that the Attorney-General is representing the public in all other cases might be where the government were to bring a criminal action for infringement of the government's copyright under copyright legislation in the U.K. and Australia respectively.

[19]  Assuming the courts characterise the type of contempt as being an interference with the administration of justice rather then breaching a court order. The Australian courts may not take the same view as the English Court of Appeal on this matter.

[20]  *The Observer and The Guardian* v *UK* (1991) 14 EHRR 153, *The Sunday Times* v *UK* *(No. 2)* (1991) 14 EHRR 229.

[21]  Senate Deb., No. 8, col. 723, 1 June 1995; Senate Deb., No. 9, col. 988, 7 June, 1995.

# References

*ACR Trading Pty Ltd* v *FAT-SEL Pty Ltd* (1987) 11 NSWLR 67.

*A-G (ex relatione Lumley) and Lumley* v *T.S. Gill* [1927] VLR 22, p. 33.

*A-G* v *Bastow* [1957] 1 QB 514.

*A-G* v *Chaudry* [1971] 3 All ER 938.

*A-G* v *Cleaver* (1811) 18 Ves. Jun. 212.

*A-G* v *Guardian Newspapers* [1987] 3 All ER 316, pp. 318-319.

*A-G* v *Harris* [1961] 1 QB 74, pp. 86, 95.

*A-G* v *Melville Construction Co. Ltd* (1969) 67 LGR 309, p. 312.

*A-G* v *Newspaper Publishing* [1987] 3 All ER 276; Court of Appeal report starts at 289.

*A-G* v *Observer Newspapers Ltd, The Guardian and Others* (1986) 136 NLJ 799, p. 799.

*A-G* v *Premier Line* [1932] 1 Ch. 303.

*A-G* v *Sharp* [1931] 1 Ch 121.

*A-G* v *Times Newspapers Ltd* [1972] 3 All ER 1136.

*A-G* v *Times Newspapers Ltd* [1973] 1 All ER 815.

*A-G* v *Times Newspapers Ltd* [1974] AC 273, pp. 301, 312, 314.

*A-G* v *Times Newspapers Ltd* [1992] 1 AC 191, p. 230.

*A-G.* v *Bastow* [1957] 1 QB 514.

*A-G.* v *Melville Construction* (1969) 67 LGR 309.

*Archaeological and Aboriginal Relics Preservation Act 1972* (Vic).

Aronson, M., and Dyer, B. (1996), *Judicial Review of Administrative Action*, Sydney.

Attorney-General's Department (1994), 'Unauthorised Disclosure of Government Information', *Legal Practice Briefing*, vol.14, Canberra, no page numbers.

*Australian Building Construction Employees' and Builders Labourers' Federation* v *David Syme* (1982) 40 ALR 518, p. 522.

Author not identified (undated), 'Injunctions and the Criminal Law', *The Laws of Australia*, vol. 2 (Administrative Law).

*Becker* v *Muldowney* (1995) 120 FLR 322.

*Brook* v *Evans* (1860) xxix LJ Ch 616.

*Coleman* v *West Hartlepool Harbour and Railway Company* (1860) 2 LT 766.

*Commonwealth* v *John Fairfax & Sons Ltd* (1980) 147 CLR 39.

*Commonwealth* v *Fairfax, David Lague, 2UE, Alan Jones and the ABC* (1995), unreported.

Contempt of Court Act 1981 (U.K.), s6.

*Cooney* v *The Council of the Municipality of Ku-ring-ai* (1963) 114 CLR 582.

*Cooper* v *Whittingham* (1880) 15 Ch 501, pp. 506-507.

*Copyright Act 1968* (Cth).

Copyright Act 1842 (U.K.), s17.

*Corvisy* v *Corvisy* [1982] 2 NSWLR 557, p. 558.

*Crimes Act 1914* (Cth), s70, s79.

*Crowder* v *Tinkler* (1816) 19 Ves. Jun. 618.

*Dean* v *Dean* [1987] 1 FLR 517.

*Egan* v *Egan* [1975] Ch 218.

*Electoral Act 1916-1966* (Cth).

*Electoral Act 1985* (SA), s132.

*Environmental Planning and Assessment Act 1979* (NSW), s124.

European Convention on Human Rights, art. 10.

Evans, J. (1980), *de Smith's Judicial Review of Administrative Action*, London, p. 457.

Fairley, D. (1990), 'D Notices, Official Secrets and the Law', *Oxford Journal of Legal Studies*, vol. 10, p. 430.

Feldman, D. (1979), 'Injunctions and the Criminal Law', *Modern Law Review*, vol. 42, p. 376.

Gibbs Committee (1991), *Review of the Commonwealth Criminal Law: Final Report*, Canberra.

*Gouriet* v *Union of Post Office Workers* [1978] AC 435, pp. 481, 489, 490-491, 494, 500.
Human Rights Act 1998 (U.K.), s12.
*Izuora* v *R* [1953] AC 327, pp. 334-335.
*John Fairfax & Sons Ltd* v *Police Tribunal of NSW* (1986) 5 NSWLR 465, p. 477.
*John Fairfax Publications Pty Ltd* v *Doe* (1995) 130 ALR 488, p. 506.
*Khorasandjian* v *Bush* [1993] QB 727 (CA).
*Kitcat* v *Sharp* (1882) 52 LJ Ch 134.
Knightley, P. (1998), *A Hack's Progress*, London.
*Lord Advocate* v *Scotsman Publications Ltd* [1990] 1 AC 812.
*Lord Advocate* v *Scotsman Publications Ltd* 1988 SLT 490, p. 491.
Lowe, N. and Sufrin, B. (1996), *Borrie and Lowe; The Law of Contempt*, London, pp. 3, 219, 499.
Meagher, R., Gummow, W. and Lehane, J. (1992), *Equity Doctrines & Remedies*, Sydney.
*Microsoft Corporation* v *Marks* (1996) 139 ALR 99.
Miller, C. (1989), *Contempt of Court*, Oxford.
*Onus* v *Alcoa of Australia* (1981) 149 CLR 27.
*Parry* v *Crooks* (1981) 27 SASR 1 (Court of Appeal), p. 9.
*Peek* v *NSW Egg Corporation* (1986) 6 NSWLR 1, pp. 3-5.
*Pidduck* v *Molloy* [1992] 2 FLR 202 (CA).
*R* v *Fletcher* (1935) 52 CLR 248, p. 258.
*Re Bramblevale* [1970] Ch 128.
Senate Deb., No. 8, col. 723, 1 June 1995.
Senate Deb., No. 9, col. 988, 7 June, 1995.
*Shamdasani* v *King-Emperor* [1945] AC 264, p. 270.
Spry, I. (1997), *The Principles of Equitable Remedies*, Sydney.
*Sunday Times (The)* v *U.K.* (1979) 2 EHRR 245.
*Sunday Times (The)* v *U.K. (No. 2)*, *Guardian* v *U.K.* (1991) 14 EHRR 229.
Sykes, E. (1953), 'The Injunction in Public Law', *University of Qld L.J.*, p. 115.
Sykes, E., Lanham, D., Tracey, R., and Esser, K. (1997), *General Principles of Administrative Law*, Sydney.
*Telecommunications (Interception) Act 1979* (Cth), s73.
The Commission of Inquiry into the Australian Secret Intelligence Service (1995), *Report on the Australian Secret Intelligence Service*, Canberra.
The Law Reform Commission (Australia) (1985), *Report No 27: Standing in Public Interest Litigation*, Canberra.
*The Mayor and Commonalty and Citizens of the City of London* v *Bolt* (1799) 5 Ves. Jun. 129.
*The Observer and The Guardian* v *UK* (1991) 14 EHRR 153.
Tilbury, M. (1990), *Civil Remedies, Vol 1: Principles of Civil Remedies*, Sydney, para. 6049.
*Trade Practices Act 1974* (Cth), s80.
*Warringah Shire Council* v *Sedevcic* (1987) 10 NSWLR 335.
*Webster* v *Dobson* [1967] VR 253.
Williams, D. (1977), 'Preventative Justice and the Courts', *Crim.L.R.*, pp. 707.
*Witham* v *Holloway* (1995) 183 CLR 525.
Zellick, G. (1985), 'Government Beyond Law', *Public Law*, p. 283.
*Zimitat* v *Douglas* [1979] Qd R 454.

# 8 The Use of the Civil Actions of Breach of Confidence and Copyright

## The civil action of breach of confidence

To obtain an interlocutory injunction to restrain publication in a breach of confidence action, the plaintiff must show that there is a good case should the proceedings eventually proceed to trial.[1] Where the plaintiff seeks to restrain publication of the confidential information by a third party, the plaintiff must show that the third party 'knew, or ought to have realised from the circumstances, that he was being given information in breach of confidence' (Cmnd 8388, 1981, para. 4.11).[2] Then an injunction may be granted both against the original party to the confidence and against third parties (*Argyll* v *Argyll* [1967] 1 Ch. 302).

Even in circumstances where a third party does not know the information is confidential an injunction may be granted (*Wheatley* v *Bell* [1982] 2 NSWLR 544; *English & American Insurance Co* v *Herbert Smith* [1988] FSR 232; Dean, 1990). Once a third party receives notice of the breach on the part of the original discloser, even if the notice comes via a writ, that knowledge will become a factor in determining any subsequent liability on the part of the third party (*Fraser* v *Evans* [1969] 1 QB 349; *Talbot* v *General Television Corp. Pty Ltd* [1980] VR 224; Gurry, 1984; Cmnd 8388, 1981; Dean, 1990). Where there is disclosure to a media defendant of confidential information relating to national security by a government servant, the defendant may thus be fixed with notice as the defendant would, in most cases (by checking the authenticity and veracity of the source) 'know, or ought to realise from the circumstances', that the information was given in breach of confidence. The principle that an innocent third party becomes liable once notified that the information is confidential may also apply to bona fide purchasers of information, regardless of the amount paid.[3]

## Breach of confidence with the government as plaintiff

Until the decision of Lord Widgery CJ in *A-G* v *Jonathan Cape Ltd* [1976]

1 QB 752 a breach of confidence action had only been applied to the protection of personal and private rights. These were 'trade secrets', that is information of a commercial and industrial nature, often learned in the course of employment, or personal confidences, for example photographs, artistic and literary confidences, etchings, the plot of a play (Gurry, 1984; Stewart, 1988; Dean; 1990). A breach of confidence action is of use to the government in the context of national security information because an interlocutory injunction may be granted to prevent disclosure of such information. As already discussed, the government may have difficulty in obtaining an injunction in these circumstances via other legal avenues.

Finn (undated) classifies government information into four types:

> The *first* is simply that stock of knowledge publicly available in the community for use by whomsoever wishes to utilise it (*'public information'*) ... The *second* is information supplied to government by third parties - individual citizens, groups, business and the like - about their private, personal or business affairs (*'third-party information'*) ... The *third* is information of and about government generated by the officers and agencies of government (*'governmental information'*). This provides the heartland of official information. The *fourth* is an exception to the third. It is what for convenience can be called the *'propriety information'* of government. Some types of governmental operation are not particularly or distinctively governmental in character at all. Government, for example, may conduct scientific research or engage in business activities (p. 19).

Information in the first category is already public knowledge and does not have 'the necessary quality of confidence' to qualify for protection in a breach of confidence action. Information in the second category, because it concerns third party information, requires regulatory safeguards to ensure it is appropriately utilised. Information relating to national security falls into the third category. Where the government seeks protection for information which falls into the fourth category it is in the same position as any other plaintiff using breach of confidence to protect personal and private rights.

The decision by Lord Widgery CJ in *A-G* v *Jonathan Cape Ltd* [1976] gave a clear indication that in certain circumstances breach of confidence might be extended to include public rights, particularly if the information related to national security. The case involved the publication of a book containing the diary kept by Richard Crossman while he had been a Cabinet Minister between 1964 and 1970. The diary fell into the third of Finn's categories, but did not contain information prejudicial to national security in the strict sense.[4] Conceding that neither defendant would be liable under the Official Secrets Act, the Attorney-General sought by means of a breach of confidence action to restrain by injunction the publication of the diary. One of the arguments put forward by the defence was that breach of confidence had previously applied only to private rights and the inclusion of public rights would be a big step, and would give the Attorney-General alarming power.

The plaintiff's case was that 'all Cabinet papers and discussion are prima facie confidential, and that the court should restrain any disclosure thereof if the public interest in concealment outweighs the public interest in a right to free publication' (p. 765). Lord Widgery said that public interest alone was insufficient for finding in favour of the plaintiff in these circumstances. Instead it was up to the court to decide whether the public interest was involved, then to balance the various factors before deciding whether to suppress the disputed material. He went on to find that the Attorney-General had made out his claim that Cabinet papers and discussion were properly matters of confidence the publication of which can be restrained by the courts.

With respect to Cabinet papers and discussion, however, the degree of protection will depend on the particular kind of information involved. Some types of information will require protection for a short period only, other types may need suppression for a longer time. As far as extending the action of breach of confidence to include public secrets he said:

> [T]hese defendants argue that an extension of the principle of the *Argyll* case to the present dispute involves another large and unjustifiable leap forward, because in the present case the Attorney-General is seeking to apply the principle to public secrets made confidential in the interests of good government. I cannot see why the courts should be powerless to restrain the publication of public secrets, while enjoying the *Argyll* powers in regard to domestic secrets. Indeed, as already pointed out, the court must have power to deal with publication which threatens national security, and the difference between such a case and the present case is one of degree rather than kind. I conclude, therefore, that when a Cabinet Minister receives information in confidence the improper publication of such information can be restrained by the court ... (pp. 769-770).[5]

It is evident from these comments that Lord Widgery was of the view that the courts may, and indeed should, grant the government an injunction to restrain the publication of information which threatens national security. Having accepted that breach of confidence was applicable to the suppression of public secrets, Lord Widgery said the Attorney-General must show:

(a) that such publication would be a breach of confidence; (b) that the public interest requires that the publication be restrained, and (c) that there are no other facts of the public interest contradictory of and more compelling than that relied upon. Moreover, the court, when asked to restrain such a publication, must closely examine the extent to which relief is necessary to ensure that restrictions are not imposed beyond the strict requirement of public need (pp. 770-771).

Factors (b) and (c) exist only in relation to government secrets and the result is that government secrets will be restrained only if it is in the public interest to do so. This is in direct contrast with private secrets the disclosure of which will be permitted only if *disclosure* is in the public interest (Gurry, 1984). In the end Lord Widgery, having read the whole of volume one of the diaries, found nothing in this particular case that warranted the restraint requested by the Attorney-General, so he refused the injunction sought.

*Commonwealth* v *John Fairfax & Sons Ltd* (1980) 147 CLR 39 is an Australian decision cited with approval by later decisions of the English courts. Again the facts concerned the disclosure of government material in the third of Finn's categories but not relating to national security in the strict sense. The plaintiff, the Commonwealth government, successfully applied ex parte for an injunction to restrain the defendant newspapers, namely *The Age* and *The Sydney Morning Herald*, from running a series of excerpts from a book called *Documents on Australian Defence and Foreign Policy* 1968-1975.

The book contained 'unpublished government memoranda, assessments, briefings and cables relating to such matters as the "East Timor Crisis", the renegotiation of agreements covering United States military bases in Australia, the presence of the Soviet Navy in the Indian Ocean, Australia's support for the Shah of Iran and predictions for the future of his regime, the security of the Butterworth base in Malaysia, outlines of the structures of the United Kingdom and United States intelligence services and the A.N.Z.U.S. Treaty' (p. 40). Before notice of the injunction had been received, about 60,000 copies of the early edition of *The Age* and a lesser amount of *The Sydney Morning Herald* containing extracts from the book had already been distributed.

At the hearing before Mason J to continue the ex parte injunctions, the defendants argued that there was a clear public interest in disclosure. In his judgment, Mason J said of the book that it held no information that had military significance, it did not fall within the D-Notice system and there was nothing in it to advantage an enemy nation. The government wanted suppression of the documents in the book because disclosure, which was not authorised, would prejudice Australia's international relations, particularly with Indonesia. The government also claimed the publication would be an offence under s79 of the *Crimes Act 1914* (Cth).

The government's case was based on three different types of action - section 79 of the *Crimes Act*, breach of confidence and copyright. First Mason J considered the requirements necessary for the issuing of an interlocutory injunction and, in doing so, he reviewed *Beecham Group Ltd* v *Bristol Laboratories Pty* (1968) 118 CLR 618 and *American Cynamid* v *Ethicon Ltd* [1975] AC 396. He concluded that the plaintiff would have to show that there is a 'probability that he will succeed at the trial, if the evidence remains the same ... [H]ow strong the probability needs to be "depends ... on the nature of the rights" asserted and "the practical consequences likely to flow from the order" sought'. Alternatively the plaintiff need only show that there is 'a serious question' to be tried (p. 49). It is not clear at this point which approach Mason J preferred, although he prefaced his remarks about *Beecham* and *American Cynamid* with the comment, 'I have only to decide whether the plaintiff has made out a sufficient case for interim relief' (p. 49). Later, however, he said, 'Consequently, the plaintiff has, in accordance with the *Beecham* test, shown a probability that it will succeed in the action' (p. 57).

As discussed in the previous chapter, Mason J quickly dispensed with the claim for an injunction to prevent a breach of section 79 of the *Crimes Act*. When considering breach of confidence, Mason J appeared to accept without question the plaintiff's argument that the government may make use of the action to protect even unclassified government information in the same way that a private person may protect his or her private secrets. There was no discussion regarding the extension of the action of breach of confidence from the protection of private secrets to the protection of public (government) secrets as there was in *A-G* v *Jonathan Cape Ltd* [1976]. The plaintiff in the present case, however, claimed the government may make use of the action even if there is no public interest in maintaining confidentiality. Mason J, while accepting that breach of confidence does apply to the protection of government information, differed on this particular approach:

> It may be a sufficient detriment to the citizen that disclosure of information relating to his affairs will expose his actions to public discussion and criticism. But it can scarcely be a relevant detriment to the government that publication of material concerning its actions will merely expose it to public discussion and criticism. It is unacceptable in our democratic society that there should be a restraint on the publication of information relating to

the government when the only vice of that information is that it enables the public to discuss, review and criticize government action.

Accordingly, the court will determine the government's claim to confidentiality by reference to the public interest. Unless disclosure is likely to injure the public interest, it will not be protected ...

If, however, it appears that disclosure will be inimical to the public interest because national security, relations with foreign countries or the ordinary business of government will be prejudiced, disclosure will be restrained. There will be cases in which the conflicting considerations will be finely balanced, where it is difficult to decide whether the public's interest in knowing and in expressing its opinion, outweighs the need to protect confidentiality (p. 52).

Mason J found support for this approach in *A-G* v *Jonathan Cape Ltd*, and cited with approval Lord Widgery's summary of the requirements to be fulfilled by a government plaintiff. The outcome in both cases with respect to the action based on breach of confidence was the same. In the instant case the plaintiff failed to obtain an interlocutory injunction because the newspapers, and copies of the book itself, that had already been sold before the defendants were notified of the injunction, had rendered the information no longer secret. The government's final argument in *Commonwealth* v *John Fairfax & Sons Ltd* was based on copyright and on this issue an injunction was granted.

The importance of this case is that it represents another incremental step in the extension of breach of confidence to suppress disclosure of government information. The ability of the government to protect its secrets, given the right circumstances, was accepted without question. Mason J, like Lord Widgery before him, did point out that different standards would apply in the use of breach of confidence by the government to restrain the disclosure of public secrets, but the door was open. Both judges say quite clearly that, providing the elements for a breach of confidence action are otherwise likely to be satisfied, the right circumstances for suppression would be confidential government information pertaining to national security.

## Disclosure of information relating to national security

*Spycatcher - the U.K. cases*

The litigation, aspects of which have already been examined in Chapter 7, centred on the memoirs, entitled *Spycatcher*, of Peter Wright, a former MI5 officer. The plaintiff was the U.K. government and the cases were attempts to restrain publication of extracts from the book by the various newspaper defendants. The government sought to obtain the injunctions on the basis that the publications were a breach of confidence, the defendants being third parties to the confidence, and release of the confidential material had national security implications. As well as permanent injunctions for the material already published by Wright, the government also sought injunctions to restrain further possible publications in the future of material as yet unwritten. Had Wright remained in the U.K. the government would have achieved a more satisfactory result by bringing the breach of confidence against him personally. He would also have been open to prosecution for breaches of the Official Secrets Act 1911.

The examination of the *Spycatcher* saga has been thorough, and from many different perspectives (Lustgarten, 1987; Brown, 1987; Arnheim 1988; Narain, 1988; Mann, 1988; Barendt, 1989; Burnet and Thomas, 1989; Howard, 1989; Lustgarten, 1989; Patfield, 1989). The *Spycatcher* cases do, however, have particular relevance to the role of D-Notices and the D-Notice system. The information at the centre of the controversy was classic D-Notice material and the government's intention was to keep the media from publishing it. There is one passing mention only of the D-Notice system in all the judgments, and that is by Sir John Donaldson MR, who commented that Parliament might wish to review the system. Donaldson MR suggested as an alternative to the system that the Home Secretary be empowered 'to issue instructions equivalent to a D notice but having the force of an ex parte injunction' (*A-G v Guardian Newspapers (No 2)* [1990] 1 AC 109, p. 200). The media would be entitled to an in camera appeal to the courts or to some specialised tribunal.

The history of the *Spycatcher* breach of confidence proceedings is as follows. On 20 July 1987 Sir Nicolas Browne-Wilkinson started hearing three interlocutory applications: the first two were made by *The Guardian* and *The Observer* to vary or discharge the interlocutory injunctions against them. The third was by the Attorney-General against *The Sunday Times* claiming 'an injunction restraining further publication of extracts ... the ground of the application in that case being that such publication would constitute a contempt of court in that it would thwart or frustrate the orders of the Court of Appeal made against *The Guardian* and *The Observer*' (*A-G v Guardian Newspapers* [1987] 3 All ER 316, p. 319). On 22 July Sir Nicolas discharged the orders, which were restored unanimously, but in a varied form, by the three judges who heard the case in the Court of Appeal. A three-two majority in the House of Lords on 30 July 1987 restored the original injunctions of Millett J, but in a more restricted form, so the interlocutory injunctions were to remain in place until the trial where the Attorney-General sought permanent injunctions.

The trial commenced before Scott J on 23 November 1987, and he gave judgment on 21 December. The Crown, through the Attorney-General, sought permanent injunctions against the three newspapers 'to prevent or restrict not only publication of the book but also publication of any comment on or of its contents' (*A-G* v *Guardian Newspapers (No 2)* [1990] 1 AC 109, per Scott J, p. 117). The Attorney-General also sought from *The Sunday Times* an account of profits made from the serialisation of *Spycatcher* and against all three defendants he sought a further general injunction restraining future publication of material emanating from Wright or other members of the security service.

Scott J held that the publication of the articles by *The Observer* and *The Guardian* did not amount to a breach of confidence, so the claim for permanent injunctions failed. He found that the first instalment of the serialisation in *The Sunday Times* was a breach of confidence, and ordered an account of profits against *The Sunday Times* in respect of the 1987 publication. Scott J did not grant an injunction to restrain further serialisation in *The Sunday Times*, and he declined to grant the general injunction as to the future with respect to any of the defendants. A two-one majority of the Court of Appeal upheld this decision, as did a unanimous House of Lords.

Arising from the U.K. *Spycatcher* decisions are a number of issues relating to the way in which confidential government information may, or may not, be restrained by the use of a breach of confidence action.

## The absent 'confidant'

It would appear that one of the major problems besetting the judges in the U.K. courts was that the parties they would have most wished to see before them, that is Wright himself and his publishers, were outside their jurisdiction. Lord Jauncey described Wright's action as reeking of turpitude, and Lord Keith was no less scathing, saying Wright was 'guilty of treachery just as heinous as that of some of the spies he excoriates in his book' (*A-G* v *Guardian Newspapers (No 2)* [1990] 1 AC 109, per Lord Jauncey, p. 294; per Lord Keith, p. 264).

## Third party defendants

Leading on from the above is the fact that in the *Spycatcher* cases the defendants were newspapers who were third parties, that is they were not privy to the original confidential disclosure. Furthermore, with the exception of *The Sunday Times*, they had not assisted the original confidant (Wright) with his breach, and this presented another new situation. When the case came to trial, and in the appeals that followed, there was general acceptance that there would be circumstances in which a third party may be restrained by injunction from publishing confidential information (for example, *A-G* v *Guardian Newspapers (No 2)* [1990] 1 AC 109, per Donaldson MR, p. 177).

In some judgments there was no apparent distinction made between a third party who assists the confidant with the breach, for example by pecuniary reward such as a publisher, and 'non assisting' third parties. It is also clear from the judgments that different standards would apply to the third party than the standards that apply between the original confider and confidant, particularly when the third party is a newspaper (*A-G* v *Guardian Newspapers (No 2)* [1990]).

*Suppressing information already in the public domain*

Another major difficulty for the judges was that as the various cases progressed through the court system, the book, and the information therein, was becoming more readily available to anyone who was interested in obtaining it. Thus it was not due to the activities of the defendants that the information which was the subject matter of the action was becoming more widely known. Many of the allegations made in *Spycatcher* had already been made by others in one or more of 12 books and 3 television programmes on MI5 and MI6 which were supplied in evidence. One of the reasons postulated for the difference in approach by the government to the allegations contained in *Spycatcher*, as compared with the lack of action in relation to the earlier revelations of the same material, was that in the book the information came directly from an 'insider' rather than second hand via a journalist, and would therefore have more weight (*A-G* v *Guardian Newspapers* [1987]; *A-G* v *Guardian Newspapers (No 2)* [1990]).

It seems that because of the desire to somehow punish Wright and his publishers, the requirements for a breach of confidence action became obscured. Certainly it became increasingly difficult to support the claim that the material remained confidential, but it was a fiction maintained in the Court of Appeal and by a majority of the House of Lords in the hearings to decide the fate of the interlocutory injunctions. The reasons were put succinctly by Lord Brandon (*A-G* v *Guardian Newspapers* [1987]):

I reached my decision solely on the ground that the Attorney General has an arguable case for the protection of an important public interest, and that it would be unjust, by discharging the temporary injunctions now, to deprive him irrevocably of the opportunity of having that case fairly adjudicated on at a proper trial (pp. 351-352).

Ultimately, however, the members of the House of Lords in the trial of the issues were forced to concede that the availability of *Spycatcher* overseas and in the U.K. had already done all possible damage to the Crown's interests, and so the injunctions were discharged.

## Breach of confidence and national security

For the first time in a breach of confidence action the subject matter of the action related to national security. In *A-G* v *Jonathan Cape Ltd* [1976] the scope of breach of confidence was extended for the first time from the protection of private secrets to include government, or public, secrets. The secrets in that case related to the activities of Cabinet. In *Commonwealth* v *John Fairfax & Sons Ltd* (1980) the extension of the action to include government secrets was accepted without question; in that case there was no material of value to a hostile power, the objection of the government to publication was largely on the basis of diplomatic embarrassment. In neither case did the breach of confidence action give rise to the injunction being sought because, in the first, the material was old and, in the second, the material was already available to the public. In both cases reference was made to the special considerations that would apply when the material related to national security.

In neither the interlocutory proceedings nor the trial of the *Spycatcher* issues was there any deliberation on the difference in principle between the protection of public secrets and the protection of private secrets. It was accepted without question that public secrets were capable of protection by a breach of confidence action, especially public secrets relating to national security.

## Who decides whether the public secrets relate to national security

There is some discussion in the judgments as to who decides the question of whether the confidential material does genuinely relate to national security, and whether the material is so sensitive that it should be subject to a suppression order. This issue is explored in a later chapter.

*The 'iniquity' defence and official clearance of material prior to publication*

The newspaper defendants claimed that the defence of 'iniquity', that is where the confidence was breached in order to reveal a wrongdoing, would override the public interest in confidence.[6] Where issues of national security are involved, it may be difficult to balance the competing public interests. The 'iniquity' defence is also referred to as the 'public interest' defence, which confuses the issues at stake.

In response to the newspapers' claim of an iniquity defence, the Crown argued that where there was a wrongdoing, there were proper authorities to whom MI5 members should take their allegations. Examples of the proper authorities were the Director General of MI5, the Home Secretary, the Prime Minister or the Cabinet Secretary. Only as a last resort should the confidential information be revealed to the media (*A-G* v *Guardian Newspapers (No 2)* [1990]).

In the opinion of Scott J there were occasions when the press were justified in revealing secret government information, although when the information pertained to national security there would have to be good reasons to publish. He was concerned that the government should not attempt to use the cloak of secrecy to be spared 'pressure and embarrassment' when such allegations were made (*A-G* v *Guardian Newspapers (No 2)* [1990], p. 167).

Scott J made reference to the issue of clearance of material prior to publication. He referred in particular to *A Matter of Trust*, a history of MI5 from 1945 to 1972, written by Nigel West, the pseudonym of Rupert Allason. The Attorney-General obtained an ex parte injunction in October 1982 preventing publication on the basis that disclosure of the information in the book would amount to a breach of confidence. The action was disposed of by a consent order in November 1982 whereby the author agreed not to publish unless in an edited version with various deletions from the manuscript. Scott J also mentioned that Sir Percy Sillitoe's autobiography, containing information about the workings of MI5, was published with the permission of the authorities. He added that it was a matter of conjecture what, if anything, Wright would have been allowed to publish had he asked for comparable authority.

Donaldson MR repeated the view that there were proper channels through which MI5 operatives should direct their concerns (*A-G* v *Guardian Newspapers (No 2)* [1990]). During the interlocutory proceedings he had said: '[I]n any event, mere allegations of iniquity can never override confidentiality. They must be proved and the burden of proof will lie on the newspapers' (*A-G* v *Guardian Newspapers* [1987], p. 337). For this he was criticised in the judgment of Bingham LJ who, while agreeing that the disclosure should in most cases be to 'one who has a proper interest to receive the information', said that in some instances the public interest required a 'wider dissemination' (*A-G* v *Guardian Newspapers (No 2)* [1990], p. 222).

Lord Griffiths took the view that all material, including trivia, relating to the service experiences of a member or ex-member of the security service should be cleared before publication. 'The only possible exception that I would countenance would be the public interest defence. Frankly, I find it very difficult to envisage the circumstances in which the facts would justify such a defence' (*A-G* v *Guardian Newspapers (No 2)* [1990], p. 269). He suggested also that newspapers receiving such information should inform the Treasury Solicitor, thus enabling the government to obtain an injunction 'so that a judge could decide whether the balance came down in favour of preserving secrecy or publication. If this is too much to hope for, and I suspect it is, then at least I would hope that an editor would first consider very closely the motive of his informant ...' (p. 279). This rather ingenuous proposition appeared to completely ignore the existence and role of the secretary of the Defence, Press and Broadcasting Committee.

In fact Wright did compile a dossier detailing the allegations against Sir Roger Hollis. This was given to the chairman of the House of Commons Select Committee on Foreign Affairs, who passed it on to Sir Robert Armstrong and the contents were considered by the security service. Seemingly this internal security service investigation of Wright's allegations was the only one that took place. There was nothing much more that Wright, or the newspapers, could have done through the official channels, except perhaps to attempt clearance through the secretary of the Defence, Press and Broadcasting Committee.[7]

It is most curious that the existence of the D-Notice system seems to have been completely ignored by all the judges involved in the *Spycatcher* cases, except for Donaldson MR whose comments regarding the D-Notice system have already been noted. The alternatives mooted in the judgments of Scott J and Lord Griffiths, that is the referral of the material to the Treasury Solicitor or 'the authorities', would undoubtedly result in a far more rigorous excision of detail than would occur through the D-Notice System. This is because the breach of confidence cases in this chapter indicate that the government, on whose behalf the Treasury Solicitor and 'the authorities' would be acting, would take a broad view of what material is 'sensitive' and should be suppressed.

*Detriment as an ingredient of a breach of confidence action*

The issue of detriment to the plaintiff, and whether or not it was an essential ingredient of a breach of confidence action, was one that taxed the minds of several of the judges. Gurry (1984), in his book on breach of confidence written before the *Spycatcher* cases, summarised the situation prior to the *Spycatcher* cases as follows:

> Several cases contain dicta that a confider may have to show detriment in order to be entitled to relief for breach of confidence. Indeed, the dicta go so far as to suggest that this may even be a constituent element of the breach of confidence action, although no judge has yet accepted that this is so. The question has been left open, and wisely so, since the existence of detriment should be relevant to the determination of the appropriate remedy rather than the existence of a breach of confidence. A confidence may be broken whether the confider suffers material detriment or not, particularly where personal confidential information is involved, since the breach here will be reflected in the confider's hurt feelings more than anything else (p. 407).

Where an injunction is being sought, whether the case is one of private secrets or trade secrets, the existence of detriment is not necessarily a prerequisite to relief being granted,[8] even though it was expressly included as a requirement by Megarry J in *Coco* v *A.N. Clark (Engineers) Ltd* [1969] RPC 41. It would seem that the context of government secrets may give rise to different considerations to cases involving private secrets or trade secrets. In *Commonwealth* v *John Fairfax & Sons Ltd* (1980), Mason J asked, 'The question then, when the executive government seeks the protection given by equity, is: What detriment does it need to show?', clearly implying that the existence of detriment will be a necessary element in a breach of confidence action being brought to protect government secrets. The answer Mason J gave to the question he posed indicates that for the government to be successful it must show detriment, and the detriment may be that national security will be prejudiced. Thus the public interest in the free flow of information relating to the government must be overridden by some superior public interest such as a threat to national security.

In the appeal from the *Spycatcher* trial, Lord Keith firstly made a distinction between the cases where the plaintiff is not the Crown and cases where the plaintiff is the Crown. In the former case he suggested that the detriment to the plaintiff may be something as nebulous as the public interest in the encouragement of respect for confidences. The latter case requires the

Crown to produce something more concrete to override the public interest in publication. Lord Keith made a further distinction between those cases where the defendant is a servant of the Crown, and those cases where the defendant is a third party. In the former situation each case will depend on the circumstances. Again he suggested that 'the general public interest in the preservation of confidentiality, and in encouraging other Crown servants to preserve it, may suffice', which appears to water down the effect and makes the Crown's task easier. Of the latter situation, where the defendant is a third party, he said:

> A communication about some aspect of government activity which does no harm to the interests of the nation cannot, even where the original disclosures has been made in breach of confidence, be restrained on the ground of a nebulous equitable duty of conscience serving no practical purpose (*A-G* v *Guardian Newspapers (No 2)* [1990], pp. 256-257).

Citing with approval Mason J's discussion of the matter in *Commonwealth* v *John Fairfax & Sons Ltd* (1980), Lord Keith said that to be successful in obtaining an injunction a government must 'show that publication would be harmful to the public interest' (p. 258). While not giving specific examples of what would constitute sufficient harm to the public interest to amount to detriment to the Crown, his conclusion that Wright could have been restrained, but the newspapers in the present case could not, may be an indication of his meaning. Had the information not already been disclosed, then the newspapers may also have been restrained.

Lord Griffiths was clearly of the opinion that detriment is an element in private breach of confidence litigation, and also that brought by the Crown. In the case of a private litigant detriment to the plaintiff may be relatively easy to establish, for Lord Griffiths gives as an example the loss of a friendship. He also agreed with Mason J's reasoning in *Commonwealth* v *John Fairfax & Sons Ltd* (1980) that the Crown 'must establish, as an essential element of the right to the remedy, that the public interest will suffer detriment if an injunction is not granted' (*A-G* v *Guardian Newspapers (No 2)* [1990], p. 270). The detriment claimed by the Crown is 'that to continue ... further publication of *Spycatcher* in this country would damage the future operation of our security and intelligence services and thus imperil national security' (p. 273). Like Lord Keith, Lord Griffiths would have restrained Wright from publication, but not the newspapers. Lord Goff, on the other hand, preferred to leave open the question of whether detriment was essential to the plaintiff's case. He said, however, that the point was immaterial in the present case because, where government secrets were involved, the Crown had to show both that the information was confidential and that publication was detrimental to the Crown.

Whatever the situation with respect to the requirements of a breach of confidence action relating to private secrets, it seems that when the government is seeking to restrain public secrets there can be little doubt that detriment in the form of injury to the public interest is an element.

## *The deterrent effect of breach of confidence*

During the interlocutory proceedings there are overtones in some of the judgments of a desire to see breach of confidence used as a deterrent - a sort of wolf in sheep's clothing. The use of an injunction to restrain the defendant from disclosing the confidential information was nothing new, and it would thus act as a deterrent to the defendant. Here it seems there was a view that the injunction could equally be used on a grander scale as an effective warning to others in the future, and not just to satisfy the requirements of the immediate situation. Again in the words of Sir Nicolas Browne-Wilkinson V-C (*A-G* v *Guardian Newspapers* [1987]):

> There remains what counsel for the Attorney General urges is the persisting public interest, namely to prevent general dissemination of the contents of this book through the press within the United Kingdom. By discouraging general dissemination those who are tempted to follow Mr Wright's example in the future and write their memoirs hot from the security service will not find it such a satisfactory or profitable business. I think there is force in that. I think that the ability to restrain the unauthorised use of confidential memoirs by those who do not mind abusing their confidence, so as to discourage others from doing it, is a real point. I do not think it can just be swept aside (p. 331).

Sir Nicolas found 'the matter to be nicely weighted and in no sense obvious' but ultimately weighed the balance of public interest in favour of freedom of the press, and, 'with considerable hesitation' dismissed the injunctions (p. 332). The three judges in the Court of Appeal unanimously, and apparently without hesitation, overturned his decision by reinstating the injunctions, but in a slightly modified form. Ralph Gibson LJ picked up on the comments of Sir Nicolas and repeated them, but did not add his own views. In the House of Lords decision, Lord Brandon and Lord Ackner, two of the three to two majority who dismissed the newspapers' appeals, examined the comments and added their views - both disagreeing with Sir Nicolas' decision.

Lord Oliver, in dissent, believed it to be a misuse of injunctive relief. Lord Bridge, also in dissent, made an impassioned plea in favour of free speech. He prophesied that if the government persisted in banning the book, which was obtainable in other countries, it would ultimately suffer humiliation when taken before the European Court of Human Rights.

The House of Lords decided by a three to two majority that the interlocutory injunctions should remain in place until trial. By the time the case came to trial the position had changed because the book and the information were increasingly available. By then discussion on the 'deterrent' effect of a breach of confidence action was limited to the remedy of an account of profits, which was imposed on *The Sunday Times* for the publication of the first instalment of the serialisation of *Spycatcher*.

*Spycatcher - the Australian cases*

There were several Australian hearings relating to *Spycatcher*. The cases in Australia were fundamentally different to the U.K. cases in that the courts in Australia were being asked to enforce the law of a foreign state. In addition the defendant was not a third party, but a party who had assisted the confidant with the breach, that is, the publisher. The former difference made the plaintiff's case more difficult, and the latter made it easier by placing the relevant parts more squarely within the well established boundaries of a breach of confidence action.

In September 1985 Helsham CJ granted an ex parte injunction against Heinemann to restrain publication of *Spycatcher*. The injunctions were not continued on the acceptance by the Attorney-General (U.K.) of an undertaking by Heinemann and Wright not to publish. The trial in N.S.W. took place before Powell J during November and December 1986. He gave judgment on 13 March 1987 - the Attorney-General (U.K.) lost, a decision affirmed by a two-one majority of the N.S.W. Court of Appeal on 24 September 1987 (*A-G (U.K.) v Heinemann Publishers Australia Pty Ltd* (1987) 8 NSWLR 341; *A-G (U.K.) v Heinemann Publishers Australia Pty Ltd* (1987) 75 ALR 353).

On 29 September 1987 Deane J declined to grant a temporary injunction pending a full hearing by the High Court. He refused the injunction on the basis that the information (contained in the book *Spycatcher*) was already freely available in other countries and could easily, and lawfully, be brought into Australia (*A-G (U.K.) v Heinemann Publishers Australia Pty Ltd* (1987) 75 ALR 461). On 13 October 1987 the book was published in

Australia. On 2 June 1988 a unanimous High Court dismissed the Attorney-General's appeal on the sole ground of not being able to enforce the governmental interests of a foreign State (*A-G (U.K.)* v *Heinemann Publishers Australia Pty Ltd* (1988) 165 CLR 30).

Breach of confidence was not examined to the same degree as in the U.K. *Spycatcher* cases because the case was lost on the threshold question of whether the plaintiff's claim was maintainable in an Australian court. In the Court of Appeal, however, Kirby P did make some comment. With respect to the defences of 'public interest' and 'iniquity', Kirby P preferred to treat 'iniquity' as an instance of the broader general principle of 'public interest' (*A-G (U.K.)* v *Heinemann Publishers Australia Pty Ltd* (1987) 75 ALR 353, p. 434). He felt that material should not be restrained 'on the ground of breach of confidence unless there is a "pressing social need" for such restraint', and he could see none, although he did point out that he was looking at public interest in an Australian context (p. 433).

*The Spycatcher cases - summary*

Several commentators, and indeed some of the judgments, note the fact that the government of the U.K. made no effort to restrain the publication of *Spycatcher* in the United States of America (Narain, 1988; Burnet and Thomas, 1989; Hocking, 1993; *A-G* v *Guardian Newspapers* [1987]; *A-G* v *Guardian Newspapers (No 2)* [1990]). The reason for this was that any such attempt arguably would have failed because of the First Amendment. Lord Ackner went so far as to remark: 'There the courts, by virtue of the First Amendment, are, I understand, powerless to control the press. Fortunately the press in this country is, as yet, not above the law, although like some other powerful organisations they would like that to be so, that is until they require the law's protection' (*A-G* v *Guardian Newspapers* [1987], p. 363).

The publication in America occurred after the first instance trial and before the Court of Appeal decision in Australia, and just before the interlocutory proceedings commenced in the United Kingdom. The ultimate undoing of the Crown's litigation in the U.K. was that once the book was published in America, people were able to bring it lawfully into the U.K. The lack of action to prevent importation was another matter which caused judicial comment (*A-G* v *Guardian Newspapers (No 2)* [1990]).

Although the government lost the battle to suppress the information in *Spycatcher*, the outcome of the cases was not all good news for the media. The government lost because the information had already become public knowledge, one way or another, and it had thereby become impossible to maintain the fiction that all the elements of a breach of confidence action were satisfied. The lesson that had been learnt by the government was that if they were able to suppress the information from the outset, then there would be a good chance of success. This was not lost on *The Sunday Times* in the U.K. which kept the first part of its serialisation of *Spycatcher* out of the early run of the relevant edition, then included it when it would be too late for the Attorney-General to obtain an injunction. Finally, and perhaps most importantly from the point of view of the U.K. government wanting to suppress information, the *Spycatcher* cases established that an injunction taken out against one newspaper would be effectively 'contra mundum', and would thus silence all newspapers (in England at any rate).

The reason for dwelling at such length on the *Spycatcher* cases in the U.K. and Australia is that, while the U.K. government ultimately failed in all its many attempts to restrain the information in that particular book, the various judgments are indicative of the judicial mindset in both countries at the time. In many of the U.K. judgments there are lengthy discussions detailing why breach of confidence was unsuccessful in these circumstances, and these give more than sufficient hints and directions on how to succeed in the future. In more propitious circumstances the government, of either the U.K. or Australia, would not always fail to restrain confidential government information in the future. This has already happened in both countries.

## *Lord Advocate* v *Scotsman Publications Ltd*

*Lord Advocate* v *Scotsman Publications Ltd* [1990] 1 AC 812 (*Cavendish*), like *Spycatcher*, was a heavy handed attempt by the U.K. government to suppress sensitive information by using breach of confidence (Burnet and Thomas, 1989; Walker, 1990). The facts of *Cavendish* have already been discussed in Chapter 4. Briefly, Mr Anthony Cavendish was an ex MI6 officer who wrote his memoirs as a book entitled *Inside Intelligence*, and having had permission for publication refused by the government, sent copies out as Christmas cards in December 1987. In late December 1987 *The Sunday Times*, having somehow obtained a copy of the book, ran an article on it. In January 1988 the Attorney-General was granted an injunction to restrain *The Observer*, *The Sunday Times* and 'any person having notice of this order' from publishing any information concerning the security and intelligence services obtained via Cavendish. Two weeks later the injunction was altered to allow publication of a modified version of *Inside Intelligence*.

In the meanwhile *The Scotsman* newspaper obtained a copy of *Inside Intelligence* and parts of the book were featured in an article. Scotsman

Publications Ltd were asked to give an undertaking not to publish any material which, if published in England, would contravene the injunction against Times Newspapers Ltd. They refused, and the Lord Advocate sought an interim interdict to restrain them, and any person having notice of the interdict, from further publication. The interim interdict was refused, a decision confirmed on appeal to the Second Division, and the case went to the House of Lords. The Court of Session and the Second Division, in effect, refused to grant an injunction 'contra mundum' in Scotland. The issue was not discussed in the House of Lords. The Lord Advocate's case was in much the same terms as those of the Attorney-General in the *Spycatcher* case, that is, the publication was a breach of confidence and release of the information was prejudicial to national security (*Lord Advocate* v *Scotsman Publications Ltd* [1990]).

The Crown conceded that the book contained nothing damaging to national security, but attempted to differentiate the present case from the *Spycatcher* case on the basis that there had been no worldwide publication of the material. Because the respondents were third parties to the confidential information, however, the appeal was dismissed. The judgments clearly implied that the failure of the Crown was due to the concession that there was nothing in the book damaging to national security.

The *Cavendish* case was heard by the House of Lords in mid 1989, not long after the House of Lords decision in the appeal from the *Spycatcher* trial (October 1988). Lord Keith, with whom Lord Griffiths and Lord Goff of Chievely concurred, repeated some of his *Spycatcher* judgment. He reiterated that 'there may be some circumstances under which a third party may come into possession of information, originally confidential, which has been revealed by a Crown servant in breach of his own duty of confidence, and yet may not be restrained from passing it on to others' (*Lord Advocate* v *Scotsman Publications Ltd* [1990], p. 822). The fact that the book was readily available worldwide, and in the U.K., was fatal to the Crown's case in *Spycatcher*. In *Cavendish* the 'particular circumstance ... which gives it a peculiar and perhaps unique character, is the abandonment by the Lord Advocate of any contention that the contents of *Inside Intelligence* include any material damage to national security' (p. 822). This coupled with the distribution of the book by Cavendish as Christmas cards was fatal to the Crown in this case also. It is clear, however, from the pointed remarks made by Lord Keith that matters may well have been different if the Crown had alleged that the book contained material damaging to national security.

Lord Templeman said that an injunction in favour of the Crown based on a breach of confidence action should be no 'different from or more severe' than the provisions of the Official Secrets Act 1989 (p. 824). Although the Act was not yet in force, Lord Templeman reviewed it to see what assistance it offered. He said section 1 would apply to Cavendish if the Act were already operative, and section 5, which relates to third parties, would apply to the respondents. Section 5 only applies if the information is 'damaging ... and he makes it knowing, or having reasonable cause to believe, that it would be damaging'. Because the Crown had conceded that publication would not cause damage to the security services, Lord Templeman found that section 5 did not apply to the respondents, and, as a result, neither did the action based on breach of confidence. Lord Templeman and Lord Jauncey of Tullichettle apparently regarded section 5 as applying to information emanating from *former* as well as present members of the security services, so two of their Lordships have seemingly chosen to ignore the anomalous application of the section to serving members of the security service only.

The *Cavendish* case had a direct connection with the D-Notice system because both *The Scotsman* and *The Glasgow Herald* sought advice from the then secretary of the Defence, Press and Broadcasting Committee, Admiral Higgins. Both were given a 'no advice' comment in response.

*Relevance of the DA-Notice system in the U.K. after Spycatcher and Cavendish*

The D-Notice system, which became the DA-Notice system in 1993, might perhaps seem obsolete after the *Spycatcher* and *Cavendish* litigation. The system was apparently ignored in the events prior to *Spycatcher* and although in *Cavendish* the advice of the secretary was sought prior to publication, with the resulting 'no advice' comment taken to signify clearance, the newspapers were subjected to legal action anyway.

Fairley (1990) suggests that the cases have left a role for the DA-Notice system, at least in any future conflicts with the Official Secrets Act 1989 where the provisions of the Act overlap the contents of the individual DA-Notices. Evidence of a 'no advice' comment from the secretary may be useful in supporting a defence under section 5(3) whereby a section 5 offence only occurs when 'the disclosure by him is damaging; and ... he makes it knowing, or having reasonable cause to believe, that it would be damaging ...'. As there was no similar wording in the 1911 Act, third parties could now use the secretary's 'no advice' comment as evidence of reasonableness when raising this defence.

Matters are not quite so clear cut with respect to DA-Notices and the law of confidence. Fairley points out that the judgments in *Spycatcher* make some attempt to strike a balance between the interests of national security and freedom of the press. He also points out that this may lead to some difficulty for the secretary (p. 434):

> Would evidence of a 'no advice' comment from the Secretary be weighed by the court on the 'freedom' of the press' side of the scale? Or, in cases where he suggested that the information was prejudicial, would his advice simply become a means whereby newspapers could avoid litigation? What, indeed, would happen if the Secretary's opinion differed from that of the Government?

The meaning of the second question posed by Fairley is not clear. If he means that as a result of the secretary's advice (that the material is prejudicial) the media do not publish it, then, yes, the media would avoid litigation. This overlooks the supposedly voluntary nature of the system, and the media's inclination to publish unless the situation is of real threat to national security. If the media were to manifest an intention to publish the prejudicial material it is hard to imagine that the government would stand by and respect the voluntary nature of the system. The government would almost certainly institute legal action of some nature, especially if it was possible to obtain an injunction in advance to prevent the publication from taking place.

As to the question of what happens when the Secretary's opinion differs from that of the government, Fairley perceives that, as a result of cases such as *Cavendish*, where this did happen, and *Spycatcher*, there appear to be two different interpretations of 'national security'. The government see the prejudice as being 'an indirect one of long term damage to the security services', whereas the secretary takes a narrower view, 'arising from the contents of particular documents' (p. 435). The government lost both cases, but the implication from the *Cavendish* case was clear enough that a contents based argument citing prejudice to national security might have led to a different result.

*Commonwealth of Australia* v *John Fairfax Publications Pty Ltd, David Lague, Radio 2UE Sydney Pty Ltd, Alan Jones and the Australian Broadcasting Corporation*

The full circumstances of what has become known as the Chinese Embassy Bugging Affair have been described in Chapter 5. Briefly, the Commonwealth, having heard in April 1995 that *The Sydney Morning Herald* was to run a story on the alleged involvement of ASIS in the bugging of the Chinese Embassy in Canberra attempted to prevent the story from being published.

*Commonwealth of Australia* v *John Fairfax Publications Pty Ltd, David Lague, Radio 2UE Sydney Pty Ltd, Alan Jones and Australian Broadcasting Corporation* (26 June 1995 - unreported)[9] raises some noteworthy issues. The first is that this is an Australian case. Apart from infrequent instances in the past, such as *Commonwealth* v *John Fairfax & Sons Ltd* (1980), the Commonwealth government has not often resorted to the courts to restrain the media from publishing information allegedly sensitive on national security grounds. This might be because the Commonwealth government has also managed to suppress the court proceedings, as initially occurred in the present case, so the whole matter remains out of public view. Alternatively it might be because the Australian media, for whatever reasons (which may include the law of defamation), does not publish material seen as being extremely sensitive or controversial. Another reason might be that the government has accepted even the most robust criticisms and embarrassing revelations without demur.

The second issue is that were it not for the persistence of the media, not to mention their downright defiance, the public would know nothing about the 1995 litigation. On 21 April 1995 the government was granted an ex parte injunction, based on breach of confidence, against the first two defendants by Bryson J, in the Equity Division of the Supreme Court of New South Wales, in these terms:

> No person shall without the approval of the Court have access either before, during or after the hearing of these proceedings to any affidavit, exhibit, pleading, information or other document used in these proceedings that is on the file in the Court or in the records of the Court (judgment delivered 26 June 1995, p. 4).

In addition Bryson J 'restrained publication and disclosure of information identifying an operation by Australian Secret Intelligence Service and identifying persons involved or the target of the operation ... [A]ll members of the public were excluded from hearings and ... no report of any part of the proceedings was to be published' (pp. 4-5). The terms of the injunction and the restrictions were as authorised by section 85B of the *Crimes Act 1914* (Cth) (*Hearing in camera etc.*). The defendants were also restrained from disposing of their documents.

On 25 May 1995 the third and fourth defendants made a radio broadcast referring to certain spying allegations and were on the same day joined in the proceedings before Bryson J on the application of the Commonwealth. On 26 May the third and fourth defendants announced on air that they could not broadcast the spy story because of legal restraints; the

Commonwealth issued a notice of motion against Jones for contempt of court in breaching the order (Author not identified, 1995). Also on 26 May the fifth defendant ran the story on the evening television news, following which the first two defendants applied to the court for the injunction against them to be dissolved. Bryson J dissolved the existing injunctions but made further injunctions against all the defendants 'restraining a narrower range of conduct', and allowing publication in *The Sydney Morning Herald* of an amended version of the story.

At the hearing on 29 May 1995 the plaintiff agreed to discontinue its action as the media coverage of the story had destroyed any chance of success in obtaining a final injunction to suppress the confidential information. The terms of this agreement remain subject to a suppression order. The defendants applied for the release of restrictions on access to various documents and affidavits supporting the Government's action to restrain publication of the allegedly confidential information. Bryson J refused the release, ordering that the defendants return all copies of the affidavits, and that the restrictions be continued.

Bryson J's judgment delivered on 26 June 1995 set out the original case for the plaintiff and defendant as follows:

> The Commonwealth as plaintiff claimed injunctions to protect alleged confidential information relating to secret activities of the Australian Security Intelligence Organisation and Australian Secret Intelligence Service. There was no statement of claim to define the alleged confidential information but it can be identified from the terms of the Summons, the interlocutory injunction of 21 April 1995 and the affidavit on which it was grounded. Shortly stated it was information relating to a technical operation mounted against a foreign diplomatic mission in Australia, information identifying the operation, persons involved or the target. The injunction obtained when the proceedings were commenced restrained the first and second defendants from publishing that information ...
> Mr Rares QC for the first and second defendants made it his principal position that it is now clear that there is no confidential information as alleged. This position has two different bases, first that the publications which have taken place were so extensive that none of the material in the plaintiff's affidavits is secret, or is confidential information, and secondly, that the plaintiff was not ever entitled to succeed because of the availability to the defendants of a number of defences relating to the conduct of the plaintiff's officers being in breach of the Diplomatic Privileges and Immunities Act 1967 and of other statutes, and to their conduct's [*sic*] being unlawful in respect of trespass on Embassy premises and in other respects. He asserted that he was ready to go on with the hearing to

determine whether these defences were well founded. He also asserted that all restraints should be removed so as to permit the exercise of a fundamental right to discuss publicly matters of public interest and the implied constitutional right of freedom of communication in relation to political discussion (pp. 1, 10-11).

This was a case where both sides strongly believed that they were right. The media defendants were convinced that the issue had little to do with national security and more to do with an attempt by the government to suppress something that was highly embarrassing with respect to its international diplomatic relations. The defendants were apparently intending to use the 'iniquity' defence. The 'iniquity' was, as already set out in the above quote, the breach by the 'plaintiff's officers ... of the Diplomatic Privileges and Immunities Act 1967 and of other statutes, and to their conduct's [*sic*] being unlawful in respect of trespass on Embassy premises and in other respects'.

On the other hand the government felt the confidential information did genuinely prejudice national security.[10] The argument was put to Bryson J that the implied constitutional guarantee of freedom of political discussion[11] should permit the release of the documents in question, but he found that a continuation of the restrictions would not breach the implied guarantee.

Bryson J found that the plaintiff's claim for public interest immunity was successful. Based on his findings that some of the material contained in the affidavits should be restricted on the basis of 'national security and foreign relations' or 'national security and diplomatic relations' considerations, he ordered the return of the documents by the defendants to the plaintiff, and continued the restrictions on reporting them. He was not prepared to excise the relevant passages from those affidavits that were only partly in need of protection as 'it would give the appearance that the Court is maintaining censorship over information' (p. 23). The comment overlooks the greater censorship imposed by proscribing all of the material rather than just parts of it. Fairfax's costs were to be paid by the government. In the meantime the contempt proceedings against Jones were discontinued, with each party to pay its own costs (Author not identified, 1995).

As mentioned above, one of the matters of greatest concern to arise from this case is that, were it not for the breaking of the story by other members of the media, that is Alan Jones on Radio 2UE and then the Australian Broadcasting Corporation, the issues may well have remained unknown to the public at large. This begs the question of how many other cases there may have been which have remained secret because of successful suppression orders.

*1996-*

In 1996, in the U.K. at least, there was some evidence that the U.K. government had perhaps learnt that breach of confidence does eventually have a 'use-by' date. In *A-G* v *Blake (Jonathan Cape Ltd, third party)* [1996] 3 All ER 903 the Attorney-General declined to frame in breach of confidence the action relating the publication of the autobiography of the ex-MI6 officer and Soviet spy, George Blake. As the material was at the time of publication some thirty years or more old, the Attorney-General, to the 'surprise' of Scott V-C, explained that the information was no longer confidential and preferred instead to base the action on copyright arising from 'a breach of fiduciary duty' (p. 907).

On 3 November 1997 *The Times* reported on a rather curious case. According to the report, by Michael Evans under the heading 'Paper told it can print spy claims - if they are untrue', an injunction was imposed on *The Mail on Sunday* earlier in the year. The application for the injunction was made by the government to prevent the publication of claims by a former MI5 officer, Mr David Shayler. Shayler alleged 'bungling' on the part of MI5 prior to the bombing of the Israeli Embassy in London in 1994. The injunction was lifted on the grounds that the allegations were untrue and 'therefore could not damage national security' (*The Times*, 3 November 1997, p. 9). It also appears from *The Times* that there was another injunction, relating to separate references to an intelligence operation against Libya, and this one remained in place.

Apparently prompted by Shayler's website coming online and providing a focus for Shayler's allegations on the Internet, the U.K. government sought to have Shayler extradited from France and he was arrested in Paris in August 1998. He was released from prison after three and a half months when the French judge found the activities of the British government to be political in nature. Shayler's website was hosted by TABnet in California, and the U.K. government wrote to TABnet asking that it comply with the injunction against Shayler. TABnet refused to shut down the site (Hollingsworth and Fielding, 1999).

At the end of September 1998 Shayler's website said he intended to publish, inter alia, 'why he was forced to become a Whistleblower'.[12] Attempts to visit the website in March 1999 came up with the message 'Forbidden/You don't have permission to access/ on this server'. A further visit in May 1999 was successful, the website containing only innocuous information such as reports from the print and broadcast media.[13] In late 1999 Shayler's revelations were published in a book entitled 'Defending the Realm – MI5 and the Shayler Affair', by Mark Hollingsworth and Nick Fielding.

Stella Rimington, former director-general of MI5, wrote her memoirs when she left the service, and in early 2000 submitted them to MI5 for vetting. Although there was little in the book that required altering on security grounds, the head of MI5, Stephen Lander, the head of MI6, Richard Dearlove, and the Cabinet Secretary, Sir Richard Wilson, asked the government to ban the book as a matter of principle. The government, while apparently sympathetic to the request, felt any such ban on publication would be challenged under the Human Rights Act 1998 (U.K.) (*The Daily Telegraph*, 20 May 2000). There was apparently no hesitation in banning a book by a former SAS soldier who wrote a book on the secret involvement of British intelligence in Srebrenica in Bosnia in 1995. The book was blocked by the Ministry of Defence, but the method used to prevent publication was not specified (*The Sunday Times*, 9 July 2000).

In October 2000 it was reported that a former member of the Special Air Service patrol Brave Two Zero was appealing in a New Zealand Court for the removal of an interim injunction, granted eighteen months earlier at the request of the U.K. government, preventing the publication of his book about the Gulf War. The U.K. government claimed the defendant had signed a confidentiality agreement before leaving the army, and publication of the book would be a breach of contract. The defendant's response was that much of the information was already in the public domain (*The Daily Telegraph*, 25 October 2000; *The West Australian*, 26 October 2000).

The apparent lack of activity in the U.K. over the issue of the publication of sensitive government information between 1989 and 1997 may indicate that potentially damaging revelations simply did not arise during this period. There are other possibilities. Perhaps the U.K. government relied on the effectiveness of the DA-Notice system, and/or turned a blind eye to leaks of this nature. Alternatively the lessons of *Spycatcher* and *Cavendish* were learnt so well that subsequent leaks were restrained effectively from the outset by way of injunction (and suppression of the legal proceedings via the Contempt of Court Act),[14] meaning that no-one dared to bring the information into the light of day for debate.

The re-emergence in the late 1990s of problems for the U.K. government with revelations by former intelligence and security service officers may be due in part to the Internet. If, as suggested in the previous paragraph, such revelations were previously restrained at the outset by injunction or through the DA-Notice system, the Internet sidesteps all this. Unlike books and media reports, which, nominally at least, go through an editing process prior to publication to maintain credibility, anyone can put anything on the Internet. Shayler used the Internet for publicity, and in May 1999 the disaffected former MI6 officer Richard Tomlinson also published information on the Internet, the names of MI6 operatives. While the government managed to persuade some Internet service providers to shut down the site, mirror sites emerged elsewhere (*The Times*, 14 May 1999).

If revenge rather than money is the object, the Internet provides the perfect means of giving the information worldwide publicity. Shayler and Tomlinson have demonstrated that the Internet now makes it almost impossible for a government to prevent sensitive information from reaching a worldwide audience. Rather than waving the big stick of the legal system at recalcitrant ex security and intelligence officers, the government may be better served by the more conciliatory approach provided by the DA-Notice system.[15]

## The use of copyright

Where the government has a claim in copyright for the material that has been published, or is about to be published, publication may be restrained by injunction if the defendant cannot convince the court that there is a good defence available. In *Commonwealth* v *John Fairfax & Sons Ltd* (1980) 147 CLR 39, while the government failed to obtain an injunction to restrain publication on the grounds of a breach of s 79 *Crimes Act 1914* (Cth) and on the grounds of breach of confidence, it succeeded with a claim in copyright.

In *Commonwealth* v *John Fairfax & Sons Ltd* (1980) Mason J accepted that the government was the owner of the copyright in the relevant documents. The issue centred on whether the defendants would 'more likely than not' be able to establish a defence pursuant to s41 of the *Copyright Act 1968* (Cth), 'fair dealing for the purpose of ... criticism or review', or s42, 'fair dealing ... for the purpose of reporting the news', or under the common law defence of public interest. Mason J was not persuaded that any of the suggested defences would prevail, and granted the injunction until the hearing of the action.

The difficulty for the government plaintiff who claims an injunction on the basis of an infringement of copyright is summed up by Mason J:

> To say that the enforcement by injunction of plaintiff's copyright in documents amounts indirectly to protection of the information contained in the documents is to confuse copyright with confidential information. Copyright is infringed by copying or reproducing the document; it is not infringed by publishing information or ideas contained in the document so

long as the publication does not reproduce the form of the literary work (p. 58).[16]

In other words if the work is summarised or paraphrased rather than reproduced verbatim, copyright may not apply. Because the Commonwealth was seeking to protect a proprietary or private right, Mason J could see no reason why a distinction should be drawn between the Commonwealth and a private citizen.

In the *Spycatcher* litigation in the U.K. there were references in several of the judgments to the issue of copyright. At no point was copyright used by the government as a basis on which injunctions might be granted to prevent the newspapers from publishing extracts from the book. Scott J, who heard the trial proceedings in the U.K., commented on the point that the government had not included copyright as a basis for the granting of an injunction, concluding that the approach would have had merit. Such a claim 'would be based on the proposition that in equity the Crown should be treated as the owner of the copyright' (*A-G v Guardian Newspapers (No 2)* [1990], p. 139). Dillon LJ, in the Court of Appeal, thought that 'there could have been strong arguments for saying that ... the copyright in *Spycatcher* belongs in equity to the Crown and is held on a constructive trust for the Crown ...' p. 211).

Sir John Donaldson MR, also in the Court of Appeal, explained why the Crown did not rely on copyright (p. 194):

> The vice of *Spycatcher* is, in the view of the Attorney General, that it purports to tear away the veil of secrecy from what the Crown was entitled in the public interest to have kept secret. A remedy based on copyright would not meet this evil. It would limit the extent to which others could quote from the text of *Spycatcher*, but, because of the statutory right of 'fair dealing' contained in s6 of the Copyright Act 1956, it would leave the media free to reveal and comment on much of its contents.

Donaldson MR was less confident than Scott LJ and Dillon LJ, in the Court of Appeal, and Lord Griffith, Lord Goff and Lord Keith, in the House of Lords, that a claim in copyright by the Crown would succeed in the *Spycatcher* circumstances.

In *A-G v Blake (Jonathan Cape Ltd, third party)*[1996] the U.K. government claimed 'an equity to the copyright in the book and to an account of the defendant's profits from the book' written by George Blake detailing his work with MI6 some thirty years earlier. The case failed on other grounds but Scott V-C, said that he would otherwise have concluded that 'the Crown was entitled in equity to the benefit of the copyright in the book and to the profits derived by the defendant therefrom' (p. 912).

There may be only limited circumstances in which copyright might apply directly to the publications in question, as it did in *Commonwealth* v *John Fairfax & Sons Ltd* (1980). The *Blake* case and some of the *Spycatcher* judgments, however, offer the government, in the U.K. at least, the alternative of a constructive trust in situations where the information was gained in the course of employment as a servant of the Crown.

## Summary - Chapters 6-8

The purpose of Chapters 6 to 8 has been to illustrate how the governments in the U.K. and Australia have attempted by means of various legal actions to suppress sensitive information that impacts on national security. When there is no clear indication that the competing interests have been given due consideration before sensitive government information is suppressed, the suspicion must arise that government interests are favoured over all other interests. Examples are where criminal offences relating to disclosure of government information do not have a public interest defence, or when judges appear to accept without question government claims that national security is an issue. In such situations the D-Notice system is a better, if not perfect, way of balancing the various interests. At least the D-Notice system allows some open and direct dialogue between the government and the media, and thus there is more likelihood of the advancement of the interests of the general public.

## Notes

1    The principles apply to the granting of injunctions generally. The High Court of Australia in *Beecham Group Ltd* v *Bristol Laboratories Pty Ltd* (1968) 118 CLR 618 required a prima facie case to be made out; the House of Lords in *American Cynamid Co* v *Ethicon Ltd* [1975] AC 396 required first an inquiry as to whether there is a serious question to be tried, then the balance of convenience should be examined. These two apparently conflicting decisions have led to some confusion in both the U.K. and Australia as to which is the correct test. For discussion on this confusion see, for example, Dean (1990) and Meagher, Gummow and Lehane (1992).

2    See also, for example, *Prince Albert* v *Strange* (1849) 41 ER 1171; *Cranleigh Precision Engineering* v *Bryant* [1966] RPC 81; Law Commission (U.K.) Working Paper No. 58 (1974).

3    The case law on this point is unclear; *Morison* v *Moat* (1851) 68 ER 492 (the defendant was found to have obtained the evidence surreptitiously and without sanction, so the question did not have to be directly answered); *Printers and Finishers Ltd* v *Holloway*

[1965] RPC 239. For discussion see Stuckey (1981), Dean (1990), Jones (1970), Gurry (1984), Law Commission (U.K.) Working Paper No. 58 (1974). Cmnd 8388 (1981) is also unclear on this point but in its recommendations it seems to take the view that the innocent third party who is a bona fide purchaser of information will become liable on notification that the information was confidential, and must seek redress against the provider of the information. In any subsequent action for breach of confidence, the courts will take these circumstances into account when determining the remedy.

4  What is meant by 'national security' is the subject of Chapter 9.

5  *Argyll* v *Argyll* [1967] 1 Ch. 302 was a breach of confidence case concerning personal and private rights, namely some highly intimate photographs.

6  For a discussion on breach of confidence, journalists and 'iniquity' prior to the *Spycatcher* cases see Grant (1985).

7  DPBAC documentation from that period will not be available in the Public Record Office until about 2016.

8  *Pollard* v *Photographic Co* (1889) 40 Ch D. 345; *Nicrotherm Electrical Co Ltd* v *Percy* [1956] RPC 272, (on appeal) [1957] RPC 207. Gurry, 1984; Dean, 1990.

9  The series of hearings, including this one, were purchased from the Supreme Court of New South Wales.

10  It has been suggested that the story of the alleged installation of bugging devices in the Embassy was originally leaked because of dissatisfaction with the arrangement - Australia allegedly taking the risks but receiving insufficient information in return. See, for example, *The Sydney Morning Herald* on 27 May 1995: 'How we spied on China - Joint operation with US to bug Embassy' by David Lague and Michael Millett. 'The US is understood to have unrestricted and direct access to all the intelligence gathered from the Chinese Embassy but has restricted Australia's access to some of this information' (p. 1).

11  As expounded in a number of High Court cases starting with *Nationwide News Pty Ltd* v *Wills* (1992) 177 CLR 1, and discussed in Chapter 10.

12  http://www.shayler.com/  The website was visited on 30 September 1998.

13  http://shayler.com./Default.htm  The website was visited on 24 May 1999.

14  Contempt of Court Act 1981 (U.K.): s4 allows 'the publication of any report of the proceedings, or any part of the proceedings, be postponed ...'; s 11 allows 'a name or other matter to be withheld from the public' and 'the court may give such directions prohibiting the publication of that ... matter in connection with the proceedings as appear to be necessary for the purpose for which it was so withheld'.

15  It seems even this would not have worked with Tomlinson who was apparently offered money in return for his silence, but perhaps by then it was too late as he had already been imprisoned for attempting to sell his memoirs: *The Times*, 14 May 1999: 'Vendetta led to leak of MI6 agents' names', by Michael Evans.

16  See also Attorney-General's Department (1994).

# References

*A-G (U.K.)* v *Heinemann Publishers Australia Pty Ltd* (1987) 75 ALR 353, pp. 433-434.

*A-G (U.K.)* v *Heinemann Publishers Australia Pty Ltd* (1987) 75 ALR 461.

*A-G (U.K.)* v *Heinemann Publishers Australia Pty Ltd* (1987) 8 NSWLR 341.

*A-G (U.K.)* v *Heinemann Publishers Australia Pty Ltd* (1988) 165 CLR 30.

*A-G* v *Blake (Jonathan Cape Ltd, third party)* [1996] 3 All ER 903, pp. 907, 912.

*A-G* v *Guardian Newspapers (No 2)* [1990] 1 AC 109, pp. 117, 139, 167, 177, 194, 200, 211, 222, 256, 257, 258, 264, 269, 270, 273, 279, 294.

*A-G* v *Guardian Newspapers* [1987] 3 All ER 316, pp. 319, 331, 332, 337, 351-352, 363.

*A-G* v *Jonathan Cape Ltd* [1976] 1 QB 752, pp. 765, 769-771.

*American Cynamid Co* v *Ethicon Ltd* [1975] AC 396.

*Argyll* v *Argyll* [1967] 1 Ch. 302.

Arnheim, M. (1988), 'The Spy in the Ointment', *Solicitors Journal*, vol. 132(43), p. 1474.

Attorney-General's Department (1994), 'Unauthorised Disclosure of Government Information', *Legal Practice Briefing*, vol. 14, (no page numbers).

Author not identified (1995), 'Gareth's suppression capers', *Gazette of Law and Journalism*, vol. 32, p. 2.

Barendt, E. (1989), 'Spycatcher and Freedom of Speech', *Public Law*, p. 204.

*Beecham Group Ltd* v *Bristol Laboratories Pty Ltd* (1968) 118 CLR 618.

Brown, B. (1987), 'Spycatcher and the Lords: The Rock and the Jellyfish', *Recent Law*, vol. October, p. 312.

Burnet, D. and Thomas, R. (1989), 'Spycatcher - the Commodification of Truth', *Journal of Law and Society*, vol. 16(2), p. 210.

Cmnd 8388 Law Commission (U.K.) Report 111 (1981), *Breach of Confidence*, para. 4.11.

*Coco* v *A.N. Clark (Engineers) Ltd* [1969] RPC 41.

*Commonwealth of Australia* v *John Fairfax Publications Pty Ltd, David Lague, Radio 2UE Sydney Pty Ltd, Alan Jones and Australian Broadcasting Corporation* (26 June 1995 - unreported), pp. 1, 4-5, 10-11, 23.

*Commonwealth* v *John Fairfax & Sons Ltd* (1980) 147 CLR 39, pp. 40, 49, 52, 57-58.

Contempt of Court Act 1981 (U.K.), s4.

*Copyright Act 1968* (Cth), s41, s42.

*Cranleigh Precision Engineering* v *Bryant* [1966] RPC 81.

*Crimes Act 1914* (Cth), s79, s85B.

Dean, R. (1990), *The Law of Trade Secrets*, Sydney.

*English & American Insurance Co* v *Herbert Smith* [1988] FSR 232.

Fairley, D. (1990), 'D Notices, Official Secrets and the Law', *Oxford Journal of Legal Studies*, vol. 10, pp. 434, 435.

Finn, P. (undated), *Integrity in Government - Interim Report 1*, Canberra, p. 19.

*Fraser* v *Evans* [1969] 1 QB 349.

Grant, W. (1985), 'In the Public Interest? The Disclosure of Confidential Information', *Media Law & Practice*, vol. 6, p. 178.

Gurry, F. (1984), *Breach of Confidence*, Oxford, p. 407.

Hocking, B. (1993), 'What Lies in the Public Interest? A Legal History of Official Secrets in Britain', *Queensland University of Technology Law Journal*, vol. 9, p. 31.

Hollingsworth, M. and Fielding, N. (1999), *Defending the Realm – MI5 and the Shayler Affair*, London.

Howard, M. (1989), 'Spycatcher Downunder: *A-G for the United Kingdom* v *Heinemann Publishers Australia*', *Western Australian Law Review*, vol. 19, p. 158.

http://www.shayler.com/

Jones, G. (1970), 'Restitution of Benefits Obtained in Breach of Another's Confidence', *The Law Quarterly Review*, vol. 86, p. 463.

Law Commission (U.K.) Working Paper No. 58 (1974), *Breach of Confidence*, London.

*Lord Advocate* v *Scotsman Publications Ltd* [1990] 1 AC 812, pp. 822, 824.

Lustgarten, L. (1987), 'Old News', *New Society*, vol. 11 September, p. 26.

Lustgarten, L. (1989), 'Learning from Peter Wright: A response to D.C. Watt', *Pol Q*, vol. 60, p. 222.

Mann, F. (1988), '*Spycatcher* in the High Court of Australia', *The Legal Quarterly Review*, vol. 104, p. 497.

Meagher, R., Gummow, W., and Lehane, J. (1992), *Equity Doctrines & Remedies*, Sydney.

*Morison* v *Moat* (1851) 68 ER 492.

Narain, B. (1988), 'Confidentiality, National Security, and the Right to Know - the *Spycatcher* Decision', *Northern Ireland Legal Quarterly*, p. 73.

*Nationwide News Pty Ltd* v *Wills* (1992) 177 CLR 1.

*Nicrotherm Electrical Co Ltd* v *Percy* [1956] RPC 272, (on appeal) [1957] RPC 207.

Official Secrets Act 1989 (U.K.), s1, s5.

Patfield, F. (1989), 'Spycatcher Worldwide - an Overview', *European Intellectual Property Review*, vol. 6, p. 201.

*Pollard* v *Photographic Co* (1889) 40 Ch D. 345.

*Prince Albert* v *Strange* (1849) 41 ER 1171.

*Printers and Finishers Ltd* v *Holloway* [1965] RPC 239.

Stewart, A. (1988), "Confidentiality and the Employment Relationship", *Australian Journal of Labour Law*, vol. 1, p.1.

Stuckey, J. (1981), 'The Liability of Innocent Third Parties Implicated in Another's Breach of Confidence', *UNSW Law Journal*, vol. 4, p. 73.

*Talbot* v *General Television Corp. Pty Ltd* [1980] VR 224.

*The Daily Telegraph*, 20 May 2000.

*The Daily Telegraph*, 25 October 2000.

*The Sunday Times*, 9 July 2000.

*The Sydney Morning Herald*, 27 May 1995, p. 1.

*The Times*, 3 November 1997, p.9.

*The Times*, 14 May 1999.

*The West Australian*, 26 October 2000.

Walker, N. (1990), 'Spycatcher's Scottish Sequel', *Public Law*, p. 354.

*Wheatley* v *Bell* [1982] 2 NSWLR 544.

# 9 'National Security' and 'The State'

## Introduction

Chapters 3 to 5 looked at the history and development of the D-Notice system. Chapters 6 to 8 discussed the legal alternatives pursued by the governments in the U.K. and Australia to prevent publication of material that might otherwise be subject to the D-Notice system. As well as showing how the two governments have circumvented the D-Notice system when looking for more failsafe methods of suppression, chapters 6 to 8 illustrate what is available in the absence of a D-Notice system.

The purpose of chapters 9 to 12 is to consider how to achieve a balance between the competing interests, and in particular how to maintain the interests of the general public, when dealing with the publication or otherwise of sensitive government information. To this end these chapters look at a number of different issues that have been mentioned earlier, but not examined in any detail. Some of these issues, such as prior restraints on speech and government manipulation of the news, are directly relevant to the D-Notice system. Others are relevant insofar as they are important factors in determining whether confidential information relating to national security will be suppressed or disseminated in the absence of an arrangement such as the D-Notice system. Some, for example prior restraints on speech, are relevant to both situations. While recognising that the issues being considered in this part are wide-ranging and have been the subject of lengthy examination in their own right, the following discussion will be kept, so far as is possible, within the narrow confines of the operation of the D-Notice system, or its alternatives.

Chapter 9 focuses on issues related to 'national security' and is divided into two parts. The first part deals with some definitions and looks at who or what is responsible for 'national security'. It can then be seen that there are difficulties in setting limits. The second part looks at who or what balances the competing public interests of suppression on the one hand and disclosure on the other.

## The meaning of 'national security' and 'the state'

This is a brief overview of a very complex area; for a description of some of the difficulties involved in attempting definition see Hanks (1988). As discussed earlier, the purpose of the D-Notice system is to prevent information detrimental to the interests of national security from being published. A narrow interpretation of national security is those matters relating to 'defence', as in military capabilities including equipment, intelligence gathering, surveillance and ciphers. A simplistic definition of 'defence' is the means by which threats to the safety or well-being of the state are prepared for, met and overcome. The word 'state' is used for want of a better word; words such as 'state', 'nation' 'government' carry different connotations, but in this particular instance 'state' is meant to carry the most general of meanings, inclusive of government, the people and geographical integrity. The phrase 'the safety or well-being of the state' was used by Lord Harris of Greenwich when defining subversion (H.L. Deb., vol. 357, col. 947, 26 February 1975). The threats may be both external or internal.

The D-Notice system was initiated to deal with matters of 'defence', but it is clear from the current D-Notices that the intention these days is to cover more than just 'defence'. For example, Australian D-Notice No 2 relates to the 'Whereabouts of Mr and Mrs Vladimir Petrov', and D-Notice No 4 relates to the 'Australian Secret Intelligence Service (ASIS)' - the functions of ASIS are to gather foreign intelligence for reasons not solely pertaining to the defence of Australia. Mr Malcolm Fraser, then Prime Minister, in the first official acknowledgement of ASIS, said: 'The main function of ASIS is to obtain, by such means and subject to such conditions as are prescribed by the Government, foreign intelligence for the purpose of the protection or promotion of Australia or its interests' (H. of R. Deb., col. 2339, 25 October 1977). The comparable U.K. DA Notice, DA Notice No 5, relates to 'United Kingdom Security and Intelligence Services and Special Forces', that is the Security Service (MI5), Secret Intelligence Service (SIS or MI6) and GCHQ (Government Communications Headquarters). The activities of MI5, SIS and GCHQ include foreign and economic policy objectives.[1]

## What is meant by 'national security'?

There are as many definitions of national security as there are attempts at definition. Lustgarten and Leigh (1994) give a broad based definition, emphasising the importance of, and different meaning attached to, national security in individual states:

> Few concepts are more complex, contentious, and of such practical importance for the exercise of political power than 'national security'. It cannot be defined, or even discussed in the abstract. Where one stands (and, politically speaking, whether one is able to stand) is critical. The unstable arena of world politics, in which co-operation, rivalry, law and anarchy coexist and overlap, is still above all a world of *states*. Each of these will vary in its character, interests, and vulnerability. Many consequences ... flow from this fact, but the point for the present is that the operative meaning of national security will therefore also vary correspondingly for each state (p. 3) [*footnote omitted*].

The media speak of the flexibility of meaning the phrase carries when used by those in power:

> National security can mean, in the vocabulary of governments, whatever they want it to mean. It is an infinitely elastic phrase (*Washington Post*, 12 August 1984, p. 1).[2]

This flexibility is reiterated by journalist Chapman Pincher (1968):

> As for national security, this is a wonderfully flexible phrase. It is occasionally used in what I consider to be its proper context - the safeguarding of secret information ... But far more often it is equated with the even more plastic phrases, 'the national interest' and the 'public interest' which so often mean the politicians' interest (p. 37).

Schauer (1982) divides threats to the national security of the state into verbal crimes, including sedition, incitement, conspiracy to overthrow the government and lists of illegal organisations, and essentially non-verbal offences that can be carried out by verbal acts, for example treason and espionage. An Australian politician's definition of national security was given in 1984 by Senator Gareth Evans (1984), at the time a Senator and Commonwealth Attorney-General. The article is the text of a speech made to the annual general meeting of the Victorian Council for Civil Liberties on 17 May 1984:

> To a very significant extent, 'national security' means just this - freedom from interference: freedom from terrorist attack, freedom from deliberately incited racial violence, freedom from espionage which itself threatens basic freedoms such as privacy, freedom from the kind of genuinely subversive

activity which is aimed - not just in theory but in fact - at destabilizing or overthrowing the very democratic system upon which the exercise of civil liberties depends (p. 451).

Dandeker (1994) talks of national security in a narrow and a broad sense:

> In the first, national security relates to politico-military processes concerned with the provision of internal peace and security to society from external or internal threats of violence through military, police, and related agencies ... A second way of defining national security is to broaden the idea of security concerns to include a whole variety of conditions concerned with national well-being, as in the provision of social welfare rights of citizenship, economic prosperity, and the protection of the ecological relationship between society and the environment (pp. 355-356).

Two articles, one by Relyea (1984) and another in the *Yale Law Journal* in which the author is not identified (1976), both trace the phrase 'national security' back to the early 1790s when Yale undergraduates debated the question 'Does the National Security depend on fostering Domestic Industries'. The *Yale Law Journal* article says that the modern usage of the term can be traced back to the period encompassing the latter part of the second world war and the start of the Cold War.

To Lord Diplock in *Council of Civil Service Unions* v *Minister for the Civil Service* [1985] 1 AC 374 (the *GCHQ* case) 'national security' was 'the defence of the realm against potential enemies' (p. 410). In *A-G* v *Guardian Newspapers (No. 2)* [1990] AC 109, Bingham LJ spoke of the 'paradigm national security case', but he does not elaborate on what that may be (p. 221). Taking Dandeker's approach, it may be possible to look at national security on a sliding scale - the narrow definition, which would no doubt include 'the defence of the realm', being the 'paradigm'.

Legislative definitions of 'national security' are uncommon but the *Australian Security Intelligence Organization Act 1979* (Cth) s4 provides:

> 'security' means:
>> (a) the protection of, and of the people of, the Commonwealth and the several States and Territories from:
>>> (i)    espionage;
>>> (ii)   sabotage;
>>> (iii)  politically motivated violence;
>>> (iv)   promotion of communal violence;
>>> (v)    attacks on Australia's defence system; or
>>> (vi)   acts of foreign interference;

whether directed from, or committed within, Australia or not;
and
(b) the carrying out of Australia's responsibilities to any foreign
country in relation to a matter mentioned in any of the
subparagraphs of paragraph (a);

It is interesting to note that there is no definition of 'national security'
or 'defence', in the following legislation: the Official Secrets Acts of 1911,
1920 and 1989 (U.K.); Security Service Act 1989 (U.K.); Intelligence
Services Act 1994 (U.K.); *Crimes Act 1914* (Cth). The *Inspector-General of
Intelligence and Security Act 1986* (Cth) s3(1) says 'security' has the same
meaning as in the *Australian Security Intelligence Organization Act 1979*
(Cth).

There is no definition of 'national security' on the U.K. DA-Notice
website, even though one of the FAQs is 'What is National Security?'. The
answer given is:

> ... [A]lthough no definition of National Security is given, the Committee
> has provided instead a context of scale, that the threat must involve 'grave
> danger to the Stage [*sic*] and/or individuals', and it is in this context that
> areas of National Security covered with some precision in the Notices
> should be read (www.dnotice.org.uk/faqs.htm).

In the context of the D-Notice system, Dandeker's narrow definition of
national security certainly applies to the type of matter that may be restrained
by a D-Notice, but the broad definition is too broad. It is unlikely that D-
Notices would be framed to include social welfare or environmental concerns.
Indeed even concepts such as 'national well-being' and 'economic prosperity'
would only fall within the D-Notice system if they were somehow included
within an aspect of the narrow sense, for example if they were brought within
the purview of organisations such as ASIS or one of the U.K. security and
intelligence services.

Even then it may be argued that the subject matter of D-Notices
should in fact remain limited to material that the system was originally
intended to cover, and relate only to material falling within the narrowest of
definitions of national security, such as that within s4(a), but *not* (b), of the
*Australian Intelligence Organization Act 1979* (Cth) above. It is not simply a
need for secrecy that identifies material that is the subject to individual D-
Notices. Perhaps the distinction between 'national well-being' and 'economic
prosperity' on the one hand and, on the other, 'national security', is one of
degree - the latter being focused on issues of imminent, or ultimate, danger to

life rather than on generalised concepts relating to quality of life.

To widen the scope of the D-Notice system, and it is unlikely the media would agree to any such proposal, would involve the media in value judgments about issues of, for example, economic policy. As will be seen in a later chapter, consideration of whether to publish or suppress material relating to these broader issues would be even less likely to engender an objective consideration of the public interest by either the government or the media than consideration of 'paradigm national security' material.

## What is meant by 'the state'?

The definitions of 'national security' also include a variety of beneficiaries to be protected by national security. These include 'the state', 'society', 'the nation', and each of these has a different nuance of meaning. In *Chandler* v *D.P.P.* [1964] AC 763 Lord Reid defined 'State' as follows:

> 'State' is not an easy word. It does not mean the Government or the Executive. 'L'Etat c'est moi' was a shrewd remark, but can hardly have been intended as a definition even in the France of the time. And I do not think that it means, as counsel argued, the individuals who inhabit these islands. The statute [*the Official Secrets Act 1911, section 1*] cannot be referring to the interests of all those individuals because they may differ and the interests of the majority are not necessarily the same as the interests of the State. Again we have seen only too clearly in some other countries what can happen if you personify and almost deify the State. Perhaps the country or the realm are as good synonyms as one can find and I would be prepared to accept the organised community as coming as near to a definition as one can get (p. 790).

In the same case Lord Devlin, on the other hand, took a different view:

> What is meant by 'the State'? Is it the same thing as what I have just called 'the country'? Mr Foster, for the appellants, submits that it means the inhabitants of a particular geographical area. I doubt if it ever has as wide a meaning as that. I agree that in an appropriate context the safety and interests of the State might mean simply the public or national safety and interests. But the more precise use of the word 'State,' [*sic*] the use to be expected in a legal context, and the one which I am quite satisfied ... was intended in this statute, is to denote the organs of government of a national community. In the United Kingdom, in relation at any rate to the armed forces and to the defence of the realm, that organ is the Crown (p. 807).

Lord Devlin did not define 'the Crown'.

Lewis (1990), comparing the Official Secrets Act 1989 and its 1911 predecessor, comments on yet another definition of 'the state', where 'the state' may be equated with the prime minister. Arnheim (1988), in the context of *Spycatcher*, also equates 'the state' with '10 Downing Street'.

Hanks (1988) talks of two different views of 'the state'. The narrow view, and the prevailing one in Australia, is 'the liberal democratic conception, which regards the state as embodied in its formal institutions of government - in the legislature, the courts, the executive government and the processes which link them with each other and with the population' (p. 120). On this view the state is neutral, in that it is not committed to any particular social or economic order, and only foreign interference or political upheaval accompanied by violence threatens the security of the state. The wider view regards the state as 'the organised political community with its associated political and social structures - the ruling political party, the established divisions of society and national priorities, whether ideological, economic or social' (p. 121). Any threat to these structures and underlying ideologies is a threat to the state, a threat which may be justifiably extinguished. This view of the state is to be found in authoritarian and totalitarian regimes.

Hanks comments that the legislature in Australia has developed a definition of 'national security' that accords with the liberal democratic and pluralist view of 'the state', and this definition tends towards a more narrow and focused approach. The courts, on the other hand, by taking the approach that 'national security' is non justiciable, and thus allowing the executive to say national security is virtually whatever the executive wants it to be, have 'adopted an approach to the concept which could well be employed to justify authoritarian, anti-democratic policies on the part of governments ...' (p. 133).

As far as the D-Notice system is concerned, the interpretation of 'the state' would most likely accord with the narrower more focused view. This is, of course, assuming that the media, and the secretary of the Committee, play their part in keeping to a minimum the amount and type of material to be the subject of restraint. As the above smorgasbord of definitions both judicial and academic will attest, the real difficulties over the definition of 'national security' and 'the state' arise when information which would otherwise be subject to a D-Notice ends up before the courts.

## Who or what is responsible for national security?

Who or what is ultimately responsible for national security is yet another issue. There are two aspects to this, one aspect relating to responsibility for carrying out operational matters and the other relating to decisions on policy. As far as the operational matters are concerned, in times of war the armed forces are responsible for the defence of the realm, which is a narrow definition of 'national security'. Censorship of material in the interests of national security is accepted as being inevitable during wartime, but it is the publication or suppression of sensitive information in peace time, when censorship requires more justification, that is the main focus here. During peace time issues of national security centre more on the security and intelligence agencies than on the armed forces. There are a number of agencies in the U.K. and Australia that carry out security and intelligence activities relating to the interests of national security during peacetime.[3] These activities range from intercepting communications between nations or within nations, espionage and personal surveillance.

In the U.K. the major agencies involved in operational activities are MI5, MI6 and GCHQ (Government Communication Headquarters). MI5, the British Security Service, is regulated by the Security Service Act 1989, and operates 'under the authority of the Secretary of State' (s1(1)). The Act does not, however, clarify what actual powers the Secretary of State has, so it could be a relationship of great influence by the minister, or of no influence at all (Leigh and Lustgarten, 1989). The Director-General, appointed by the Secretary of State, reports annually to the Prime Minister and the Secretary of State.

MI6, the British Secret Intelligence Service, and GCHQ, which intercepts communications, are regulated by the Intelligence Services Act 1994, which placed these two agencies on a statutory footing for the first time. Like MI5, the Secret Intelligence Service and GCHQ operate 'under the authority of the Secretary of State' (s1(1) and s3(1)). The Chief of the Secret Intelligence Service and the Director of GCHQ are appointed by the Secretary of State, and report annually to the Prime Minister and the Secretary of State.

In Australia, the Australian Security Intelligence Organisation (ASIO) has a legislative basis, namely the *Australian Security Intelligence Organisation Act 1979* (Cth). The Director-General reports to the Minister annually and the report is laid before each House of Parliament. The Office of National Assessments (ONA) operates under the *Office of National Assessments Act 1977* (Cth). The functions of the ONA are to 'assemble and correlate information relating to international matters that are of political, strategic or economic significance to Australia ...' (s5(1)(a)).

There is no regulatory legislative framework for the Australian Secret Intelligence Service (ASIS), the Defence Signals Directorate (DSD), and the Defence Intelligence Organisation (DIO). One of the recommendations of the Commission of Inquiry into the Australian Secret Intelligence Service (1994) was that legislation should be introduced to continue ASIS in existence and to provide authority for its activities. The Commission of Inquiry commented: 'It is no longer appropriate that the formal conferral of authority for the exercise of these functions should be the exclusive province of the executive arm of government' (para. 3.29).

ASIO is under the direction of the Attorney-General, to whom the Director-General must report annually (*ASIO Act*). ASIS is under the direction of the Minister of Foreign Affairs, and DSD and DIO the Minister of Defence (Richelson and Ball, 1990). ONA is an autonomous body reporting directly to the Prime Minister (*ONA Act*).

All these Australian agencies are, however, covered by the *Inspector-General of Intelligence and Security Act 1986* (Cth). The Act established the position of the Inspector-General of Intelligence and Security to whom complaints about these agencies may be made. The objects of the Act are, inter alia, 'to assist Ministers in the oversight and review of the compliance with the law by, and the propriety of particular activities of, Australian intelligence or security agencies' (s4). The Act gives the Inspector-General of Intelligence and Security the power to inquire into the compliance with directions or guidelines given to these agencies by the responsible Minister. The Inspector-General reports annually to the Prime Minister.

Thus there is statutory recognition in both the U.K. and Australia that the intelligence and security agencies are subject to the direction of the responsible Minister. Clearly then, the general policy decisions as to the remit of these agencies lies with the executive. This is reflected in the legislation which places ultimate responsibility for the activities of these agencies in the executive, although in the case of the security organisations in the U.K. this responsibility may not be well defined (Leigh and Lustgarten, 1989). The directives as to specifics of policy may be limited in some way by the legislation itself which leaves the head of the relevant agency with some discretionary powers. An example is the *Australian Security Intelligence Organisation Act 1979* (Cth), which, while saying the Director General of ASIO is subject to the general directions of the Minister, also says that the Minister is not empowered to override the opinion of the Director General.

The judiciary in both the U.K. and Australia has acknowledged that policy decisions relating to national security issues are the responsibility of the executive. In *A v Hayden* 156 CLR 532, Gibbs CJ said the executive is responsible for national security. Murphy J had much the same view, as did Wilson and Dawson JJ. There is, however, a certain inconsistency in the terminology used in the various judgments: Gibbs CJ refers to 'the executive' (p. 548), Murphy J to 'the executive government through its Minister' (p. 564), and Wilson and Dawson JJ to the 'Commonwealth' or 'the Commonwealth Government' (pp. 577-578).

To Lord Diplock in the *GCHQ* case, 'National security is the responsibility of the executive government' (p. 412). While both these cases related to security and intelligence organisations, the quotes illustrate that the judgments did not limit executive government responsibility to these organisations only, but referred instead to policy decisions on national security issues in general. The question as to the justiciability of these executive decisions is examined later in this chapter.

## Who decides which of the above definitions of 'national security' and 'the state' should apply in a particular situation?

Following on from these definitions which show a diversity of views, both academic and judicial, it would be possible to conclude that, in respect of matters relating to national security at least, 'the state' is whatever the government, or the executive, says it is. According to some of the above definitions, they may say as well that 'the state' equates to the government, or the executive, or even the Prime Minister. In addition 'national security' is whatever the government, or the executive says it is. Some issues relating to national security would be relevant to any government, but other, different, issues would be relevant to particular governments depending on different factors such as the political persuasion of the party in power. Expediency would probably dictate exactly what is to be included in the definition of national security at any given time, but expediency would probably also dictate that it should include a very broad range of matters which threaten the continued existence in power of that particular government.

## Who or what balances the interests of national security against competing public and private interests?

The question then follows as to how material subject to suppression by the government can be monitored to ensure that publication would genuinely be contrary to the interests of national security, and the suppression is not a cover-up for ineptitude, corruption or some other embarrassment. Three possibilities are the D-Notice system, Parliament and the courts.

### *The D-Notice system*

As far as the D-Notice system is concerned, the Defence, Press and Broadcasting Committee (DPBC) in Australia and the Defence, Press and Broadcasting Advisory Committee (DPBAC) in the U.K. formulate the actual D-Notices or DA-Notices. The media representatives on the respective committees have the responsibility of ensuring that the individual D-Notices are tightly framed to cover only matters genuinely relating to national security. In the U.K. the secretary of the DPBAC is independent, the government side of the committee is represented by departmental officials from the civil service, and there are no members of the executive government on the committee. Thus in the U.K. it may be easier for the media to make out their case for publication than in Australia. There is, however, no independent member of the committee whose only role is to objectively represent the interests of the general public. While both sides currently on the committee purport to represent the public interest, that is the interests of the general public, they in fact represent their own interests. These self serving interests of the government and the media are, in some instances, in direct conflict with the interests of the general public. The addition of one or more genuinely independent committee members whose only role is to represent the interests of the general public would ameliorate the situation.

In Australia the Chairman of the DPBC (assuming it were to operate as before) is the Minister for Defence and the Executive Secretary comes from within the Department of Defence. Again where the interpretation of individual D-Notices is concerned, the independent secretary in the U.K. may find it easier to be objective and more inclined to see the media point of view than in Australia where the secretary in effect represents the government side and is therefore more likely to favour suppression. If the government has so much potential to influence the committee in Australia the competing interests are not as balanced as they are in the U.K., and the interests of the general public are even less likely to be properly represented.

*Parliament*

There are legislative provisions which provide some mechanisms for Parliamentary scrutiny of the security and intelligence agencies in the U.K. and Australia. In the U.K., the Director-General of the Security Service reports annually to the Prime Minister and the Secretary of State (Security Service Act 1989 (U.K.). Lustgarten and Leigh (1994, p. 442) describe the reports as 'terse documents' compared with the equivalent Australian reports. The Chief of the Secret Intelligence Service and the Director of GCHQ also report annually to the Prime Minister and the Secretary of State (Intelligence Services Act 1994 (U.K.)). There is no requirement that these reports be laid before Parliament, so the information therein is not available to Parliament.

The Security Service Act 1989 (U.K.) makes provision for the Prime Minister to appoint a Security Service Commissioner, someone who holds or has held high judicial office. One of the functions of the Security Service Commissioner is the review of the exercise by the Secretary of State of his powers relating to the applications for warrants by the Security Service. Another function is the investigation of complaints referred to him by the Tribunal established by the Security Service Act 1989 (U.K.). The Tribunal, consisting of three to five longstanding members of the legal profession, investigates complaints regarding the activities of the Security Service. The Tribunal does not give reasons for its decisions except in a report to the Secretary of State and to the Commissioner where the decision is in the complainant's favour. Decisions of the Tribunal and the Commissioner are not subject to appeal or liable to be questioned in court. Whereas there is no requirement that the annual reports to the responsible Minister from the heads of the security and intelligence agencies be tabled in Parliament, the annual report of the Commissioner to the Prime Minister must be laid before each House. In consultation with the Commissioner the Prime Minister may edit the version to be laid before Parliament; the report is then accompanied by a statement as to whether any matter is excluded. This report does to some extent allow Members of Parliament to question the activities of the Security Service.

The Intelligence Services Act 1994 (U.K.) makes provision, identical to that in the Security Service Act, for the appointment of a Commissioner and the establishment of a Tribunal in relation to the operations of the Secret Intelligence Service and GCHQ. The wording of the respective provisions in the two Acts is almost verbatim. The Intelligence Services Act 1994 (U.K.) also established the Intelligence and Security Committee, 'to examine the expenditure, administration and policy of (a) the Security Service; (b) the

Intelligence Service; and (c) GCHQ' (s10(1)). The nine member Committee, none of whom can be a Minister, is appointed by the Prime Minister in consultation with the Leader of the Opposition. The members are drawn from both Houses, but there is no stipulation for any balance of representation from the parties. The head of each agency, and in some instances the Secretary of State, decides on what information should be disclosed to the Committee. Certain information may be not be disclosed, for example information which may identify operational methods or particular operations. The Committee reports annually to the Prime Minister who lays the report, which may be edited, before each House.

In Australia the Inspector-General of Intelligence and Security reports annually to the Prime Minister (*Inspector-General of Intelligence and Security Act 1986* (Cth)). The report is subsequently laid before each House of Parliament, but the Act allows 'such deletions ... as the Prime Minister considers necessary in order to avoid prejudice to security' (s35(5)). The Leader of the Opposition is given an unedited version, but must treat as secret the edited parts. The Leader of the Opposition receiving the full version of the report may safeguard against too much editing (Lee, Hanks and Morabito, 1995).[4] The *Office of National Assessments Act 1977* (Cth) provides that the Director-General report annually, but there is no requirement for the report to be tabled in Parliament or shown to the Leader of the Opposition.

The Director-General of the Australian Security Intelligence Organisation (ASIO) must report annually to the Minister, and an edited version of the report is tabled in Parliament (*ASIO Act 1979* (Cth)). In addition an unedited version of the report is shown to the Leader of the Opposition. In 1986 an amendment to the *Australian Security Intelligence Organization Act 1986* (Cth) established a Parliamentary joint committee 'to review aspects of the activities of the Organization that are referred to the Committee' by the Minister or by a motion passed by either House (s92C (1) and (2)). Part IVA was included in the Act by the *Australian Security Intelligence Organisation Amendment Act 1986* (Cth). Lee (1989) doubts the efficacy of the Parliamentary joint committee as do Lee, Hanks and Morabito (1994). The latter remark, 'it really is difficult to see how a body whose membership and investigative powers are so closely controlled by the executive can be said to offer independence of the executive' (p. 242).

The Commission of Inquiry into the Australian Secret Intelligence Service (1995) recommended that the Australian Secret Intelligence Service (ASIS) be placed on a statutory basis and that the Opposition be included in formal briefings on ASIS. The Commission recommended that there be established a single Parliamentary intelligence and security committee to review the activities of both ASIS and ASIO. By late 2000 these recommendations had not yet been implemented.

Where the relevant legislation requires reports to be laid before Parliament there is the opportunity for concerned members of Parliament in both the U.K. and Australia to acquaint themselves with the issues, albeit in a censored version, and then to pursue the relevant government Minister over national security matters.[5] Where the leader of the opposition is able to look at an unedited version of a report, there is further scope for questioning as to why material should be left out when the report is presented to Parliament. Whether or not members of Parliament avail themselves of the opportunity is a different matter.

Scrutiny of government activity in the U.K. Parliament is dismissed, one might say contemptuously, by Zellick (1985). While not quite so extreme in their view of Parliamentary scrutiny of government activity, Lustgarten and Leigh (1994) share some of Zellick's doubts as to its effectiveness, at least as far as the U.K. is concerned. They comment, 'despite recent moves to greater openness ... it is all too easy for ministers to slip back behind the national security shield to cover political embarrassment: as the Prime Ministerial refusals to answer questions during the "Spycatcher" affair ... well illustrate' (p. 442) [*footnote omitted*]. They also express doubts about the effectiveness of Parliamentary select committees. Miller (1994) is similarly sceptical about the situation in Australia.

## The courts

In recent years the civil law actions of breach of confidence and breach of copyright have been used by the government in both the U.K. and Australia to suppress sensitive information. The government applies to the court for an injunction preventing a media defendant from publishing the allegedly sensitive material pending a trial for breach of confidence or breach of copyright or both. This then, is the point at which the judiciary faces the weighty task of evaluating government claims for suppression in the interests of national security. Sometimes a quick decision must be made by a judge if the media have a story which is on the verge of being published and the government wants it stopped immediately. Once the information is published to a mass audience the situation is irretrievable. Publication may even destroy the possibility of a successful trial if the action is breach of confidence, as illustrated by the *Spycatcher* cases.

There has been a tendency for the courts, particularly in the U.K., to accept the claims of the executive, whoever 'the executive' is, that national security is an issue, and to stand back from any further investigation of the authenticity of the claim. In the words of Lord Diplock: 'It is par excellence a non-justiciable question. The judicial process is totally inept to deal with the type of problem which it involves' (*GCHQ* case, p. 412). Lee, Hanks and Morabito (1995, p. 182) warn against allowing this attitude of 'judicial deference' to slide into 'judicial subservience'. Evans (1980, p. 457fn88) speaks of 'Curial deference to ministerial views ...'.

*The situation in the U.K. - The development of the national security 'trump'* [6]

*The Zamora* [1916] 2 AC 77 is the case in which judicial deference in matters of national security was supposedly initiated. It was in this case that Lord Parker of Waddington said:

> Those who are responsible for the national security must be the sole judge of what the national security requires. It would be obviously undesirable that such matters should be the subject of evidence in a court of law or otherwise discussed in public (p. 107).

The case, which the Crown lost, was a decision of the Privy Council sitting as a Prize Court and deciding a matter of international law. While Lord Parker's dictum has been relied on in later cases, there is a strong argument that it is relevant only to prize law and should not be used as the basis for any extended principle of judicial quarantine of national security issues (Forsyth, 1985; Lustgarten and Leigh, 1994).

Lord Parker's quote from *The Zamora* is repeated in *Chandler* v *D.P.P.* [1964] AC 763 (*Chandler*) in which the defendants (the appellants in the House of Lords) were charged under section 1 of the Official Secrets Act 1911. The appellants were members of the Committee of 100, formed to promote the aims of the Campaign for Nuclear Disarmament. They planned a demonstration with the objective of immobilising the Wethersfield Royal Air Force base in Essex which was then occupied by squadrons of the United States Air Force. The appeal was based on the trial judge's refusal to allow counsel for the defence to cross examine a prosecution witness, or to put the defendants' case that they were acting 'in the interests of the State'.

The House of Lords found that once a discretionary power was exercised by the Crown, in this case the deployment and operation of the armed forces, it became a policy issue. Thus in deciding how to interpret 'purposes prejudicial to the safety or interests of the State', the House of

Lords found that it was for the Crown (being the 'State') to give evidence as to what its interests were, and differing views of the 'interests of the State', such as those of the defendants, were irrelevant. Lord Devlin hedged this rather bald analysis with some provisos, saying that the Crown may exaggerate the extent of its interests and so it was the duty of the courts to prevent abuse of the prerogative in this way.

Thompson (1963) takes a very critical look at the House of Lords decision in *Chandler*. He is kindest to Lord Devlin, of whom he says in relation to the above comments: 'A personal reaction to this is like that of the football enthusiast who watches one of his side dribble through the opponents' defence and finally miss an open goal: one would have been less disappointed had there not been the original exciting run. For even Lord Devlin in the end enabled the Crown to have the decisive, though for him not the only, say in what the interests of the state were ...' (pp. 225-226). Even so, the decision in *Chandler* did not give trump status to issues of national security (Forsyth, 1985).

In a leap backwards, however, the House of Lords decision in the *GCHQ* case elevated government invocations of national security to trump status. GCHQ monitors electronic transmissions in and out of Britain for intelligence purposes, and is a branch of the civil service. The Prime Minister, as Minister for the Civil Service, issued an oral instruction in 1983, without consulting the relevant unions, prohibiting staff members at GCHQ from being members of national trade unions because industrial action, strikes, were not in the interests of national security. The unions sought judicial review of the instruction on the basis that there was a procedural obligation for the Minister to act fairly by consulting those affected as had been the practice in the past.

The unions were successful at first instance, but lost in the Court of Appeal and House of Lords. The question of national security was not raised until the case went to the Court of Appeal, after the government lost at first instance, giving 'rise to a widespread suspicion at the time that it was an exercise in *ex post facto* rationalization' (Lustgarten and Leigh, 1994, p. 331fn69). Much of the importance of the case has to do with judicial review of the prerogative. Previously the court would only look at whether or not the prerogative existed, and its extent, but, having established these factors, would not then look at the way in which it had been exercised. The *GCHQ* decision indicated that the test of reviewability would now depend on the content rather than the source, but did not make clear what content would be reviewable. Lord Roskill offered some enlightenment by saying what would *not* be reviewable:

Prerogative powers such as those relating to the making of treaties, the defence of the realm, the prerogative of mercy, the grant of honours, the dissolution of Parliament and the appointment of ministers as well as others are not, I think, susceptible to judicial review because their nature and subject matter are such as not to be amenable to the judicial process. The courts are not the place wherein to determine whether a treaty should be concluded or the armed forces disposed in a particular manner or Parliament dissolved on one date rather than another (p. 418).

Having found that, in certain circumstances, the prerogative would be reviewable, although Lord Roskill's list did not leave much, their Lordships turned to the facts of the instant case. In looking to balance the plaintiff's claim of the requirement for procedural fairness against the defendant's claim that she had acted in the interests of national security, the House of Lords found unanimously that the latter claim outweighed the former. As Forsyth (1985) sums it up:

This national security 'trump' appears to be a doctrine of general application and the only question for the court was one of evidence: had the Prime Minister established that this was in fact the reason for her acting without consultation (pp. 29-30) [*footnote omitted*].

Furthermore, Forsyth finds that the doctrine was not justified by either of the main cases relied on, *The Zamora* and *Chandler*. Lustgarten and Leigh (1994) say the *GCHQ* case was decided at a time when the Cold War affected political thinking to such an extent that it may even have permeated the collective subconscious of the Law Lords.

*The situation in the U.K. – 'public interest immunity'*

Public interest immunity is where the court is asked to consider restricting access to information during the pre-trial and trial stages of litigation on the basis that the interests of suppression outweigh the interests of disclosure. A claim for public interest immunity requires the court to balance the competing interests of suppression on the one hand and disclosure on the other. If successful such a claim restricts the evidence that would otherwise be available to the parties. There is no limit to the type of public interest to which such a claim may apply, and each case will require differing factors to be taken into account when the balancing process is carried out. Private litigants may claim public interest immunity, but it is usually associated with claims by the government. Government claims may be made in relation to a wide range of information, but the most obvious is high level information, such as Cabinet deliberations, policy advice, diplomatic relations and, of course, national security (Ligertwood, 1993; Aronson and Hunter, 1998).

In cases where the sensitive information is the subject of a breach of confidence or copyright action, the essence of the litigation is the information itself. Not all cases where there is a claim for public interest immunity are centred on the information itself; often the information is a peripheral factor, but is required as evidence to strengthen the position of one of the parties. Where the government is a plaintiff in a breach of confidence action a claim for public interest immunity is an additional tool in the quest for suppression.

*The situation in the U.K. - the evidence required*

The next issue that arises is the evidence required to persuade the court that the sensitive government information should be suppressed. This may be in order to claim public interest immunity, or in an application for an injunction, or during a trial.

In the U.K. there was a time, in 1942 at the height of the second world war, when the House of Lords accepted that an affidavit deposed by a Minister of the Crown was by itself sufficient evidence to give rise to a successful claim for public interest immunity. The judiciary would not question a claim of national security, or any other claim in favour of the government, that such a certificate may make (*Duncan* v *Cammell Laird & Co* [1942] AC 624). The decision was acceptable during wartime,[7] but these 'conclusive certificates' were subsequently used, and misused, by governments until the decision in *Conway* v *Rimmer* [1968] AC 910.

In *Conway* v *Rimmer*, a case relating not to national security but to the discovery of documents, the House of Lords decided that the certificate of a Minister would not necessarily be accepted without further investigation. The plaintiff was a former probationary police constable who required the documents in an action for malicious prosecution he had started against his superintendent. Lord Reid made a distinction between class claims and contents claims in cases where the Crown wishes certain documents to be suppressed:

> [E]ither because it would be against the public interest to disclose the contents of the particular document or documents in question, or because the document belongs to a class of documents which ought to be withheld, whether or not there is anything in the particular document in question disclosure of which would be against the public interest (p. 943).

The result was that their Lordships ordered that the documents 'should be produced but only for inspection in the first place in order to determine whether the facts discoverable by their production would be prejudicial or detrimental to the public welfare in any justifiable sense' (p. 980).

A contents claim is made on the basis that the information is secret and disclosure would harm the public interest, for example where the information relates to national security. The justification for the 'class category' is that the government, or other organisation claiming the immunity, cannot operate effectively if that particular class of information is disclosed. There is a presumption of secrecy for all documents within that class, although disclosure of individual documents may not harm the public interest. Cabinet documents are often cited in this context.

There may be little to distinguish a class claim from a contents claim, and certain documents may fall into both categories, but the effect is different. Contents claims ordinarily involve inspection of the documents by the court in order for the competing interests to be balanced. Class claims, on the other hand, give rise to different considerations. Since *Conway* v *Rimmer* class claims no longer provide automatic immunity, but the House of Lords remains reluctant, and unlikely, to order disclosure in class claims relating to government decision making at the highest levels. Where the lower levels of government are concerned the court may order inspection of the documents, as happened in *Conway* v *Rimmer*, to balance the competing interests (Ligertwood, 1993).

In *A-G* v *Jonathan Cape Ltd* [1976] 1 QB 752 Lord Widgery took a closer look at Cabinet documents in a case involving the publication of the memoirs of a former Cabinet Minister. The case was the first time in which the government had sought to restrain the disclosure of sensitive information by means of the civil action of breach of confidence. Lord Widgery said:

> [I]t seems to me that the degree of protection afforded to Cabinet papers and discussion cannot be determined by a single rule of thumb. Some secrets require a high standard of protection for a short time. Others require protection until a new political generation has taken over (p. 767).

The evidence to support non-disclosure, which included affidavits 'from a large number of leading politicians', was not sufficient to convince Lord Widgery that the Diaries should be suppressed. Instead he read volume one for himself before deciding that there was nothing in it to warrant continued restraint. It is of interest to note that while *Conway* v *Rimmer* was cited in argument by counsel for the Attorney-General and counsel for the *Sunday*

*Times*, the case was not referred to in Lord Widgery's judgment. His judgment, nonetheless, does appear to reflect the approach advocated by *Conway* v *Rimmer*.

In the *GCHQ* case the evidence relied on was provided in an affidavit by Sir Robert Armstrong (p. 422):

> To have entered such consultations would have served to bring out the vulnerability of areas of operations to those who had shown themselves ready to organise disruption and consultation with individual members of staff at GCHQ would have been impossible without involving the national unions.

This was sufficient to satisfy the House of Lords that national security was an issue. As has already been noted, the government success was due only to the national security reasons. Lustgarten and Leigh (1994) describe the standard as being 'a low one, made lower still by the inevitable difficulty of the other party in contradicting it' (p. 330) [*footnote omitted*].[8] Lee, Hanks and Morabito (1995) continue the criticism of the finding that the claim to national security was sufficiently established by the affidavit:

> [I]t would appear that the burden cast upon the Crown to justify a national security claim is really not an onerous one at all ... In constructing their role as one of determining whether the evidence supports the involvement of a national security interest, the courts may undermine such a role if they adopt a less than critical evaluation of the evidence (pp. 193-194).

It was an affidavit deposed by the ubiquitous Sir Robert Armstrong, the then Secretary to the Cabinet and leading Crown witness, that set out the national security concerns in the *Spycatcher* cases. The *Spycatcher* cases were, of course, about the suppression of documents, or a document, namely the book *Spycatcher*. The depositions in Sir Robert Armstrong's affidavit were relied on by the plaintiff, the Attorney-General, at all stages of the proceedings. The affidavit was not contested or cross examined (*A-G* v *Guardian Newspapers* [1987] 3 All ER 316). Clearly it was sufficient to satisfy the requirements for the imposition of the original injunctions and to sustain continued operation of the injunctions through a number of separate hearings in parallel proceedings until trial.

By the time *Spycatcher* came to trial, the publication of the information had destroyed the possibility of the breach of confidence action succeeding, at least against these third party defendants. In the House of Lords the specific issue of the evidence required to show the material should be suppressed in the interests of national security was not addressed by their Lordships. Lord Goff, while discussing freedom of speech under art 10 of the Convention for the Protection of Human Rights and Fundamental Freedoms, said the right would be limited in the interest of national security where there was a 'pressing social need'. He did not elaborate on the evidence that would be required to establish the 'pressing social need'.

*The situation in Australia - the national security 'trump'*

The *Zamora* principle ('Those who are responsible for the national security must be the sole judges of what the national security requires') at one time had the support of the High Court of Australia (*Commonwealth* v *Colonial Combing, Spinning and Weaving Co Ltd* (1922) 31 CLR 421). This approach has been questioned in more recent cases, and, in the High Court at least, there has been no ready acceptance of a national security trump. As far as the courts' ability to determine issues of national security, Mason J had the following to say in *Church of Scientology* v *Woodward* (1982) 154 CLR 25:

> It is one thing to say that security intelligence is not readily susceptible of judicial evaluation and assessment. It is another thing to say that the courts cannot determine whether intelligence is 'relevant to security' and whether communication of intelligence is 'for purposes relevant to security'. Courts constantly determine issues of relevance (p. 59-60).

Mason J recognised that determining 'relevance to security' is not without difficulties. One difficulty is that security is a 'fluctuating concept', and another is that a party attempting to establish that there is *no* connection with security in cases such as the present one will have a 'formidable task' (pp. 60-61). In *A* v *Hayden* (1984) 156 CLR 532 Gibbs CJ said:

> In *The Commonwealth* v. *Colonial, Combing, Spinning and Weaving Co. Ltd*, Isaacs J. said that the well-known dictum in *The Zamora*, that 'those who are responsible for the national security must be the sole judges of what the national security requires' is 'unquestionable law'. The statement would nowadays be regarded as too absolute. It does not mean that when the executive seeks a special privilege or immunity on grounds of national security the courts will defer without question to the judgment of the executive as to what the national security requires ... (pp. 548-549) [*footnotes omitted*].

*The situation in Australia – 'public interest immunity'*

The Australian courts, especially the High Court, have shown a far more investigative approach than the U.K. courts to government claims of public interest immunity, including claims for suppression of information relating to the highest level of government. The common law relating to public interest immunity has been affected to some extent by the *Evidence Act 1995* (Cth). Chapter 3 of the *Evidence Act 1995* (Cth) relates to the admissibility of evidence in proceedings. Section 130, which falls within chapter 3, applies to 'admitting into evidence information or a document that relates to matters of state', and is a virtual restatement of the common law with respect to public interest immunity. Section 130(4) sets out the circumstances where the information is taken to relate to matters of state, and these include, inter alia, 'if adducing it as evidence would ... prejudice the security, defence or international relation of Australia'. Section 130(5) lists matters which may be taken into account when the balancing process is being carried out, and these include, inter alia, 'the importance of the information of the document in the proceeding' and 'whether the substance of the information or document has already been published'. Part 3 of the Act gives the court a general discretion to exclude or limit the use of evidence. The common law covers those aspects of public interest immunity to which the Act does not apply.

*The situation in Australia – the evidence required*

In *Sankey* v *Whitlam* (1978) 142 CLR 1 the government wished to prevent certain documents from being produced or admitted in evidence in a case where a private citizen, Mr Sankey, alleged that the then Prime Minister, Mr Gough Whitlam, and three other members of the Federal Executive Council had each committed an offence against the *Crimes Act 1914* (Cth) and were involved in a conspiracy at common law.

The documents in question were not 'in any way concerned with the defence of the Commonwealth or with the conduct of the nation's foreign affairs' but were, however, 'very much concerned with the highest level of the executive government' (p. 51). The documents related to a meeting of the Executive Council, interdepartmental memoranda and documents, a memorandum from a senior official of the Treasury to the Treasurer, programmes submitted to the Loan Council by the Commonwealth, programmes approved by the Loan Council and minutes of the Loan Council. The government's claim for nondisclosure was based on a class claim.

Gibbs ACJ, having reviewed Lord Reid's examination of the principles of document disclosure in *Conway* v *Rimmer*, concluded that '[t]he fundamental principle is that documents may be withheld from disclosure only if, and to the extent, that the public interest renders it necessary'. This included 'cabinet documents and other papers concerned with policy decisions at a high level' (p. 41). Gibbs ACJ said that where an affidavit has been sworn claiming disclosure would be contrary to the public interest, it is essential for the documents to have been seen by the person making the claim. He added that the court had the power to inspect the documents privately to assist in the decision as to whether production should be ordered.

Mason J reiterated the view that it was for the court to determine what material should be produced, and if necessary the court should inspect the documents in order to make the decision. As for claims that the material should not be disclosed, regardless of age, because it fell within a certain class of document, such as cabinet papers, Mason J set out what would be required if he were to agree to such a claim:

> I have gained little assistance from the affidavits sworn by ministers and heads of departments in support of the objection to production. They have sought refuge in the amorphous statement that non-disclosure is necessary for the proper functioning of the Executive government and of the public service, without saying why disclosure would be detrimental to their functions, except for the reference to want of candour. Perhaps affidavits in this form were acceptable in the days when it was thought that the court should uphold an objection once made by the Crown through its appropriate representative. But they are plainly unacceptable now that the court is to resolve the issue for itself, after an inspection of the documents when that is thought to be appropriate. An affidavit claiming Crown privilege should state with precision the grounds on which it is contended that documents or information should not be disclosed so as to enable the court to evaluate the competing interests. The affidavits in this case fall far short of this standard and I must therefore look beyond them for the considerations which tend to support non-production (pp. 96-97).

Drawing a distinction between documents relating to important matters of policy and other policy matters, Mason J felt only the former should be granted protection from disclosure. Presumably 'important matters of policy' would include issues relating to national security.

Following examination of the documents by the court, the documents relating to a meeting of the Executive Council, inter-departmental memoranda and documents, and the memorandum from a senior official of the Treasury to the Treasurer were found not to be privileged from production. The programmes submitted to the Loan Council by the Commonwealth, programmes approved by the Loan Council and minutes of the Loan Council, were to be produced in part only.

Mason J had the opportunity to look again at issues relating to the nondisclosure of confidential government information in *Commonwealth* v *John Fairfax & Sons Ltd* (1980) 147 CLR 39, a case which has been considered earlier on in this book. The hearing was a motion to continue the interlocutory injunctions for which the Commonwealth government had successfully applied ex parte to Mason J. The injunctions restrained the material in question on the basis that disclosure would prejudice Australia's relations with other countries.

The Commonwealth argued its case for restraint on the alternate bases of a breach of section 79 of the *Crimes Act 1914* (Cth), breach of confidence and infringement of copyright. The first two grounds failed, but the government was successful in obtaining interlocutory injunctions based on copyright. As far as the evidence was concerned, '[t]he officers of the Commonwealth upon whose affidavits the injunctions were granted were cross-examined by Mason J' (p. 41), but because the proceedings were interlocutory some of the evidence was incomplete. The application under the *Crimes Act* was rejected, and the issue of national security was then discussed in connection with the breach of confidence action. From what Mason J said in his judgment it seems that he did not accept without question the evidence given on behalf of the government. He spoke as follows of Mr Pritchett, the Secretary of the Department of Defence, and Mr Henderson, the Secretary of the Department of Foreign Affairs:

> Mr Henderson has testified that publication of parts of the book would be detrimental to relations with foreign countries. He was not cross-examined on his opinion because this has been an interlocutory hearing. At a trial the soundness of his opinion would be strenuously contested.
>
> Mr. Pritchett did not state that the disclosure of any particular documents would be prejudicial to national defence. He said, however, that a number of documents in the book were Defence Department documents with a security classification ranging from 'TOP SECRET' downwards. According to the plaintiff's 'Protective Security Handbook', the classifications accorded to some of these documents indicate that disclosure would be prejudicial to national security. But in the absence of evidence from Mr. Pritchett, I am not prepared to assume that publication of any of the documents will now prejudice national security, except perhaps in the limited sense suggested by Mr Henderson, that publication might make

other countries less willing to provide information on a confidential basis (p. 53).

Because of the publication that had already taken place, Mason J found that the action for breach of confidence would fail. The suspicion shown by Mason J in his judgments in *Sankey* v *Whitlam* and *Commonwealth* v *John Fairfax & Sons Ltd* about the 'amorphous' statements offered in evidence on behalf of the government is to be preferred to deference. This approach is more likely to lead to a thorough investigation of the evidence which in turn protects the interests of the general public by weeding out the claims for suppression that do not genuinely relate to national security.

*Alister* v *The Queen* (1984) 154 CLR 404 concerned an appeal to the High Court from the NSW Supreme Court. Following a foiled bomb attack, the three appellants, Mr Paul Alister, Mr Anthony Dunn and Mr Timothy Anderson, who were members of the Ananda Marga organization, had been convicted of conspiracy to murder and Alister and Dunn were also convicted of attempted murder. Another person, Mr Richard Seary, had taken part in the activities but had informed the police in advance of the plot; the appellants believed Seary was working as an agent for the Special Branch of the NSW police and also for ASIO. The appellants claimed they had been framed by ASIO, and caused a subpoena to be issued against the Officer in Charge of ASIO requiring production of all files, notes and memoranda relating to the investigation of the Ananda Marga by Seary. The appellants did not know whether the documentary evidence requested, if indeed there was any such evidence available, would assist in their defence.

The subpoena had been set aside by the trial judge, Lee J. In deciding to set aside the subpoena Lee J at first ruled that he should read the documents before forming an opinion. However, after an overnight adjournment, during which time he considered *Conway* v *Rimmer* and *Sankey* v *Whitlam*, he changed his mind and decided to accept the affidavit of the Attorney-General (applying for the subpoena to be set aside) without more.

The appeal, based on the issue of the disallowed subpoena and also on the cross examination during the trial, was dismissed by the NSW Court of Criminal Appeal. In the High Court Gibbs CJ, Murphy and Brennan JJ found that the trial judge had erred, Wilson and Dawson JJ dissenting. Gibbs CJ referred to *Sankey* v *Whitlam* and discussed at length the two conflicting interests at stake when one party seeks production of documents and the other party claims that production is contrary to the public interest. He noted that an anterior question arose before the balancing exercise could take place, and that was, 'should the court look at the documents to assist it in answering these questions?' (p. 412).

Wilson and Dawson JJ gave a joint judgment. Their dissent was based not on the justiciability of the activities of ASIO, or of the ability of the court to examine the evidence that might result from the subpoena. For them the claim for discovery failed because the appellants were unable to show what, if any, admissible evidence would eventuate to assist the case for the defence. In coming to this conclusion Wilson and Dawson JJ said that the interests of national security 'raise issues of great importance, issues which will seldom be wholly within the competence of a court to evaluate' and the view of the responsible Minister as to what constituted national security would carry considerable weight (p. 435). Some of their comments indicate that they are not closing out the possibility of there ever being review of the evidence by the court for itself when national security was a factor, and there would be occasions, where there was more substance to the claim, when the court might view the documents for itself.

The court ordered ASIO to produce 'any documents which were supplied by Richard John Seary or which relate to any investigation made by him and which refer to the applicants or any of them or to the crimes of which they have been convicted' (p. 468). Following examination of the material produced as a result, Gibbs CJ, Wilson, Brennan and Dawson JJ found that there was nothing which would have assisted the appellants, and had the trial judge also examined it he would correctly have found it to be privileged. They therefore dismissed the appeal.

The *Spycatcher* litigation that took place in Australia has been examined in earlier chapters. Again it was the affidavits sworn by Sir Robert Armstrong that provided much of the evidence for the U.K. government's case. In addition Sir Robert Armstrong was cross examined at length. Street CJ, in the New South Wales Court of Appeal, said 'the assertion of damage to the British national security ... made by Sir Robert Armstrong in his affidavit ... was the subject of vigorous attack in cross-examination' (*A-G (U.K.)* v *Heinemann Publishers Australia Pty Ltd* (1987) 75 ALR 353, p. 371). This already seems to be different to the *Spycatcher* litigation in the U.K., where the original injunctions were granted on the strength of Sir Robert Armstrong's affidavit, and upon which he was apparently not cross-examined (*A-G* v *Guardian Newspapers* [1987] 3 All ER 316).

The U.K. government based its claim on the argument that the book belonged to a class of documents that should not be disclosed, and even during cross-examination Sir Robert Armstrong 'was not prepared to descend to specify particular parts of the contents of *Spycatcher* which attracted concern on behalf of the United Kingdom Government' (*A-G (U.K.)* v *Heinemann*

*Publishers Australia Pty Ltd* (1987) 75 ALR 353, p. 369). Despite this, Street CJ, finding for the U.K. government in a dissenting judgment, said the claim, which he characterised as an 'aggregated contents objection', managed to successfully 'run the gauntlet' of *Conway* v *Rimmer* (p. 369-370).

The judgments of Kirby P and McHugh JA were less enthusiastic about the claims of the two governments, both justices dismissing the appeals but for different reasons. Kirby P characterised the claim as an attempt to enforce public law of a foreign state and found the court had no jurisdiction to deal with the case. He did, however, discuss in some detail the issue of what would be required to convince the court that national security detriment was at stake.

After referring to the change in approach brought about by the decisions in *Conway* v *Rimmer* and *Sankey* v *Whitlam*, Kirby P commented: '[T]he courts neither in the United Kingdom nor in Australia have surrendered to unexaminable assertions of national security detriment made by or on behalf of the Government ... But it is sufficient to say that neither in national security nor in other claims by the Crown to withhold documents will the court accept a neutered role' (p. 420). He said that it might have been easier to understand the appellant's assertions of damage to national security in the present case had the claim been based on references to specific parts of the contents rather than a general class claim. After thoroughly analysing the claim made on behalf of the Australian government, Kirby P concluded that he could not give it the weight that the government did. McHugh J based his decision on different findings, and he did not look at the issue of the evidence supplied by the respective Governments relating to national security. The High Court dismissed the appeal of the A-G (U.K.) from the decision of the New South Wales Court of Appeal, also on different grounds, so did not look at this particular issue either.

The most recent judgment to look at what evidence would be required to persuade the court that national security interests would be damaged was that of Bryson J in *Commonwealth* v *John Fairfax Publications Pty Ltd, David Lague, Radio 2UE Sydney, Alan Jones and Australian Broadcasting Corporation* (15 May 1995) unreported: Supreme Court of New South Wales 2033/95.[9] The plaintiff's case was based on breach of confidence. The defendants were intending to raise the defence of iniquity, alleging that the plaintiff's officers had breached *Telecommunications (Interception) Act 1979* (Cth) and the *Diplomatic Privileges and Immunities Act 1967* (Cth) and in addition their conduct had been unlawful as they had trespassed on the Chinese Embassy premises.

In this hearing, one of a series that took place within a period of weeks, the plaintiff applied for an order that the defendants' Notice to Produce be set aside. The Notice to Produce related to certain documents (namely warrants, warrant requests and authorisations) permitting the activities of ASIO with respect to the alleged bugging of the Chinese Embassy in Canberra. When the proceedings initially commenced the plaintiff was successful in obtaining an injunction to restrain the defendants from publishing during the interlocutory period any information about the operation, and restrictions were imposed on the availability of information to the defendants.

Bryson J found the defendants had a legitimate forensic purpose for requiring the documents, so he dismissed the plaintiff's claim that the Notice to Produce was a fishing expedition and therefore an abuse of process. He said the documents should be produced, subject to the plaintiff's claim of public interest immunity on the basis that the documents should be withheld as disclosure would be prejudicial to national security. Bryson J then had to balance the competing public interest claims. The plaintiff's claim was for suppression on the grounds that publication was not in the public interest because of prejudice to national security. The defendants' claim was for production on the grounds of being able to prepare themselves fully for trial and the public interest in publication on matters of international relations and safety. The defendants' counsel agreed that the identities of those involved in the operation should not be disclosed.

The government's argument for continued suppression was based on affidavits from the Director-General of ASIS, the Deputy Director-General of ASIS, the then Attorney-General Mr Michael Lavarch, and the then Minister for Foreign Affairs (and Minister responsible for ASIS) Senator Gareth Evans. Bryson J did not look at the documents, finding the credentials of these deponents sufficient to obviate the requirement for him to assess the contents for himself:

> In my opinion I do not need to inspect the documents to accept that their production and disclosure to anyone would be seriously adverse to the public interest with respect to national security and also with respect to international relations. The subject matter and the nature of the documents show to a high degree of probability and even without looking at them that they have important implications for those matters, and I have before me verified statements by high public officers which show that they have considered the matter, and they expressed their views in firm and strong terms. In the case of the Deputy Director-General, his view is more fully reasoned that [sic] those of the Ministers, who adopt his view, and in the case of Senator Evans the witness expresses further cogent considerations. The Ministers have high responsibilities and are the persons in the best

position to voice an Executive objection and an Executive perception of public interest. The view of the Minister for Foreign Affairs on the effect which a disclosure would have on foreign affairs must be accorded great respect, while the Attorney General is himself the Minister who decided to issue the warrants: he must have seen the warrant requests and is in an extremely good position to form the views which he has expressed (pp. 7-8).[10]

Bryson J recognised the high value that must be placed in a democracy on the availability to the general public of information relating to public affairs, and commented that the matters of national security and diplomatic affairs in the instant case were of the most serious kind. However, mentioning a number of cases to which he had been referred,[11] he said that 'judicial expressions ... evaluate national security and international relations very highly'. Concluding that the balancing exercise was a difficult one, he upheld the government's claim for immunity.

> I find the balancing exercise a difficult one because of the strength of the considerations ranged on each side and the high values which must be attributed to them. It is not right to say that national security and international relationships are the sum of things which must be saved on a day of crisis today if the community life and the administration of civil justice within it are to continue; there is no threat of that order of acuteness, while civil justice is a very prominent part of the values which must be preserved. The impediment to the opportunity to defend the proceedings will be marked if the defendants do not have access to important documents close to the heart of the controversy. Still it is my judgment on the balance of the public interests that the claim for immunity must be upheld (p. 11).

The rather tentative approach of Bryson J appears to be a drawing back from some of the previous Australian decisions, and in particular from the more investigative approach espoused by the High Court in cases such as *Sankey* v *Whitlam,* and by individual judges such as Mason J in *Commonwealth* v *John Fairfax & Sons Ltd.*

This judgment, as with the previous hearings, was itself subject to a suppression order until 29 May 1995 by which time the media had defied the injunctions and published the story. Following the publication of the story in the electronic and print media, the plaintiff, the government, agreed to discontinue its action which would be doomed to failure as the confidential information was no longer secret. The original injunctions against the defendants were dissolved, and new injunctions put in place restraining a narrower range of conduct. In his judgment dated 26 June 1995,[12] following a directions hearing on 31 May 1995, Bryson J ordered that some of the affidavits, for example the affidavits of Senator Gareth Evans and the Deputy General-Director of ASIO, should be returned to the plaintiff's solicitor and remain the subject of suppression for reasons of national security and diplomatic relations. By then it would appear that Bryson had read the contents of some of the warrants, or those warrants at least which were annexed to an affidavit.

*The role of the courts in the U.K. and Australia - conclusion*

Hanks (1988) summarises the situation in Australia, at least as at 1988, as follows:

> Australian courts have also accorded primacy to 'national security' considerations, but have tended towards a more sceptical view of government assertions of the interest, generally insisting that such assertions are justiciable ...
> Australian decisions suggest a more robust approach, at least superficially, to government assertions of national security interests. But they share with the overseas decisions a superficial approach to the concept, and an uncritical adoption of an ill-defined justification for government action which would otherwise be without legal foundation (pp. 116-117).

Judges have a critical role in weighing up the various interests that come before the courts. When the government resorts to the legal system to suppress the type of information that might otherwise be subject to a D-Notice, it is judges who must diligently probe the claims of the government that the interests of national security are at stake. If necessary, judges should request access to the information rather than simply relying on the evidence in an affidavit. This is not to suggest that the courts should enter into the realm of assessing government policy. There are undoubtedly difficulties in engaging in an inspection of whether national security interests are genuinely involved without entering into policy areas, but judges should be able to identify the difference between the interests of national security and the covering up of other interests which have nothing whatever to do with national security. If the government objects to access to the information being granted to a judge in one of the lower courts, it can request a stay of proceedings and have the issue decided by the judiciary at the highest level (*Sankey* v *Whitlam*).

## Notes

1    Security Service Act 1989 (U.K.), s1(3); Intelligence Services Act 1994 (U.K.), s1(2)(a)(b) and s3(2)(a)(b). See also Lustgarten and Leigh (1994).

2    Cited in Lee, Hanks and Morabito (1995), p. 19.

3    These agencies also operate during wartime and some, notably the intelligence agencies, have direct connections with the military. It is outside the parameters of this book to identify all of these agencies; for a detailed list see Richelson and Ball (1990).

4    See also Lee (1989).

5    In both countries the legislation covering the security and intelligence agencies is relatively recent. For a fuller discussion of the development of Parliamentary scrutiny in both countries and a comparison with other jurisdictions, see Miller (1994).

6    National security 'trump' is an expression used by Schauer (1982, p. 197). See also Forsyth (1985), Hanks (1988), Lustgarten and Leigh (1994).

7    For a discussion on the production of documents by the Crown during that era, and a comparison with other jurisdictions, see Street (1951).

8    See also Drewry (1985).

9    The decision is also unavailable electronically.

10   The quote is copied directly from the text; the rather convoluted second sentence has been re-checked for accuracy in transposition.

11   Bryson made reference to *Church of Scientology* v *Woodward* (1982) 154 CLR 25, per Brennan J, p. 76; *Sankey* v *Whitlam* (1978) 142 CLR 1, per Gibbs ACJ, pp. 38-39 (referring to *Conway* v *Rimmer* [1968] AC 910, per Lord Reid, p. 940); *Australian National Airlines Commission* v *Commonwealth* (1975) 132 CLR 582, per Mason J, p. 591; *Sankey* v *Whitlam* (1978) 142 CLR 1, per Stephen J, p. 57; *Alister* v *The Queen* (1984) 154 CLR 404, per Wilson and Dawson JJ, pp. 435-436.

12   Hearing date: 31 May 1995. Delivered: 26 June 1995: Supreme Court (NSW) Equity Division 2033/95. Unreported but available electronically.

## References

*A* v *Hayden* (1984) 156 CLR 532, pp. 548-549, 564, 577-578.

*A-G (U.K.)* v *Heinemann Publishers Australia Pty Ltd* (1987) 75 ALR 353, pp. 369-371, 420.

*A-G* v *Guardian Newspapers (No. 2)* [1990] AC 109, p. 221.

*A-G* v *Guardian Newspapers* [1987] 3 All ER 316.

*A-G* v *Jonathan Cape Ltd* [1976] 1 QB 752, p. 767.

*Alister* v *The Queen* (1984) 154 CLR 404, pp. 412, 435-436, 468.

Arnheim, M. (1988), 'The Spy in the Ointment', *Solicitors Journal*, vol. 132(43), p. 1474.

Aronson, M. and Hunter J. (1998), *Litigation Evidence and Procedure*, Sydney.

*Australian National Airlines Commission* v *Commonwealth* (1975) 132 CLR 582, p. 591.

*Australian Security Intelligence Organisation Act 1979* (Cth), s4, s92.

*Australian Security Intelligence Organisation Amendment Act 1986* (Cth).

Author not identified (1976), 'National Security and the Amended Freedom of Information Act', *Yale Law Journal*, vol. 85, p. 401.

*Chandler* v *D.P.P.* [1964] AC 763, pp. 790, 807.

*Church of Scientology* v *Woodward* (1982) 154 CLR 25, pp. 59-61, 76.

*Commonwealth* v *Colonial Combing, Spinning and Weaving Co Ltd* (1922) 31 CLR 421.

*Commonwealth* v *John Fairfax & Sons Ltd* (1980) 147 CLR 39, pp. 41, 53.

*Commonwealth* v *John Fairfax Publications Pty Ltd, David Lague, Radio 2UE Sydney, Alan Jones and Australian Broadcasting Corporation*, unreported (15 May 1995) 2033/95, pp. 7-8, 11.

*Conway* v *Rimmer* [1968] AC 910, pp. 940, 943, 980.

*Council of Civil Service Unions* v *Minister for the Civil Service* [1985] 1 AC 374 , pp. 410, 412, 418, 422.

*Crimes Act 1914* (Cth), s79.

Dandeker, C. (1994), 'National Security and Democracy: The United Kingdom Experience', *Armed Forces and Society*, vol. 20 (3), pp. 355-356.

*Diplomatic Privileges and Immunities Act 1967* (Cth).

Drewry, G. (1985), 'The GCHQ Case - A Failure of Government Communications', *Parliamentary Affairs*, vol. 38, p. 371.

*Duncan* v *Cammell Laird & Co* [1942] AC 624.

Evans, G. (1984), 'National Security and civil liberties: the role of ASIO', *Australian Foreign Affairs Record*, vol. May, p. 451.

Evans, J. (1980), *de Smith's Judicial Review of Administrative Action*, London, p. 457fn88.

*Evidence Act 1995* (Cth), s130.

Forsyth, C. (1985), 'Judicial Review, The Royal Prerogative and National Security', *Northern Ireland Legal Quarterly*, vol. 36(1) Spring, pp. 29-30.

*GCHQ* case (see under *Council of Civil Service Unions* v *Minister for the Civil Service* [1985] 1 AC 374).

H. of R. Deb., col. 2339, 25 October 1977.

H.L. Deb., vol. 357, col. 947, 26 February 1975.

Hanks, P. (1988), 'National Security - A Political Concept', *Monash University Law Review*, vol. 14, pp. 116-117, 120-121, 133.

*Inspector-General of Intelligence and Security Act 1986* (Cth), s3, s4, s35.

Intelligence Services Act 1994 (U.K.), s1, s3, s10.

Lee, H. (1989), 'The Australian Security Intelligence Organisation - New Mechanisms for Accountability', *International and Comparative Law Quarterly*, vol.38, p. 890.

Lee, H., Hanks, P., and Morabito, V. (1995), *In the Name of National Security: the Legal Dimensions*, Sydney, pp. 19, 182, 193-194, 242.

Leigh, I. and Lustgarten, L. (1989), 'The Security Service Act', *Modern Law Review*, vol. 52, p. 801.

Lewis, N. (1990), 'Undemocratic Centralism and Neo-Corporatism', *Alberta Law Review*, vol. XXVIII No. 2, p. 540.

Ligertwood, A. (1993), *Australian Evidence*, Sydney.

Lustgarten, L., and Leigh, I. (1994), *In From the Cold: National Security and Parliamentary Democracy*, Oxford, pp. 3, 330, 331fn69, 442.

Miller, R. (1994), 'What Should Parliament Know?', in A. Bergin and R. Hall (eds), *Intelligence and Australian National Security*, Canberra.

*Office of National Assessments Act 1977* (Cth), s5.

Official Secrets Acts 1911, 1920, 1989 (U.K.).

Pincher, C. (1968), 'Press Freedom and National Security', *Journalism Today*, vol. Spring, p. 37.

Relyea, H. (1984), 'National Security and Freedom of Information', *Media Law and Practice*, vol. 5(3), p. 238.

Richelson, J., and Ball, D. (1990), *The Ties that Bind*, Sydney.

*Sankey* v *Whitlam* (1978) 142 CLR 1, pp. 38, 39, 41, 51, 57, 96, 97.

Schauer, F. (1982), *Free speech: a philosophical enquiry*, Cambridge, p. 197.

Security Service Act 1989 (U.K.), s1, s2.

Street, H. (1951), 'State Secrets - A Comparative Study', *Modern Law Review*, vol. 14(2), p. 121.

*Telecommunications (Interception) Act 1979* (Cth).

The Commission of Inquiry into the Australian Secret Intelligence Service (1995), *Report on the Australian Secret Intelligence Service*, Canberra, para. 3.29.

*The Zamora* [1916] 2 AC 77, p. 107.

Thompson, D. (1963), 'The Committee of 100 and the Official Secrets Act, 1911', *Public Law*, pp. 225-226.

*Washington Post*, Vol 131, No 7 (12 August 1984), p. 1 (cited in Lee, H., Hanks, P., and Morabito, V. (1995), *In the Name of National Security: the Legal Dimensions*, Sydney, p. 19).

www.dnotice.org.uk/faqs.htm

Zellick, G. (1985), 'Government Beyond Law', *Public Law*, p. 283.

# 10 Free Speech and National Security

## Introduction

Chapter 1 of the book looks at the three main philosophical arguments that may be used to justify a free speech principle. The purpose is to demonstrate that free speech is a legitimate interest to be weighed against the government's desire to restrict publication of confidential information on national security grounds. While Chapter 1 is couched in general terms, this chapter is more specific in that it examines the impact of both the D-Notice system and national security on free speech issues. These issues lie at the heart of whether the D-Notice system is a legitimate way of restricting speech in the interests of national security. These issues also lie at the heart of the extent to which the government may legislate to restrict speech in the interest of national security.

## The D-Notice system and the right to free speech

For Barendt (1996, p. 15), '[f]reedom of speech is primarily a liberty against the state'[1] and it is suppression of speech by the state that appears to be at the core of the three main theories formulated to justify a free speech principle. In accepting that freedom of speech is a right worthy of protection from interference by the state, it must also be recognised that it is not an absolute right and in some cases interference may be legitimate. The recognition that freedom of expression is not an absolute right is reflected in the relevant provisions of the International Covenant on Civil and Political Rights (ICCPR) and the European Convention on Human Rights (ECHR). ICCPR Art. 19(3): 'It may therefore be subject to certain restrictions, but these shall only be such as are provided by law and are necessary ... for the protection of national security ...'. ECHR Art. 10(2) allows restrictions 'as are prescribed by law and are necessary... in the interests of national security'.

One situation is where the interference relates to the protection of a private right rather than protection of the 'public interest'. Another situation where interference may be legitimate is where there is a distinction to be made in the kind of speech to be protected from interference. This is so even when the government is a party and the public interest is, prima facie, best served by openness. In other words there are certain types of speech that should be subject to some form of control because of the harm that may ensue from a lack of control. Speech on matters relating to national security is an example of speech that, if uncontrolled, may cause harm at the higher end of the scale. For this reason there is a possible justification for control and it is clear from the judgments examined later that the judiciary recognise that information pertaining to matters of national security may warrant different treatment to other types of government information.

## D-Notices as prior restraints on speech

There is a further distinction to be made with respect to the circumscription of the right to free speech, and this is to do with the form of the restraint rather than the content of the speech. While certain types of speech may legitimately be subject to control, the control is usually in the form of punishment that occurs after publication has taken place. Here there is the opportunity, in theory at least, for the information to be properly evaluated because it is available to the public. In the historic sense, 'censorship' meant the control took place before publication by a system of licensing, and thus the flow of information to the public at large was controlled. The act of publication without approval gave rise to an offence regardless of the content of the publication; the content itself might give rise to another offence (Schauer, 1982). In his *Areopagitica* Milton (1644) said licensing puts a book in the position of having 'to stand before a jury ere it be born to the world, and undergo yet in darkness the judgment of Radamanth and his colleagues, ere it can pass the ferry backward into light ...' (p. 14). For Milton and Blackstone (1765) prior restraints were wrong, but once publication had occurred any subsequent punishment did not offend their respective free speech principles.

A reason for finding prior restraints offensive is that the decision as to which material can or cannot be published lies in the hand of an administrative official who may not act objectively, and who may make political rather than legal decisions (Schauer, 1982). These decisions are made behind closed doors, 'on vague and imprecise standards, with no right of appeal and little effective judicial review' (Barendt, 1996, p. 118). Officials may also be over zealous as it is in their own interests to justify their existence by aggressively exercising their authority (Schauer, 1982).

On the other hand it may be argued that the distinction between prior restraint and subsequent punishment, 'based on the temporal aspects of the official action', cannot be justified (Schauer, 1982, p. 150). The deterrent effect of potential liability in civil or criminal law for the publication of material may act as an equally efficient censor as any licensing scheme (Schauer, 1982; Chafee, 1969). It may in fact be preferable to avoid the prospect of legal action by submitting material for clearance before publication, thus avoiding both the cost and consequences of a trial. This is an argument in favour of an arrangement such as the D-Notice system.

For Schauer (1982), much of the debate on the distinction between prior restraint and subsequent punishment focuses wrongly on the issue of timing; in his view fear of subsequent punishment may deter publication just as much as any prior restraint. Conversely anyone who feels strongly enough about something will publish in contravention of a prior restraint. He sees the fixation with timing as obscuring the real issue which is the 'identity and discretion of the restrainers' (p. 152). Barendt (1996) comments that this argument 'seems to underestimate the possible (perhaps likely) abuses of censorship systems' (p. 120fn21).

Schauer's writing is centred on the United States experience where free speech is guaranteed by the Constitution. There it would be difficult for a prior restraint to survive a challenge as to its constitutional validity, even when government secrets are the subject matter of the restraint (Barendt, 1996). In the U.K. until the Human Rights Act (1998) came into operation there was no similar constitutional protection of free speech, and sovereignty of parliament meant that prior restraints, censorship, would be far more likely to survive judicial scrutiny. In Australia the courts have dealt with free speech issues on a case by case basis. The situation in the U.K. and Australia is covered more fully later in this chapter.

According to Barendt, there are three factors to be taken into account when determining whether a prior restraint is reasonable. The first factor is how the censoring body is constituted and its procedure. For Barendt restraints put in place by a judge are 'generally more tolerable' than those put in place by an administrative body, 'but not so much as to justify the frequent refusal of the English courts to recognize an injunction prohibiting publication as a form of previous restraint' (p. 122). Barendt finds judges 'more tolerable' than administrative censors because the former 'should not suffer from the same degree of institutional bias' (p. 119). The second factor is the length of time for which the prior restraint is operative. The third factor is the content of the restrained material, which may need to be suppressed before publication as the only way of preventing harm, such as injunctions to prevent the disclosure of sensitive government information.

In *The Observer and the Guardian* v *U.K.* (1991) 14 EHRR 153 the European Court of Human Rights said that Article 10 of the European Convention of Human Rights, relating to freedom of expression:

> does not in terms prohibit the imposition of prior restraints on publication, as such ... On the other hand, the dangers inherent in prior restraints are such that they call for the most careful scrutiny on the part of the Court. This is especially so as far as the press is concerned, for news is a perishable commodity and to delay its publication, even for a short period, may well deprive it of all its value and interest (p. 191).

When applying Barendt's factors to the D-Notice system, the following may be observed. Two of the main characteristics of prior restraints are that publication does not take place and, as noted earlier, if publication without approval does take place it gives rise to an offence regardless of the content, which may be subject to a separate offence (or liability in civil law). Certainly the D-Notice system prevents material from being published, but representatives of the media themselves are able to assist in the formulation of what is included in each D-Notice, and to negotiate with the secretary of the D-Notice Committee on what may, or should not, be published in individual cases. Because the system is voluntary and extra legal, no offence is committed when material is published in defiance of a D-Notice, although subsequent liability for content may well arise in either the criminal or civil law. For these reasons the D-Notice system is not typical of a prior restraint. If, however, lack of publication is the essence of prior restraint, and it may well be so for the major criticism of prior restraints is that they prevent issues being opened up for debate by the public at large, then the D-Notice system is indeed a prior restraint. This is so regardless of how voluntary it is and how much the media itself participates in the self censorship.

> [N]o such system can be justified simply on the ground that it is convenient to, and preferred by, the publishers; otherwise the public interest in receiving information may be entirely ignored. From a constitutional point of view, a voluntary system of censorship accepted by the publishers is surely the very worst; no individual will have an opportunity to challenge it in the courts, and particular decisions are effectively insulated from judicial review ...
> A potential reader wishing to challenge decisions under such a system may be met by the arguments that he has no standing, and probably that in the absence of a legally binding decision, there is no justiciable issue for the court to determine ...(Barendt, 1996, pp. 135-136).

If the media is involved in censorship, the question must arise as to whether it can also claim to represent the 'public interest'. This issue will be examined in the next chapter. The uneasiness about the alliance between the government and the media is echoed by Chadwick (1995):

> Journalists gamble with their credibility when they collude with government to withhold information from the same people on whose behalf the media claims to be a watchdog, scrutinising government and holding it to account (p. 6).

These objections to the nature of the censorship body which decides on the material to be proscribed by the D-Notices are exacerbated by the second factor relating to the reasonableness of the prior restraint, that is, the length of time during which material is to be suppressed. In some instances it is legitimate for journalists to withhold information in the short term at the request of the authorities, but once the moment has passed the content, and the fact that it was suppressed, should be made public (Chadwick, 1995).[2]

With respect to the D-Notice system, the relevant material is not to be published for an indefinite period and some D-Notices seem to remain in perpetuity regardless of the content. An example of this is Australian D-Notice No 2, relating to the '*Whereabouts of Mr and Mrs Vladimir Petrov*'. D-Notice No 2 was last reconfirmed on 1st December 1982 and is included among the handbook entitled *Australian D-Notices*, the most recent edition of which was published in 1983 and which was still being sent out in 1996. Mr Petrov died in Melbourne in 1991 and while Mrs Petrov was still alive in 1995 (*The Sydney Morning Herald*, 27 May 1995), it is believed she has died since then. In September 1984, some thirty years after the Petrovs' defection, the *Truth* ran an article on Mr Petrov who was then seventy-seven, complete with a photo said to be a recent one, in direct contravention of the D-Notice. The next day *The Age* had a similar story also in direct contravention of the D-Notice. The story included the name of the geriatric hospital where Mr Petrov was believed to be a patient, and his reported alias, Sven Allyson (*The Age*, 24 September 1984). An official response was immediate. The executive secretary of the Defence Press and Broadcasting Committee said that publication of the information had been a deliberate breach of a D-Notice, and the matter would be raised at the next DPBC meeting (*The Age*, 25 September 1984).

To overcome the criticism of indefinite prohibition, the individual D- or DA-Notices should be subjected to regular review to ensure their subject matter has not become innocuous or so out of date as to bring the system into disrepute. Regular review does happen with the DA-Notice system in the U.K.

The third factor relating to reasonableness, that of content, is the only one that favours the D-Notice system, because the subject matter of the D-Notices relates to issues of national security. Information relating to national security is one of the few types of information that it may be legitimate to restrain on the basis that the harm done by disclosure outweighs the harm done by restraint (Barendt, 1996; Cowen, 1984; ICCPR).[3] With respect to the D-Notice system this of course makes the assumption that the media participants agree not to publish only that information genuinely relating to national security. There is always the danger that editors may be bluffed into withholding other material which the government wants restrained for different reasons, or that the atmosphere of cooperation engendered by the system may result in an agreement to restrain such information.

Given that the D-Notice system fails two of the three factors put forward by Barendt for determining the reasonableness of a prior restraint, it may be argued that there must be more appropriate ways to restrain publication relating to national security. Campbell and Whitmore (1975) make the additional point that the secrecy surrounding the early days of the D-Notice system is not helpful to its reputation:

> Perhaps the most unsatisfactory aspect of this particular exercise in security censorship is that it existed for so long without the general public being informed of its existence. Both the Government and the press were at fault. It is the ultimate in censorship to conceal the very existence of a system of censorship however informal it might be (p. 333).

A final noteworthy point in the context of prior restraints of speech. When the governments in either the U.K. or Australia have turned to the law to prevent publication of information that might also be subject to a D-Notice, injunctions have provided the necessary means of restraint. By framing an action in breach of confidence, the government is able to obtain an injunction to suppress the information pending the trial of the issues. This type of prior restraint may well sit better within the three factors to determine reasonableness than the D-Notice system. The censoring body is a judge, or judges, who will act objectively without self-interest. The suppression is not indefinite as the injunction is only in place until the trial or a fixed date, and the judge must be satisfied that content relates to national security or otherwise warrants suppression. It is also possible to appeal the decision. The interlocutory stages of the *Spycatcher* litigation are a good example. In the

House of Lords two of the three majority judges who were in favour of continuing the interlocutory injunctions until trial made much of the fact that it was not for an indefinite period (*A-G* v *Guardian Newspapers* [1987] 3 All ER 316).

A criticism of the procedure itself is that once an injunction is granted, a breach of the injunction may lead to an action for contempt of court, resulting in a complete shift in direction and emphasis away from the original issues. In addition the decision in *A-G* v *Newspaper Publishing* [1987] 3 All ER 276[4] effectively made such an interlocutory injunction, initially obtained against one newspaper, 'contra mundum'. This is a very unreasonable prior restraint (Robertson and Nicol, 1990).

## National security and the right to free speech

Where there is no recognised 'constitutional' right to freedom of speech, it may be viewed as a comparative lightweight in any judicial, or even legislative or executive, balancing process made between the interests of free speech and the interests of national security.

Dicey (1945) said, '[a]s every lawyer knows, the phrases "freedom of discussion" or "liberty of the press" are rarely found in part of the statute-book nor among the maxims of the common law. As terms of art they are indeed quite unknown to our courts' (p. 239). Following a review of defamation, sedition and blasphemy, he remarked, '[f]reedom of discussion is, then, in England little else than the right to write or say anything which a jury, consisting of twelve shopkeepers, think it expedient should be said or written' (p. 246).

Dicey's comments remain apt today, certainly as far as Australia is concerned. It is only very recently that the U.K. has incorporated the European Convention of Human Rights into domestic law so the full ramifications of that incorporation are yet to be seen. Australia has no domestic law protecting the right to free speech as a general proposition; it exists only when not limited by some legal constraint, for example defamation, copyright or breach of confidence (Cowen, 1984; Neville Brown, 1977).[5] Defamation, breach of confidence and copyright are private law rights, and publication is more likely to be restrained as there is no third party, or 'public' interest in publication. In both countries, however, serious judicial consideration of freedom of speech has become more likely in cases where restraints on publication are being sought, even in defamation, copyright and breach of confidence actions.

*The situation in the U.K.*

The U.K. played a major role in the drafting of the European Convention on Human Rights (ECHR) after the Second World War. The U.K. was one of the first countries to sign the ECHR and in March 1951 was the first country to ratify the ECHR. In 1966 the U.K. accepted that an individual, rather than other States only, had standing to bring an action (Cm 3782). It was not until November 1998, however, that the U.K. incorporated the ECHR into domestic law, by way of the Human Rights Act (1998) (the Act), as part of the Blair Labour government's pledge to modernise British politics (Cm 3782). The Act became operational in Scotland in July 1999 and in England on 2 October 2000.

Section 3(1) of the Act provides: 'So far as it is possible to do, primary legislation and subordinate legislation must be read and given effect in a way which is compatible with the Convention rights.' Section 4 of the Act provides that a court may make a declaration of incompatibility if the provision is incompatible with a Convention right. Section 6 says '[i]t is unlawful for a public authority to act in a way which is incompatible with a Convention right', and defines 'public authority' as including a court or tribunal and 'any person certain of whose functions are functions of a public nature', but excluding either House of Parliament or anyone exercising functions connected with proceedings in Parliament. Section 7 deals with standing for s6 proceedings, limiting it to a person who is (or would be) a victim of the unlawful act. Nothing in the Act creates a criminal offence, and a court may grant 'such relief or remedy, or make such order, within its powers as it considers just and appropriate' (s8(1)). Damages may be awarded in some circumstances. Ministers in charge of a Bill before either House of Parliament must make a statement in writing to the effect that the provisions are compatible with Convention rights (s19).

Declarations of incompatibility will not alter the legality of primary legislation, and as a result the government somehow hopes to preserve parliamentary sovereignty. A declaration of incompatibility will, however, 'have the effect of putting the issues squarely to the Government and Parliament for further consideration' (Cm 3782, para. 2.17). The courts are empowered to strike down subordinate legislation, providing the primary legislation does not prevent removal of the incompatibility (Human Rights Act (1998); Cm 3782). For reasons of parliamentary sovereignty the Act is not entrenched, and can be repealed or amended in the same way as any other Act (Cm 3782).

On 24 July 1997 *The Times* reported a speech made the evening before by the Lord Chancellor, Lord Irvine of Lairg, at the judges' annual dinner. The Lord Chancellor 'proposed a new partnership between judges and ministers to give the judiciary an opportunity to contribute to government policymaking on the justice system and end tensions between them'. In what appears to be a desire to make possible the impossible, he said:

> What is critical is that the form of incorporation (of the European Convention) sits comfortably with our United Kingdom institutions. It must not disturb the supremacy of Parliament.
> It must not put the judges in a position where they are seen as at odds with Parliament. That would be a recipe for conflict and mutual recrimination (*The Times*, 24 July 1997, internet version).

The Articles of the ECHR are set out in Schedule 1 of the Act. Article 10 reads:

> 1. Everyone has the right to freedom of expression. This right shall include freedom to hold opinions and to receive and impart information and ideas without interference by public authority regardless of frontiers ...
> 2. The exercise of these freedoms, since it carries with it duties and responsibilities, may be subject to such formalities, conditions, restrictions or penalties as are prescribed by law and are necessary in a democratic society, in the interests of national security, territorial integrity or public safety, for the prevention of disorder or crime, for the protection of health or morals, for the protection of the reputation or rights of others, for preventing the disclosure of information received in confidence, or for maintaining the authority and impartiality of the judiciary.

The margin note for s12 of the Human Rights Act is 'Freedom of expression'. Section 12 reads:

> 12. (1) This section applies if a court is considering whether to grant any relief which, if granted, might affect the exercise of the Convention right to freedom of expression.
> (2) If the person against whom the application for relief is made ('the respondent') is neither present nor represented, no such relief is to be granted unless the court is satisfied-
> > (a) that the applicant has taken all practicable steps to notify the respondent ; or
> > (b) that there are compelling reasons why the respondent should not be notified.

(3) No such relief is to be granted so as to restrain publication before trial unless the court is satisfied that the applicant is likely to establish that publication should not be allowed.

(4) The court must have particular regard to the importance of the Convention right to freedom of expression and, where the proceedings relate to material which the respondent claims, or which appears to the court, to be journalistic, literary or artistic material (or to conduct connected with such material), to-

    (a) the extent to which-

        (i) the material has, or is about to, become available to the public; or

        (ii) it is, or would be, in the public interest for the material to be published;

    (b) any relevant privacy code

(5) In this section-

'court' includes a tribunal; and

'relief' includes any remedy or order (other than in criminal proceedings).

This provision is of particular relevance to any application by the government for an interlocutory injunction, based on an action for breach of confidence, to restrain prior to publication what is alleged to be confidential government information. The provision makes express reference to journalistic material, and if the application is ex parte it will be interesting to see whether national security interests provide 'compelling reasons' why the respondent should not be notified. The government may rely on the national security trump to argue that the nature of the information requires that the hearing be conducted with speed and, more importantly, secrecy.

Prior to the passing of the Act the ECHR conferred no direct rights on a party and the U.K. courts were not obliged to take the ECHR into account when deciding the issues before them (*Malone* v *Metropolitan Police Commissioner* [1979] 2 All ER 620). While this factor limited the relevance of the ECHR to the courts in the U.K., the ECHR did nonetheless impact on the legal system in two different ways. Firstly a party who had exhausted all possible remedies in the U.K. was able to petition the European Commission on Human Rights. The Commission decided if the petition was admissible and, if it was admissible, then decided if there had been a breach of the ECHR. If the Commission decided there had been a breach, the case was then referred to the European Court of Human Rights in Strasbourg for a final decision. State parties to the ECHR agree to be bound by the Court's decisions even though it has no power to enforce them. The second way in which the ECHR impacted on the legal system was that in the case of an ambiguous local statute, the court should interpret the statute in a way not inconsistent with the ECHR. An examination of how this worked in practice may indicate the approach of the courts to ECHR rights, in particular the right to freedom of expression, following the passing of the Human Rights Act.

Lustgarten and Leigh (1994) are of the view that the European Court of Human Rights has itself limited the usefulness of the ECHR by its interpretation of the restrictions which may, under the terms of the ECHR, legitimately derogate from the designated rights. One of the restrictions listed in 10(2), in fact the first one listed, is 'national security':

> The concern is to see that the member state has acted within its 'margin of appreciation' and only where it is beyond the bounds of this discretion, or where the restriction lacks a legal basis at all, will it be found to be in breach of the Convention. This is a direct international counterpart to the judicial reluctance to interfere with subjective exercises of executive discretion at the national level. Not surprisingly, in view of the fundamental state interests at stake, the national security margin of appreciation has been liberally construed ... Where the United Kingdom *has* been found to violate the Convention, it is because of the absence of a legal basis for the purported power and not the substance of its use - the obvious implication is that the defect may be simply remedied by wide discretionary legislation ... (Lustgarten and Leigh, 1994, pp. 344-345).

Whereas 'proportionality' has been an issue, and a ground of review, when the effects of the other types of restriction have been in dispute before the European Court of Human Rights,[6] the principle does not seem to have been applied consistently to cases where the state is claiming a restriction based on national security. Proportionality means that the restriction, or derogation from the right, should be no more extensive than is necessary to achieve the aim, that is, it should be proportionate to the objective. Neither is there any definition of national security by which to measure the state's actions.[7]

In the *Spycatcher* series of cases the relevance of the ECHR was considered in the U.K. courts. The newspapers also successfully petitioned the European Court of Human Rights following the loss in the House of Lords in round one when the interlocutory injunctions were continued (*The Observer and the Guardian* v *U.K.* (1991) 14 EHRR 153; *Sunday Times* v *U.K. (No. 2), Guardian* v *U.K.* (1991) 14 EHRR 229). The time lapse between the House of Lords decision being handed down, in 1987, to the European Court hearing in 1991, illustrates another criticism of the procedure and that is the prolonged period of litigation (Cm 3782), especially in cases such as

*Spycatcher* where disclosure of information is concerned. At the end of four or five years much, if not all, of the subject matter of the action will have become public knowledge perhaps of historic interest only, and it will certainly have lost its newsworthiness. For a government intent on hiding information under the mantle of national security when in reality the disclosure would only be prejudicial to the government in a political sense, it allows scope for other burning issues to take precedence, such as, for example, a Falklands or Gulf War. As it happened in *Spycatcher* the injunctions were lifted by the House of Lords at the trial in 1988, so for the media it was a triumph of principle only.

It is of interest to see how the various judgments in the *Spycatcher* interlocutory proceedings dealt with the ECHR, because, despite the fact that the U.K. courts were not at the time obliged to take the Convention into account, in this case the House of Lords did just that. The judgments may give some indication of how the incorporation of the ECHR into domestic law will affect cases relating to the opposing interests of free speech and national security.

Lord Bridge, dissenting, commented that until he read the decisions of the majority he had not seen any need to adopt the Convention into U.K. law because he 'had confidence in the capacity of the common law to safeguard the fundamental freedoms essential to a free society including the right to freedom of speech which is specifically safeguarded by art 10 of the convention' (*A-G v Guardian Newspapers* [1987] 3 All ER 316, p. 346). Lord Bridge commented, somewhat presciently, that if the government persisted in its attempts at suppression, 'they will face inevitable condemnation and humiliation by the European Court of Human Rights in Strasbourg' (p. 347). Lord Brandon, in the majority, saw the exception of national security provided for by art 10(2) as overriding the public right to freedom which 'cannot, even in a democratic country such as the United Kingdom, be absolute' (p. 348).

Lord Templeman, in the majority, found the restraints imposed by the injunctions satisfied the tests of the Convention for three reasons. First: '[O]nce mass circulation takes place ... then members of the security service will be liable to be harassed with accusations to which they cannot respond.' Second: 'If the injunctions are discharged it must follow that any disgruntled public servant or holder of secret or confidential information relating to the security service can achieve mass circulation in this country of damaging truths and falsehoods by the device of prior publication anywhere else abroad.' Third:

> All the newspapers reports between 27 April and 14 July 1987 were contrary to the object and purpose of the Millet injunctions ... and were

intended to bring pressure on the English courts to allow *Spycatcher* to be published here. The Millet injunctions cannot now be discharged without surrendering to the press an untrammelled, arbitrary and irresponsible power to evade an order of the court designed for the safety of the realm to protect the confidentiality of information obtained by a member of the secret service' (pp. 356-357).

Lord Ackner, in the majority, approved what Lord Templeman had said on this issue, and found that because the injunctions in place were temporary only and the government had a good case for permanent injunctions, the Convention would not be of help to the newspapers. Lord Oliver, dissenting, said nothing directly about the convention, but found, like Lord Bridge, that because so much publication had already taken place, further restraint was unacceptable.

The newspapers' petition to the European Commission on Human Rights ultimately resulted in the finding by the European Court of Human Rights that, once *Spycatcher* had been published in the United States, the claim of national security interests by the Government to support the continuation of the injunctions was unsustainable (*The Observer and the Guardian* v *U.K.* (1991) 14 EHRR 153; *Sunday Times* v *U.K. (No. 2)*, *Guardian* v *U.K.* (1991) 14 EHRR 229).[8] The majority judgment in *The Observer and the Guardian* v *U.K.* (1991) discussed issues of proportionality and national security, but there was no attempt to define 'national security', except perhaps to accept the argument of the Attorney-General that it was 'secret'. The Court found that prior to publication of *Spycatcher* in the U.S.A. the restraint was legitimate. After publication in the U.S.A. the restraint was not legitimate because the material was no longer secret. As a consequence it is tempting to wonder if the Court accepted that the material related to national security interests simply because the government claimed it was secret. Several partly dissenting judgments, whilst agreeing that the second period violated Article 10, found the first period of restraint also violated Article 10.

The *Sunday Times* v *U.K. (No. 2)*, *Guardian* v *U.K.* (1991) case was decided in very similar terms to the majority opinion in *The Observer and the Guardian* v *U.K* (1991). This was the first time a state's claim of national security had been rejected by the European Court (Lustgarten and Leigh (1994). Indeed subsequent to their loss in the House of Lords in the *GCHQ* case (*Council of Civil Service Unions* v *Minister for the Civil Service* [1985] 1 AC 374), the trade unions were unsuccessful in their petition to the European Commission on Human Rights. They did not even get past first base because the government's 'nationality security trump' worked at that level also.

More recent cases in the U.K., not involving national security interests, have shown that freedom of speech has become an important factor in the outcome. In *Derbyshire County Council* v *Times Newspapers Ltd* [1993] AC 534 the House of Lords, upholding the decision of the Court of Appeal, found that a local authority should not be allowed to sue for libel as it was 'contrary to the public interest because to admit such actions would place an undesirable fetter on freedom of speech' (p. 549). Where the Court of Appeal had relied on art. 10 of the ECHR, the House of Lords simply relied on the common law to reach the same decision.

Hoffman LJ said in *R* v *Central Independent Television* [1994] 3 All ER 641: 'It cannot be too strongly emphasised that outside the established exceptions ... there is no question of balancing freedom of speech against other interests. It is a trump card that always wins' (p. 652).[9] In the previous paragraph of his judgment, however, Hoffmann LJ had listed the exceptions in Art. 10(2) of the European Convention, which include national security.

*Conclusion - U.K.*

Even following incorporation of the ECHR into U.K. domestic law via the Human Rights Act one can only speculate as to whether a claim of national security interests by the government would still out-trump freedom of speech.

*The situation in Australia*

Free speech as a distinct right is not protected by any domestic law in Australia. Even so, the judiciary has taken the interests of free speech into account in a number of cases.[10] The notion that there are implied rights in the Constitution was put forward in the High Court judgments of Murphy J from 1976 to 1986,[11] but at that stage Murphy J was the only High Court justice to formulate judgments using this approach.

A series of High Court cases decided in the 1990s, starting with *Nationwide News* v *Wills* (1992) 177 CLR 1 (*Nationwide News*) and *Australian Capital Television Pty Ltd* v *Commonwealth* (1992) 177 CLR 106 (*ACTV*), established the concept that within the Constitution there is, by implication, a guarantee of freedom of political discourse.[12] These cases were foreshadowed in 1988 by the decision in *Davis* v *Commonwealth* (1988) 166 CLR 79 (*Davis*). In *Davis* the plaintiffs challenged the validity of certain sections of the *Australian Bicentennial Authority Act 1980* (Cth) which allowed the Authority constituted by the Act to control the use of its symbol and certain expressions. The defendants demurred and succeeded in part, but not entirely, as part of one of the disputed sections, containing the expression '200 years', was found by the whole court to be invalid.

There was a wide divergence in the views of the High Court justices on these issues during the 1990s, and the analysis below is done on the basis of an examination of individual judgments. As it is likely that the views of new High Court justices will fall within the existing wide range of opinion, some conclusions may be drawn. Between 1995 and 1998 Mason CJ, Deane, Dawson, Toohey JJ and Brennan CJ[13] retired from the High Court and were replaced by Gummow, Kirby, Hayne, Callinan JJ and Gleeson CJ.

*Issues arising from the cases*

The relevant issues are those that may play a part in any High Court consideration of a case involving the suppression or publication of information that the government considers sensitive on national security grounds. Many of the concepts examined below are intertwined, so the divisions are to some extent artificial.

*1. Implied rights and freedoms in the Constitution*

During the 1990s there were a number of decisions that charted the ebb and flow of the finding of implied rights and freedoms in the Constitution. Most of these decisions related to an implied guarantee of freedom of political discourse, but some related to attempts to extend the findings of implied rights into other areas, such as equality of voting power. Only the former will be examined.

*(i) Cases developing the concept of an implied guarantee of freedom of political discourse* In *Nationwide News*, decided by the High Court in 1992, the applicant, *The Australian* newspaper, had published an article attacking the integrity of the Australian Industrial Relations Commission. Consequently an information was laid before the Federal Court by Wills, an officer of the Australian Federal Police, alleging that the applicant had breached section 299(1)(d)(ii) of the *Industrial Relations Act 1988* (Cth): 'a person shall not ... by writing or speech use words calculated ... to bring a member of the Commission or the Commission into disrepute'. The matter was referred to the Full Court of the High Court by way of case stated for consideration of whether the particular clause was *ultra vires* the legislative powers of the

Commonwealth Parliament and therefore invalid. The High Court struck down the clause, all seven justices finding it to be ultra vires and invalid, but for different reasons. For Mason CJ the clause failed on the issue of proportionality, and there was therefore no necessity to consider the argument based on the implied guarantee within the Constitution. Brennan J, on the other hand did consider the issue and found such a guarantee to exist.

Deane and Toohey JJ delivered a joint judgment. They said that the Constitution sets out a doctrine of representative government and within that was to be found 'an implication of freedom of communication of information and opinions about matters relating to the government of the Commonwealth'. For Deane and Toohey JJ this operated on two levels, the first being communication between 'the represented and their representatives' and the second being 'between the people of the Commonwealth' (pp. 73-74).

Dawson J thought that the concept of reasonable proportionality was of limited assistance; in his view the question to be asked was whether there was sufficient connection between the head of power and the measure in dispute. Once a sufficient connection is established the Court should not judge whether or not it is appropriate, that being a question for Parliament not the Court. Because the provision was too widely drawn for Dawson J to discern any connection between its provisions and conciliation and arbitration in industrial disputes, he found it to be invalid.

Gaudron J found the impugned section was not 'appropriate and adapted for the protection of the Commission and its proceedings', and agreed with the reasoning of both Mason CJ and McHugh J in coming to this conclusion (p. 95). McHugh J found the section was not reasonably incidental to the power given in the Constitution for the purposes of arbitration and conciliation because it went beyond what was reasonable and appropriate.

Only the judgments of Brennan, Deane and Toohey JJ made direct reference to an implied right to discussion of political matters. A number of the judgments made reference to Mason J's comments in *Commonwealth v John Fairfax & Sons Ltd* (1980) 147 CLR 39.

> It is unacceptable in our democratic society that there should be a restraint on the publication of information relating to government when the only vice of that information is that it enables the public to discuss, review and criticise government action (p. 52).[14]

The decision in *ACTV*[15] was handed down at the same time as *Nationwide News*. This second case involved the hearing of demurrers to the statements of claim of the plaintiffs seeking a declaration that Pt IIID of the

*Broadcasting Act 1942* (Cth) (the Act) was invalid. Pt IIID introduced a new Part into the Act purporting to regulate political advertising on radio and television. Schauer (1994) describes *ACTV* as 'in several ways an exemplary free speech controversy ... the case is highly typical of contemporary free speech disputes in using the principle of free speech to block what would otherwise appear to be a well intentioned action instituted in the service of public good ...' (p. 1). The plaintiffs' case was that the regulations restricted the discussion of public and political affairs, and the Commonwealth's response was that it was intended to reduce the pressure on political parties and candidates to raise money for the purpose of advertising.

The majority, Mason CJ, Deane, Toohey and Gaudron JJ, found Pt IIID to be invalid. Mason CJ based his judgment solely on the issue of an implied guarantee of freedom of communication in relation to public and political discussion because he saw that as overarching all the other issues argued by the parties. While acknowledging that the framers of the Constitution deliberately left citizens' rights in general to the protection of the common law, Mason CJ agreed with the plaintiffs' characterisation of the argument in the present case as being freedom of expression in relation to public and political affairs which was an essential concomitant of representative government as provided for in the Constitution. He also saw it as operating on two levels, between elected representatives and the electorate, and between members of the community, reflecting the approach of Deane and Toohey JJ in *Nationwide News*.

Deane and Toohey JJ in a joint judgment also reaffirmed their view that freedom of communication on matters relating to the government of the Commonwealth was implied in the Constitution as a result of the doctrine of representative government. For them any legislation impinging on the implication would be beyond the scope of the relevant grant of legislative power. The exception would be where:

> [I]t is justified as being in the public interest for the reason that the prohibitions and restrictions on political communications which it imposes are either conducive to the overall availability of the effective means of such communications or do not go beyond what is reasonably necessary for the preservation of an ordered and democratic society or for the protection or vindication of the legitimate claims of individuals to live peacefully and with dignity in such a society (p. 169) [*footnote omitted*].

Presumably prohibitions imposed on the grounds of national security interests would fall within the exception outlined.

Deane and Toohey were unmoved by the Commonwealth's claim that the public interest lay in removing the pressure for massive spending on advertising by political parties. This was because Part IIID prevented those parties not allocated free time (free time was to be allocated to parties already represented in Parliament) from using the most effective means of political communication, that is radio and television. They found the whole of Part IIID invalid, but like Mason CJ, their judgment hinted that more specific regulations might succeed.

Gaudron J said that freedom of discourse was an essential part of free elections, thus such a freedom must necessarily be implied in the Constitution. The implication is not without limits:

> Recourse to the general law reveals that freedom of speech (which, of course, is wider than freedom of political discourse) is not absolute, but may be regulated and, in certain circumstances, may be severely restricted. As the implied freedom is one that depends substantially on the general law, its limits are also marked out by the general law. Thus, in general terms, the laws which have developed to regulate speech, including the laws with respect to defamation, sedition, blasphemy, obscenity and offensive language, will indicate the kind of regulation that is consistent with the freedom of political discourse (p. 217).

For Gaudron J, if the Commonwealth is legislating under a head of power conferred by s51, and the legislation regulates political discourse, then, in order to be valid the regulation must be 'reasonably and appropriately adapted' to the end to be achieved. On examination, Gaudron J found the measures were not reasonable and appropriate, and so Part IIID was invalid.

In the minority, Brennan J found it to be partly invalid, McHugh J found it to be invalid except in relation to the Territories and Dawson J found it to be wholly valid. Brennan J reaffirmed his finding in *Nationwide News* that there exists within the Constitution an implied guarantee of freedom of discussion of political matters. Basing his judgment on whether the provisions of the Part were proportionate to the interest to be served, he found that all but two subsections, relating to the governments of the states, were valid. Saying it was, 'both simplistic and erroneous to regard any limitation on political advertising as offensive to the Constitution' (p. 159), the matter for him then became an exercise in deciding which sections of the disputed Part were 'appropriate and adapted' to their ends.

A review of these two cases (*Nationwide News* and *ACTV*) show that Dawson J was the only justice to reject outright the notion of implied rights in the Constitution, preferring instead a formalistic approach. The justices who did discern a guarantee of political discourse within the Constitution made it clear it was a limited right only; McHugh's definition was the narrowest, as he restricted the application of the implied right to 'federal elections' (*ACTV*, p. 227). For Brennan J a competing public interest might override the right, but for any legislative curtailment to be effective, the curtailment must be reasonably and appropriately adapted to the end to be achieved.

Two 1994 High Court cases, *Theophanous* v *Herald & Weekly Times* (1994) 182 CLR 104 (*Theophanous*) and *Stephens* v *West Australian Newspapers Ltd* (1994) 182 CLR 211 (*Stephens*) considered whether the implication of freedom of political discourse would extend to the civil law of defamation. The plaintiffs were Federal and state politicians respectively. The defendants claimed in their defence that the material was published pursuant to a freedom guaranteed by the Constitution. In *Theophanous* the allegedly defamatory material was contained in a letter to the editor, and in *Stephens* it was in a newspaper report repeating allegations about the plaintiffs made by another politician.

The question for the High Court in these two cases was whether the implication could make the transition from being a restriction on legislative and executive power, as decided in previous cases, to providing relief for a defendant in the civil action of defamation. A bare majority in both cases, Mason CJ, Toohey and Gaudron JJ who gave a joint judgment in both cases, and Deane J, found the implication would extend to defamation. For the remaining three justices, Brennan, Dawson and McHugh JJ, the Constitution did not contain any general guarantee of freedom of communication and in *Theophanous* that, for them, was an end to the matter. In *Stephens*, however, with its different fact situation, Brennan, Dawson and McHugh JJ, whilst finding for the plaintiffs, did suggest that the defence of qualified privilege might extend to such communications, providing that it was reasonable to believe that the source of the defamatory material was in possession of special knowledge.

*Lange* v *Australian Broadcasting Corporation* (1997) 189 CLR 520 (*Lange*), another defamation case involving a politician, albeit a member of the New Zealand Parliament, was decided in 1997 by a differently constituted High Court. Mason CJ and Deane J had been replaced by Gummow and Kirby JJ, with Sir Gerald Brennan now Chief Justice. The defendant relied on the decisions in *Theophanous* and *Stephens*. Because two of the majority in *Theophanous* and *Stephens* were not present in the instant case, the Court, having heard a large number of submissions regarding the correctness of these two decisions, decided to reconsider them. Brennan CJ, Dawson, Toohey, Gaudron, McHugh, Gummow and Kirby JJ handed down a unanimous joint decision, described by the then Australian Press Council chairman, Professor David Flint, as 'a very good decision, a very clever decision' (*The Australian*, 9 July 1997, p. 5).[16] The judgment dispensed with the 'constitutional defence', advocated in the previous two cases by Mason CJ, Deane, Toohey and Gaudron JJ, and developed instead a wider category of qualified privilege, as already proposed by Brennan J in *Stephens*, which would assist media defendants.

In the meanwhile other cases concerning the validity of legislation had been decided. In *Cunliffe* v *Commonwealth* (1994) 182 CLR 272 (*Cunliffe*)[17] the plaintiffs, two solicitors, unsuccessfully challenged the validity of Part 2A of the *Migration Act 1958* (Cth) which provided a regulatory scheme for the giving of immigration advice. The plaintiffs argued on the basis that the impugned sections of the Act did not have a direct connection with the subject of either s51(xix), 'Naturalization and aliens', or s51(xxvii), 'Immigration and emigration', of the Constitution. They argued further that the impugned sections infringed the implied guarantee of freedom of communication by being disproportionate to the ends to be achieved. Brennan, Dawson, Toohey and McHugh JJ found Part 2A to be wholly valid. Mason CJ, Deane and Gaudron JJ found certain sections to be invalid, because they infringed the implied guarantee of political discourse, but considered that these sections could be read down. Toohey J, in the majority, also found the implied guarantee to apply to the impugned provisions, but, for him, the provisions were valid because they were not disproportionate.

The plaintiff in *Langer* v *Commonwealth* (1996) 186 CLR 302 (*Langer*) unsuccessfully challenged the validity of s329A *Commonwealth Electoral Act 1918* (Cth) which makes it an offence to encourage an elector to fill in a ballot paper otherwise than in accordance with s240 of the Act. The plaintiff claimed that s329A denied Australian voters the right to freely choose their Parliamentary representatives, that it was beyond legislative power and it infringed the implied freedom of political discourse. Reference was made to the point that the plaintiff did not press the last argument, but it was still considered in the judgments. Brennan CJ, Toohey, Gaudron, McHugh and Gummow JJ found the section to be valid, Dawson J dissenting.

*Muldowney* v *State of South Australia* (1996) 186 CLR 352 (*Muldowney*) concerned a similar situation to *Langer*, but on a State level. The decision was handed down two months after the *Langer* decision. Consistent with the decision in *Langer*, the impugned provisions were found to be valid. In *Langer* Dawson J gave the only dissenting judgment, in *Muldowney* the decision was unanimous. For Dawson J the difference between the two provisions was that in *Langer* the legislation prevented advice on how to cast a *formal* vote, albeit not one in accordance with full preferential voting. In *Muldowney* the advice related to the casting of an *informal* vote. In the first case the vote still had value, in the second it did not.

The decision in *Levy* v *State of Victoria* (1997) 189 CLR 579 (*Levy*) was handed down in 1997 some three weeks after *Lange*. In *Levy* the plaintiff was charged with offences under regulation 5(1) of the Wildlife (Game) (Hunting Season) Regulations 1994 (Vict). For public safety reasons access to duck hunting areas during the hunting season is restricted to persons carrying a valid game licence. The plaintiff committed the offences when, without a valid game licence, he entered into a hunting area. The plaintiff's purpose was to protest against laws permitting duck hunting. The plaintiff then commenced a proceeding in the High Court for a declaration that the regulation was invalid. The plaintiff argued that it was invalid because, inter alia, it restricted political communication, that is, the ability to protest at the site, and thus infringed the implied freedoms contained in the Commonwealth and Victorian Constitutions. The defendants demurred. All seven justices found the regulation to be valid on the basis that it was reasonably appropriate and adapted to the protection of public safety. All, except Dawson J, spoke in terms of the implied guarantee. For the first time in one of his individual judgments, Dawson J's position on the implied guarantee was ambivalent, in that he referred to it without overtly denying its existence, although he based his own decision on the freedom being 'a residual freedom owing its existence to a restriction upon legislative power' (p. 607).

*Brown & Ors* v *Members of the Classification Review Board of the Office of Film and Literature Classification* (1998) 82 FCR 225 (*Brown*) was decided by the Federal Court in March 1998. On 11 December 1998 an application for special leave to appeal to the High Court was refused. The three presiding Federal Court judges unanimously dismissed an appeal by the editors of *Rabelais*, the student newspaper of the La Trobe University Student Representative Council. The appeal was against the decision of the Commonwealth Office of Film and Literature to refuse classification of the July 1995 edition because it contained an article detailing how to shoplift. The lack of classification effectively prohibited its distribution. One of the grounds of appeal was that the article was protected by the implied freedom of political discourse. French J found it 'arguable that in some aspects the article would fall within a broad understanding of political discussion' (p. 238). Heerey and Sundberg JJ found that the article did not fall within any understanding of political discussion and all three were agreed that the *National Classification Code* and the supporting provisions of the

*Classifications (Publications, Films and Computer Games) Act 1995* (Cth) were appropriate and adapted to a legitimate end.

*(ii) Some conclusions on the development of implied rights and freedoms in the Constitution*   There are two schools of thought on the development by the High Court of implied rights and freedoms in the Constitution. Douglas (1993) writing after the decision in *ACTV*, thinks there is a strong argument that any general guarantee of fundamental rights and freedoms is excluded, expressly and by implication, from the Constitution. The argument is based on the narrow scope of subject matters chosen by the founders for protection in the Constitution, and the 'issue was simply whether the courts should have a supervisory role over the Commonwealth Parliament in those matters' (p. 320). Douglas concludes that the 'greatest objection' to the *ACTV* decision is that the High Court 'unilaterally imposed' a significant change on the Australian people without there being any opportunity for public debate on the issue (p. 350). Creighton (1993) says much the same as Douglas, pointing out that a referendum on a proposal to prohibit laws restricting free speech was soundly defeated.

Bork (1971) says the following, albeit in the United States context but arguably it applies more generally:

> It follows that the choice of 'fundamental values' by the Court cannot be justified. Where constitutional materials do not clearly specify the value to be preferred, there is no principled way to prefer any claimed human value to any other. The judge must stick close to the text and the history, and their fair implications, and not construct new rights ...
>
> The reason is obvious. Every clash between a minority claiming freedom and a majority claiming power to regulate involves a choice between the gratifications of the two groups. When the Constitution has not spoken, the Court will be able to find no scale, other than its own preferences, upon which to weigh the respective claims to pleasure (pp. 8-9).

A judicial answer to this argument (not specifically to Bork's article), is given by Justice Toohey (1993) in a paper discussing the role of the courts in upholding the rule of law in the face of an increasingly powerful executive.

Barker (1995) commends the decisions in *Nationwide News* and *ACTV* in the context of the judiciary acting as a check on the abuse of executive power. As a result of *Nationwide News* and *ACTV*, Barker sees the High Court as demonstrating a willingness to play an important role in holding the executive government accountable for its actions, and this accountability in turn protects human rights in Australia.[18] The media enthusiastically welcomed the decisions finding an implied guarantee of free speech in the Constitution. *Nationwide News, ACTV, Theophanous* and *Stephens* were heralded with front page banner headlines such as 'High Court strikes down libel law/ Free speech breakthrough' (*The Australian Financial Review*, 13 October 1994, p. 1), 'Landmark ruling backs right to criticise politicians/ Court extends free speech' (*The Australian*, 13 October 1994, p. 1) and 'High Court rules for free speech' (*The West Australian*, 13 October 1994, p. 1).

Clearly some of the judgments in the earlier cases such as *Nationwide News* and *ACTV* gave rise to optimism that the implications recognised by the High Court would go further than merely the right to freedom of political discourse. However later cases that sought to test the limits of the implications, such as *McGinty* v *State of Western Australia* (1996) 186 CLR 140 (*McGinty*) and *Kruger* v *Commonwealth* (1997) 190 CLR 1 (*Kruger*) showed that the optimism was unfounded.[19] Indeed, the later cases also illustrate that even the implied guarantee of freedom of political discourse is not as expansive as may have been indicated by cases such as *Nationwide News, ACTV, Theophanous* and *Stephens.*

## 2. References to national security

There is little reference to national security in the cases relating to implied rights in the Australian Constitution. In *Davis, Nationwide News, ACTV* and *Theophanous* Brennan J commented how national security interests may limit freedom of speech:

> The circumstances which may affect the extent to which the freedom can be curtailed include the exigencies of defence or national security and the contemporary risk to other interests which are in need of protection (*Nationwide News*, p. 51).

In *Cunliffe* Gaudron J spoke of sedition as being 'an area in which discussion has traditionally been curtailed in the public interest' (p. 389). In *Kruger* she mentioned sedition as being an example of a 'pressing social need' which legitimately restricts speech (p. 128). From the comments of Brennan and Gaudron JJ it would seem that those restrictions on free speech that are based on the related public interest areas of national security and sedition are the type of restrictions that are more likely to be justifiable.

## 3. Government by the people versus parliamentary supremacy

The issue of government by the people versus parliamentary supremacy is closely connected with issues of proportionality, discussed immediately below. In the implied rights cases the judgments contained two, possibly three, approaches as to where power ultimately lies. It is worth noting at the outset that Dawson J throughout all the cases, with one exception, has clung steadfastly to the notion of parliamentary supremacy, that is, that power resides with the Parliament. The one exception was in *Lange* where the Full Court was straitjacketed into a joint judgment, but in the later case of *Kruger* Dawson J returned to his previous approach.

Deane and Toohey JJ, on the other hand, were of the view that 'all powers of government ultimately belong to, and are derived from, the governed' (*Nationwide News*, p. 70).[20] This was also the view of Mason CJ (*ACTV*). Describing this approach as 'a republican notion of representative government', Fitzgerald (1993) says:

> More than the rest of the Court, those three judges defined representative democracy as a system of government driven by and accountable to the people. It is fair to say they (literally) deconstructed Diceyan parliamentary sovereignty and in its place planted a republican thesis of government by the people[21] (p. 266).

The position of Brennan J, later CJ, is less clear. In *Nationwide News* he appeared to be of the same view as Mason CJ, Deane and Toohey JJ. In *Cunliffe*, however, he seemed more inclined to favour the approach of Dawson J, but this could have been in support of Dawson J's approach to characterisation and proportionality rather than Dawson J's approach to where power resides. McHugh took a similarly ambiguous position.

Kirby J made reference to the notion that sovereignty resides only in the people of Australia saying, without expressing a view either way, '[t]hat view is not without conceptual and historical difficulties[22]' (*Levy*, p. 634). The joint judgment handed down in *Lange* made the following reference to the issue:

> The Constitution displaced, or rendered inapplicable, the English common law doctrine of the general competence and unqualified supremacy of the legislature. It placed upon the federal judicature the responsibility of deciding the limits of the respective powers of State and Commonwealth governments (p. 564) [*footnote omitted*].

The High Court's decision as to where ultimate power resides is important to the question of the validity or otherwise of any legislation relating to national security issues. An example would be an amendment to the *Crimes Act 1914* (Cth) making secondary disclosure by the media of confidential government information an offence, as was mooted by the Keating Labor Government in 1995. If Parliament is supreme it can make any law, however draconian or secretive, with respect to a topic within a head of power without the High Court being able to strike it down. If, on the other hand, supremacy lies with the governed, the High Court may take into account factors such as proportionality when deciding on the constitutionality of such laws.

## 4. Characterisation and proportionality

Proportionality in this context means that the legislation should be no more extensive than is necessary to achieve the aim or objective. The application of proportionality is not necessarily limited to legislation and may also apply to the common law. Another phrase used instead of proportionality is 'appropriate and adapted' (*Cunliffe*, p. 321).

Where the validity of a Commonwealth law is the issue, a process of characterisation is required to determine whether the law falls within a head of power. In the cases examined above, one of the sharpest divisions of opinion in the judgments of the various justices was over the application of the concept of proportionality to the characterisation process. What follows is an overview of the main themes that emerge from the different approaches.

*(i) The narrow view* Dawson J's approach is the least complicated and gives proportionality the narrowest scope. In accordance with his view that Parliament is supreme, Dawson J considered, at least until the decision in *Lange* (the joint judgment in *Lange* contained some views not previously, or subsequently, ascribed to Dawson J) that proportionality is not relevant to the assessment of the validity of legislation unless the head of power is purposive. Purposive powers are those powers in the Constitution that involve a legislative 'purpose' rather than a 'subject matter', for example s51(vi), 'the defence power', is generally accepted as being a purposive power.[23]

If it is not a purposive power, then for Dawson J the only question is whether the legislation has a sufficient connection with the head of power:

> Establishing the requisite connection is often a matter of degree, but once it is established, it does not matter that the legislature has chosen a means of achieving its aim which goes further than is necessary or desirable. That is

a matter for the legislature (*Leask* v *Commonwealth* (1996) 187 CLR 579, p. 602 (*Leask*)).

With this approach characterisation of non-purposive powers is simply a matter of sufficient connection. Where the power is purposive, the additional test of proportionality may be required to test whether the legislation is valid. Brennan J's approach was the same as that of Dawson J (*Cunliffe*). There were, however, some significant differences between the two in their interpretation as to what constitutes a purposive power. In *Cunliffe* Brennan J took s51 (xxix) 'external affairs' and s51 (xxxix) 'incidental powers' of the Constitution to be purposive powers; Dawson J in *Nationwide News* was of the opposite opinion. Gummow J, who came to the High Court in 1995 on the retirement of Sir Anthony Mason, stated clearly in *Leask* that proportionality had no role to play in the characterisation of a non-purposive power.

*(ii) The application of proportionality where the head of power is restricted by express or implied rights*    Brennan J was of the view that the test of proportionality also applied to cases where the power was restricted by constitutional limitation, express or implied, such as the implied guarantee of freedom of political discourse (*Nationwide News*). The difference between Brennan and Dawson JJ on this issue is that the latter found no guarantee of any right or freedom implied in the Constitution.[24] Both Brennan and Dawson JJ made reference more than once in their judgments to 'a margin of appreciation' in favour of the Parliament (*ACTV*; *Theophanous*; *Cunliffe*).

In joint judgments in *Nationwide News* and *ACTV*, Deane and Toohey JJ found proportionality relevant where the case concerned the validity of a law which constrained the implied freedom of communication and, as a result, held the respective legislative provisions invalid in both cases. In *Cunliffe* McHugh J said that proportionality was relevant in the characterisation of laws related to s92 of the Constitution. In *Levy* McHugh J said that proportionality applied to those laws constrained by a freedom implied in the constitution, as did Toohey and Gummow JJ.

The use of proportionality where the head of power is restricted by an implied right was given the endorsement of a single unanimous High Court decision in *Lange*:

> When a law of a State or federal Parliament or a Territory legislature is alleged to infringe the requirement of freedom of communication ... two questions must be answered before the validity of the law can be determined. First, does the law effectively burden freedom of

communication about government or political matters either in its terms, operation or effect? Second, if the law effectively burdens that freedom, is the law reasonably appropriate and adapted to serve a legitimate end the fulfilment of which is compatible with the maintenance of the constitutionally prescribed system of representative and responsible government ... If the first question is answered 'yes' and the second is answered 'no' the law is invalid (pp. 567-568) [*footnote omitted*].

*(iii) The application of proportionality to test sufficient connection with the head of power*   Brennan J said proportionality may also be used to test whether there is a sufficient connection with the head of power:

> In the context of a challenge to a law on the ground that its operation and effect do not reveal a sufficient connection to the subject of a head of power, proportionality is a concept used to ascertain whether an Act achieves an effect or purpose within power. So used, proportionality has nothing to say about the appropriateness, necessity or desirability of the law to achieve an effect or purpose or to attract the support of the power (*Leask*, p. 593) [*footnote omitted*].

McHugh J had a similar approach, saying that once there is a sufficient connection between the head of power and the legislation it is not for the court to interfere, but proportionality is relevant in determining if there is a connection (*Nationwide News*). Toohey was of the same opinion in *Leask*, and so was Kirby J, who came to the High Court in 1996 when Sir William Deane left. Kirby J meticulously set out the various approaches to assessing the constitutional validity of legislative provisions, including the application of proportionality. While he concluded it might sometimes be helpful in characterisation, it afforded no authority 'for judging the desirability of the law or the means employed by the law maker. Provided the law is within power, the means adopted will not ordinarily be a matter for the Court' (*Leask*, p. 636).

*(iv) The wider view*   Mason CJ, took the widest view of the applicability of proportionality to characterisation:

> [I]n characterizing a law as one with respect to a permitted head of power, a reasonable proportionality must exist between the designated object or purpose and the means selected by the law for achieving that object or purpose. The concept of reasonable proportionality is now an accepted test of validity on the issue of ultra vires (*Nationwide News*, p. 29).

From what Gaudron J said in *Nationwide News* it would appear that, for her, reasonable proportionality is a test both of connection and of validity. While Gaudron J's approach may fall a little short of Mason CJ's, it is still wider than most of the other High Court justices.

*(v) Summary*    Except perhaps for Dawson J who favoured the most conservative approach, the judgments discussed here show much common ground between the justices over the applicability of proportionality. For example all were agreed that it applied to purposive powers, although there was disagreement as to what constituted a purposive power. Most were agreed that proportionality applied to non-purposive powers where an implied freedom was involved. For all the talk about the wideness of application of proportionality in some of the judgments, in the event there was not much difference in the result because the cases involved implied freedoms and all the justices, except Dawson J, agreed that proportionality applied. The main difference between Mason CJ, Deane, Gaudron and Toohey JJ, and the other High Court justices is that the former seemed prepared to be more generous in their interpretation of the limits of the implied guarantees in the Constitution. Thus, for them, proportionality had a greater role to play.

In the previous section the issue of where ultimate power lies was discussed. One criticism of the use of proportionality as a test of validity is that, in a sense, it gives ultimate power to the High Court (*Nationwide News*; *Cunliffe*; Fitzgerald, 1993; Lindell, 1994). Lee (1994, p. 127) asks: 'In the final analysis, is the concept merely a legal facade for judicial usurpation of parliamentary functions?' Lee's answer to this question is:

> [T]he allegation of a usurpation of the role of Parliament ignores the unstated assumption of the Australian constitutional order, namely, the Parliament, just like any other institutions of government, is subject to the rule of law (p. 148) [*footnote omitted*].

Any amendment to the *Crimes Act*, as mentioned under the previous heading (making secondary disclosure by the media of confidential government information an offence), would most likely be reliant for its validity on Constitution s51(vi), the defence power. Even the most 'orthodox' approach to purposive powers took the defence power to be a purposive power, so proportionality would apply in the characterisation process. Because the implied guarantee of political discussion would be an issue, proportionality would apply again on this basis. As the implied freedom is a constitutional guarantee, it should prevail over the amendment if the amendment survives the test of proportionality during the characterisation process. It would, however, be interesting to see whether the proportionality for the 'characterisation' of the amendment (that is, to determine if it is a law with respect to defence) becomes intertwined with the proportionality principle by reference to the implied freedom.

If, for some reason, some other head of power was relied upon in any challenge to the validity of such an amendment, the implied guarantee of freedom of political discourse would apply. It is arguable that a majority, at the very least, of the High Court justices would accept the application of proportionality in these circumstances. A challenge in the High Court to the constitutionality of such an amendment to the *Crimes Act* would raise some interesting issues. From the cases examined in this section it would seem that, for the provisions to be valid, the restriction on speech must be proportionate to the end to be achieved. However, the fact that the end to be achieved relates to the interests of national security may shift the balance towards validity. Even so, although the court may give the government a margin of appreciation because of the public interest in national security, proportionality remains an issue and will require the judiciary to take into account the public interest favouring disclosure.

## 5. The implied guarantee of freedom of political discourse (the guarantee)

There are a number of different issues that arise from the development of the implied guarantee of freedom of political discourse (the guarantee):

*(i) The application of the guarantee to the common law* The great majority of the cases in which the guarantee has been an issue have been cases involving the validity or otherwise of legislation, either at a Commonwealth or State level. The three common law cases in which the freedom has been discussed are the defamation cases of *Theophanous*, *Stephens* and *Lange*. As mentioned earlier, *Lange* clawed back the application of the freedom to the common law action of defamation from a 'constitutional defence' to a limited expansion of the defence of qualified privilege.

As far as issues of national security are concerned *Lange* is relevant as follows. *Lange* has probably squashed any potential that there may have been after *Theophanous* and *Stephens* for a media defendant in a breach of confidence action involving government information to claim a defence on the basis of an implication in the Constitution of the guarantee. Similarly it now seems unlikely that the guarantee would successfully be utilised in an argument by the media against the granting of an injunction to prevent publication of confidential government information. In *Commonwealth* v *John Fairfax Publications Pty Ltd, David Lague etc.* (31 May 1995, unreported), Bryson J had already reached his own conclusion on this issue, and the decision in *Lange*, some two years later, vindicates his approach:

> Interlocutory injunctions and procedural directions restricting access to evidence and diffusion of information are indispensably necessary for the exercise of jurisdiction to protect confidential information and to decide proceedings in which the existence of confidential information is alleged. This is so whether the Commonwealth or any other person is the plaintiff ...
>
> The events which have overtaken this case have furnished very full exemplification of the amplitude of freedom available. In my opinion there will be no breach of the implied guarantee if I continue the restrictions under Order 6 and the undertakings; what will take place will be an instance of the workings of a law, in no way an extraordinary law, in an ordered society.

*(ii) The guarantee as a restriction on legislative and executive power* Some of the judgments contain a mention of the extent of the application of the guarantee, that is, does it apply only to legislative power? In *Theophanous* Mason CJ, Toohey and Gaudron JJ say '[t]he decisions in *Nationwide News* and *Australian Capital Television* establish that the implied freedom is a restriction on legislative and executive power' (p. 125). The joint judgment of the Full Court in *Lange* takes this further by including not only Ministers and the public service, but also statutory authorities and public utilities which report to a Minister or to the legislature. This is relevant to national security information, as much of the decision making is done by the executive, by Ministers, or by the public service.

*(iii) The guarantee as a negative not a positive right* Following on from the previous point, the judgments make it plain that the guarantee is a negative right, a limitation on Commonwealth power, rather than a free standing private right (*Theophanous*; *Lange*).

*(iv) Direct or consequential effect of any restriction on the guarantee* The court is more likely to strike down those restrictions that directly affect ideas or information, rather than those restrictions where the effect is incidental (*ACTV*; *Langer*; *Levy*). The question arises as to whether a restriction relating to national security issues, such as an amendment to the *Crimes Act* as mentioned above, or even some litigated issue related to the D-Notice system,

would be characterised as having a direct or consequential effect on the guarantee. Would the prosecution of journalists for secondary disclosures under an amended *Crimes Act* be a law about political discourse or a law about national security with the restriction on political discourse an incidental by-product? Even if the restriction is found to have a direct effect, which is likely as the provisions would directly target ideas and information, it is possible that the competing public interest in national security may trump the guarantee.

## Conclusion - Australia

The difficulty for the media defendant is always going to be that the information allegedly relates to national security, and this alone may shift the balance in favour of the government and the suppression of the material. Whatever the approach during the 1990s of individual High Court justices to issues such as implied freedoms or guarantees, or to characterisation, it is clear that limits will apply to even the most generous interpretation of such implications. These limits are most likely to be cited as national security, which lies at the heart of this book.

If the government amends the *Crimes Act* to make secondary disclosure by the media of confidential government information an offence and the validity of the amendments is challenged, issues of proportionality will be critical. It may be the case that the limits of the guarantee are reached in the interests of national security and the legislation is found to be valid, however unreasonable and draconian its terms. This is unlikely as the implied guarantee of political discourse, sourced in the constitution, will be relevant. Because of this, the proportionality test will constrain the judiciary to take into account the public interest in free speech, that is, to limit the effect of the provisions to be no more restrictive than is necessary. Should the amendments be found to be valid and any media defendant tried for a secondary disclosure offence, the judiciary's role in assessing whether the information is genuinely sensitive for national security reasons is crucial in ensuring a just outcome.

After the decision in *Lange* it does not seem likely that the media defendant in a breach of confidence case can either prevent the granting of an injunction to suppress the material or mount a defence based on the implied guarantee. The role of the judiciary in ensuring that the competing interests are properly balanced will again be crucial.

## Notes

1    Macmillan Patfield (1996) comments in response: 'It is arguable that the State is not necessarily the repository of all power in society' (p. 206). It is, however, unnecessary to pursue this proposition here.

2    Chadwick (1995) gives the example of hostage crises. On the issue of withholding information until the danger passes, Newman (1984) says: 'Perhaps the most outstanding examples of media/police co-operation occur in a case of kidnapping when an agreement worked out in a meeting at New Scotland Yard with editors in 1975 following the Lesley Whittle case, serves to obviate the dangers of splashing vital information across the front pages. A voluntary news blackout with the aim of reducing risks to the victim has now operated in six kidnap cases' (p. 16). From the Australian perspective, Grabowsky and Wilson (1989) say: 'Journalists are often in a position to do favours for police by tailoring a story in a particular way ... This self-censorship of good intent is usually engaged in by editors if they regard it to be "in the public interest". But agreements reached with the police not to run items conflict starkly with the media's ethos of free and open coverage of news events. Some journalists also fear that what may start off as good intent could develop into chronic inhibition' (p. 31). The Australian Press Council (1994) announced the adoption by the media of guidelines on reporting major crime incidents which included the following: 'Reporting of sieges, hostage taking and criminal activities of a similar nature must not knowingly endanger lives, hamper attempts by authorities to conclude the event, offer comfort and support to the perpetrators or provide them with vital information' (p. 24).

3    Sir Zelman Cowen was at the time Chairman of the Press Council in the U.K.

4    Discussed in Chapter 7.

5    For a detailed discussion of the U.S.A experience in balancing secrecy against the need for openness when national security is involved see Author not identified (1990). For the situation in Canada see Rankin (1986).

6    See, for example, *Sunday Times (The)* v *U.K.* (1979) 2 EHRR 245, in the context of an injunction granted to restrain publication of an article about the drug Thalidomide on the grounds that publication would amount to a contempt of court. This case, and this particular point, is also mentioned in Chapter 7. Using terms such as a 'pressing social need' and whether it was 'proportionate to the legitimate aim pursued' (para. 62), the European Court of Human Rights (ECHR) found the provisions of the injunction 'not to be proportionate to the legitimate aim pursued ...' (para. 67). In *Dudgeon* v *U.K.* (1981) 4 EHRR 149 the applicant, a homosexual, complained of the laws in Northern Ireland which had the effect of making criminal offences of certain homosexual acts between consenting adult males. The ECHR found 'the restriction imposed on Mr. Dudgeon ... by reason of its breadth and absolute character, is, quite apart from the severity of the possible penalties provided for, disproportionate to the aims sought to be achieved' (para. 61).

7    In *Klass* v *Federal Republic of Germany* (1978) 2 EHRR 214, the applicants claimed that the contested legislation, which permitted authorities to open mail and listen to telephone conversations violated Art. 6 (right to a fair hearing) and Art. 8 of the ECHR. The surveillance was to be carried out in secret and once the surveillance was completed the subject was to be notified, but only if notification did not jeopardise the objective of the surveillance. One of the aims of the legislation was to safeguard national security

and the initial decision to place someone under surveillance was in the hands of the supreme *Land* authority or a Federal Minister. Art. 8(1) says: 'Everyone has the right to respect for his private and family life, his home and his correspondence.' Art. 8(2) allows interference 'with the exercise of this right ... where necessary ... in the interests of national security'. The issue under Art. 8 for the European Court was whether the interference was justified. The Court found telephone conversations to be included in Art. 8(1). While noting that 8(2), because it provides an exception to the right guaranteed by the ECHR, is be narrowly interpreted, the Court found one of the aims of the legislation was to safeguard national security. The Court concluded that the legislation was necessary in a democratic society, and there was no breach of Art. 8.

The applicants in *Klass* claimed that Art. 6 had been violated because 'it does not require notification ... in all cases after the termination of surveillance measures and excludes recourse to the courts to test the lawfulness of such measure' (para. 74). The Court held that, 'as long as it remains validly secret, the decision placing someone under surveillance is thereby incapable of judicial control on the initiative of the person concerned, within the meaning of Article 6; as a consequence, it of necessity escapes the requirements of that Article' (para. 75). Once someone had been notified, there were several legal remedies available, so again Art. 6 was not violated.

The Court made no comment about what was meant by 'national security', apparently satisfied to leave this decision to the supreme *Land* authority or Federal Minister. The issue of proportionality as such is not mentioned, the Court saying instead it 'must be satisfied that, whatever system of surveillance is adopted, there exist adequate and effective guarantees against abuse' (para. 50). Once the Court had found that Art. 8 had not been violated, the somewhat circular reasoning applied to the alleged violation of Art. 6 allowed a neat sidestepping of the issue of the rights of those who were *not* notified that they had been the subject of surveillance.

See also *Leander* v *Sweden* (1987) 9 EHRR 433. The applicant unsuccessfully contended breaches of Articles 8, 10, and 13 following the refusal of the Naval Museum at Karlskrona to give him permanent employment. The refusal was on the basis of some information in a secret police register, and he claimed he should have been given the opportunity to refute this. Again without determining what is meant by 'national security' the Court unanimously found no violation of Art. 8 and 10 and by four votes to three no violation of Art. 13. On the issue of whether the interference with the applicant's rights was proportionate, the Court said that, because the aim was the protection of national security, 'the margin of appreciation available to the respondent State ... in the present case ... was a wide one' (para. 59). The question was more one of whether the Court was satisfied that adequate safeguards against abuse existed.

In *Wingrove* v *the United Kingdom* (1996) (ECHR internet version) the ECHR reiterated that the margin of appreciation accorded to a State would differ in each particular case. Where Art. 10 was involved, a narrow margin of appreciation would apply where political speech was to be restricted. A wider margin would apply where personal convictions were the issue, such as those of a religious or moral nature. In *Wingrove* the Court found no breach of Art. 10 where the applicant's video, depicting the ecstasy of Saint Teresa of Avila, was refused classification by the British Board of Film Classification on the grounds that it infringed the criminal law of blasphemy.

It is interesting to note that in recent times the High Court of Australia has utilised the ECHR terminology with respect to proportionality.

8    For comment on the case in the European Commission and Court of Human Rights see McDermott (1991) and Coliver (1992).

9    The case concerned an application to restrict the broadcasting of material which would identify the child of a man convicted of indecency involving two young boys.

10    See, for example, defamation cases such as *Waterhouse* v *Australian Broadcasting Corporation* (1986) 61 ALJR 24 (there is no CLR report of this case which included issues of contempt as well as defamation); *Lovell* v *Lewandowski* [1987] WAR 81; *National Mutual Life Association of Australasia Ltd* v *G.T.V. Corporation Pty Ltd* [1989] VR 747; *Chappell* v *TCN Channel Nine Pty Ltd* (1988) 14 NSWLR 153. Each case concerned an application for an interlocutory injunction to restrain the allegedly defamatory material. Only in the last case was the application successful. In that case the defamatory imputations related to the plaintiff's private life and while the defendant may have had an arguable defence of justification at trial, Hunt J concluded that 'the plaintiff's private behaviour alleged against him here did not amount to a matter of public interest or concern' (p. 171). A unanimous, and single, judgment of the High Court in *John Fairfax & Sons Ltd* v *Cojuangco* (1988) 165 CLR 346 considered the 'newspaper rule' and the attendant free speech interests. The New South Wales Court of Appeal in *Ballina Shire Council* v *Ringland* (1994) 33 NSWLR 680 held by a majority that the plaintiff local government authority had no right to sue for defamation. Both Gleeson CJ and Kirby P, in the majority, found persuasive the House of Lords decision in *Derbyshire County Council* v *Times Newspapers Ltd* [1993] AC 534. In *Ballina* the free speech interests which prevailed over the plaintiff's rights in defamation were found not to have the same effect on injurious falsehood, also pleaded by the plaintiff, per Gleeson CJ, per Mahoney JA; Kirby P dissenting on this point. Some examples of references to free speech interests in contempt of court cases are *Gallagher* v *Durack* (1983) 152 CLR 238, and there is repeated mention made of the public interest in freedom of discussion in *Hinch* v *A-G (Vic)* (1987) 164 CLR 15. Note also the judgment of Mason J in *Commonwealth* v *John Fairfax & Sons Ltd* (1980) 147 CLR 39; Mason J speaks of 'the public's interest in knowing and in expressing its opinion' (p. 52) in deciding not to grant an application for an interlocutory injunction to restrain the publication of government information on the basis of a breach of confidence claim. An interlocutory injunction was, however, granted to restrain a breach of copyright in the material.

11    For example, *R* v *Director-General of Social Welfare (Vic); Ex p. Henry* (1975) 133 CLR 369; *Buck* v *Bavone* (1976) 135 CLR 110; *Sillery* v *R* (1981) 180 CLR 353. In two cases the implied right was a right of communication; *Ansett Transport Industries (Operations) Pty Ltd* v *Commonwealth* (1977) 139 CLR 54 and *Miller* v *TCN Channel Nine Pty Ltd* (1986) 161 CLR 556. Murphy J died in October 1986.

12    'Freedom of political discourse' is the wording used by Gaudron J in *ACTV* (p. 208). The guarantee has been variously described in the relevant High Court judgments, for example: 'freedom of expression in relation to public and political affairs' by Mason CJ in *ACTV* (p. 136); 'freedom of political discussion' by Deane and Toohey JJ in *Nationwide News* (p. 75); 'freedom of communication on matters of government and politics' by the full court in *Lange* (p. 559). Note Schauer's (1994, p. 4) discussion on the word 'discourse'.

13    For a review of the role played by Brennan CJ in the development of human rights law in Australia see Justice M. Wilcox (1999).

14 This repeats a quote in Chapter 8.

15 For a critique of *ACTV* based on various free speech theories see Cass (1994).

16 For discussion of the *Lange* case see Walker (1998) and Chesterman (1998).

17 *Cunliffe* was handed down on the same date as *Theophanous* and *Stephens*.

18 Smallbone (1993) comments that concerns about the failure of Parliament to control the executive go back as far as Bagehot in 1888.

19 Except, perhaps, for the judgments of Toohey and Gaudron JJ in cases such as *Kruger*. It is freedom of political discourse that is most relevant to the book, so these other freedoms will not be examined in any detail.

20 For further comment on this concept, see Zines (1995) and Smallbone (1993).

21 Footnote from Fitzgerald's text: 'One might immediately question why such a reformulation of representative government ignores corporatist, feminist or public choice theories of government. What of government by big business or trade unions? Does the sexual contract rate a mention? Is government really necessary? These are questions people are currently asking in response to the recent High Court decisions.'

22 Footnote from Kirby J's text: 'See, eg, *McGinty and Others* v *The State of Western Australia* (1996) 186 CLR 140 at 237, per McHugh J; at 274-275, per Gummow J; Zines, *The High Court and the Constitution*, 4th ed (1997), pp 395-396; Aroney, "The Gestative Propensity of Constitutional Implications" Autumn [1997] *Policy*, 26 at p 28 points out that at the time when the Australian Constitution was drafted most women and Aboriginals were denied the right to vote in national elections.'

23 The following have also been put forward as purposive powers, although not all are universally accepted as such: s51 (xxix) 'external affairs' (the aspect enabling the implementation of international treaties and conventions); s51 (xxxvi), s51 (xxxix) incidental powers, s122, s31 (*Cunliffe*; *Langer*, Lee, 1994; Blackshield and Williams, 1998). As far as s51 is concerned, note that there is some criticism, judicial and academic, of the notion that the s51 powers can be thus separated, and that, as a result, different criteria apply to the assessment of their respective validity (Blackshield and Williams, 1998). In *Leask* v *Commonwealth* (1996) 187 CLR 579 Kirby J said: 'It is difficult, in principle, to embrace the proposition that proportionality might be an appropriate criterion for some paragraphs of s 51 ... yet impermissible in respect of others' (p. 635).

24 Note, however, that Dawson J found the concept of proportionality useful when the freedom was not found by implication but stated clearly in the terms of the section, for example s 92 of the Constitution (*ACTV*; *Cunliffe*).

# References

*A-G* v *Guardian Newspapers* [1987] 3 All ER 316, pp. 346-348, 356-357.

*A-G* v *Newspaper Publishing* [1987] 3 All ER 276.

*Ansett Transport Industries (Operations) Pty Ltd* v *Commonwealth* (1977) 139 CLR 54.

*Australian Bicentennial Authority Act 1980* (Cth).

*Australian Capital Television Pty Ltd* v *Commonwealth* (1992) 177 CLR 106, pp. 136, 159, 169, 208, 217, 227.

Australian Press Council (1994), *Annual Report No. 18*, Sydney, p. 24.

Author not identified (1990), 'Keeping Secrets: Congress, the Courts, and National Security Information', *Harvard Law Review*, vol. 103, p. 906.

*Ballina Shire Council v Ringland* (1994) 33 NSWLR 680.

Barendt, E. (1996), *Freedom of Speech*, Oxford, pp. 15, 114, 118-119, 120fn21, 122, 135-136.

Barker, M. (1995), 'Accountability to the Public: Travelling Beyond the Myth', in P. Finn (ed), *Essays on Law and Government, Vol 1, Principles and Values*, Sydney.

Blackshield, T. and Williams, G. (1998), *Australian Constitutional Law & Theory: Commentary & Materials*, Sydney.

Blackstone, W. (1765), *Commentaries*, Book IV.

Bork, R. (1971), 'Neutral Principles and Some First Amendment Problems', *Indiana Law Journal*, vol. 47, pp. 8-9.

*Broadcasting Act 1942* (Cth).

*Brown v Members of the Classification Review Board of the Office of Film and Literature Classification* (1998) 82 FCR 225, p. 238.

*Buck v Bavone* (1976) 135 CLR 110.

Campbell, E. and Whitmore, H. (1975), *Freedom in Australia*, Sydney, p. 333.

Cass, D. (1994), 'Through the Looking Glass: The High Court of Australia and the Right to Political Speech', in T. Campbell and W. Sadurski (eds), *Freedom of Communication*, Aldershot.

Chadwick, P. (1995), 'Pressure on to replace D-notices', *Communications Update*, vol. June, p. 6.

Chafee, Z. (1969), *Free Speech in the United States*, New York.

*Chappell v TCN Channel Nine Pty Ltd* (1988) 14 NSWLR 153, p. 171.

Chesterman, M. (1998), 'The Common Law Rules in Defamation - OK?', *The Tort Law Review*, vol. March, p. 9.

*Classifications (Publications, Films and Computer Games) Act 1995* (Cth).

Cm 3782 (1997), *Rights Brought Home: The Human Rights Bill*, para. 2.17.

Coliver, S. (1992), 'Spycatcher - the legal and broader significance of the European Court's judgment', *Media Law and Practice*, p. 142.

*Commonwealth Electoral Act 1918* (Cth).

*Commonwealth v John Fairfax & Sons Ltd* (1980) 147 CLR 39, p. 52.

*Commonwealth v John Fairfax Publications Pty Ltd, David Lague etc* (31 May 1995, unreported).

*Council of Civil Service Unions v Minister for the Civil Service* [1985] 1 AC 374 (*GCHQ* case).

Cowen, Z. (1984), 'Protecting Press and Public' in C. Bainbridge (ed), *One Hundred Years of Journalism*, London.

Creighton, P. (1993), 'The Implied Guarantee of Free Political Communication', *Western Australian Law Review*, vol. 23, p. 163.

*Crimes Act 1914* (Cth).

*Cunliffe v Commonwealth* (1994) 182 CLR 272, pp. 321, 389.

*Davis v Commonwealth* (1988) 166 CLR 79.

*Derbyshire County Council v Times Newspapers Ltd* [1993] AC 534, p. 549.

Dicey, A. (1945), *Introduction to the Study of the Law of the Constitution*, London, pp. 239, 246.

Douglas, N. (1993), 'Freedom of Expression under the Australian Constitution', *UNSW Law Journal*, vol. 16(2), pp. 320, 350.

*Dudgeon v U.K.* (1981) 4 EHRR 149, para. 61.

European Convention on Human Rights (ECHR), arts. 6, 8, 10, 13.

Fitzgerald, B. (1993), 'Proportionality and Australian Constitutionalism', *University of Tasmania Law Review*, vol. 12(2), p. 266.

*Gallagher v Durack* (1983) 152 CLR 238.

Grabowsky, P. and Wilson, P. (1989), *Journalism and Justice: How Crime is Reported*, Sydney, p. 31.

*Hinch v A-G (Vic)* (1987) 164 CLR 15.

Human Rights Act 1998 (UK), s3, s4, s6, s7, s8, s12, s19.

*Industrial Relations Act 1988* (Cth), s299.

International Covenant on Civil and Political Rights (ICCPR), art.19.

*John Fairfax & Sons Ltd v Cojuangco* (1988) 165 CLR 346.

*Klass v Federal Republic of Germany* (1978) 2 EHRR 214, para. 50, 74, 75.

*Kruger v Commonwealth* (1997) 190 CLR 1, p. 128.

*Lange v Australian Broadcasting Corporation* (1997) 189 CLR 520, pp. 559, 564, 567-568.

*Langer v Commonwealth* (1996) 186 CLR 302.

*Leander v Sweden* (1987) 9 EHRR 433, para. 59.

*Leask v Commonwealth (Leask)* (1996) 187 CLR 579, pp. 593, 602, 634-635.

Lee, H. (1994), 'Proportionality in Australian Constitutional Adjudication' in G. Lindell (ed), *Future Directions in Australian Constitutional Law*, Sydney, pp. 127, 148.

*Levy v State of Victoria* (1997) 189 CLR 579, pp. 607, 634.

Lindell, G. (1994), 'Recent Developments in the Judicial Interpretation of the Australian Constitution', in G. Lindell (ed), *Future Directions in Australian Constitutional Law*, Sydney.

*Lovell v Lewandowski* [1987] WAR 81.

Lustgarten, L. and Leigh, I. (1994), *In From the Cold; National Security and Parliamentary Democracy*, Oxford, pp. 344-345.

Macmillan Patfield. F. (1996), 'Towards a Reconciliation of Free Speech and Copyright', in E. Barendt, S. Bate, J. Dickens (eds), *The Yearbook of Media and Entertainment Law*, Oxford, p. 206.

*Malone v Metropolitan Police Commissioner* [1979] 2 All ER 620.

McDermott, J. (1991), ' "Spycatcher": success before the European Commission in Strasbourg', *Media Law and Practice*, vol. 12, p. 14.

*McGinty v State of Western Australia* (1996) 186 CLR 140.

*Migration Act 1958* (Cth).

*Miller v TCN Channel Nine Pty Ltd* (1986) 161 CLR 556.

Milton, J. (November 1644), *Areopagitica*, reprinted by Cambridge University Press (1918), Cambridge, p.14.

*Muldowney v State of South Australia* (1996) 186 CLR 352.

*National Mutual Life Association of Australasia Ltd v G.T.V. Corporation Pty Ltd* [1989] VR 747.

*Nationwide News v Wills* (1992) 177 CLR 1, pp. 29, 51, 70, 73, 74, 75, 95.

Neville Brown, L. (1977), 'A Bill of Rights for the United Kingdom?', *The Parliamentarian*, vol. LVIII No. 2, p. 79.

Newman, K. (1984), 'The Media and Public Order' in C. Bainbridge (ed), *One Hundred Years of Journalism*, London, p. 16.

*R v Central Independent Television* [1994] 3 All ER 641, p. 652.

*R v Director-General of Social Welfare (Vic); Ex p. Henry* (1975) 133 CLR 369.

Rankin, M. (1986), 'National Security: Information, Accountability, and the Canadian Security Intelligence Service', *University of Toronto Law Journal*, vol. 36, p. 249.

Robertson, G. and Nicol, A. (1990), *Media Law*, London.

Schauer, F. (1982), *Free speech: a philosophical enquiry*, Cambridge, pp. 150, 152.

Schauer, F. (1994), 'Free Speech in a World of Private Power', in T. Campbell and W. Sadurski (eds), *Freedom of Communication*, Aldershot, pp. 1, 4.

*Sillery v R* (1981) 180 CLR 353.

Smallbone, D. (1993), 'Recent Suggestions of an Implied "Bill of Rights" ', *Federal Law Review*, vol. 21, p. 255.

*Stephens v West Australian Newspapers Ltd* (1994) 182 CLR 211.

*Sunday Times (The) v U.K.* (1979) 2 EHRR 245, para. 62, 67.

*Sunday Times (The) v U.K. (No. 2), Guardian v U.K.* (1991) 14 EHRR 229.

*The Age*, 24 September 1984.

*The Age*, 25 September 1984.

*The Australian Financial Review*, 13 October 1994, p. 1.

*The Australian*, 13 October 1994, p. 1.

*The Australian*, 9 July 1997, p. 5.

*The Observer and the Guardian v U.K.* (1991) 14 EHRR 153, p. 191.

*The Sydney Morning Herald*, 27 May 1995.

*The Times*, 24 July 1997 (internet version).

*The West Australian*, 13 October 1994, p. 1.

*Theophanous v Herald & Weekly Times* (1994) 182 CLR 104, p. 156.

Toohey, Justice J. (1993), 'A Government of Laws, and Not of Men?', *Public Law Review*, vol. 4, p. 158.

Walker, S. (1998), '*Lange v ABC*: the High Court rethinks the "constitutionalisation" of defamation law', *Torts Law Journal*, vol. 6, p. 9.

*Waterhouse v Australian Broadcasting Corporation* (1986) 61 ALJR 24.

Wilcox, M. (1999), 'Sir Gerard Brennan's Contribution to the Human Rights Law in Australia', *The Law Society of Western Australia Brief*, vol. 26(1), p. 15.

Wildlife (Game) (Hunting Season) Regulations 1994 (Vic).

*Wingrove v the United Kingdom* (1996) (ECHR internet version).

Zines, L. (1996), 'Constitutionally Protected Individual Rights', in P. Finn (ed), *Essays in Law and Government, Vol 2, The Citizen and the State in the Courts*, Sydney.

# 11 The Government, Media and Judiciary

This book examines the issue of suppression or publication of information that the government alleges is prejudicial to national security. So far the book has looked at how the determination of whether material should be suppressed or published is carried out in a practical sense, that is through the operation of the D-Notice system or through the alternative which is by recourse to the legal system. The underlying question is who safeguards the 'public interest', in the sense of the interests of the general public in having only the information suppressed that is genuinely prejudicial to national security. The two parties involved, the government wanting suppression of the information and the media wanting publication, both claim to represent the public interest. This chapter focuses on the issue of the 'public interest', and how it is, or rather is not, objectively ascertained by the two parties. To this end the chapter contains an investigation of which side, if any, does actually represent the public interest. There is an examination of the way in which the government and the media manipulate the news while purporting to represent the public interest, followed by a look at the role of the judiciary.

## Government manipulation of the news

Government manipulation of the news is tied up with government secrecy, or the suppression of information that may harm what the government perceives to be the public interest, whatever the public interest may be in the circumstances.

> Conflicts over secrecy - between state and citizen, as in this case, or parent and child, or in journalism or business or law - are conflicts over power: the power that comes through controlling the flow of information. To be able to hold back some information about oneself or to channel it and thus influence how one is seen by others gives power ... (Bok, 1982, p. 18).

Some secrecy in government is inevitable, and acceptable, but the difficulty arises in ascertaining the degree of secrecy that is acceptable and there is a continuous tension between suppression and disclosure (Bok, 1982; Rowat, 1981).[1] The longer a government is in power the more likely it is to be convinced of its right to be in office and to be correct in its own interpretation of events and issues. An increase in secrecy follows, with a resulting increase in the inherent dangers.

> Secrecy can harm those who make use of it in several ways. It can debilitate judgment, first of all, whenever it shuts out criticism and feedback, leading people to become mired down in stereotyped, unexamined, often erroneous beliefs and ways of thinking. Neither their perception of a problem nor their reasoning about it then receives the benefit of challenge and exposure ... (Bok, 1982, p. 25).

The government may, and does, claim that the material should be suppressed or disclosed in the manner of their choosing because their interests are the same as those of the public and there are quite genuine reasons for their actions. This is particularly so, and in fact may well often be true, when the information relates to national security. In some instances, however, these interests may be viewed more cynically as simply being in the interests of the government in optimising its prospects of re-election (Michael, 1982; Rowat, 1981).[2]

Pincher (1968) speaks of politicians 'bending the truth':

> It is regrettable but true that some journalists are now more inclined to believe their information is correct when it has been officially denied.
> The Parliamentary lie, which denies or deliberately appears to deny a newspaper report for political purposes constrains press freedom in two ways - first by interfering with the dissemination of the truth and secondly by making journalists and their newspapers appear to be unreliable (p. 46).

In general the media asserts that when it can be convinced that an issue genuinely has implications that would be damaging to national security, it will back off and refrain from publication (Pincher, 1968; Fairley, 1990; Lustgarten and Leigh, 1994).[3] The kind of self censorship that most often takes place is when individual lives may be put in danger if publication takes place (Michael, 1982). As mentioned in an earlier chapter, Schauer (1982, pp. 198-199) talks of the 'clear and present danger' doctrine in the United States, which includes not only danger but imminence.

Tension between the media and the government occurs when the suspicion arises that the government is using national security as an excuse to cover up something else such as ineptitude, corruption or some other cause of embarrassment. One major criticism of the D-Notice System is that, by participating, the media is actively promoting government manipulation of the news by publishing only what is acceptable to the government. The answer to that is that the System is voluntary, in theory at any rate, and the media need not, and does not, always comply. Even so, it is difficult to overcome the misgiving that the media is being fed a certain line which they are then promoting on behalf of the government.

With respect to the situation in the U.K., Lustgarten and Leigh (1994) comment on media self censorship in these terms:

> Its defenders would describe it as 'discretion'; a less polite word would be collusion. It is the attitude which underpins both the Lobby system and the D notice system ... Within this structure editors and politicians know each other on social terms and frequently meet informally. They share the same social background and outlook, which produces a consensual, implicit understanding and permits substantial voluntary agreement about what is and is not fit to become public knowledge ... (p. 260).

Though they are not included, the description of social background and outlook also encompasses highly placed officials within government departments in the U.K. Mutually beneficial relationships between media proprietors and government Ministers, even Prime Ministers, are also a possible way for the government to manipulate the media, and the news (Henningham, 1991).

It is obvious, and understandable, that those in government wish to see the better side of themselves appearing in the media, and promote this angle unashamedly. Many writers are firmly of the view that government manipulation of the news is as institutional as it is insidious. The practice is not confined to governments of any one particular political persuasion. In the U.K. both Conservative and Labour governments have used both the DA-Notice system and the courts to suppress material on the basis that restraint is 'in the interests of national security'.

This is no less so in Australia, with the D-Notice system being established by the Menzies Liberal government in 1952, and the existence of the system being kept a secret by successive Liberal governments until it became public in 1967. The 1995 Chinese Embassy Bugging Affair occurred while the Keating Labor government was in power. During the furore Gareth Evans Q.C., then a Senator and Minister for Foreign Affairs, was given the task of responding to the Samuels Report on ASIS on behalf of himself and on behalf of the Minister for Defence, Senator Robert Ray, and the Attorney-

General, Michael Lavarch. Senator Evans was fiercely critical of the role of the media, and contemplated amending the *Crimes Act 1914* (Cth) to introduce the offence of secondary disclosure to punish the media (Senate Deb., No. 8, col. 722-723, 1 June 1995). In return Senator Evans faced equally fierce criticism in and out of Parliament (Senate Deb., No. 9, col. 988, 7 June 1995):

> Senator MacGIBBON - Given the minister's entry to the parliament as a great civil libertarian and bearing in mind that T.J. Ryan memorial lecture of 1982 - which I read this week with great interest - in which he promulgated the case for civil liberties, I would have thought there would have been more effort put into modifying or amending the Crimes Act and making alternative strategies before resorting to the draconian penalties which he has promulgated.

The *Gazette of Law and Journalism* headed its story on the events as 'Gareth's suppression capers' (July 1995, p. 2). In the editorial of 14 December 1995 the *Sydney Morning Herald* commented:

> There is obviously room for disagreement over what information truly damages the national interest and what does not. There is, however, no doubt that governments are inclined to want far more information suppressed than can properly be justified on national interest grounds, if only because of the natural tendency of governments to equate their own political interests with the national interest. Moreover, there is also no doubt that the courts will often give more weight to a government's assertions of the need to protect the national interest than to a newspaper's arguments in favour of the free flow of information.

For some commentators government manipulation of the news in the U.K. reached a peak during the years of Conservative government when Margaret Thatcher was Prime Minister (Ewing and Gearty, 1990):

> Questions of national security and governmental secrecy have not been fetishes peculiar to the Thatcher administrations. It is easy to forget that two American journalists, Philip Agee and Mark Hosenball, were deported in 1977 by Mr Merlyn Rees, then Home Secretary, on the ground that their departure would be conducive to the public good in the interests of national security. It is also easy to forget that it was during the life of the last Labour Government that attempts were made to ban the publication of the Crossman diaries and that criminal prosecutions were instituted against Crispin Aubrey, John Berry, and Duncan Campbell in connection with an interview given by Berry about his work with SIGINT, a governmental

service dealing with the interception and analysis of radio communications. Yet while all British Governments this century have been obsessed by questions of secrecy and security, the last ten years have seen these obsessions carried to remarkable lengths ... in several instances the Government and the Prime Minister were helped rather than hindered by Her Majesty's judges (p. 129).

Keane (1991) is equally outspoken in his appraisal of the Thatcher years. Lewis (1990), who describes Mrs Thatcher's style as 'increasingly presidential' (p. 543), charts the shift of power from Parliament, at its strongest in the early eighteenth century, to the dominant party in Parliament, then to the leader of that party who appointed the cabinet and the ever more powerful cabinet committees.

The concentration of power facilitates the manipulation of information; because the information is known only to the trusted few it can be kept secret or fed out in whatever form is necessary for the occasion. One such method is the selective, and politically motivated, leaking of information by Ministers (Thomas, 1995; Author not identified, 1987). Eisenschitz (1985) examines a number of U.K. cases[4] where information has been suppressed, most often by the government but sometimes by big organisations such as Distillers (over the Thalidomide settlements). She concludes:

These are just a selection of what appears to be a deluge of Government-related information-supply cases. Either a Government department is involved or there is some interaction with Government in all the cases. The OSA may or may not be involved. The common feature appears to be the manipulation of the law to suit political office holders. Occasionally the courts question and oppose this, sometimes they support the political line. The law is inevitably drawn into the political arena and loses its impartiality or at least its perceived impartiality (p. 257).

Two cases which illustrate this are *R* v *Ponting* [1985] Crim LR 318, discussed in Chapter 6, and *Chandler* v *DPP* [1964] A.C. 763, discussed in Chapter 9, both of which involved prosecutions under the Official Secrets Act, and in which the courts refrained from looking behind the bald words of the statute to evaluate any wider context of 'interest of the State' which would benefit the respective defendants (Hocking, 1993).

Campbell and Whitmore (1973) discussed the restrictions on the manipulation of the flow of government information in the Australian context. At the time a new Labor government had recently come to power with Prime Minister Whitlam giving a commitment to open government, hence the comment 'until recently the view' in the passage quoted below. Although in the intervening years a number of initiatives have taken place with respect to access to government information, where the interests of national security are involved nothing has changed:

> The overall Australian picture is one of fairly effective and thoroughgoing repression of comment. The problem for the future is to reconcile the undoubted public interest in being informed on public issues, with the equal public interest in the maintenance of confidence in the Government and loyalty in the public service. Until recently the view of all Australian Governments seems to have been that the latter public interest is to have precedence ... Ministers took the view that they, and they alone should be permitted to discuss official policy, and have access to official information
> ...
> It is hardly necessary to point out that administrative efficiency and integrity in government depend upon free and open discussion of public issues. Members of the Opposition can scarcely mount effective criticisms when they have no access to vital information which can only be disclosed by public service comment. The newspapers are similarly limited in their effectiveness. Above all members of the public cannot form any assessment of official policy when large sections of that policy are shielded from public view by the twin limitations on disclosure of information and comment by public servants. Ministers and senior public servants have a vested interest in covering up their mistakes, shortcomings and occasional dishonesties. This vested interest must not be allowed to prevail over the wider public interest (p. 352).

Campbell and Whitmore's last paragraph is a fitting summary of the issues involved in the discussion of government manipulation of the news, and in particular the issue of the protection of the interests of the general public.

## Media manipulation of the news

The previous section examines government manipulation of the news, but the other extremely influential force that manipulates the news to suit its own interests is the media. This section is written in the knowledge that the selection of material to be included necessarily involves a form of 'manipulation'.

> Despite the multitude of positions taken by journalists, scholars, politicians, and the public, the news remains a puzzle. On the one hand, few things are

as much a part of our lives as the news. With the advent of sophisticated mass communication, the news has become a sort of instant historical record of the pace, progress, problems, and hopes of society. On the other hand - and here's the puzzle - the news provides, at best, a superficial and distorted image of society. From the tremendous number of events occurring ... each day, the typical news fare covers only a narrow range of issues, from the viewpoints of an even narrower range of sources, with emphasis placed on drama over depth, human interest over social significance, and formula reporting over perceptive analysis (Lance Bennett, 1988, p. xi).

Lance Bennett's reference is to the United States, but the quote is apt for the U.K. and Australia also.

It must be said at the outset that what is newsworthy for each organisation depends largely on its place in the market, 'news' being a commodity (Lance Bennett, 1988; Hartley, 1989[5]). With the exception of a few national broadcasters which are paid for by the taxpayer, media organisations are commercial enterprises, and therefore their existence is dependent on a particular readership or viewership. The national broadcaster in the U.K. is the BBC, and the ABC and SBS in Australia. Even these organisations are not entirely free to ignore ratings (Hartley, 1989).

It is outside the scope of this book to examine the finer distinctions that exist in news selection between the print and electronic media, radio and TV, and the commercial and national broadcasters.[6] In a nutshell, 'content must always fit the format, and it is therefore always secondary to the format' (Ericson, Baranek and Chan, 1991, p. 21). What follows is a brief discussion of some of the more general ways in which the news may be manipulated by the media. It should be noted, however, that the broadcast media in both the U.K. and Australia is subject to a statutory regulatory regime requiring broadcasters to observe rules on impartiality.

Because of the huge amount of information available to the news media, the process of selection of news items is in itself a manipulation. Fowler (1991) sees the interests of the print media as being in promoting the interests of capitalism, because of the commercial nature of newspaper organizations. This would apply equally to the broadcast media. The notion that the interests of the media lie in promoting the interests of capitalism is explored in Curran (1978).

Hartley (1989) looks at news selection in terms of the news-maker rather than the news-reporter. He also speaks of 'autonomy and influence' in the relationship between the broadcast media and the government, in particular when the two are at odds:

Clearly there is autonomy from government viewpoints if an item is covered in a way that arouses government fury. But on the other hand a full-scale public row is damaging to the news organization's reputation - it has often been argued that as a result, editors-in-charge practice 'self-censorship' in sensitive areas. That is, they tailor their comments or coverage to keep within the limit of what is believed to be tolerable to the government (p. 52).

Hartley lists twelve 'general news values' which were identified in a study by Galtang and Ruge (1973). These assist the journalist to select items from the plethora of potentially newsworthy events that occur daily. Some of these news values are general the world over, and some are dependent on the culture of the news gatherer. The list includes such matters as 'frequency', which is the time-span an event takes. Murders, for example, take little time and the meaning is easily and quickly understood. A murder fits daily newspapers and daily television and radio programmes, whereas social and cultural trends take longer to unfold and understand. Another inclusion on the list is 'threshold', meaning the size of the event; some events are too small to be reported and this threshold varies between local and national news. The more of the listed categories that a single item falls into, the more likely it is to be selected as newsworthy and the higher it will be ranked in priority (Hartley, 1989; Golding and Elliott, 'News Values and News Production', 1996; Bell, 1991; Fowler, 1991; Ericson, Baranek, and Chan, 1987).

Ericson, Baranek and Chan (1987) suggest that 'deviance', defined broadly as 'the behaviour of a thing or person that strays from the normal ... is *the* defining characteristic of what journalists regard as newsworthy ...' (p. 4) [*their emphasis*]. Furthermore, by designating what deviance is, '[t]he journalistic search for procedural strays and signs of disorder is a means of charting the consensual boundaries of society and acknowledging order', and in this way 'journalists become part of the control institutions they report on' (p. 8) (see also Ericson, Baranek and Chan, 1991; Hartley, 1989; Golding and Elliott, 'Bias, Objectivity and Ideology', 1996).

Briefly, most journalists have been socialised into, and internalise, the dominant values of society. Indeed they have tended, on the basis of the available evidence, to be 'centrist' in political orientation, and they also work within organisational settings and codes of professional practice that inhibit radical journalism. [*endnotes omitted*] (Curran, 1978, p. 74).

According to Lance Bennett (1988), there are four information biases in the way news content is dealt with. Most of the criticisms of the failings of the news can be attributed to these biases. The first is 'personalized news', defined as 'the journalistic bias that gives preference to the individual actors and human interest angles in events while downplaying institutional and political considerations that establish the social contexts for those events' (p. 26). Personalised news may be part of corporate policy of the news organisation. The example given is of the American CBS evening news. The second bias is 'dramatised news'; 'the potential for drama is a virtual guarantee that an event will become a major news story' (p. 35). Dramatised news sits well with personalised news and both trivialise news content. The third bias is 'fragmented news':

> Events in fragmented news exist in self-contained dramatic capsules, isolated from each other in time and space. The impression given off by the news is that of a jigsaw puzzle that is out of focus and missing many pieces. When focus is provided it is on the individual pieces, not on how they fit the surrounding picture (p. 44).

The fourth bias is 'normalised news', where the 'potential for confusion and disorientation inherent in personalized, dramatized, and fragmented news leaves people vulnerable to old, familiar, reassuring images of how the world works - images that drive bothersome details out of mind' (p. 51). In other words the bombardment of small, superficial, bits of information makes informed analysis unlikely.

Taylor (1992) writing on the media coverage of the Gulf War, makes the following observation:

> Because journalists are neither sociologists nor historians, their concern is more with the detail than the overall picture. They work for news organisations the role of which is to bring to the public the extraordinary rather than the typical, the 'newsworthy' rather than the commonplace. The pressure therefore to produce competitive stories tends to make them focus upon what they consider to be 'news' which can produce good copy and headlines. But perhaps the biggest casualty of all in wartime news reporting, focusing as it does on the spectacular incident or speech around which the story can be framed, is context (pp. 12-13).

While Taylor applies the comment about context to wartime reporting, it is pertinent to other reporting also.

Each news story starts with a journalist writing copy, although television newsreaders also write some or all of what they read out. The information for the stories comes from a number of different sources, and is rarely the compiler's original work in the sense of coming from firsthand experience. International news usually comes from Reuters, Associated Press, United Press International and Agence France Press, and domestic news, which is not obtained by the media outlet directly, comes from internal news agencies. Many local news stories are simply rewritten news releases from politicians, companies and other organisations with information they want publicised (Bell, 1991). These news releases are written to suit the message or image that the particular organisation wishes to promote.

Information for stories initiated by the journalist comes in the main from sources. These are most likely to be official sources from within the court system, the police, the legislature and the private sector (Ericson, Baranek and Chan, 1989). The source is someone in authority, someone in a senior position who can be recognised as representing their organisation, because this is seen as giving the information credibility, even though there may be others in a better position to know the facts (Ericson, Baranek and Chan, 1989; Ericson, Baranek and Chan, 1991).

> News is what an authoritative source tells a journalist ... they wear a general mantle of authority and are part of the institutional network where journalists expect to get information. The world of journalists' sources is, as M. Fishman argues, 'bureaucratically organized' (1980:51).
> The corollary to this is equally well attested in the research: unofficial news sources are little use (Kress 1983b). Alternative sources tend to be ignored: individuals, opposition parties, unions, minorities, fringe groups, the disadvantaged. Among politicians it is ministers who have overwhelming access to the media ... (Bell, 1991, pp. 191-192).

Fowler (1991) is of the view that the concentration on a particular level of source necessarily leads to partiality in what is reported and how it is reported. Ericson, Baranek and Chan (1989) comment on the relationship between the media and sources from within the police, a relationship they see as being one of mutual interests. This approach ties in with their (Ericson et al) notion, discussed above, of 'deviance' being newsworthy. By designating what amounts to 'deviance' journalists are part of the established order. The police also are part of the established order and the co-operation between the police and the media serves to foster the public interest. In this context the public interest is the 'general good' (Ericson, Baranek and Chan, 1989, p. 92).

The choice of language in the story also carries a message about the position of the writer. The words carry signs about the meaning intended for them. Hartley (1989) gives an example of the use of the word 'terrorist' rather than 'freedom fighter'. He points out that it is unlikely that 'terrorists *liberated*' would be used together because, although grammatically correct, the two words have different connotations (p. 21). Note the connotation in the word 'manipulation' used in the heading of the sections in this chapter. Hartley also speaks of stereotyping and cites industrial disputes as an example of the 'us : them' approach (p. 116):

us : them
management : strikers
government : unions

When the journalist has written the story, it usually goes through an editorial chain before it is published. The editor, or editors, may make a number of changes to the original story, the editorial function being to maximise the news value (Bell, 1991). The input of another party, the editor, again denotes that a choice is being made - manipulation in a broad sense. The element of choosing between alternatives, inevitable as it is in the process of news production, gives rise to the criticism of potential bias because the decisions may be value laden (Golding and Elliott, 1996, 'Bias, Objectivity and Ideology'; Fowler, 1991).

In Australia the current standard of journalism is criticised by one of their own in *The Sydney Morning Herald* on 14 November 1998. Under the heading 'A daily diet of scorn and derision' Paul Sheehan comments on the replacement of 'mild disdain' with 'something more hostile' in the attitude of the public to journalists. He says 'society must now deal with an omnivorous media that is more intrusive, more ubiquitous and more opinionated than ever before' (p. 43). While there is much criticism of media proprietors, journalists themselves are not so good at introspection (Henderson, 1990).

Some journalists, however, are of the view that it is possible for journalists to be both objective and impartial, and bias at this level is more likely to be unconscious rather than deliberate. There is also a distinction to be made between objectivity and impartiality (Golding and Elliott, 1996, 'Bias, Objectivity and Ideology'; Hartley, 1989). The Australian journalists' Code of Ethics preamble speaks of '[r]espect for truth and the public's right to information'. The Code of Ethics requires journalists to report news honestly and without distortion, but, as Bowman (1990) points out, adherence to the Code may be shortlived if the media employer has different requirements. Bowman also points out, however, that most journalists are ethical.

At a higher level than the journalists and sub-editors, conscious bias is evident in the approach of some media outlets. In the U.K. 'the *Sun* is known to be consistently hostile in its treatment of trades unions, and of what it calls "the loony Left", the *Guardian* is generous in its reporting of CND' (Fowler, p. 11). The increasing control of the media by a small number of proprietors is cited as a cause for concern, and as being good for neither democracy or for journalists (Chadwick, 1990; Henningham, 1991). This concern about the dangers of the powerful few controlling the press is not new, and the situation has been likened to the days when authoritarian governments ruled the press (Siebert, Peterson and Schramm, 1976). Chadwick (1990) says the objections do not depend on proof of abuse, but on the potential power for abuse.

There is also the issue of deliberate bias, political bias, by media proprietors. Media proprietors have, through their news media outlets, immense power to influence public opinion and, if so minded, can shape politics and social policies (Hartley, 1989). In the U.K. Robert Maxwell, who died in November 1991, had been a Labour member of Parliament in the 1960s, but lost his seat in the general election of 1970. In the 1980s his Mirror Group newspapers supported the Labour party, and Maxwell is reported to have ordered the editor of the *Daily Mirror* to print an unsubstantiated story unfavourable to Margaret Thatcher, then the Prime Minister. The editor refused to print the story, and resigned shortly afterwards. The *Daily Mirror* traditionally held a lunch, hosted by Maxwell himself, at Labour Party conferences (Bower, 1995).

In Australia, Sir Keith Murdoch through his newspapers assisted Joseph Lyons into power as Prime Minister in 1931 as the leader of a non-Labor party. Lyons had previously been a Labor Member of Parliament. Keith Murdoch later received a knighthood for his efforts. Sir Keith supported the Liberal party after the war, and the 'Murdoch press' supported Robert Menzies to victory in the 1949 election. Sir Keith died in 1952. In 1968 son Rupert's papers ran a successful campaign to see John Gorton head the Liberal party after the death of Harold Holt. When William McMahon ousted Gorton as Prime Minister in 1971, Murdoch, who did not like McMahon, turned to the Labor party, although by that time he had already begun to discreetly support Labor. In the run-up to the 1972 election the Murdoch press supported the victorious Labor party, led by Gough Whitlam. The support included an unsigned column written by Murdoch in the Sydney *Daily Mirror* denigrating the media support for McMahon. The column appeared in the *Daily Mirror* on 23 November 1972 under the heading 'Mirror Election Viewpoint'. Whitlam believed 'that Murdoch had backed him in 1972, as he later backed Malcolm Fraser in 1975, in order to take credit for the victory' (Munster, 1987, p. 103). In 1975-76 Murdoch fell out with Whitlam Labor and supported the Liberal party headed by Malcolm Fraser to power. In 1983 Murdoch altered his allegiance yet again and assisted the Hawke Labor party into power. In the meanwhile he had been a confirmed backer of the Margaret Thatcher Conservative government in the U.K. since 1979 (Munster, 1987; Henningham, 1991).

The Packer family in Australia also openly campaigned in favour of a particular political party. Sir Frank Packer was a staunch supporter of the Right (Barry, 1994):

> For nigh on four decades he used the newspaper [*the Sydney Telegraph*] as his own personal soapbox from which to harangue politicians, attack his rivals or declaim on whatever subject had lately caught his eye ... For almost forty years he fought a shameless campaign to keep the Labor Party out of office, denigrating and ridiculing its policies and politicians, while financing and encouraging its opponents. Packer and the politicians in Canberra believed it was within his capacity to make and break prime ministers and to bring down governments, and there was evidence to suggest they were right. Thanks in part to his newspapers, the Liberal-Country Party coalition remained in government in Australia for a record twenty-three years on the trot, from 1949 to 1972, and on more than one occasion its leaders thanked Packer for their election victory (pp. 56-57).

Denis O'Brien, who spent ten years writing for Packer publications, says Frank Packer's interventionist style was most evident in the manner he ran his newspapers. Journalists 'could expect to be peremptorily sacked if they dared publish anything which was not in line with his views' (*The Weekend Australian*, Review, 21-22 October 2000, p. 13). Munster (1987) recounts how anxious Prime Minister McMahon was in 1972 when he was told that Sir Frank Packer had sold the *Daily* and *Sunday Telegraph* to Rupert Murdoch's News Limited. The assumption 'that Murdoch was making another move to unseat the Government was accordingly widespread. It was also false' (p. 97).

Kerry Packer took over from his father in 1974, and initially supported the Liberal party especially during the 1975 election. Although Packer was 'deeply conservative' he was also pragmatic and, like Rupert Murdoch, his allegiances shifted to Labor during the 1980s (Barry, 1994). In February 1999 Ken Cowley, former News Limited executive chairman, and Kerry Packer denied allegations made by a former NSW government minister that they had agreed not to report on the 'duchessing' (fawning over) members of the International Olympic Committee during Sydney's Olympic bid. In light of the just quoted views of the biographers and other media commentators the responses are interesting. Packer is quoted as saying the claims were 'absolute bullshit ... and if you want a rude reply I'll give you one of those' and 'there was "no way" he would give any undertaking to restrict the reporting of his television network or magazine interests' (*The Sydney Morning Herald*, 19 February 1999). Cowley said:

> It's rubbish. Neither myself or News Ltd has never [*sic*] made any arrangements or agreements with politicians. We have never been part of clandestine or secret arrangements. Proprietors or managers of businesses never speak for editors (*The Sydney Morning Herald*, 19 February 1999).

These responses do not bode well for any revival of the D-Notice system in Australia.

It is clear from the above brief review that there are a great number of different ways in which the media might approach the treatment of government information that is sensitive on the grounds of national security. As the media in this case is a party, in that the government may wish to prevent the material from being published by the media, it is potentially an 'us : them' or 'media : government' situation. However, because the media is on the side of established order, they may not wish to alienate the government too seriously by trumpeting their grievances and the information. Much would depend on the political colour of the government and its particular allegiances with the media at the time. In the context of whistleblowers, through whom this type of sensitive information usually surfaces, Dempster (1997, pp. 208-209) uses a quote from de Maria, founder of the Whistleblowers Action Group:

> Conflicts between sensationalism and investigative journalism; snapshot coverage and sustained reporting; and victim-focused versus system-focused stories swim below the surface, usually out of sight of the whistleblower. Such conflicts are resolved by media management against the public interest more times than is realised. The fiercely free media, exposing wrongdoing wherever it finds it, is largely a myth that we and whistleblowers hold on to along with the myth of accountability and integrity in government. Bar some spectacular cases ... the government does not have much to worry about with the media, which is driven more by economic considerations: will the largely conservative media consumer 'buy' the whistleblower's story, and therefore buy the newspaper or item in the electronic news?

There are differing views on the question of the extent to which the media does actually influence society and political processes. Knightley (1998), for example, says '[t]he truth is that the power of the press is greatly overrated ... the power to report or not to report could not be compared with the power of judges, ministers, civil servants, corporate directors or trade union leaders' (p. 177). Henningham (1991), on the other hand, says '[t]here can be no doubt that the media do affect society and politics - it is nonsense to cast media in the role of passive observers' (p. 266).

In the context of this book the issue is whether the media do actually represent the public interest, that is the interests of the general public, where the government alleges that material should not be published on the grounds of national security. Given all the other factors that are taken into account when a news story is put together it is arguable that the public interest is not treated as a separate value in its own right. Any consideration of the public interest, in the sense used in this book, may be entirely coincidental or because it coincides with some of the other news values.[7]

### The role of the judiciary

One of the threads that runs through the discussion of balancing the competing interests when national security is involved is that of the role of the judiciary. The judiciary become involved when the government, rather than using the voluntary D-Notice system which may not bring about the required result, resorts to the law to suppress confidential information. The role of the judiciary is a topic by itself and one not confined just to cases relating to national security issues, but it is the context of national security that is relevant here.[8]

Chapter 9 looked in detail at how judges in the U.K. and Australia deal with cases relating to national security and how they determine what evidence is required to establish that national security is indeed an issue. It is therefore already clear that judges have a vital role to play in looking after the interests of the general public when the government wishes to suppress information on the grounds of national security and the media want publication. The previous sections of this chapter have determined that the government and media, while both expressing conviction that they are representing the public interest, in fact have other interests at heart which may, or may not, coincide with the public interest.

The print and electronic media are able to shape and present a story to communicate any message they wish, and on occasion shamelessly and ruthlessly promote their own particular causes. The tension between the media and the legal system is at its greatest in cases involving free speech issues, and the public at large is left in no doubt of the media point of view when judges make disagreeable decisions, that is when the media loses a case.

When the House of Lords decided by a 3-2 majority in the interlocutory stages of *Spycatcher* that the interim injunctions should remain in place to restrain further publication until trial, the full judgments were not handed down until some weeks after the decision was announced (*A-G* v *Guardian Newspapers* [1987] 3 All ER 316). The reasoning in the full judgments showed that, in essence, the majority felt it necessary in the interests of justice to preserve the plaintiff's case until the full trial could take place; they stressed that the measures were not at that stage permanent and they hoped that the trial would commence without too much of a time lapse. Following the initial announcement, and without knowing the reasoning of the majority, the *Daily Mirror* printed photographs of Lord Ackner, Lord Brandon and Lord Templeman upside down with the headline 'You Fools' and included wording in the story such as 'monstrous act of censorship'. This particular decision 'led to unprecedented criticism of the judiciary from the British press (not surprisingly since they lost), from commentators around the world where legal systems had allowed publication of Wright's allegations, and even from within the British judiciary itself' (Lee, 1988, p. 109). In an article on the *Spycatcher* case, Lord Oliver of Aylmerton (1991, p. 23) struck back at the media, his criticism including the following anonymous poem:

> You cannot hope to bribe or twist,
> Thank God, the British journalist,
> But seeing what the man will do unbribed,
> There's no occasion to.

A letter to *The Times* on 5 November 1997 from Leslie Hinton, Executive Chairman, News International plc, illustrates that, even after ten years, segments of the U.K. press retain a distrust of the judiciary. The letter was sent with reference to the tension between press freedom and some of the provisions of the European Convention on Human Rights. It followed reassurances by the Lord Chancellor on this issue that press freedom 'will be in "the safe hands of British judges" '. In the letter, headed 'Press Freedom', Hinton speaks of the 'idiosyncratic behaviour of judges in their media decisions' and remarks on the 'often narrow and out of date experiences' of the judiciary (p. 23). The content of the letter is ironic given the previous section covers media manipulation of the news; one wonders if the editor of *The Times* could have refused to print it.

Criticism of the judiciary also comes from academic circles (Lee, Hanks, and Morabito, 1995; Halliwell, 1991; Ewing and Gearty, 1990; Lewis, 1990; Walker, 1990). This is particularly so with respect to some of the U.K.

decisions where national security is an issue, as is evident from earlier chapters. One of the most trenchant of these critics has been Griffiths (1997), and he makes the following comments in relation to the *Spycatcher* litigation:

> The *Spycatcher* litigation exposed the political bias of some of the most senior members of the judiciary in the most blatant way. The case was pursued by the government with great vigour in this country and in Australia long after any useful purpose could be achieved. Before it was concluded, the action had become an abuse of the judicial process. And for much of the time a majority of the judges sitting in the Court of Appeal and the House of Lords gave support to the government in circumstances which grossly interfered with the right and duty of the national press to report matters of the greatest public concern.
>
> The serious charge to be laid against the judiciary is that they rarely do more than pay lip service to freedom of expression. That is why the outburst by Lord Bridge in *Spycatcher* where he spoke of totalitarianism ... seemed so remarkable. For once an English judge hit the table hard, almost as if he were one of the great liberal judges of the Supreme Court of the United States. The shock was considerable; but the mood passed and the impulse died (pp. 298-299).

The 1991 edition had a paragraph in the middle of the two quoted here which contained the most blistering criticism.

Lustgarten (1989) is also very critical of the judiciary in the context of decisions relating to national security, describing their performance as 'dreadful' (p. 230). Lustgarten goes on to claim that from the mid 1980s the U.K. government had a 'legal strategy', part of which was to seek to have its cases heard before 'obliging' judges. Referring to *R* v *Ponting* [1985] Crim LR 318, Lustgarten describes Mr Justice McCowan as being 'known to be sympathetic to the Government' (pp. 230-231). When the government failed in this case because the jury acquitted Ponting, notwithstanding McCowan J's sympathies for the prosecution's case, the government thereafter avoided the use of juries by turning to the civil law of breach of confidence. By using breach of confidence the government obtained, in all except one instance, an interim or interlocutory injunction, often ex parte, to prevent publication (Lustgarten, 1989; Lustgarten and Leigh, 1994).

There is also the use of judges in extra judicial roles which relate to national security matters. For example, judges are appointed to chair, or otherwise take part in, one-off inquiries into a specific security matter; they are appointed to sit on tribunals which hear security related issues and some security organisations may have a judge as Director (Lustgarten and Leigh,

1994). Serious criticisms may arise if a judge were to take part in some extra judicial activity relating to national security, then hear a case involving the same or similar issues. An example is that of Lord Radcliffe who heard the appeal in *Chandler* v *DPP* [1964] AC 763 directly after chairing the inquiry into *Security Procedures in the Public Service* (Cmnd 1681, 1962). While making it clear that they are not suggesting any judicial wrongdoing, Lustgarten and Leigh make the point that 'there is a curious paradox between the self denying judicial ordinance on substantive consideration of issues of national security in court and the preparedness to use the judiciary to consider identical issues extra-judicially' (p. 491). A further point about the use of judges in extra judicial roles is that it may cast doubt on their impartiality, particularly in situations that become highly politicised (Leigh and Lustgarten, 1991; Lustgarten and Leigh, 1994).

Hanks (1988) says the refusal of the courts to examine the intricacies of national security as a concept, and to try to balance the competing interests, may be due to a reluctance to become involved in political issues. This means that the concept of national security is given a broad interpretation because the courts do not require governments to be specific about the risks to the state when national security is an issue. As a result governments are able to determine for themselves what national security is, and can therefore connect national security with their own security for their own political ends.

One accusation which is sometimes directed at the judiciary, particularly the Court of Appeal and the House of Lords in the U.K., is that they, or a large majority at least, come from a certain (privileged) background, a background very often shared with senior members of the executive. The criticism implies that this background and upbringing is reflected in their decisions (Griffiths, 1997). Griffiths makes the point also that it is politicians who appoint the judiciary.

Finding favourable comment is more difficult, but Lee's assessment of the judicial approach is extensive and, despite the rather weighted title of his book, *Judging Judges*, he is not entirely negative. He dismisses the criticism about privileged background influencing outcomes as 'too simplistic' (1988, p. 33). As an example of the fallibility of this proposition he uses the House of Lords judgment in the interlocutory *Spycatcher* judgment;[9] if the theory about background were correct then Lord Bridge, who went to Marlborough, an English public school, should have decided in favour of the establishment, instead of which he decided for the press. Lord Templeman, who went to a government school, should have decided for the press against the government, but he instead found for the government.

Lee examines the decision in the *GCHQ* case[10] and suspects that the

Law Lords allowed themselves to advance the judicial scope to look at the prerogative in the full knowledge that the government would win the case anyway on the issue of national security. Later on Lee turns again to the interlocutory House of Lords *Spycatcher* judgments. While saying that he was not a supporter of the Government's case, he roundly criticises those who rushed into print in condemnation of the majority without waiting for the reasoning behind their decision that the injunctions should remain in place. Of the majority decisions he says: 'Their judgments made sense. Given that the Law Lords were only being asked to preserve the status quo until the full trial, the decision was not unreasonable' (p. 113). Brown (1987) says much the same about the reasoning of the majority, but he adds a sting:

> Altruists or self-servers; the Peter Wrights of England, like Clive Ponting, will never enlist the sympathy of English Judges: at any rate, not until the Judges come to be recruited from a much broader spectrum of the society. (Jurors, as illustrated by the Ponting trial, may have a different attitude.) Whether or not he is an honest-to-goodness exposer of the 'real traitors' in high places, to the Establishment Mr Wright exemplifies the penultimate cad: not the very worst kind, because he did not betray his own precise social class. Nevertheless he has let the side down, and has compounded his own brand of professional 'treachery' from a safe desk at the nether-end of the world (pp. 315-316).

Support for the judiciary does, however, also come from an unexpected quarter; Michael correctly points out that a few cases have been surprisingly decided in a manner favourable to the respective defendants as a result of the presiding judge, and mentions in particular *R* v *Cairns, Aitken, Roberts and the Sunday Telegraph* (1971) (unreported) and *R* v *Aubrey, Berry and Campbell* (1978) (unreported). Robertson (1998) also commends Mars Jones J for his decision in *R* v *Aubrey, Berry and Campbell* although this is probably understandable as Robertson was one of the defence team for Duncan Campbell.

The difficulty in finding material favourable to the judiciary to make this discussion more evenly balanced is worthy of comment. Traditionally judges in office do not explain themselves to their critics, eliminating the most obvious source of response to criticism. Criticism of the judiciary has not been confined to cases involving national security, but that is the relevant context here. There is a perception that 'national security' is only really a serious issue in wartime, and during peacetime it is just another unjustifiable excuse for censorship. The conflict between free speech and censorship is one which gives rise to strong opinions, especially where it appears, rightly or wrongly, that the government is being abetted by the courts in its efforts to keep the public in the dark about its activities. The media, often ignorant of the processes of the law, can be less than objective in presenting the issues and will castigate anyone seen as obstructing the right to publish freely. It is clear also that some of the above criticism emanates from those whose political views are hostile to the establishment, in the general sense of the word, which would include judges.

## Summary

When the government uses the legal system to suppress allegedly sensitive information the judiciary play a pivotal role in balancing the various competing interests. The criticism would be less strident if judges were more convincing in their role as guardians of the public interest, particularly in cases relating to government claims of prejudice to national security. The public interest at the centre of this book is the interests of the general public in having all information available except for information that genuinely threatens national security. If the judiciary were always to approach with scepticism government claims for suppression in the interests of national security, the public interest would be much better served.

The last three chapters have examined a range of concepts which underlie the issues discussed in the earlier chapters. The common theme is the difficulty inherent in balancing the various interests when the government wishes to suppress material on the basis that publication would be prejudicial to national security. When the voluntary D-Notice system is used the parties with the competing interests in suppression or publication, that is the government and the media, are directly involved in the decision making process. When the issues arise in the courts, judges make the decisions. The last three chapters have illustrated that neither the government nor the media is entirely objective in their respective claims to represent the public interest, their own interests submerging what may be in the interests of the general public. These chapters have also illustrated that the judiciary may not always be relied on either to safeguard the interests of the general public when a case involving national security comes to the courts.

## Notes

[1]    Bok (1982) chapters XII 'Secrets of State', XIII 'Military Secrecy' and XIV 'Whistleblowing and Leaking' contain an excellent analysis of the dilemmas, moral and otherwise, posed by secrecy in the respective contexts.

2   The Blair Labour government in the U.K. is opening up government to scrutiny with the Public Interest Disclosure Act 1998 and the Freedom of Information Bill 1998, albeit with exemptions for national security information, but at the same time initiating the first prosecutions under the Official Secrets Act 1989. In Australia the *Freedom of Information Act 1982* (Cth) establishes a right of public access to the documents of Commonwealth agencies and Ministers; s33(1) exempts documents 'if disclosure ... would be contrary to the public interest for the reason that the disclosure - (a) could reasonably be expected to cause damage to (i) the security of the Commonwealth; (ii) the defence of the Commonwealth ...'. The Act was amended in 1983 to exempt documents originating with, or received from, ASIS, ASIO, ONA, DSD or JIO; *Freedom of Information Act 1983* (Cth), s4.
      For a discussion on the position of whistleblowers in Australia see McMillan (1994). At present, in 2000, there is no protection for whistleblowers in Australia at the Commonwealth level.

3   This was evident through conversation with several Australian journalists during 1996 and 1997.

4   Among the cases examined by Eisenschitz (1985) are *R* v *Aubrey, Berry and Campbell* unreported, *R* v *Ponting* [1985] Crim LR 318, both discussed in Chapter 6, and *Council of Civil Service Unions* v *Minister for the Civil Service* [1985] 1 AC 374, discussed in Chapter 9.

5   With respect to Hartley, note Windschuttle's (1998) scathing criticism of media theorists in general and Hartley in particular.

6   For discussion of the differences see Ericson, Baranek and Chan (1991) and Bell (1991).

7   In the course of researching this book, two relevant examples of journalistic inaccuracy came to light. Whitton (1991) says: 'In Australia, the Fraser government sought an injunction in 1981 to stop *The Sydney Morning Herald* publishing certain Foreign Affairs documents and cables concerning Indonesia, but the Australian High Court's position on secrecy proved more sensible than that of the House of Lords. Refusing the injunction, Sir Anthony Mason ruled that ...' (p. 281). As has been discussed in Chapter 8, in *Commonwealth* v *John Fairfax & Sons Ltd* (1980) 147 CLR 39, the case in question, an interlocutory injunction was refused on the basis of breach of confidence, but granted with respect to the claim in copyright. Whitton's (p. 281) source is '(Turnbull, 1988, p. 12)'. Turnbull's exact words are (1988): 'Sir Anthony Mason had refused an injunction to the Government, saying that governments could only restrain the publication of confidential information if they could establish that the information was still secret, and most importantly, that its publication would cause real detriment, not just embarrassment and public debate and controversy' (p. 12). No mention is made of the interlocutory injunction granted with respect to the copyright claim. As the *Spycatcher* case did not involve any alleged breach of government copyright, and only related to breach of confidence, Turnbull may have considered it unnecessary to be pedantic about detail.
      The second instance is an article in *The Bulletin* by Fred Brenchley, referring to the publication of the memoirs of ex Australian Cabinet Minister, Neil Blewett (*The Bulletin*, 15 December 1998, p. 26). Brenchley says: 'Blewett has carefully exorcised security matters from his book to avoid breaching the Official Secrets Act' (p. 27). While Brenchley may be talking of the Official Secrets Act in the U.K., which is most unlikely in the circumstances, this is not mentioned. The context gives rise to the

impression that Australia has an Official Secrets Act at the Commonwealth level, and of course it does not.

8   For an analysis of the role of the justices in the High Court of Australia, at least until the mid 1980s, see Galligan (1987), in particular the final chapter. For an analysis of the Law Lords and the House of Lords from 1800 to 1976 see Stevens (1979).

9   *A-G* v *Guardian Newspapers* [1987] 3 All ER 316.

10   *Council of Civil Service Unions* v *Minister for the Civil Service* [1985] 1 AC 374.

## References

*A-G* v *Guardian Newspapers* [1987] 3 All ER 316.

Author not identified (1987), 'Current Topics - The constitutionality of "leaks" or disclosures by Ministers of the Crown', *The Australian Law Journal*, vol. 61(3), p. 107.

Author not identified (1995), 'Gareth's Suppression Capers', *Gazette of Law and Journalism*, vol. 32, p. 2.

Aylmerton, Lord Oliver of (1991), 'Spycatcher Case: Confidence, Copyright and Contempt', in S. Shetreet (ed), *Free Speech and National Security*, Dordrecht, p. 23.

Barry, P. (1994), *The Rise and Rise of Kerry Packer*, Sydney, pp. 56-57.

Bell, A. (1991), *The Language of the News Media*, Oxford, pp. 191-192.

Bok, S (1982), *Secrets - On the Ethics of Concealment and Revelation*, New York, pp. 18, 25.

Bower, T. (1995), *Maxwell - the Final Verdict*, London.

Bowman, D. (1990), 'The AJA code', in J. Henningham (ed) *Issues in Australian journalism*, Melbourne.

Brown, B. (1987), 'Spycatcher and the Lords: the Rock and the Jellyfish', *Recent Law*, vol. October, pp. 315-316.

Campbell, E. and Whitmore, H. (1975), *Freedom in Australia*, Sydney, p. 352.

Chadwick, P. (1990), 'The ownership disaster: how journalism failed', in J. Henningham (ed), *Issues in Australian journalism*, Melbourne.

*Chandler* v *D.P.P.* [1964] A.C. 763.

Cmnd 1681 (1962), *Security Procedures in the Public Service*.

*Commonwealth* v *John Fairfax & Sons Ltd* (1980) 147 CLR 39.

*Council of Civil Service Unions* v *Minister for the Civil Service* [1985] 1 AC 374.

*Crimes Act 1914* (Cth).

Curran, J. (1978), 'The Press as an Agency of Social Control: an Historical Perspective', in G. Boyce, J. Curran and P. Wingate (eds), *Newspaper History from the Seventeenth Century to the Present Day*, London, p. 74.

*Daily Mirror*, 23 November 1972 (cited in Munster, 1987, p. 295).

de Maria, W. (1995), 'Whistleblowing', *The Alternative Law Journal*, vol. 20 No 6, p. 270.

Dempster, Q. (1997), *Whistleblowers*, Sydney, pp. 208-209.

Eisenschitz, T. (1985), 'Secrecy and the Free Flow of Information in the UK', *European Intellectual Property Review*, vol. 9, p. 257.

Ericson, R., Baranek, P. and Chan, J. (1987), *Visualising Deviance: A Study of News Organization*, Milton Keynes, pp. 4, 8.

Ericson, R., Baranek, P. and Chan, J. (1989), *Negotiating Control: A Study of News Sources*, Milton Keynes, p. 92.

Ericson, R., Baranek, P. and Chan, J. (1991), *Representing Order: Crime, Law, and Justice in the News Media*, Buckingham, p. 21.

Ewing, K. and Gearty, C. (1990), *Freedom Under Thatcher: Civil Liberties in Modern Britain*, Oxford, p. 129.

Fairley, D. (1990), 'D Notices, Official Secrets and the Law', *Oxford Journal of Legal Studies*, vol. 10, p. 430.

Fowler, R. (1991), *Language in the News: Discourse and Ideology in the Press*, London, p. 11.

*Freedom of Information Act* 1982 (Cth), s33.

*Freedom of Information Act* 1983 (Cth), s4.

Freedom of Information Bill 1998 (U.K.).

Galligan, B. (1987), *Politics of the High Court: A Study of the Judicial Branch of the Government in Australia*, Brisbane.

Golding, P. and Elliott, P. (1996), 'Bias, Objectivity and Ideology', in P. Marris and S. Thornham (eds), *Media Studies: A Reader*, Edinburgh.

Golding, P. and Elliott, P. (1996), 'News Values and News Production', in P. Marris and S. Thornham (eds), *Media Studies: A Reader*, Edinburgh.

Griffith, J. (1991), *The Politics of the Judiciary*, London.

Griffith, J. (1997), *The Politics of the Judiciary*, London, pp. 298-299.

Halliwell, M. (1991), 'Judicial Review and Broadcasting Freedom: the Route to Europe', *Northern Ireland Legal Quarterly*, vol. 42(3), p. 246.

Hanks, P. (1988), 'National Security - A Political Concept', *Monash University Law Review*, vol. 14, p. 114.

Hartley, J. (1989), *Understanding News*, London, pp. 21, 52, 116.

Henderson, G. (1990), 'The nine myths of Murdochphobia', in J. Henningham (ed), *Issues in Australian Journalism*, Melbourne.

Henningham, J. (1991), 'Mass Media', in J. Henningham (ed), *Institutions in Australian Society*, Brisbane, p. 266.

Hocking, B. (1993), 'What Lies in the Public Interest? A Legal History of Official Secrets in Britain', *Queensland University of Technology Law Journal*, vol. 9, p. 31.

Keane, J. (1991), *The Media and Democracy*, Cambridge.

Knightley, P. (1998), *A Hack's Progress*, London, p. 177.

Lance Bennett, W. (1988), *News - The Politics of Illusion*, New York, pp. xi, 26, 35, 44, 51.

Lee, H., Hanks, P. and Morabito, V. (1995), *In the Name of National Security: The Legal Dimensions*, Sydney.

Lee, S. (1988), *Judging Judges*, London, pp. 33, 109, 113.

Lewis, N. (1990), 'Undemocratic Centralism and Neo-Corporatism', *Alberta Law Review*, vol. XXVIII, No. 2, p. 543.

Lustgarten, L. (1989), 'Learning from Peter Wright: a Response to D.C. Watt', *Pol. Q.*, vol. 60, pp. 230-231.

Lustgarten, L. and Leigh I. (1994), *In From the Cold: National Security and Parliamentary Democracy*, Oxford, pp. 260, 491.

McMillan, J. (1994), 'The Whistleblower versus the Organization - Who should be Protected?', in T. Campbell and W. Sadurski (eds), *Freedom of Communication*, Aldershot.

Michael, J. (1982), *The Politics of Secrecy*, Harmondsworth.

Munster, G. (1987), *Rupert Murdoch - A Paper Prince*, Ringwood, pp. 97, 103.

Official Secrets Act 1989 (U.K.).

Pincher, C. (1968), 'Press Freedom and National Security', *Journalism Today*, vol. Spring, p. 46.

Public Interest Disclosure Act 1998 (U.K.)

*R v Aubrey, Berry and Campbell* (1978) (unreported).

*R v Cairns, Aitken, Roberts and the Sunday Telegraph* (1971) (unreported).

*R v Ponting* [1985] Crim LR 318.

Robertson, G. (1998), *The Justice Game*, London.

Rowat, D. (1981), 'The Right to Government Information in Democracies', *Media Law and Practice*, vol. 2, p. 314.

Schauer, F. (1982), *Free speech: a philosophical enquiry*, pp. 198-199.

Senate Deb., No. 8, col. 722-723, 1 June 1995.

Senate Deb., No. 9, col. 988, 7 June 1995.

Siebert, F., Peterson, T. and Schramm, W. (1976), *Four Theories of the Press*, Urbana.

Stevens, R. (1979), *Law and Politics: The House of Lords as a Judicial Body, 1800-1976*, London.

Taylor, P. (1992), *War and the Media - Propaganda and Persuasion in the Gulf War*, Manchester, pp. 12-13.

*The Bulletin*, 15 December 1998, p.27.

*The Sydney Morning Herald*, 14 November 1998, p. 43.

*The Sydney Morning Herald*, 19 February 1999 (internet version).

*The Times*, 5 November 1997, p. 23.

*The Weekend Australian*, Review, 21-22 October 2000, p. 13.

Thomas, Justice E. (1995), 'Secrecy and Open Government', in P. Finn (ed), *Essays on Law and Government, Vol. 1, Principles and Values*, Sydney.

Turnbull, M. (1988), *The Spycatcher Trial*, Melbourne, p. 12.

Walker, N. (1990), 'Spycatcher's Scottish Sequel', *Public Law*, p. 354.

Whitton, E. (1991), 'Journalism and the Trade of Authority', in J. Henningham (ed), *Institutions in Australian Society*, Brisbane, p. 281.

Windschuttle, K. (1998), 'The Poverty of Media Theory', *Quadrant*, vol. March, p. 11.

# 12 Recommendations and Conclusion

This book examines the various interests at stake when the governments in either the U.K. or Australia wish to suppress confidential information on the grounds of prejudice to national security. The opposing parties are the government, seeking suppression, and the media, seeking publication, both at the same time claiming to represent the public interest. The underlying question is whether the parties do in fact represent the public interest, in the sense of the interests of the general public in having only that material suppressed which is genuinely prejudicial to national security.

The public interest in publication of confidential government information raises issues of free speech. At the outset of this book it was established that free speech is a principle worthy of protection, at least where it is political speech. In this context the most relevant justification is the argument from democracy, as it holds that in order for the general public to effectively participate in the democratic process they must be properly informed about the activities of their government.

The focus of the book has been twofold. Firstly the focus has been on the D-Notice system, where the government and the media meet to discuss whether the material in question is to be suppressed or published. Chapters 1 to 5 examine the history and present operation of the D-Notice system in the U.K. and Australia. From this it can be seen that the interests of the general public have never been impartially represented in the development of the D-Notice system in the U.K. and even less so in Australia. The interests of the general public are not independently represented in the current operation of the DA-Notice system in the U.K. The D-Notice system in Australia has been inoperative for some years, although in the latter part of the 1990s there was some attempt by the government to reinvigorate it. In Australia decisions on whether or not to publish are made by journalists and editors.

As the D-Notice system is voluntary and has no legal backing, the governments in both the U.K. and Australia have resorted to the law to suppress confidential government information. The second focus of the book has therefore been on the legal alternatives to the D-Notice system. Here it falls to the judiciary to balance the competing interests of the government and the media. Once again the underlying question is whether the interests of the general public are sufficiently safeguarded, this time by the judiciary. Chapters 6 to 8 examine the legal protection, through criminal or civil actions, of confidential government information. These chapters illustrate how, in both criminal and civil actions against the media, the judiciary have had the vital role of balancing the competing interests. In the absence of an operative D-Notice system in Australia, and the continuing sidestepping of the DA-Notice system in the U.K., it is the judiciary who must look after the interests of the general public. It is shown that that the judiciary in the U.K. and Australia have not consistently balanced the competing interests, some judges seeming to be too easily persuaded by government claims that national security is at stake.

Chapters 9 to 11 analyse a number of different concepts that are interwoven through the issues already considered. Chapter 9 looks at what is meant by 'national security' and 'the state', then inquires into whom or what balances the competing interests of national security against the competing public interest of openness in government, manifested by publication. This again clearly illustrates that some judges who carry out the role of balancing these interests, may be too easily persuaded by the governments' side of the argument. Chapter 10 examines the tension between freedom of speech and the suppression of information, and considers the question of what circumstances justify censorship. It determines that the D-Notice system is a prior restraint on speech, as are injunctions to prevent publication of confidential government information. Chapter 10 also determines that national security is one of the few legitimate reasons for suppression of government information and this may qualify these prior restraints as 'reasonable'. The constitutional issues explored indicate that, both in the U.K. and Australia, any government imposed restriction that affects free speech must now be 'proportionate' to withstand judicial scrutiny as to its validity. This is so even where the restriction on speech is imposed on the basis of harm to the public interest on the grounds of national security. While the government may be allowed a margin of appreciation, the test of proportionality will nonetheless constrain the judiciary to take into account the competing public interest in free speech. Chapter 11 looks at manipulation of the news by government and the media, thus showing that neither side objectively represents the interests of the general public. Finally the role of the judiciary is assessed.

The book identifies that neither the voluntary D-Notice system nor the legal alternatives give sufficient weight to the interests of the general public. The following conclusions may be drawn:

## 1. The DA-Notice system in the U.K.

The DA-Notice system currently operates in a satisfactory way in the U.K. for the participants, that is the government and the media, but the interests of the general public are not sufficiently represented on the Defence, Press and Broadcasting Advisory Committee. This can be overcome by the appointment of additional members to the committee whose role it is to represent the interests of the general public.

### Proposed reform: the appointment of independent members to the committee

*Additional independent members*

Two additional members, and a third to deputise, should be appointed to the Defence, Press and Broadcasting Advisory Committee. Appointments would require a two thirds vote of all the members of the committee. The reason for suggesting the appointments be made by the committee itself is to enhance the prospect of success of the proposal. There may be considerable difficulties in identifying a suitably impartial body with sufficient status to make the appointments and any appointments made by parties external to the committee may be resisted by the committee itself. The appointments would be for a three year term, renewable twice only, and staggered so that the first appointments are for one three year and one six year term, the deputy for a six year term. This ensures continuity in the event that one appointee is not reappointed.

The nominees must have no connections, direct or indirect, past or present, with the executive government, the civil service, the armed forces (needless to say this includes the various secret services, such as, but not limited to, MI5, MI6 and GCHQ), or the media. Their only role is to represent the interests of the general public by ensuring only government information which is genuinely prejudicial to national security interests is suppressed. When it comes to the actuality of suppressing material, it is usually a confidential matter between the secretary and the particular editor or journalist. Prior to advocating suppression of all or part of any material, the secretary must consult with at least one of the independent members. The resulting opinion of the independent member is to be made known to the particular journalist, editor or author in each case.

It follows that, to be fully informed, at least one of the independent members must be allowed to examine the material that the government wants to suppress and be privy to the reasons why the government wants it to be suppressed. While the secretary of the DPBAC spends most of his time examining material, it does not need to be so time consuming for the independent members. Apart from attendance at the two meetings per year, and other ad hoc business involving all members, the members need only be involved if suppression is recommended by the secretary.

If the extra members are sufficiently independent, as is the point of this recommendation, there will be occasions on which the media, for whatever reasons, may agree to suppress material at the request of the government, but the independent member(s) will advocate its publication. The independent members' role is merely to advise, the media individually still has the choice as to whether or not to publish, but they may precipitate a rethink on the part of either the government or media or both. Having independent members does not necessarily guarantee that any additional allegedly sensitive government information is in fact published, but this may happen. As important is the fact that the general public have a stake in the decision. Having an independent member may also encourage the likes of Peter Wright, David Shayler and Richard Tomlinson to have confidence in the DA-Notice system, although this may be a vain hope.

*Candidates for nomination to the positions of independent membership*

Among the most obvious candidates for nomination to the independent representatives' positions on the committee would be retired members of the judiciary. As in the past some have been seemingly reticent to approach government requests for suppression of information with the necessary cynicism, they may not all be sufficiently independent. Other candidates are:

- The Ombudsman;
- Nominees proposed by DPBAC members;
- Nominees proposed by other interested parties, such as free speech and human rights organisations;
- Nominees proposed by the Ombudsman;
- Members of academia with a proven interest in free speech issues. Preferably such academics should have a legal background for a basic understanding of the legal issues involved if the information ultimately goes before the courts.

Consideration was given to including members of Parliament from the major opposition party. The arguments against such individuals being nominated may outweigh the arguments in favour. The arguments against are:

- It may be one of the few situations where the major parties are in agreement over tactics, and suppression is favoured so that when either party is in power they can rely on the support of at least one of the independent members;
- the party to which such a member belongs may be voted into power during the term of the candidate's appointment. In this case the independent committee member would be required to resign and this would be unnecessarily disruptive;
- an opposition member may have to deal with incidents that took place when his or her party was in power.

The arguments in favour are:

- The member may be in a position to be permitted to view sensitive government material. It is equally likely that the government may resist this;
- the member would have an understanding of the competing issues involved;
- the member may favour publication if the material has little or nothing to do with national security but shows the government in a less than favourable light.

Alternatively one independent member may come from the membership of one of the standing sub-committees of Parliament that deals with defence matters; such a nominee may come from any party but would require a two third majority endorsement of the particular committee. No more than one independent member should be a current Member of Parliament.

Because of the requirement that at least one of the independent members be given access to sensitive government material, retired senior members of the judiciary, some members of the major Opposition party, and the Ombudsman are the candidates that most readily qualify. It may be necessary for all other candidates to undergo some sort of screening process, and without wishing to add further burdens to the office, this could be done by the Ombudsman. The requirement for access to material must not be allowed to become an insuperable problem put up by the government of the day as an argument against having independent members. If necessary it need only be one of the members at any given time that has this access, the other member being present for more routine decisions such as general drafting of D-Notices.

## Other reforms

One proposal is that the committee should report annually to Parliament, and these reports should be available to the public. Chadwick (1995) recommends some reforms in the context of the Australian system and these apply equally to the DA-Notice system. Some of his proposals already operate, for example he says committee members should be named and a general description of the matters covered by D-Notices should be published.[1] Chadwick's remaining proposals should be adopted. These are that committee members should serve for a limited term only; the criteria for deciding the subject matter of individual D-Notices should be disclosed and such criteria should include a precise definition of 'national security'; D-Notices should expire on a fixed date unless specifically renewed after a re-examination; the system as a whole should be reviewed regularly. Chadwick says, 'any damage to national security said to justify suppression be immediate, direct, inevitable and irreparable, a test applied by the US Supreme Court in *Pentagon Papers*, a national security case' (p. 7).[2]

## 2. The D-Notice system in Australia

The D-Notice system has been inoperative in Australia for a number of years. When the system did function in Australia the Defence, Press and Broadcasting Committee was too heavily weighted in favour of government interests. The system should be revived, but the structure should be changed to reflect the operation of the system in the U.K.

## Proposed reform: composition of the DPBC

In a revitalised D-Notice system the secretary must be independent from the government and the media. No committee members should be Ministers, or members of Parliament from the party, or the coalition parties, holding the balance of power in the House of Representatives. There must be additional independent members on the committee, the same number and criteria to apply as those put forward for the suggested reform of the U.K. committee under 1(i) above.

## Other reforms

The reform proposals mentioned above for the DA-Notice system in the U.K. should also apply to the Australian system. In addition there must be no amendment of the *Crimes Act* 1914 (Cth) to make secondary disclosures by the media an offence.

## 3. Examination of the evidence by the judiciary

In the event that the government in either country applies for an injunction to restrain publication by the media of allegedly sensitive government information, the judiciary must carefully examine the evidence, that is *examine the information itself*, to ensure it does in fact represent a genuine threat to national security. This applies also to any criminal action that may be instigated against the media for the publication, or intended publication, of any such information. In addition:

- all applications for injunctions to suppress publication in the interests of national security must be heard inter partes;
- no injunction shall operate 'contra mundum'.

Consideration was given to recommending that the above suggestions be given statutory force. As this would give rise to criticism on the basis that it interferes with the independence of the judiciary, and compromises the separation of powers doctrine, the proposal was discounted.

## Conclusion

It is acknowledged that there is no perfect solution to the question of when confidential government information is to be suppressed in the interests of national security. With the advent of the Internet, it is now almost impossible for a government to suppress secret information. Conciliation with disgruntled possessors of sensitive government information may be more effective than heavy handed use of the legal system. Despite the criticisms of the D-Notice system, it does allow the issues to be discussed by the parties involved, and ultimately leaves the decision with respect to publication in the hands of the media or author. A system reformed in the way proposed above would permit negotiation by representatives of all the stakeholders and thus do more to balance the competing interests than any of the alternatives.

## Notes

[1]    The names and business addresses of the members of the DPBAC, and the DA-Notices, are published on the DPBAC website; http://www.dnotice.org.uk/index.htm

The names, business addresses and phone numbers of the members of the DPBC, and the D-Notices, were included in the last published booklet by Defence, Press and Broadcasting Committee (1983), *Australian D-Notices*, Canberra.

[2]    Chadwick gives no reference for the *Pentagon Papers* case; it is *New York Times Co* v *US*, 403 US 713 (1971) the quote is per Stewart J, p. 730.

## References

Chadwick, P. (1995), 'Pressure on to replace D-notices', *Communications Update*, vol. June, p. 7.

Defence, Press and Broadcasting Committee (1983), *Australian D-Notices*, Canberra.

*New York Times Co* v *US*, 403 US 713 (1971), p. 730.

www.dnotice.org.uk/index.htm

# Bibliography

Aitken, J. (1971), *Officially Secret*, London.

Arnheim, M. (1988), 'The Spy in the Ointment', *Solicitors Journal*, vol. 132(43), p. 1474.

Aronson, M. and Hunter J. (1998), *Litigation Evidence and Procedure*, Sydney.

Aronson, M., and Dyer, B. (1996), *Judicial Review of Administrative Action*, Sydney.

Attorney-General's Department (1994), 'Unauthorised Disclosure of Government Information', *Legal Practice Briefing*, vol.14, Canberra, no page numbers.

Aubrey, C. (1981), *Who's Watching You?*, London.

Australian Press Council (1994), *Annual Report No. 18*, Sydney.

Australian Press Council (1996), *Annual Report No. 20*, Sydney.

Author not identified (1976), 'National Security and the Amended Freedom of Information Act', *Yale Law Journal*, vol. 85, p. 401.

Author not identified (1987), 'Current Topics - The constitutionality of "leaks" or disclosures by Ministers of the Crown', *The Australian Law Journal*, vol. 61(3), p. 107.

Author not identified (1987), 'News – Spy in the sky', *Media Law and Practice*, vol. 8, p. 34.

Author not identified (1987), 'UK News', *Media Law and Practice*, vol. 8, p. 118.

Author not identified (1990), 'Keeping Secrets: Congress, the Courts, and National Security Information', *Harvard Law Review*, vol. 103, p. 906.

Author not identified (1995), 'Gareth's Suppression Capers', *Gazette of Law and Journalism*, vol. 32, p. 2.

Author not identified (1995), 'News', *Australian Press Council News*, vol. August, p. 4.

Author not identified (undated), 'Injunctions and the Criminal Law', *The Laws of Australia*, vol. 2 (Administrative Law).

Aylmerton, Lord Oliver of (1991), 'Spycatcher Case: Confidence, Copyright and Contempt', in S. Shetreet (ed), *Free Speech and National Security*, Dordrecht.

Bainbridge, C. (1984) 'One Hundred Years of Journalism', in C. Bainbridge (ed.), *One Hundred Years of Journalism*, London.

Barendt, E. (1996), *Freedom of Speech*, Oxford.

Barker, M. (1995), 'Accountability to the Public: Travelling Beyond the Myth', in P. Finn (ed), *Essays on Law and Government, Vol 1, Principles and Values*, Sydney.

Barry, P. (1994), *The Rise and Rise of Kerry Packer*, Sydney.

Bell, A. (1991), *The Language of the News Media*, Oxford.

Blackshield, T. and Williams, G. (1998), *Australian Constitutional Law & Theory: Commentary & Materials*, Sydney.

Blackstone, W. (1765), *Commentaries*, Book IV.

Bok, S. (1982), *Secrets - On the Ethics of Concealment and Revelation* , New York.

Bork, R. (1971), 'Neutral Principles and Some First Amendment Problems', *Indiana Law Journal*, vol. 47, p. 1.

Bower, T. (1995), *Maxwell - the Final Verdict*, London.

Bowman, D. (1990), 'The AJA code', in J. Henningham (ed), *Issues in Australian journalism*, Melbourne.

Brown, B. (1987), 'Spycatcher and the Lords: The Rock and the Jellyfish', *Recent Law*, vol. October, p. 312.

Bulloch, J., and Miller, H. (1961), *Spy Ring, The Full Story of the Naval Secrets Case*, London.

Burnet, D. and Thomas, R. (1989), 'Spycatcher - the Commodification of Truth', *Journal of Law and Society*, vol. 16(2), p. 210.

Campbell, E. (1967), 'Public Access to Government Documents', *The Australian Law Journal*, vol. 41, p. 73.

Campbell, E. and Whitmore H. (1975), *Freedom in Australia*, Sydney.

Campbell, T. (1994), 'Rationales for Freedom of Communication', in T. Campbell and W. Sadurski (eds), *Freedom of Communication*, Aldershot.

Carne, G. (1993), 'Official Secrets and the Gibbs Report: A Charter for Reform or a Tug of the Legal Forelock?', *University of Tasmania Law Review*, vol. 12(1), p. 11.

Cass, D. (1994), 'Through the Looking Glass: The High Court of Australia and the Right to Political Speech', in T. Campbell and W. Sadurski (eds), *Freedom of Communication*, Aldershot.

Chadwick, P. (1990), 'The ownership disaster: how journalism failed', in J. Henningham (ed), *Issues in Australian journalism*, Melbourne.

Chadwick, P. (1995), 'Pressure on to replace D-notices', *Communications Update*, vol. June, p. 6.

Chafee, Z. (1919), 'Freedom of Speech in War Time', *Harvard Law Review*, vol. 32, p. 932.

Chafee, Z. (1969), *Free Speech in the United States*, New York.

Chapman, B. (1963), *British Government Observed*, London.

Chapman, R. and Hunt, M. (eds) (1987), *Open Government*, Beckenham.

Chesterman, M. (1998), 'The Common Law Rules in Defamation - OK?', *The Tort Law Review*, vol. March, p. 9.

Clark, W. (1986) *From Three Worlds*, London.

Cm 3782 (1997), *Rights Brought Home: The Human Rights Bill.*

Cm 3818 (1997), *Your Right to Know: Freedom of Information.*

Cmnd 1681 (1962), *Security Procedures in the Public Service.*

Cmnd 3309 (1967), *Report of Committee of Privy Councillors appointed to inquire into 'D' Notice matters.*

Cmnd 3312 (1967), *The 'D' Notice System.*

Cmnd 5104 (1972), *Departmental Committee on s.2 of the Official Secrets Act 1911.*

Cmnd 8129 (1981), *The D Notice System, Observations presented by the Secretary of State for Defence.*

Cmnd 8388 (1981), Law Commission (U.K.) Report 111, *Breach of Confidence.*

Coliver, S. (1992), 'Spycatcher - the legal and broader significance of the European Court's judgment', *Media Law and Practice*, p. 142.

Cowen, Z. (1984), 'Protecting Press and Public' in C. Bainbridge (ed), *One Hundred Years of Journalism*, London.

Creighton, P. (1993), 'The Implied Guarantee of Free Political Communication', *Western Australian Law Review*, vol. 23, p. 163.

Curran, J. (1978), 'The Press as an Agency of Social Control: an Historical Perspective', in G. Boyce, J. Curran and P. Wingate (eds), *Newspaper History from the Seventeenth Century to the Present Day*, London.

*Daily Express*, 19 October 1967.

*Daily Express*, 21 February 1967.

*Daily Mirror*, 23 November 1972.

Dandeker, C. (1994), 'National Security and Democracy: The United Kingdom Experience', *Armed Forces and Society*, vol. 20 (3), p. 353.

de Maria, W. (1995), 'Whistleblowing', *The Alternative Law Journal*, vol. 20 No 6, p. 270.

Dean, R. (1990), *The Law of Trade Secrets*, Sydney.

Defence, Press and Broadcasting Committee (1983), *Australian D-Notices*, Canberra.

Dempster, Q. (1997), *Whistleblowers*, Sydney.

Dicey, A. (1945), *Introduction to the Study of the Law of the Constitution*, London.

Douglas, N. (1993), 'Freedom of Expression under the Australian Constitution', *UNSW Law Journal*, vol. 16(2), p. 315.

Drewry, G. (1985). 'The GCHQ Case - A Failure of Government Communications', *Parliamentary Affairs*, vol. 38, p. 371.

Dulles, A. (1963), *The Craft of Intelligence*, New York.

Dworkin, R. (1977), *Taking Rights Seriously*, London.

Eisenschitz, T. (1985), 'Secrecy and the Free Flow of Information in the UK', *European Intellectual Property Review*, vol. 9, p. 254.

Ericson, R., Baranek, P. and Chan, J. (1987), *Visualising Deviance: A Study of News Organization*, Milton Keynes.

Ericson, R., Baranek, P. and Chan, J. (1989), *Negotiating Control: A Study of News Sources*, Milton Keynes.

Ericson, R., Baranek, P. and Chan, J. (1991), *Representing Order: Crime, Law, and Justice in the News Media*, Buckingham.

European Convention on Human Rights.

Evans, G. (1984), 'National Security and civil liberties: the role of ASIO', *Australian Foreign Affairs Record*, vol. May, p. 451.

Evans, J. (1980), *de Smith's Judicial Review of Administrative Action*, London.

Ewing, K. and Gearty, C. (1990), *Freedom under Thatcher*. Oxford.

Fairley, D. (1990), 'D Notices, Official Secrets and the Law', *Oxford Journal of Legal Studies*, vol.10, p. 430.

Feldman, D. (1979), 'Injunctions and the Criminal Law', *Modern Law Review*, vol. 42, p. 369.

Finn, P. (undated), *Integrity in Government - Interim Report 1*, Canberra.

Fitzgerald, B. (1993), 'Proportionality and Australian Constitutionalism', *University of Tasmania Law Review*, vol. 12(2), p. 263.

Forsyth, C. (1985), 'Judicial Review, The Royal Prerogative and National Security', *Northern Ireland Legal Quarterly*, vol. 36(1) Spring, p. 25.

Fowler, R. (1991), *Language in the News: Discourse and Ideology in the Press*, London.

Galligan, B. (1987), *Politics of the High Court: A Study of the Judicial Branch of the Government in Australia*, Brisbane.

Gibbs Committee (1991), *Review of Commonwealth Criminal Law: Final Report*, Canberra.

Golding, P. and Elliott, P. (1996), 'Bias, Objectivity and Ideology', in P. Marris and S. Thornham (eds), *Media Studies: A Reader*, Edinburgh.

Golding, P. and Elliott, P. (1996), 'News Values and News Production', in P. Marris and S. Thornham (eds), *Media Studies: A Reader*, Edinburgh.

Gowing, M. (1974), *Independence and Deterrence - Britain and Atomic Energy, 1945-1952 Vol. 2*, London.

Grabowsky, P. and Wilson, P. (1989), *Journalism and Justice: How Crime is Reported*, Sydney.

Grant, W. (1985), 'In the Public Interest? The Disclosure of Confidential Information', *Media Law & Practice*, vol. 6, p. 178.

Griffith, J. (1991), *The Politics of the Judiciary*, London.

Griffith, J. (1997), *The Politics of the Judiciary*, London.

Gurry, F. (1984), *Breach of Confidence*, Oxford.

H. of R. Deb. col. 265 and 269, 21 October 1914 (Second Reading).

H. of R. Deb., col. 1643, 4 October 1967.

H. of R. Deb., col. 2865, 8 & 9 November 1967 (Answers to Questions).

H. of R. Deb., col. 2339, 25 October 1977.

H.C. Deb., 4th series, vol. LXXXI, col. 1593-1597, 27 July 1900.

H.C. Deb., 4th Series, vol. 188, col. 673-674, 11 May 1908.

H.C. Deb., vol. 47, col. 388-389, 22 January 1913.

H.C. Deb., vol. LXVI, col. 8, 25 August 1914.

H.C. Deb., vol. LXVI, col. 372-374 and col. 453-511, 31 August 1914.

H.C. Deb., vol. 68, col. 123-139, 12 November 1914.

H.C. Deb., vol. 640, col. 636-638, 11 May 1961.

H.C. Deb., vol. 676, col. 26, 23 April 1963.

H.C. Deb., vol. 676, col. 27, 31, 23 April 1963.

H.C. Deb., vol. 742, col. 274, 28 February 1967.

H.C. Deb., vol. 743, col. 160-161 (Written Answers to Questions), 17 March 1967.

H.C. Deb., vol. 748, col. 1989, 2080, 2084, 2085, 2088-2089, 22 June 1967.

H.L. Deb., vol. 250, col. 904, 29 May 1963.

H.L. Deb., vol. 284, col. 775-783, 6 July 1967.

H.L. Deb., vol. 357, col. 947, 26 February 1975.

Halliwell, M. (1991), 'Judicial Review and Broadcasting Freedom: the Route to Europe', *Northern Ireland Legal Quarterly*, vol. 42(3), p. 246.

Hanks, P. (1988), 'National Security - A Political Concept', *Monash University Law Review*, vol. 14, p. 114.

Hartley, J. (1989), *Understanding News*, London.

HC 773 (1980), *Third Report from the Defence Committee (Session 1979-80), The D Notice System*, London.

Heath, E. (1989), 'A State of secrecy', *New Statesman & Society*, vol. 10 March, p. 10.

Hedley, P. and Aynsley, C. (1967), *The D-Notice Affair*, London.

Henderson, G. (1990), 'The nine myths of Murdochphobia', in J. Henningham (ed), *Issues in Australian Journalism*, Melbourne.

Henningham, J. (1991), 'Mass Media', in J. Henningham (ed), *Institutions in Australian Society*, Brisbane.

Hocking, B. (1993), 'What Lies in the Public Interest? A Legal History of Official Secrets in Britain', *Queensland University of Technology Law Journal*, vol. 9, p. 31.

Hollingsworth, M. and Fielding, N. (1999), *Defending the Realm – MI5 and the Shayler Affair*, London.

Hooper, D. (1987), *Official Secrets*, London.

Howard, M. (1989), 'Spycatcher Downunder: *A-G for the United Kingdom* v *Heinemann Publishers Australia*', *Western Australian Law Review*, vol. 19, p. 158.

International Covenant on Civil and Political Rights.

Jaconelli, J (1982), 'The "D" Notice System', *Public Law*, p. 37.

Joint Working Party of JUSTICE and the British Committee of the International Press Institute (1965), *The Law and the Press*, London.

Jones, G. (1970), 'Restitution of Benefits Obtained in Breach of Another's Confidence', *The Law Quarterly Review*, vol. 86, p. 463.

Kalugin, O. (with Fen Montaigne) (1994), *Spymaster*, London.

Keane, J. (1991), *The Media and Democracy*, Cambridge.

Knightley, P. (1998), *A Hack's Progress*, London.

Lance Bennett, W. (1988), *News - The Politics of Illusion*, New York.

Law Commission (U.K.) Working Paper No. 58 (1974), *Breach of Confidence*, London.

Lee, H. (1989), 'The Australian Security Intelligence Organisation - New Mechanisms for Accountability', *International and Comparative Law Quarterly*, vol.38, p. 890.

Lee, H. (1994), 'Proportionality in Australian Constitutional Adjudication' in G. Lindell (ed), *Future Directions in Australian Constitutional Law*, Sydney.

Lee, H., Hanks, P. and Morabito, V. (1995), *In the Name of National Security: The Legal Dimensions*, Sydney.

Lee, S. (1988), *Judging Judges*, (1988) London.

Leigh, I. and Lustgarten, L. (1989), 'The Security Service Act', *Modern Law Review*, vol. 52, p. 801.

Lewis, N. (1990), 'Undemocratic Centralism and Neo-Corporatism', *Alberta Law Review*, vol. XXVIII No. 2, p. 540.

Ligertwood, A. (1993), *Australian Evidence*, Sydney.

Lindell, G. (1994), 'Recent Developments in the Judicial Interpretation of the Australian Constitution', in G. Lindell (ed), *Future Directions in Australian Constitutional Law*, Sydney.

Lovelace, C. (1978), 'British press censorship during the First World War', in G. Boyce, J. Curran, and P. Wingate (eds), *Newspaper History from the 17th Century to the Present Day*, London.

Lowe, N. and Sufrin, B. (1996), *Borrie and Lowe; The Law of Contempt*, London.

Lustgarten, L. (1987), 'Old News', *New Society*, vol. 11 September, p. 26.

Lustgarten, L. (1989), 'Learning from Peter Wright: A response to D.C. Watt', *Pol Q*, vol. 60, p. 222.

Lustgarten, L. and Leigh, I. (1994), *From the Cold: National Security and Parliamentary Democracy*, Oxford.

Macmillan Patfield, F. (1996), 'Towards a Reconciliation of Free Speech and Copyright', in E. Barendt, S. Bate, J. Dickens (eds), *The Yearbook of Media and Entertainment Law*, Oxford.

Maher, L. (1995), 'ASIS "D" Notice Controversy', *Media Law Reporter*, vol.2, p. 139.

Mann, F. (1988), '*Spycatcher* in the High Court of Australia', *The Legal Quarterly Review*, vol. 104, p. 497.

Margach, J. (1978), *The Abuse of Power: The War between Downing Street and the Media from Lloyd George to Callaghan*, London.

Marshall, G. (1961) 'Comment' *Public Law*, p. 225.

Marshall, G. (1967), 'Comment', *Public Law*, vol. Winter, p.261.

McDermott, J. (1991), ' "Spycatcher": success before the European Commission in Strasbourg', *Media Law and Practice*, vol. 12, p. 14.

McGinness, J. (1990), 'Secrecy Provisions in Commonwealth Legislation', *Federal Law Review*, vol. 19, p. 49.

McMillan, J. (1994), 'The Whistleblower versus the Organization - Who should be Protected?', in T. Campbell and W. Sadurski (eds), *Freedom of Communication*, Aldershot.

Meagher, R., Gummow, W. and Lehane, J. (1992), *Equity Doctrines & Remedies*, Sydney.

Mercer, D., Mungham, G. and Williams, K. (1987), *The Fog of War*, London.

Michael, J. (1982), *The Politics of Secrecy*, Harmondsworth.

Mill, J.S. (1859), *On Liberty*, reprinted by The Legal Classics Library (1992), New York.

Miller, C. (1989), *Contempt of Court*, Oxford.

Miller, R. (1994), 'What Should Parliament Know?', in A. Bergin and R. Hall (eds), *Intelligence and Australian National Security*, Canberra.

Milton, J. (November 1644), *Areopagitica*, reprinted by Cambridge University Press (1918), Cambridge.

Ministry of Defence Open Government Document No. 93/06, *The Defence Advisory Notices: A Review of the D Notice System*.

*Morning Post*, 2 September 1911.

Munster, G. (1987), *Rupert Murdoch - A Paper Prince*, Ringwood.

Narain, B. (1988), 'Confidentiality, National Security, and the Right to Know - the *Spycatcher* Decision', *Northern Ireland Legal Quarterly*, p. 73.

*Nation Review*, 9-15 February 1978.

*Nation Review*, 16-22 February 1978.

*Nation*, 15 July 1967.

Neville Brown, L. (1977), 'A Bill of Rights for the United Kingdom?', *The Parliamentarian*, vol. LVIII No. 2, p. 79.

*New Statesman*, 11 February 1971.

Newman, K. (1984), 'The Media and Public Order' in C. Bainbridge (ed), *One Hundred Years of Journalism*, London.

Nicol, A. (1979), 'Official Secrets and Jury Vetting', *Crim.L.R.*, p. 284.

O'Higgins, P. (1972), *Censorship in Britain*, London.

Palmer, A. (1984), 'The History of the D-Notice Committee', in C. Andrew and D. Dilks (eds), *The Missing Dimension: Government and Intelligence Communities in the Twentieth Century*, London.

Palmer, S. (1990), 'Tightening Secrecy Law: The Official Secrets Act 1989', *Public Law*, p. 243.

Patfield, F. (1989), 'Spycatcher Worldwide - an Overview', *European Intellectual Property Review*, vol. 6, p. 201.

Pincher, C, (1968), 'Press Freedom and National Security', *Journalism Today*, vol. Spring, p. 37.

Pincher, C. (1978), *Inside Story: A Documentary of the Pursuit of Power*, London.

Pincher, C. (1981), *Their Trade is Treachery*, London.

PRO ADM 1/20905.

PRO ADM 116/1058.

PRO ADM 116/4082.

PRO CAB 16/27.

PRO CAB 17/91.

PRO CAB 4/8, 368-B CID.

PRO DEFE 53/1.

PRO DEFE 53/2.

PRO DEFE 53/3.

PRO DEFE 53/4.

PRO DEFE 53/5.

PRO DEFE 53/6.

PRO DEFE 53/7.

PRO DEFE 53/8.

PRO DEFE 53/9.

PRO DEFE 53/10.

PRO DEFE 53/19.

PRO WO 32/6381.

Rankin, M. (1986), 'National Security: Information, Accountability, and the Canadian Security Intelligence Service', *University of Toronto Law Journal*, vol.36, p. 249.

Relyea, H. (1984), 'National Security and Freedom of Information', *Media Law and Practice*, vol. 5(3), p. 238.

Richelson, J., and Ball, D. (1990), *The Ties that Bind*, Sydney.

Robertson, G. (1989), *Freedom, the Individual and the Law*, London.

Robertson, G. (1998), *The Justice Game*, London.

Robertson, G. and Nicol, A. (1990), *Media Law*, London.

Rowat, D. (1981), 'The Right to Government Information in Democracies', *Media Law and Practice*, vol. 2, p. 314.

Royal Commission on the Press (U.K.) (1977), *Final Report*, London.

Scanlon, T. (1979), 'Freedom of Expression and Categories of Expression', *U. Pittsb. L.R.*, vol. 40, p. 519.

Scanlon, T. (1986), 'A Theory of Freedom of Expression', in R. Dworkin (ed), *The Philosophy of Law*, Oxford.

Schauer, F. (1982), *Free Speech: a Philosophical Enquiry*, Cambridge.

Schauer, F. (1994), 'Free Speech in a World of Private Power', in T. Campbell and W. Sadurski (eds), *Freedom of Communication*, Aldershot.

Seegal, Z. (1991), 'Security Censorship: Prior Restraint (After the Schnitzer Decision)', in S. Shetreet (ed), *Free Speech and National Security*, Dordrecht.

Seely, J. (1930), *Adventure*, London.

Senate Deb., vol. 101, col. 3615-3616, 9 December 1983.

Senate Deb., No. 8, col. 716-726, 1 June 1995.

Senate Deb., No. 9, col. 987-988, 7 June 1995.

Siebert, F., Peterson, T. and Schramm, W. (1976), *Four Theories of the Press*, Urbana.

Smallbone, D. (1993), 'Recent Suggestions of an Implied "Bill of Rights" ', *Federal Law Review*, vol. 21, p. 255.

Spry, I. (1997), *The Principles of Equitable Remedies*, Sydney.

Stevens, R. (1979), *Law and Politics: The House of Lords as a Judicial Body, 1800-1976*, London.

Stewart, A. (1988), "Confidentiality and the Employment Relationship", *Australian Journal of Labour Law*, vol. 1, p. 1.

Street, H. (1951), 'State Secrets - A Comparative Study', *Modern Law Review*, vol. 14(2), p. 121.

Stuckey, J. (1981), 'The Liability of Innocent Third Parties Implicated in Another's Breach of Confidence', *UNSW Law Journal*, vol. 4, p. 73.

Supperstone, M. (1981), *Brownlie's Law of Public Order and National Security*, London.

Sykes, E. (1953), 'The Injunction in Public Law', *University of Qld L.J.*, p. 114.

Sykes, E., Lanham, D., Tracey, R., and Esser, K. (1997), *General Principles of Administrative Law*, Sydney.

Taylor, P. (1992), *War and the Media - Propaganda and Persuasion in the Gulf War*, Manchester.

Ten, C. L. (1980), *Mill on Liberty*, Oxford.

*The Age*, 24 September 1984.

*The Age*, 25 September 1984.

*The Australian Financial Review*, 13 October 1994.

*The Australian*, 13 October 1994.

*The Australian*, 15 September 1997.

*The Australian*, 9 July 1997.
*The Bulletin*, 15 December 1998.
The Commission of Inquiry into the Australian Secret Intelligence Service (1995), *Report on the Australian Secret Intelligence Service*, Canberra.
*The Daily Telegraph*, 20 May 2000.
*The Daily Telegraph*, 22 August 2000.
*The Daily Telegraph*, 25 October 2000.
*The Guardian*, 19 November 1998.
*The Guardian*, 13 April 1999.
The Law Reform Commission (Australia) (1985), *Report No 27: Standing in Public Interest Litigation*, Canberra.
*The National Times*, 12-17 February 1973.
*The National Times*, 19-24 February 1973.
*The National Times*, 6-11 August 1973.
*The National Times*, 20-25 August 1973.
*The National Times*, February 25-March 2 1974.
*The National Times*, October 31-November 5 1977.
*The Sunday Times*, 2 August 1998.
*The Sunday Times*, 1 November 1998.
*The Sunday Times*, 9 July 2000.
*The Sydney Morning Herald*, 27 May 1995.
*The Sydney Morning Herald*, 14 December 1995.
*The Sydney Morning Herald*, 14 November 1998.
*The Sydney Morning Herald*, 19 February 1999 (internet version).
*The Times*, 19 September 1907: cited in PRO ADM 116/1058.
*The Times*, 7 July 1967.
*The Times*, 4 February 1971.
*The Times*, 24 July 1997 (internet version).
*The Times*, 3 November 1997.
*The Times*, 4 November 1997.
*The Times*, 5 November 1997.
*The Times*, 25 November 1997.
*The Times*, 12 December 1998.
*The Times*, 14 May 1999.
*The Weekend Australian*, Review, 21-22 October 2000.
*The West Australian*, 13 October 1994.
*The West Australian*, 27 May 1995.
*The West Australian*, 26 October 2000.
Thomas, Justice E. (1995), 'Secrecy and Open Government', in P. Finn (ed), *Essays on Law and Government, Volume 1, Principles and Values*, Sydney.
Thomas, R. (1986), 'The British Official Secrets Acts 1911-1939 and the Ponting Case', *Crim.L.R.*, p. 491.
Thompson, D. (1963), 'The Committee of 100 and the Official Secrets Act, 1911', *Public Law*, p. 201.
Thomson, G. (undated), *Blue Pencil Admiral*, London.
Tilbury, M. (1990), *Civil Remedies, Vol 1: Principles of Civil Remedies*, Sydney.

*Time*, 17 August 1998.

Toohey, B. (1994), 'A Case for Greater Openness', in A. Bergin and R. Hall (eds), *Intelligence and Australian National Security*, Canberra.

Toohey, B. and Pinwill, W. (1989), *Oyster: The Story of the Australian Secret Intelligence Service*, Melbourne.

Toohey, Justice J. (1993), 'A Government of Laws, and Not of Men?', *Public Law Review*, vol. 4, p. 158.

Towle, P. (1975), 'The Debate on Wartime Censorship in Britain 1902-14', in B. Bond and I. Roy (eds), *War and Society Vol I*, London.

Turnbull, M. (1988), *The Spycatcher Trial*, Melbourne.

Vincent, D. (1998), *The Culture of Secrecy - Britain, 1832-1998*, Oxford.

Walker, N. (1990), 'Spycatcher's Scottish Sequel', *Public Law*, p. 354.

Walker, S. (1998), '*Lange* v *ABC*: the High Court rethinks the "constitutionalisation" of defamation law', *Torts Law Journal*, vol. 6, p. 9.

*Washington Post*, Vol 131, No 7 (12 August 1984) (cited in Lee, H., Hanks, P., and Morabito, V. (1995), *In the Name of National Security: the Legal Dimensions*, Sydney, p. 19).

Whitmore, H. (1968), 'Censorship of the Mass Media: The "D" Notice System', *The Australian Law Journal*, vol. 41, p. 449.

Whitton, E. (1991), 'Journalism and the Trade of Authority', in J. Henningham (ed), *Institutions in Australian Society*, Brisbane.

Wilcox, M. (1999), 'Sir Gerard Brennan's Contribution to the Human Rights Law in Australia', *The Law Society of Western Australia Brief*, vol. 26(1), p. 15.

Wildlife (Game) (Hunting Season) Regulations 1994 (Vic).

Williams, D. (1965), *Not in the Public Interest: the Problem of Security in Democracy*, London.

Williams, D. (1968), 'Official Secrecy in England', *Federal Law Review*, p. 22.

Williams, D. (1977), 'Preventative Justice and the Courts', *Crim.L.R.*, p. 703.

Williams, F. (1946), *Press, Parliament and People*, London.

Windschuttle, K. (1998), 'The Poverty of Media Theory', *Quadrant*, vol. March, p. 11.

www.1underground.com/Features/features253tomlinson.shtml

www.1underground.com/Features/mi6-diana.shtml

www.dnotice.org.uk/index.htm

www.shayler.com/

Zellick, G. (1985), 'Government Beyond Law', *Public Law*, p. 283.

Zifcak, S. (1989), 'What Sir Harry Gibbs should decide: the disclosure of official information in Australia (Part 1)', *Freedom of Information Review*, vol. August, p. 38.

Zifcak, S. (1989), 'Secrecy, disclosure and the public interest: the disclosure of official information in Australia (Part 2)', *Freedom of Information Review*, vol. October, p. 50.

Zines, L. (1996), 'Constitutionally Protected Individual Rights', in P. Finn (ed), *Essays in Law and Government, Vol 2, The Citizen and the State in the Courts*, Sydney.